# International Applications
# of U.S. Income
# Tax Law

# International Applications of U.S. Income Tax Law

## Inbound and Outbound Transactions

### ERNEST R. LARKINS

WILEY

John Wiley & Sons, Inc.

*Library of Congress Cataloging-in-Publication Data:*

Larkins, Ernest R. (Ernest Radford)
   International applications of U.S. income tax law : inbound and outbound transactions /
by Ernest R. Larkins.
      p.   cm.
   Includes index.
   ISBN 0-471-46449-X (cloth : acid-free paper)
   1. Income tax—United States—Foreign income.   2. Investments, Foreign—Taxation—
Law and legislation—United States.   3. Aliens—Taxation—Law and legislation—United
States.   4. Foreign tax credit—United States.   5. Double taxation—United States.
   I. Title: International applications of US income tax law.   II. Title.
   KF6419.L37 2004
   343.7305′248—dc21
                                                          2003014219

10 9 8 7 6 5 4 3 2 1

My wife, Nancy, has acted as cheerleader (and unofficial press agent) throughout the process. She has my appreciation for her confidence and enthusiasm. I dedicate this text to the three people I have enjoyed teaching the most—my own children—Joshua, Esther, and Hannah. I also thank the many Georgia State University students who have taken my international tax class, and wish them well in their lives and careers.

# About the Web Site

As the purchaser of this book, *International Applications of U.S. Income Tax Law: Inbound and Outbound Transactions*, you have access to the supporting Web site:

www.wiley.com/go/internationaltax

The Web site contains a Word file for the "U.S. Model Income Tax Treaty (September 20, 1996)."

The password to enter this site is: international.

# Contents

# Preface

**G**lobalization means that increasingly few tax professionals can avoid international tax issues. The daily capital that flows into and out of the United States exceeds $14 billion. Many of these flows involve tax issues. Without an understanding of international tax issues, tax professionals can easily overlook benefits or inadvertently stumble into tax pitfalls. Beyond the legal text, professionals must consider the marginal tax rate applicable to international transactions.

An extraordinarily broad topic, international taxation includes the study of many countries' tax laws and the international agreements among those countries affecting tax liabilities. This book explores a less-ambitious area: the international aspects of U.S. income tax law. Thus, the 17 chapters focus on the U.S. income tax laws and international agreements affecting cross-border transactions of both U.S. and foreign persons. The tax systems of other nations receive attention only to illustrate overall tax concepts or the application of U.S. law.

U.S. international taxation involves two major types of activities crossing national borders: inbound and outbound transactions. Inbound transactions occur when foreign persons conduct business in the United States or make U.S. investments. Outbound transactions occur when U.S. persons conduct business abroad or make foreign investments.

For both inbound and outbound transactions, knowledge of certain "generic" topics is crucial. Thus, Part One explains topics applicable to both inbound and outbound activities: tax policy objectives, jurisdiction, tax treaties, source of income rules, and allocation and apportionment procedures. Part Two discusses inbound transactions, including the determination of residency status, U.S. taxation of foreign persons, meaning of effectively connected income, U.S. tax consequences when foreign persons dispose of U.S. real estate, and the U.S. branch profits tax. Some concepts involving the taxation of foreign persons (e.g., effectively connected income) facilitate the study of outbound transactions. Also, the statutory and regulatory law dealing with inbound transactions is less voluminous and complex than the tax law dealing with outbound transactions. For these reasons, outbound topics follow inbound topics. Part Three covers the foreign tax credit, antideferral rules, and incentives for exporting and working abroad. Finally, Part Four deals with related person issues such as transfer pricing and international reorganizations. These rules may affect inbound and outbound transactions but are not essential to the understanding of either. Thus, the text covers related person issues last.

The text contains many special features:

- *Empirical Evidence:* Located primarily in footnotes, this feature references studies linking tax law changes and the managerial reaction of multinational companies.
- *Examples:* Apply points of law discussed in the text. Many illustrate application of U.S. provisions with examples based on foreign tax laws.
- *Exhibits:* Assist readers in visualizing and understanding fundamental provisions.
- *Flashbacks:* Relate the current text to materials appearing earlier in the book and, thus, assist the reader in synthesizing rules and concepts.
- *Important Terms:* Appear in bold type within the text and are defined in the glossary.
- *Key Cases:* Summarize most important judicial opinions.
- *Marginal Tax Rate Analyses:* Numerous equations and formulas facilitate the reader's understanding and synthesis through focus on aggregate economic effects of legal rules.
- *Pointers:* Showcase compliance-related matters, planning ideas, research materials, comparative tax systems, and cultural issues.

I hope this text whets the appetite of the international tax novice, and provides practical guidance to those with international experience. To this end, I invite and welcome all comments, suggestions, and corrections. The reader can send correspondence to Ernest R. Larkins, P.O. Box 4050, School of Accountancy, Georgia State University, Atlanta, GA 30303-4050 or to elarkins@gsu.edu.

# International Applications
# of U.S. Income
# Tax Law

# Generic Topics

# Policy and Overview

To assist readers in viewing this book's contents from the proper perspective, this chapter begins with a brief explanation of international tax policy and its economic effects. Next the chapter discusses an essential topic that does not fit neatly into other chapters but underlies many tax strategies: the taxpayer's choice of business entities for its international activities. The remainder of the chapter provides a brief overview of topics covered throughout the book to give readers a frame of reference to which they can relate materials in later chapters.

To facilitate discussions in each chapter, the text often refers to "nations" as either "home" or "host countries." The **home country** is the country where the taxpayer under consideration resides. The **host country** is the country (other than the home country) where the taxpayer conducts business or makes investments and, thus, is sometimes called the **source country**.

## INTERNATIONAL TAX POLICY

Governments formulate international tax law to accomplish economic objectives. The more prominent international aspects of U.S. tax law find their roots in three neutrality standards. The first, **capital export neutrality (CEN)**, seeks to assure that the global tax burden is identical on a given amount of income earned domestically and an identical amount of income earned abroad. From the perspective of U.S. persons, CEN means that the tax law creates neither an incentive nor a disincentive to conduct business or invest abroad.[1] So, the tax law remains neutral on capital outflow issues and becomes a nonfactor. When CEN exists, U.S. persons make foreign business and investment decisions based on market analyses, production

---

[1] The Internal Revenue Code and many works on international taxation follow the legal practice of defining "U.S. person" and "foreign person" to include both individuals and entities. Thus, **foreign persons** in this text refers collectively to foreign individuals and foreign entities, and **U.S. persons** refers to both U.S. individuals and U.S. entities.

costs, business risks, and other nontax factors. That is, capital follows the highest risk-adjusted, before-tax rates of returns, wherever located. Achieving CEN leads to more efficient uses of U.S. economic resources and, thus, higher productivity levels. When perfect competition exists, CEN assures optimal resource allocations and productivity levels.

---

### EXAMPLE

In addition to its U.S. activities, Anchor, Inc., a Delaware corporation, conducts business through its branch in Singapore. Anchor earns $100,000 Singaporean profit and $900,000 U.S. profit. The tax rates in Singapore and the United States are 24.5 and 35 percent, respectively.[2]

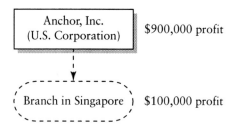

The United States taxes the worldwide income of Anchor, including the foreign branch profits, but provides a credit for the Singaporean taxes Anchor pays. The calculation of tax liability appears as follows:

|  | *Singapore* | *United States* |
| --- | --- | --- |
| Taxable income | $100,000 | $1,000,000 |
| Tax rates | × .245 | × .35 |
| Income tax before credit |  | $ 350,000 |
| Foreign tax credit |  | − 24,500 |
| Tax liability | $ 24,500 | $ 325,500 |

On a worldwide basis, Anchor pays $350,000 ($24,500 + $325,500) income tax on its $1 million profit. If Anchor had earned the entire $1 million in the United States, the U.S. income tax would have been $350,000 ($1,000,000 × 35%) also. Thus, U.S. tax policy for this scenario is capital-export-neutral. Anchor owes the same total tax regardless of where it earns the $100,000.

---

[2]PricewaterhouseCoopers, *Corporate Taxes: Worldwide Summaries 2002–2003* (Hoboken, NJ: John Wiley & Sons, Inc., 2002), p. 737.

The second primary objective, **capital import neutrality (CIN)**, focuses on the market where individuals or entities conduct business or make investments and, when present, fosters global competitiveness. CIN exists when individuals or entities bear the same tax burdens as individuals or entities from other countries operating within the same market. The focal market might be the United States or a foreign host country. CIN allows businesses to compete globally on an equal footing with similar businesses from other countries. Like CEN, equalizing the tax burden for business operations within a given market causes businesses to focus on nontax factors when making decisions. This focus results in a more efficient allocation of host country resources.

---

### EXAMPLE

Returning to the first example, suppose Anchor, Inc. decides to conduct business in Singapore through a foreign subsidiary rather than a foreign branch. As long as the multinational does not directly or indirectly repatriate the earnings, U.S. law effectively shields the foreign subsidiary's $100,000 profit from U.S. taxation. Thus, the worldwide tax burden on the $100,000 foreign profit is $24,500 ($100,000 × 24.5%). In comparison, France exempts the profit of foreign subsidiaries conducting business in Singapore, meaning that they also face an effective worldwide tax rate of 24.5 percent.[3] In this situation, U.S. tax law is CIN vis-à-vis French tax law for business conducted in Singapore. Also, U.S. tax law is CIN for U.S. businesses competing in Singapore with Singaporean companies.

---

The third standard, **national neutrality (NN)**, finds less acceptance among policy makers, at least on a broad scale, than either CEN or CIN. This standard recognizes that individuals and entities must share international business and investment returns with the U.S. government, a silent partner that, nonetheless, demands payment. NN assures that the United States always gets the same percentage cut from the "tenuous partnership," regardless whether the taxpayer commits capital domestically or abroad. Under this standard, U.S. persons deduct foreign government levies (e.g., foreign property taxes, import duties, and other noncreditable taxes) the same as other business expenses. In contrast to the credit benefit in the first example and the exemption benefit in the second example, merely permitting taxpayers to deduct foreign taxes represents a disincentive to conduct

---

[3]PricewaterhouseCoopers, *Corporate Taxes: Worldwide Summaries 2002–2003* (Hoboken, NJ: John Wiley & Sons, Inc., 2002), p. 737.

business or invest abroad; comparable U.S. business and investment activities avoid this foreign tax expense. In effect, NN induces a U.S. person to engage in international activities only when the risk-adjusted, before-tax return abroad exceeds the return available in the United States and, thus, does not result in the most efficient allocation of resources. However, in comparison with CEN and CIN, NN preserves the U.S. tax revenue from foreign activities.

---

### EXAMPLE

Bitter Jitters, Inc., a U.S. company, sells delectable candy products for $140 a crate. Each crate of candy products costs $70 to manufacture, and related selling and administrative expenses total $30. The U.S. tax rate is 35 percent. On a recent foreign sale, Bitter pays a $20 foreign government levy. Bitter deducts the foreign levy, an application of NN. As the table following illustrates, deducting the $20 results in a $20 before-tax profit and allows Bitter to pay the U.S. government its 35 percent share, or $7. In contrast, allowing Bitter to credit the $20 foreign levy (if indeed the levy qualifies as a foreign income tax) precludes the U.S. government from sharing in the $20 profit.

|  | Foreign Tax Deducted | Foreign Tax Credited |
| --- | --- | --- |
| Selling price | $140 | $140 |
| Cost of goods sold | − 70 | − 70 |
| Selling and administrative | − 30 | − 30 |
| Foreign levy as deduction | − 20 |  |
| Taxable income from sale | $ 20 | $ 40 |
| U.S. corporate tax rate | × 35% | × 35% |
| U.S. tax before credit |  | $ 14 |
| Foreign levy as credit |  | − 20 |
| U.S. tax liability | $ 7 | $ 0 |

---

Other objectives also play significant roles in formulating U.S. tax policy. For instance, the United States exempts the nonbusiness interest income of foreign persons derived from deposits in U.S. banks, savings institutions, and insurance companies.[4] This exemption provides tax benefits to foreign

---

[4] IRC §§871(i), 881(d).

investors that U.S. investors do not enjoy and, thus, violates CIN. The objective seeks to attract foreign capital to support the U.S. economy. Also, qualified U.S. individuals working abroad can exempt up to $80,000 of their foreign earnings from U.S. tax.[5] This benefit contravenes CEN. A U.S. individual performing the same services within the United States does not qualify for the $80,000 exemption. In short, the international provisions under U.S. tax law evidence a hodgepodge of sometimes-conflicting economic objectives. Nonetheless, CEN and CIN play more important roles than the other objectives.

## ENTITY SELECTION

The tax consequences of international business transactions often depend on the business form through which such activities occur. Foreign branches (or divisions or offices) represent extensions of businesses, not separate legal or taxable entities. Foreign branch losses flow through to offset profits on the entity's domestic return. Similarly, foreign branch profits flow through to the entity's domestic return, as does income tax the foreign branch pays on such profits. In addition to an income tax, some foreign countries impose a branch profits tax (analogous to a dividend withholding tax) on estimated remittances from the foreign branch to its home office. U.S. multinationals often decide not to conduct business abroad through a branch since the branch form does not protect domestic assets from legal claims arising abroad. However, banks and other financial institutions sometimes use foreign branches to meet capital reserve requirements in host countries.

---

### EXAMPLE

Short Sport, Inc., a U.S. company, provides instructional training in various athletic events for individuals under age 13. Three years ago, it established a Canadian division, hoping to duplicate its domestic success. The division experienced losses during the first two years. Short Sport deducted the losses against its U.S. profit. During the current year, the division shows a profit, which Canada taxes. On its U.S. return, Short Sport reports the profit and claims the Canadian income tax as a foreign tax credit.[6]

---

[5]IRC §911.

[6]As Chapter 11 explains, a recapture provision may prevent Short Sport from claiming the full Canadian income tax as a foreign tax credit. Also, as Chapter 10 discusses, a branch profits tax might apply in the profitable year.

For international joint ventures, U.S. multinationals often use **fiscally transparent entities** such as foreign partnerships. Like branches, partnerships flow through losses, profits, and foreign income tax to their U.S. owners. In contrast to corporate joint ventures, U.S. multinationals experience fewer problems claiming foreign tax credits when they use partnership joint ventures. Also, foreign partnership remittances avoid dividend withholding taxes. However, like branches, foreign partnerships do not limit owners' liabilities.

Foreign subsidiaries possess two advantages over foreign branches and partnerships. First, they allow U.S. parent companies to defer U.S. tax on foreign earnings until actually or constructively received as dividends. The longer the deferral, the smaller the present value of the U.S. tax when finally paid. However, this sword cuts two ways: U.S. parent companies cannot claim any credit for foreign income tax the subsidiary pays until the parents actually or constructively receive dividends. Also, unlike branches and partnerships, foreign subsidiaries do not allow U.S. parent companies to deduct foreign losses. Second, incorporating abroad effectively shields assets of U.S. parent companies from legal claims against foreign subsidiaries. Exhibit 1.1 summarizes the characteristics of the three business forms just discussed.

Exhibit 1.1 highlights the key trade-off when selecting foreign business structures—to obtain flow-through treatment exposes the U.S. owners to legal liability claims from abroad. However, **check-the-box** procedures allow many foreign businesses to select their own treatment under U.S. law, but only if they are not **per se corporations**.[7] Exhibit 1.2 lists some examples of per se corporations, which U.S. law always treats as corporations.

Except for per se corporations, foreign business entities with only one owner can elect treatment as either branches or corporations under check-the-box procedures. Similarly, foreign business entities with two or more owners can elect treatment as either partnerships or corporations.[8] The ability to choose extends to general and limited partnerships, joint ventures, lim-

**EXHIBIT 1.1**    Foreign Business Structures

|                    | Branch               | Partnership          | Subsidiary          |
|--------------------|----------------------|----------------------|---------------------|
| Operating loss     | Flow through         | Flow through         | Defers deduction    |
| Operating profit   | Flow through         | Flow through         | Defers U.S. tax     |
| Foreign income tax | Flow through         | Flow through         | Defers tax credit   |
| Asset protection   | Unlimited liability  | Unlimited liability  | Limited liability   |

---

[7] Reg. §301.7701-2(b)(8).
[8] Reg. §301.7701-3(a).

**EXHIBIT 1.2**  Selected Per Se Corporations

| Jurisdiction | Foreign Business Entity |
| --- | --- |
| Australia | Public Limited Company (Ltd.) |
| Canada | Corporation (Inc., Ltd., or SCC) |
| France | Société Anonyme (SA) |
| Germany | Aktiengesellschaft (AG) |
| India | Public Limited Company (Ltd.) |
| Italy | Società per Azioni (SpA) |
| Japan | Kabushiki Kaisha (KK) |
| Mexico | Sociedad Anónima (SA) |
| Netherlands | Naamloze Vennootschap (NV) |
| Norway | Allment Aksjeselskap (ASA) |
| Sweden | Publika Aktiebolag (AB) |
| Switzerland | Aktiengesellschaft (AG) |
| United Kingdom | Public Limited Company (Ltd.) |

ited liability companies, and other business entities that are not per se corporations. Exhibit 1.3 provides some examples of foreign business entities that can select their treatment under check-the-box regulations.

Regulations provide default classifications for business entities failing to choose, which depend on the number of owners and whether foreign jurisdictions treat entities as possessing limited liability. By default, regulations classify business entities with two or more owners as partnerships if the foreign jurisdiction considers at least one owner to possess unlimited liability. Similarly, U.S. law disregards single-member entities in which the owner has unlimited liability (i.e., treats such entities as foreign branches or **tax nothings**). Otherwise, the default provisions classify business entities as corporations.[9]

**EXHIBIT 1.3**  Selected Foreign Entities That Can "Check the Box"

| Jurisdiction | Foreign Business Entity |
| --- | --- |
| France | Société à Responsabilité Limitée (SARL) |
| Germany | Gesellschaft mit beschränkter Haftung (GmbH) |
| Italy | Società a Responsabilità Limitata (SARL) |
| Japan | Yugen Kaisha (YK) |
| Mexico | Sociedad de Responsabilidad Limitada (S de RL) |
| Switzerland | Gesellschaft mit beschränkter Haftung (GmbH) |

---

[9]Reg. §301.7701-3(b).

**COMPLIANCE POINTER:** Business entities file Form 8832, Entity Classification Form, to select their classification. Once selected, an entity cannot change its classification for five years without IRS consent.[10]

Check-the-box elections often produce **hybrid entities** that the foreign jurisdiction treats as limited liability companies but that the United States recognizes as flow-through structures. Conversely, when foreign jurisdictions recognize business entities as flow-through structures but the United States treats them as corporations, **reverse hybrid entities** result. Hybrids and reverse hybrids sometimes provide U.S. multinationals with tax arbitrage opportunities or the ability to reduce global taxes further than if all jurisdictions characterized business entities similarly.

## GENERIC TOPICS

Governments impose taxes on individuals and entities only when they have jurisdiction to tax. National laws define jurisdiction and establish global or territorial tax systems. Countries with global systems, such as the United States, tax the worldwide income of their residents and domestic entities. Countries with territorial systems, such as France, tax only income from within their borders. More than one nation sometimes has jurisdiction to tax the same income from international transactions, giving rise to possible double taxation. **Income tax treaties** represent one means of addressing double tax situations.

Income tax treaties mitigate the effect of double taxation. For instance, treaties prevent host countries from taxing treaty partner residents on specified income. For these transactions, CEN results if the residents' home country taxes the income at regular rates. For instance, the United States-Spain income tax treaty prevents Spain from taxing income a U.S. business derives within Spain as long as the income is not attributable to a Spanish permanent establishment.[11] The treaty overrides Spanish law, which otherwise might tax such income in addition to U.S. law, resulting in double taxation. Most treaty provisions are reciprocal, so the same treaty article restricts U.S. jurisdiction to tax income a Spanish business derives from the United States, assuming the business's income is not attributable to a U.S. permanent establishment.

Source rules dichotomize income between U.S. and foreign sources. Each type of income (e.g., compensation for services or dividends) follows a

---

[10]Reg. §301.7701-3(c).
[11]United States-Spain income tax treaty (Feb. 22, 1990), art. 7(1).

different source rule. U.S. taxpayers can credit any foreign income tax they pay subject to a formulary limit that depends on foreign source taxable income. The higher the foreign source taxable income, the more likely U.S. taxpayers can credit all their foreign income taxes. Foreign persons use the source rules for a different purpose: to determine their U.S. tax liabilities. The United States taxes foreign persons on U.S. source income, though exceptions exist.

As U.S. law sources income, it allocates and apportions deductions. U.S. taxpayers subtract apportioned deductions from their foreign source *gross* income to determine foreign source *taxable* income, an input to the foreign tax credit limit just mentioned. Likewise, the United States taxes the U.S. business income of foreign persons after deductions, requiring allocation and apportionment procedures to convert gross business income to taxable business income.

## INBOUND TRANSACTIONS

**Inbound transactions** involve foreign persons conducting business or investing in the United States. Foreign persons include foreign corporations and nonresident aliens. Foreign corporations are corporations organized or created abroad. Nonresident aliens are non-U.S. citizens residing outside the United States. Nonresident aliens do not include alien individuals: (1) to whom U.S. immigration authorities grant permission to reside permanently in the United States or (2) who spend substantial time in the United States based on an objective day-counting test.

The United States taxes foreign persons on two types of income: (1) nonbusiness, primarily investment, income from U.S. sources and (2) income effectively connected with a U.S. trade or business, including personal service income. The Code allows no deductions against U.S. source investment income and taxes such income at 30 percent or a lower treaty rate. Payors of U.S. source investment income withhold this tax when making payment. The Code taxes U.S. business income at regular rates applicable to U.S. persons, an application of CIN since the law treats both U.S. and foreign persons the same in the U.S. market.

Special rules apply to foreign persons' gains from disposing of U.S. real property. The Code taxes such gains as though effectively connected with a U.S. business. Also, when a domestic corporation holds a substantial amount of U.S. real estate, and a foreign shareholder sells the corporate stock, Section 897 taxes the gain as effectively connected income. Without this provision, some foreign persons might avoid U.S. tax on gain from indirect holdings of U.S. real estate, a result differing from the treatment of U.S. persons with similar gains. Thus, Section 897 attempts to achieve CIN.

The United States imposes a branch profits tax on foreign persons conducting U.S. business activities through U.S. branches (or divisions or offices). The tax provides parity between foreign persons operating through U.S. subsidiaries and U.S. branches. Since the United States collects a dividend withholding tax on profit remittances from U.S. subsidiaries, the branch profits tax attempts to collect a similar amount through estimating annual remittances from the U.S. branch to its foreign home office. Section 884 bases the estimate on the change in the U.S. branch's assets between years. For instance, declining asset balances, unless operating losses accompany the declines, suggest that the branch remits U.S. profits to its foreign home office.

## OUTBOUND TRANSACTIONS

Provisions dealing with **outbound transactions** either prevent abuses or provide incentives. Antiabuse provisions include the rules for controlled foreign corporations, passive foreign investment companies, and foreign personal holding companies that prevent U.S. taxpayers from deferring U.S. tax liabilities indefinitely. Incentive provisions include the foreign tax credit to mitigate double tax problems, the foreign earned income exclusion for U.S. individuals working abroad, and the extraterritorial income exclusion and domestic international sales corporation deferral for export activities.

Outbound transactions involve U.S. citizens, U.S. residents, and domestic entities conducting business or investing abroad. The United States taxes these U.S. persons on their worldwide income. Since outbound business and investment activities often result in foreign income tax also, U.S. persons depend on the foreign tax credit to mitigate the double tax impact.

The foreign tax credit provides U.S. taxpayers with a dollar-for-dollar credit on their U.S. returns for foreign income tax they pay. Also, U.S. corporations claim a credit for foreign income tax their foreign subsidiaries pay when the former receive dividends. Section 904 limits the foreign tax credit to the result of Equation 1.1:

$$\text{Limit} = \frac{\text{Foreign source taxable income}}{\text{Worldwide taxable income}} \times \text{U.S. tax before the credit} \quad (1.1)$$

When the equation limits the foreign tax credit, U.S. taxpayers pay an effective tax rate equal to the foreign tax rate, a result consistent with CIN. When the limit is high enough to enable U.S. persons to credit all their foreign income tax, their effective tax rate equals the U.S. tax rate, a result consistent with CEN.

In the global arena, IRS personnel sometimes trace taxpayer abuse to **controlled foreign corporations (CFCs)** and their use in conducting international business activities and making offshore investments. CFCs are foreign corporations that U.S. shareholders control through owning more than 50 percent of either stock value or voting power. As separate entities, CFCs provide the opportunity for U.S. shareholders to defer U.S. taxes indefinitely, often providing substantial present value benefits. With some exceptions, as long as CFCs do not remit their foreign profits as dividends to their U.S. owners, no U.S. tax liability results. However, the exceptions are broad. When CFCs earn Subpart F income, their U.S. shareholders report a constructive dividend. That is, they report CFCs' foreign profit as **gross income** even though they receive none of the profit as actual dividends. Subpart F income comes in many varieties, but generally it represents foreign income earned in a way suggesting strong tax avoidance motives behind the CFC's location and operation.

---

### EXAMPLE

Oliver Enterprises, Inc., a domestic corporation, establishes a wholly owned foreign subsidiary, Dodger, Ltd., in the Cayman Islands, which does not impose income taxes. Thus, Dodger is a CFC. Oliver sells its products to Dodger, which, in turn, resells the products to foreign customers. None of Dodger's customers reside in the Cayman Islands. Also, Dodger undertakes no significant manufacturing, assembling, or packaging activities in the Cayman Islands. Thus, one might wonder what business purpose Dodger serves other than to capture income in a no-tax jurisdiction. Based on the lack of business activities and customer base in the Cayman Islands, the foreign profit Dodger earns is Subpart F income. Even if Dodger pays no dividends to Oliver, the latter must recognize a constructive dividend for Dodger's foreign profits. The constructive dividend precludes Oliver from deferring U.S. tax through a structure without a clear business purpose.

---

The indefinite deferral of U.S. tax on foreign profits, when Subpart F income does not exist, is consistent with CIN since the U.S. multinational's marginal tax rate approximates the foreign country's tax rate. When Subpart F income causes U.S. shareholders to recognize all foreign profits as constructive dividends, the marginal tax rate equals the U.S. tax rate, a result consistent with CEN.

The Code contains other provisions designed to thwart U.S. tax deferrals besides those affecting CFCs. Two of the more potent antideferral weapons are the **foreign personal holding company (FPHC)** and **passive foreign investment company (PFIC)** rules. The FPHC rules operate similarly to those of CFCs—U.S. shareholders receive constructive dividends when FPHCs earn specified types of passive income. PFICs, however, work differently from CFCs and FPHCs. Rather than tainted earnings causing constructive dividends, the PFIC legislation allows U.S. tax deferrals, but retroactively imposes an interest charge to gain from disposing of PFIC stock and certain distributions exceeding prior-year dividends. In effect, the Code eliminates the deferral benefit after the fact through interest charges on U.S. deferred taxes.

U.S. tax law provides two incentives for U.S. exporters: the **extraterritorial income exclusion (EIE)** and the **domestic international sales corporation** (DISC). On most export sales, the EIE reduces U.S. tax by 15 percent. Thus, a $100 tax bill on a U.S. sale would fall to $85 on a similar export sale. In contrast to the EIE, the DISC legislation allows U.S. exporters to defer U.S. tax on export profits. The Code imposes an interest charge on the U.S. tax deferral. In effect, the DISC benefit mimics a low-interest loan from the government.

U.S. individuals with foreign income can claim the foreign tax credit if they qualify. Alternatively, the United States allows U.S. individuals working abroad to claim a foreign earned income exclusion. This provision exempts up to $80,000 of foreign earnings from U.S. taxation each year. U.S. citizens and residents qualify for the exclusion if they demonstrate foreign presence in approximately 11 out of 12 months or foreign residency. When foreign earnings fall below the $80,000 threshold, the individual only pays income tax to the foreign host country on earnings. Thus, this provision often achieves CIN in the host country's market.

## RELATED PERSON TRANSACTIONS

When multinational companies transact international business with unrelated persons, the market sets an **arm's-length price**. However, when multinational companies deal with related persons, the market no longer acts as an unbiased arbiter. An incentive exists to manipulate transfer prices between related persons so profits fall under the jurisdiction of countries with very low or zero tax rates. Without some constraint, multinational companies can eliminate the tax on many international transactions simply through setting advantageous transfer prices. To prevent such abuses, regulations require U.S. and foreign taxpayers to set transfer prices according to acceptable methods, each bearing some semblance to arm's-length standards.

Substantial penalties apply for serious transfer pricing infractions. Taxpayers desiring more confidence that the IRS finds their transfer pricing acceptable can negotiate advance pricing agreements.

International reorganizations often involve transfers of appreciated properties. Under many Code provisions, companies realizing gain on such transfers defer the gain through carryover basis rules, even though the properties' final destinations might exceed the reach of U.S. jurisdiction, preventing the United States from ever taxing the gain. Absent some remedy, companies restructuring internationally might permanently avoid U.S. taxation on their appreciated assets. Section 367 addresses this problem, overriding the Code provisions providing for nonrecognition treatment and allowing the United States to tax the realized gain immediately on a variety of transactions.

# CHAPTER 2

# Jurisdiction to Tax

**A** government's power to impose its taxes on persons or transactions is its jurisdiction to tax. Jurisdiction in international tax parlance is analogous to *nexus* under state and local tax laws. However, the criteria for establishing jurisdiction differ from the standards states use to determine nexus.

National tax laws vary in the way they demarcate their power to tax. As explained in the first section, some countries define jurisdiction primarily on the basis of the persons involved in cross-border transactions. Other countries focus principally on economic transactions in establishing their jurisdiction. Thus, countries exercise their powers to tax in different ways.

## TALE OF TWO SYSTEMS

National tax laws are either global or territorial in nature. The primary distinction lies in their treatment of resident individuals and domestic entities.[1] A global system, as the phrase implies, taxes the worldwide income of a nation's residents and domestic entities, though a credit mechanism often provides double tax relief. Under a territorial system, taxation stops at the border. Developing countries often manage territorial systems more easily since revenue agencies need not enforce compliance on a worldwide basis.

Countries with global systems exercise jurisdiction primarily over persons. Specifically, global systems tax the worldwide income of their individuals and entities. The rationale for taxing worldwide income asserts that countries confer certain benefits on their individuals and entities for which they reasonably expect some return in the form of tax revenue. For individuals, benefits include protection when abroad and the right to return to their homeland whenever they choose. For entities, benefits include domestic laws defining business relationships and protecting entities from unfair practices.

---

[1] In the tax laws of many countries, the term *resident* can apply to either individuals or entities. Under U.S. law, it generally applies to individuals only.

Most developed nations use global tax systems. The United States is one example, though recent trade controversies with the European Union (EU) and the desire to be more competitive with other nations have tempted some Congressional members to convert to a territorial system. Other examples of global systems include Japan and the United Kingdom.

Global systems tax individuals on the basis of citizenship or residence. That is, countries with global systems tax the worldwide income of their individual citizens or residents. Citizenship is a relatively objective concept, deeply rooted in most countries' national laws. As a result, few tax disputes arise turning on an individual's citizenship. In contrast, a country's definition of residency often depends on subjective criteria, spawning frequent tax controversies involving large tax assessments. Also, one country's definition of residency may vary significantly from the meaning of residency in other countries. No universally accepted concept of residency exists. Thus, some individuals may be residents of two or more countries simultaneously, a situation discussed in Chapter 6.

Under global systems, countries exercise jurisdiction over corporations based on where the entity organizes or incorporates (known as legal domicile), establishes its central management (known as fiscal domicile), or some combination of the two criteria. Controversies normally do not arise about where a corporation organizes—it depends on the place where the entity files articles of incorporation or similar documents. However, the place of a corporation's central management (or seat of effective management) is not always easy to determine. Some national tax laws indicate that a corporation's central management exists in the same place as the corporation's head office, where its board meetings occur, or according to a similar yardstick.

> **PLANNING POINTER:** When countries base jurisdiction solely on the location of central management, corporations can shift future income between jurisdictions by moving management functions to another country. Most countries consider the movement of management functions to be a nontaxable event. (In contrast, changing legal domicile through selling or exchanging shares may result in a taxable gain.) To discourage the movement of management functions to garner tax benefits, some national tax laws assert jurisdiction based on both legal and fiscal domicile, as illustrated in the next example.

Most governments do not tax partnerships and other fiscally transparent (or flow-through) entities. Of course, whether a country treats an entity as fiscally transparent depends on the country's internal laws. A given entity might be fiscally transparent under one country's tax laws but not another's. However, assuming fiscal transparency, a country may exercise jurisdiction

**EXAMPLE**

Germany taxes the worldwide income of corporations organized in Germany or managed and controlled from Germany.[2] Thus, Germany taxes the U.S. income of a company performing its management activities in the United States if the company incorporates in Germany. Likewise, Germany taxes the U.S. income of a company incorporated in the United States if the company conducts its management activities from Germany.

over the entity's owners or beneficiaries. Specifically, whether a country has jurisdiction to tax flow-through income often depends on the owners' or beneficiaries' citizenship, residence, organization situs, or place of central management, rather than similar characteristics about the **flow-through entity** itself.

**EXAMPLE**

Normative Nutrients Company is a U.S. general partnership earning $200,000 foreign source profit during the current year. Normative has two individual owners, Kenneth and Barbara, who share profit in a 3:2 ratio. Kenneth is a U.S. citizen: Barbara's citizenship and residency is in Bermuda. The United States cannot tax the full $200,000 of Normative's profit since it arose from foreign sources. Normative's organization in the United States is irrelevant. However, since Kenneth is a U.S. citizen, the United States has jurisdiction to tax his $120,000 share of the partnership's profit.

**COMPLIANCE POINTER:** Though a fiscally transparent entity's place of organization or management may be irrelevant in determining a country's jurisdiction to tax the entity's income, these factors may be very important in determining the liability for withholding tax on payments to the entity. Thus, U.S. law requires withholding on dividends paid to a foreign partnership while exempting similar payments to a domestic partnership.

---

[2]PricewaterhouseCoopers, *Corporate Taxes: Worldwide Summaries 2002–2003* (Hoboken, NJ: John Wiley & Sons, Inc., 2002), p. 269.

**EXHIBIT 2.1** Concepts of Jurisdiction

| Tax System | Jurisdiction Over | Basis for Taxation | Examples |
|---|---|---|---|
| Global | Persons | Citizenship<br>Residence<br>Place of organization<br>Central management | United States<br>Japan |
| Territorial | Transactions | Source of income<br>Relation to trade<br>or business | France<br>Ecuador |

In contrast to global systems, some countries focus primarily on transactions rather than the persons involved. Countries with territorial systems tax only income from transactions occurring within their borders, and exempt income from outside their borders. Thus, territorial nations often use an income stream's source as the basis for taxation; they tax domestic source income but exempt foreign source income. To prevent abuse, some territorial nations tax foreign source income if it relates to a domestic trade or business. Alternatively, they may define all income related to a domestic **trade or business** as domestic source income, even if the taxpayer otherwise earns the income abroad. France, Hong Kong, and several countries in Latin America use territorial systems. Exhibit 2.1 summarizes the concepts related to global and territorial tax systems.

Though the prior discussion suggests that countries fall either into the global or territorial camp, the distinction is not always clear. The tax laws in many countries contain aspects of both systems. A continuum might more realistically portray the variety of national tax laws. The continuum might show global systems at the left pole, territorial systems at the right, and the world's tax systems scattered from one extreme to the other.

---

## EXAMPLE

Australia exempts most foreign branch profit and foreign dividends received from **listed countries**, which include primarily countries with income tax treaties in force. This is the territorial aspect of Australian taxation. In contrast, Australia taxes foreign income received from non-listed countries, which is the global facet.[3] Other countries have similar mixed systems.

---

[3]PricewaterhouseCoopers, *Corporate Taxes: Worldwide Summaries 2002–2003* (Hoboken, NJ: John Wiley & Sons, Inc., 2002), p. 17.

## U.S. JURISDICTION

As indicated earlier in "Tale of Two Systems," the United States taxes income on a global basis, primarily emphasizing jurisdiction over individuals and entities. The government taxes U.S. individuals and domestic corporations on their worldwide income.[4] U.S. individuals include both U.S. citizens and U.S. residents.[5] As Chapter 6 discusses in more detail, U.S. residents (or resident aliens) include permanent immigrants to the United States and individuals remaining in the United States for a substantial time.[6] U.S. law treats incorporated entities organized or created within the United States or the District of Columbia as domestic corporations.[7]

## KEY CASE

The taxpayer, a U.S. citizen and Mexican resident, derives income from personal and real property located in Mexico. He contends that the United States cannot tax his income since he resides, and his property exists, beyond U.S. territorial limits. In rejecting the taxpayer's contention, the Supreme Court observes that U.S. law does not constrain the federal government's jurisdiction to tax. Since the U.S. government provides benefits to its citizens and their property wherever located, the United States possesses the power to tax the income from such property.[8]

In contrast, the Code taxes foreign persons only on two types of income: U.S. source investment income and income effectively connected with a U.S. trade or business. Foreign persons include nonresident aliens and foreign corporations. **Nonresident aliens** are non-U.S. citizens not residing in the United States. U.S. law treats incorporated entities organized or created abroad as foreign corporations.

---

[4]Reg. §§1.1-1(b), 1.11-1(a). The statutory authority for taxing worldwide income is a bit more cryptic. IRC §61(a) considers all income to be gross income. The section draws no distinction between domestic and foreign source income. IRC §§872(a) and 882(b) exempts foreign parties from U.S. taxation on foreign source income. Since no similar exemption applies to U.S. parties, the Code taxes U.S. individuals and domestic corporations on both domestic and foreign income.
[5]Many nations tax the worldwide income of its residents. However, the United States is the only developed country to also tax the worldwide income of its citizens.
[6]IRC §7701(b)(1)(A).
[7]IRC §7701(a)(4), (10). In relationship to the U.S. tax system, "domestic" means the same as "U.S." Thus, a domestic corporation is the same as a U.S. corporation, and a domestic partnership is equivalent to a U.S. partnership.
[8]*Cook v. Tait*, 265 US 47 (1924).

**EXAMPLE**

Dunkirk Deliveries, Ltd. is a foreign corporation specializing in intercontinental parcel shipments and conducting business in the United States and the United Kingdom. During the current year, Dunkirk earns taxable profit of $24 million (one-third attributable to its U.S. office). The United States can tax $8 million of Dunkirk's profit since it is effectively connected with its U.S. business.

## DOUBLE TAXATION

Though tax systems may possess similarities, no two are exactly alike. Double tax problems arise because each country exercises its jurisdiction to tax in different ways. Two countries may seek to tax the same income stream because each claims jurisdiction to tax the same persons or the same transactions. Alternatively, one country may claim jurisdiction to tax the person to a transaction while another country claims jurisdiction to tax the transaction itself.

Absent some remedy, the potential **double taxation** illustrated in the preceding examples would dissuade many individuals from investing or doing business abroad. Economic theory, of course, maintains that anything

**EXAMPLE**

Ike is a U.S. citizen residing in Canada for the last four years. The United States claims jurisdiction to tax Ike's worldwide income because of his citizenship. Canada taxes his worldwide income based on his residence.

**EXAMPLE**

Enoch is a U.S. citizen. During two months this year, he works in Bolivia. He does not live abroad long enough to become a Bolivian resident. The United States claims jurisdiction to tax Enoch's worldwide income, including the personal service income from abroad, based on his citizenship. Bolivia asserts its right to tax Enoch's personal service income since he performs the work within its borders.

hindering trade (e.g., double taxation) is bad. Fortunately, remedies exist. As a bilateral solution, tax treaties grant jurisdiction to tax certain transactions solely to the home country and reduce the tax rates on other transactions. As a unilateral remedy, the foreign tax credit often provides relief from double income taxation to taxpayers under global tax systems. Another unilateral approach, especially among countries with territorial systems, is the exemption method. The **exemption method** forgoes taxation on foreign source income (under territorial systems) or specified types of profit (e.g., international transportation income), especially if another country likely will tax the income. Chapter 3 discusses income tax treaties, and Chapter 11 explains the foreign tax credit under U.S. law.

# CHAPTER 3

# Income Tax Treaties

**T**ax treaties (or conventions) are negotiated agreements between two countries establishing reciprocal rules for each nation to tax residents from the other country. The most important agreement for business and investment planning is the income tax treaty. The United States has over 50 income tax treaties in force. Also, several U.S. treaties are pending or in various stages of negotiation.

Each treaty has two objectives. The primary goal is to reduce double taxation so international commerce can flourish. To this end, treaties limit the host country's right to tax income. For instance, the treaty may preclude the host country from taxing personal service income and business profit when the recipient meets certain requirements (as discussed later). Also, treaties usually reduce the withholding tax on investment income.

---

### FLASHBACK

From Chapter 2, recall that double taxation discourages foreign commerce, and tax treaties provide bilateral remedies. Unilateral responses to double tax issues include the **foreign tax credit** and the exemption method.

---

The second goal is to facilitate cooperation between taxing authorities in the home and host countries. Virtually all treaties contain an **exchange of information article,** which makes hiding income and, thus, tax evasion more difficult. Treaties also promote cooperation through **mutual agreement articles,** which provide means of settling disputes between a taxpayer and the host country's taxing authority and clarifying issues on which the tax treaty is unclear. When countries need help in collecting taxes from a taxpayer residing in a treaty country, they often rely on the **administrative assistance article** to enlist the treaty country in the collection effort.

Though outside this chapter's scope, other international agreements also affect tax liabilities. The following list summarizes these other agreements:

- The United States maintains approximately 17 estate tax treaties, several of which cover gift taxes also. These treaties reduce instances of double estate (and, in some cases, double gift) taxation.
- Totalization agreements are growing in importance and number. The United States has about 20 in force. These agreements mitigate the effect of double Social Security taxation and provide for an aggregated, or "totalized," benefit when individuals pay Social Security taxes to more than one country.
- The United States negotiates **exchange of information agreements** with low- or no-tax countries in the Caribbean and Latin America. From the U.S. perspective, these agreements discourage tax evasion. The United States has approximately 14 of these agreements in force.
- The United States has concluded about 30 **international shipping and aviation agreements**. These agreements restrict or eliminate host country taxation of cross-border transportation income.

While these various agreements are important, this chapter focuses on income tax treaties. Since each income tax treaty differs, a general discussion of this topic is broad. Thus, this chapter uses the U.S. Model Treaty as the primary basis for discussion.[1] Following brief descriptions of how treaties become law and what authoritative weight tax professionals can ascribe to treaties, this chapter explains specific provisions of U.S. income tax treaties.

## TREATY CREATION AND AUTHORITY

Treaty negotiations begin with a model treaty, which often reflects the preferred positions of each country's negotiators. As noted, the United States has its own **model treaty**. Other model treaties include those of the **Organization for Economic Cooperation and Development (OECD)**, which most developed countries favor, and the United Nations (U.N.), which **developing countries** prefer. Under the premise that the host or source country should relinquish its jurisdiction to tax most cross-border transactions, the United

---

[1] Treasury Department Model Income Tax Convention (September 20, 1996) [hereafter, U.S. Model Treaty]. *Tax Treaties* (Chicago: Commerce Clearing House, 2002), *U.S. Tax Treaties* (New York: Warren, Gorham & Lamont, 2002), and the *Tax Notes International* (TNI) file in LEXIS contain copies of all U.S. tax treaties signed or in force.

States and OECD models favor capital-exporting nations. These models reduce withholding tax rates on royalties and other investment income to low levels, decreasing the host country's tax revenue from these income streams. In contrast, the U.N. model provides more favorable terms for capital-importing countries. The U.N. model preserves the host country's jurisdiction to tax some income items that the U.S. and OECD models do not. Also, the U.N. model provides for higher withholding tax rates.

> **CULTURAL POINTER:** Some may find references to developing nations as "undeveloped countries" or "third world countries" offensive since these phrases suggest that economic development is not occurring or the country otherwise is backward.

After agreeing on an initial text, tax treaty negotiators send the proposed agreement to their respective countries for approval or ratification. In the United States, the **Senate Foreign Relations Committee** examines all proposed treaties and, for those it views favorably, recommends that the Senate give its advice and consent.[2] In the United States, a treaty needs a two-thirds vote of the Senate for ratification; the House of Representatives does not participate in the process. After ratification, the income tax treaty becomes effective according to its own terms (e.g., January 1 of the next year). Treaties remain in force indefinitely until one of the countries decides to terminate the agreement. To provide taxpayers with some measure of predictability, the treaty's terms normally prohibit each country from terminating the agreement during the first five years. Later changes often take the form of protocols, which are treaty amendments that, as freestanding documents, taxpayers read with the related treaty.

> **RESEARCH POINTER:** The Senate Foreign Relations Committee Report assists the tax professional to interpret and apply the treaty's provisions correctly. The Treasury Department and the Joint Committee on Taxation prepare separate explanations of each treaty. The TNI file in the FEDTAX library of LEXIS contains these valuable research documents.

Treaties possess the same authoritative weight as the Internal Revenue Code (hereafter, the Code). Article VI, clause 2 of the U.S. Constitution (i.e., the supremacy clause) refers to both treaties and the Code as the

---

[2]Article II, Section 2(2) of the U.S. Constitution requires the president to obtain the Senate's advice and consent before making a treaty.

"supreme law of the land." Thus, tax professionals resolve conflicts between treaties and regulations or revenue rulings in favor of treaties. Conflicts between treaties and the Code are more problematic. The later-in-time rule often controls.[3] If Congress enacted a treaty most recently and intended it to override conflicting Code provisions, it typically prevails. However, if Congress enacted the Code provision last and intended for it to override conflicting treaty articles, the Code receives precedence.[4] If the Code provision is more recent and the legislative history does not evidence an intent to override the conflicting treaty provision, the treaty prevails. Based on these principles, treaty rules usually apply when in conflict with the Code, especially for cross-border transactions that are common.

---

### EXAMPLE

A U.S. company pays a $1,000 dividend to a Swiss national and resident. Section 871(a)(1) subjects the $1,000 to a 30 percent tax. However, article 10(2)(b) of the U.S.-Switzerland Treaty provides for a 15 percent tax. In routine transactions of this sort, the treaty almost always overrides the conflicting Code provision either because the Senate ratified the treaty more recently than the Code provision or because Congress did not intend for more recent changes to the Code to override existing treaties. Thus, the United States imposes only a 15 percent tax on the dividend.

---

**COMPLIANCE POINTER:** If it conflicts with the Code, taxpayers must disclose any tax return position based on a treaty using Form 8833, Treaty-Based Return Position.[5] However, Treasury waives disclosure for many common transactions, such as the dividend payment in the preceding example.[6] Taxpayers pay a $1,000 penalty ($10,000 for C corporations) for each failure to disclose, which is in addition to all other penalties.[7]

---

[3] *Whitney v. Robertson*, 124 US 190 (1888), contains one of the earliest expressions of the later-in-time rule.
[4] *U.S. v. Lee Yen Tai*, 185 US 213 (1902), clarified that the later-in-time rule cannot be applied blindly. For the most recently enacted provision to prevail, congressional intent must be clearly stated or inferred from the legislative history. IRC §894(a)(1) codified this clarification through its "due regard" language.
[5] IRC §6114.
[6] Reg. §301.6114-1(c).
[7] IRC §6712.

## TREATY SCOPE

Tax benefits from treaties depend on two broad issues related to coverage. First, the individual or entity involved must establish whether the treaty covers them. Second, they must ascertain which taxes the treaty covers. Whether a treaty provides benefits, and the extent of those benefits, depends on conclusions from these issues.

U.S. income tax treaties indicate that only individuals and entities qualifying as "residents" receive treaty benefits.[8] For instance, treaties reduce tax rates on investment income residents derive from the host country and eliminate tax on certain business profit and personal service income residents earn in the host country. Thus, establishing that an individual or entity resides in a treaty country is the first step to identifying treaty benefits.

### KEY CASE

The taxpayer, a citizen of Sweden, boxes Floyd Patterson for the world heavyweight championship on three separate occasions. Each bout takes place in the United States. A Swiss entity (established the year before the first bout) contracts to fight Patterson. The taxpayer is the Swiss entity's only employee and sole source of revenue, and he receives 70 percent of the Swiss entity's gross income plus pension benefits. Since he maintains a Swiss apartment and bank account, the taxpayer contends that he resides in Switzerland. Swiss residence, if established, would exempt his boxing income from U.S. taxation under the then-existing U.S.-Swiss Treaty. (The U.S.-Sweden Treaty did not provide such benefits.) However, the court disagrees, holding that the taxpayer's other social and economic ties establish his residency in Sweden. Thus, the U.S.-Swiss treaty does not shelter his income from U.S. taxation.[9]

Differing domestic laws in each treaty country can cause a taxpayer to be a resident of both countries simultaneously, a status known as dual residency. If not addressed, dual residency can exacerbate double tax problems

---

[8]As noted in Chapter 2, "Jurisdiction to Tax," the Code applies the term "residents" only to individuals, not entities. In contrast, U.S. treaties use the term in referring to both individuals and entities.

[9]*Johansson v. U.S.*, 336 F.2d 809 (CA-5, 1964). For similar shell corporation schemes that "loan out" employees, see Rev. Rul. 74-330, 1974-2 CB 278, and Rev. Rul. 74-331, 1974-2 CB 281. The special treaty articles applicable to athletes and entertainers (discussed later in this chapter) prevent many loan-out schemes among these individuals.

or, in some cases, create loopholes permitting unintended benefits. Thus, income tax treaties contain a series of tie-breaker rules for classifying dual residents, whether individuals or entities, as residents of only one country. When applying treaty provisions, assigning residency under the tie-breaker rules to only one country also identifies the taxpayer's home and host countries.

Resolving this residency issue is very important since treaty benefits flow in only one direction—treaties reduce host country taxes, not those in the home country. The U.S. Model Treaty classifies individuals as residents according to the following hierarchy:

- If the taxpayer has a permanent home in only one of the treaty countries, the treaty assigns residency to that country.
- When the individual has a permanent home in both countries, residency depends on the center of vital interests (e.g., place of social and economic ties).
- When the taxpayer has a permanent home in neither country or his or her center of vital interests is unclear, residency depends on the individual's habitual abode (i.e., where he or she usually lives).
- When the individual has habitual abodes in both treaty countries or neither treaty country, citizenship determines residency.
- When the taxpayer has citizenship in both treaty countries or neither country, the competent authorities in each country resolve the issue through the treaty's mutual agreement procedures.[10]

---

### EXAMPLE

Paige is a U.S. resident and German resident under the IRC and German tax law, respectively. Paige has a permanent home in both countries and spends approximately one-half of her time in each place. However, her immediate family resides, and her business interests center, in the United States. Article 4(2)(a) of the U.S.-German Treaty considers an individual with a permanent home in both countries as a resident in the country that is the "center of vital interests." Thus, Paige is a U.S. resident under the treaty.

---

A U.S. corporation is a dual resident if its management activities occur in another country and, as a result, that country treats the company as one of its residents. For applying treaty rules, the U.S. Model Treaty regards dual

---

[10]U.S. Model Treaty, Article 4(2).

resident corporations as residents in the country of incorporation.[11] However, several U.S. treaties do not follow the model on this point.

---

## EXAMPLE

International Hobbies, Inc. incorporates in Delaware but centrally manages operations from the Czech Republic. Under the respective U.S. and Czech laws, International Hobbies is both a U.S. and a Czech corporation (i.e., a dual resident).[12] To apply the treaty, International Hobbies must determine whether it is a U.S. resident or a Czech resident. Article 4(5) of the U.S.-Czech Treaty considers dual resident corporations as residents in the country of incorporation. Thus, International Hobbies is a U.S. resident for treaty purposes.

---

Once individuals and entities assure their coverage under a treaty's residency rules, the next step is to determine which host country taxes the treaty covers. For foreign residents (i.e., inbound transactions), U.S. income tax treaties explicitly cover the federal income tax but not state and local income taxes in the United States. Also, income tax treaties do not cover U.S. Social Security and self-employment taxes, though separate totalization agreements may confer coverage (as discussed in Chapter 15). Newer treaties extend coverage to the accumulated earnings tax and personal holding company tax, even though earlier treaties treated them as nonnegotiable penalties.[13]

> **RESEARCH POINTER:** Since many state and local jurisdictions in the United States piggyback on the federal calculation, treaties may indirectly affect state and local income taxes through reductions in federal adjusted gross income or taxable income, the starting points with some state calculations. Consult the laws in each jurisdiction to determine whether they restrict treaty benefits.

For U.S. residents (i.e., outbound transactions), U.S. income tax treaties cover our treaty partner's national income tax. Some treaties also extend coverage to property, capital, local income, and other taxes.

---

[11]U.S. Model Treaty, Article 4(3).

[12]PricewaterhouseCoopers, *Corporate Taxes: Worldwide Summaries 2002–2003* (Hoboken, NJ: John Wiley & Sons, Inc., 2002), p. 189.

[13]U.S. Treasury Department Technical Explanation of the United States Model Income Tax Convention (September 20, 1996) [hereafter, U.S. Model Treaty Explanation], Article 2.

## PERSONAL SERVICE INCOME

In most countries, the source of personal service income depends on where the taxpayer performs the work. Countries treat compensation from personal services rendered within their borders as domestic income and often tax such income. However, taxing the personal service income every time a **nonresident** performs cross-border services imposes considerable administrative burdens on both the country and the taxpayer. The country, if it has such a rule, must enforce it. Also, taxing income from all domestic services forces nonresidents to keep records, file returns, and pay taxes on nominal income attributable to minimum host country contact. Further, a policy of taxing all income from services nonresidents render domestically can discourage foreign travel and, thus, international commerce. To minimize administrative burdens and assist foreign commerce, treaties exempt personal service income from host country taxation when the contact is immaterial.

Many treaties distinguish between dependent and independent personal service income. Dependent services are generally those employees render. The host country cannot tax dependent service income (including salaries, wages, bonuses, and in-kind compensation) if the individual meets certain conditions. Under the **commercial traveler article** of the U.S. Model Treaty, the income is exempt if:

- The employee is present in the host country no more than 183 days during the year,
- The employer is not a host country resident, and
- A permanent establishment of the employer in the host country does not bear the expense of the compensation.[14]

---

### EXAMPLE

The commercial traveler article in the U.S.-Slovakia Treaty is similar to the one in the U.S. Model Treaty. Lena, a Slovakian national and resident, works as an employee in the United States from April 1 to August 31 during the current taxable year (first requirement in the preceding list). Her employer, Whispering Wilderness Wear (WWW), organizes in

---

[14]Article 15(2). Generally, corporations are "residents" wherever they are organized. Article 4(3). If a foreign corporation employs a nonresident alien who performs services in the United States, the second requirement is satisfied.

and manages operations from Slovakia. Thus, the employer is not a U.S. resident (second requirement in the list). WWW has branch operations in the United States, which pay Lena's compensation for the five months of her visit. The Slovakian home office reimburses the U.S. branch for the amount paid to Lena and, thus, bears the cost of her compensation. So, WWW does not deduct Lena's compensation against the portion of its business profit the U.S. taxes (third requirement). Under Article 15(2) of the U.S.-Slovakia Treaty, Lena excludes her personal service income for U.S. tax purposes.

**PLANNING POINTER:** The 183-day rule in some of the older U.S. treaties applies strictly on a year-by-year basis. Under these treaties, an employee present in the host country continuously from July 2, 2002 to July 2, 2003 qualifies for the exemption during both 2002 and 2003, assuming no further presence in either year.

Usually, only home countries tax independent contractors and self-employed individuals. However, a host country can tax independent personal service income if attributable to a fixed place of business regularly available within the host country.[15] In many treaties, the time independent contractors spend in the host country and the compensation they receive do not affect their eligibility for the treaty exemption.

### EXAMPLE

The independent personal service article in the U.S.-Sweden Treaty is similar to the one in the U.S. Model Treaty. Sabrina, a U.S. citizen and resident, works as an independent tax consultant for several technology companies. During the year, she stays in Sweden for 200 days and earns $235,000 while there. If Sabrina works in a fixed Swedish office, Article 14 of the U.S.-Sweden Treaty allows Sweden to tax her professional fees. However, if she does not remain in one location, and hotel rooms double as temporary office space for her consulting activities, Sweden cannot tax her $235,000.[16]

---

[15]U.S. Model Treaty, Article 14.
[16]U.S. Model Treaty Explanation, Article 14.

**COMPLIANCE POINTER:**    Employees and independent contractors whose personal service earnings are exempt in the host country benefit administratively, too. The exemption relieves them from keeping host country tax records and filing host country tax returns. Also, they avoid foreign withholding taxes and the necessity to claim a foreign tax credit, if otherwise available, on their home country returns.

If an individual does not meet the exemption requirements, the host country can tax personal service income. When the home country has a territorial tax system, no double taxation usually results since only the host country taxes the service income. However, when the home country uses a global tax system, both the home and host country tax the same income stream. To reduce or prevent double taxation in this latter case, the home country allows a foreign tax credit (as explained in Chapter 11).

Special treaty provisions often apply to government workers, retirees, divorcees, entertainers, athletes, students, apprentices, trainees, and teachers receiving service income. These provisions vary considerably among treaties and usually override the general rules applicable to dependent and independent personal service income (as discussed earlier). Excepting the last bulleted point in the following list, the U.S. Model Treaty rules are:

- Under most circumstances, only the home country of government employees (e.g., military and embassy personnel) tax government pay.[17]
- Only the country where payments originate taxes Social Security benefits.[18]
- The home country taxes pensions, annuities, and alimony, even if the recipient renders the services giving rise to the payment in the host country.[19]
- The general personal service rules exempt income from host country taxation when the visit is relatively short. The presumption is that short visits result in little revenue loss. However, professional entertainers and athletes often can earn large amounts of income in short time spans. Thus, treaties allow host countries to tax the income of professional entertainers and athletes whose gross receipts during the year from host country services exceed $20,000. When gross receipts do not exceed $20,000, treaties typically consider entertainers and athletes to be amateurs who must follow the general rules for dependent or independent personal services.[20]

---

[17] U.S. Model Treaty, Article 19.
[18] U.S. Model Treaty, Article 18(1)(b).
[19] U.S. Model Treaty, Article 18(1)-(3).
[20] U.S. Model Treaty, Article 17(1).

- Only the home country can tax the income of students, apprentices, and trainees temporarily present in a host country for full-time education or training at an accredited institution. However, this exemption from host country taxation applies only to the income received in relationship to education or training and only when the payment arises from someplace outside the host country.[21] In the case of students, the lost revenue from this exemption is usually trivial.
- To encourage the cross-cultural exchange of ideas and values, many treaties prevent host countries from taxing professors and teachers on host country income related to teaching or research if their foreign stay does not exceed two years.[22] Though many U.S. treaties allow this exemption, the U.S. Model Treaty does not.

---

### EXAMPLE

The Social Security, pension, and alimony provisions in the U.S.-Spain Treaty are similar to the ones in the U.S. Model Treaty. Samantha is a Spanish national and resident. During the year, she receives U.S. Social Security benefits, pension benefits, and alimony. Before her retirement, Samantha worked 30 years in New Jersey. After her retirement, Samantha renounced her U.S. citizenship and moved to Spain. Samantha's ex-husband lives in Florida. Under Article 20 of the U.S.-Spain Treaty, only Spain taxes Samantha's pension and alimony; the United States taxes her Social Security benefits.

---

## BUSINESS PROFIT

An individual or entity engages in business when it regularly and continuously conducts considerable activities to make a profit.[23] Absent a treaty, the United States taxes income of foreign persons effectively connected with a U.S. trade or business, and many countries have similar rules for taxing

---

[21]U.S. Model Treaty, Article 20.

[22]For an analysis of the issues, see Ernest R. Larkins, "Professors Who Teach Outside the United States: Tax Planning and Policy Analysis," *Journal of the American Taxation Association*, 9 (Fall 1987), pp. 48–74.

[23]*Lewenhaupt v. Comm.*, 20 TC 151 (1953), *aff'd per curiam*, 221 F.2d 227 (CA-9, 1955).

business profit.[24] However, when a treaty exists, the bar for taxing business profit inches up a notch. Under most U.S. income tax treaties, the host country cannot tax business profit unless it is attributable to a **permanent establishment (PE)** in the host country.[25]

---

### EXAMPLE

Richie, a foreign national residing abroad, and his prize bull visit several ranches in Houston and Dallas, Texas, Wichita, Kansas, and Albuquerque, New Mexico over a two-month period. For the bull's services, Richie nets $125,000 after expenses. Richie is conducting a U.S. business if the activities are regular, continuous, and considerable. If Richie resides in Honduras, the United States can tax the $125,000 since it is effectively connected with the U.S. business and no treaty exists between the United States and Honduras. However, if Richie resides in Mexico, Article 7(1) of the U.S.-Mexico Treaty prevents the United States from taxing Richie's $125,000 since the U.S. business does not have a PE to which income can be attributed.

---

**COMPLIANCE POINTER:**  The IRS ordinarily will not rule in advance on whether a taxpayer has a PE or whether income is attributable to a PE.[26]

When a partnership conducts business through a PE, U.S. law treats its general and limited partners as though they derive their partnership income through a PE.[27] Thus, the partnership's way of doing business carries over to each of its owners. As a result, U.S. law treats any partnership income attributed to the PE the same in the hands of each partner. When a treaty exists, host countries can tax foreign partners on their distributive shares of partnership income attributed to host country PEs.

---

[24]IRC §§871(b), 882(a). For examples of taxpayers with effectively connected income but not through a permanent establishment, see *de Amodio v. Comm.*, 34 TC 894 (1960), *aff'd*, 299 F.2d 623 (CA-3, 1962); Rev. Rul. 58-63, 1958-1 CB 624; and Rev. Rul. 67-321, 1967-2 CB 470.

[25]U.S. Model Treaty, Article 7(1).

[26]Rev. Proc. 2003-7, §4.01(9), 2003-1 IRB 233.

[27]*Donroy, Ltd. v. U.S.*, 301 F.2d 200 (CA-9, 1962); Rev. Rul. 90-80, 1990-2 CB 170.

---

**EXAMPLE**

---

Deer Lick Enterprises is a partnership with two equal partners. Buck is a U.S. citizen, and Fawn is a foreign national and resident. During the year, Deer Lick derived $230,000 profit effectively connected with its U.S. business. The company earned all but $30,000 of this profit through its U.S. PE. Of Fawn's $165,000 distributive share of Deer Lick's business profit, she derives $150,000 through a U.S. PE. If Fawn resides in a nontreaty country such as Bermuda, the United States taxes Fawn on her $165,000 share of U.S. business income. If instead she resides in France, Article 7(1) of the U.S.-France Treaty exempts the $15,000 of business profit not attributed to the U.S. PE. Thus, the United States taxes Fawn on only $150,000 of U.S. business income.

---

PEs come in three varieties: fixed places, dependent agents, and long-term projects. The most common PE form is the fixed place of business. Specifically, PEs include facilities such as warehouses, offices, stores, factories, branches, workshops, mines, oil or gas wells, quarries, or other locations where the taxpayer extracts natural resources.[28] PEs do not include temporary business uses of fixed locations (e.g., hotel rooms).[29] However, as the following case suggests, one must consider each situation on its merits.

---

**KEY CASE**

The taxpayer (a French citizen, resident, and well-known author) lives and works in the United States. He promotes his rights as an author, negotiates with publishers, and supervises translations. These continuous and regular pursuits occur in the author's U.S. home office, constitute business activities, and result in royalty income. The taxpayer deducts home office expenses on

*1 home office = PE*

---

[28]U.S. Model Treaty, Article 5(2).

[29]U.S. Model Treaty Explanation, Article 5. As mentioned earlier, most treaties prevent host countries from taxing independent personal service income absent a "fixed place of business." The primary difference between a permanent establishment and fixed place of business is that the latter may lack permanence. Thus, temporary office space that an accounting firm makes available to an independent contractor may constitute a fixed place of business but is not a permanent establishment.

his U.S. tax return, suggesting that he conducts the U.S. business from his home, a fixed location. Thus, the Tax Court attributes the royalty income to the author's U.S. home office, which it holds is a U.S. PE.[30]

---

### EXAMPLE

American Jigsaws, Inc., a domestic corporation, mails its puzzle catalogue to retail outlets in Germany and solicits the same outlets through telephone. When American Jigsaw sells puzzle products to German buyers, the export profit avoids German income tax. Under Article 7(1) of the U.S.-German Treaty, American Jigsaw maintains no German PE to which Germany can attribute the export profits.

---

Treaties regard business operations as PEs when conducted through dependent agents (e.g., employees) routinely exercising authority to conclude contracts for their principals (e.g., employers).[31] Independent agents (e.g., commission agents, brokers, and independent distributors) typically work for multiple principals in the course of their own businesses and are not PEs.

### KEY CASE

A Canadian national and resident manufactures a novelty item in Canada that he sells to a U.S. company with exclusive distributor rights. The U.S. firm distributes the item to newsstands that, in turn, sells them to the public. The Canadian individual periodically sends an employee to check on newsstand displays and pricing. The Tax Court held that the U.S. distributor acted as a dependent agent of the Canadian individual and, thus, constituted a U.S. PE. The court based its conclusion primarily on the language of the distribution contract. First, the contract did not state that the U.S. company "buys" the item. Second, the U.S. business reserved the right to pull the items from newsstands and return them to the taxpayer in certain cases. Third, the contract referred to the "exclusive distribution" through the U.S. company. Fourth, the contract specified the price at which the U.S. business must sell to the newsstands and the price at which the newsstands must sell

---

[30]*Simenon v. Comm.*, 44 TC 820 (1965).
[31]U.S. Model Treaty, Article 5(5).

to the public. Fifth, all items were "fully returnable" for full credit, regardless of their condition. Sixth, the U.S. company had to account for only the items sold. Seventh, the taxpayer bore all transportation charges, both to and from Canada. Since the court treated the U.S. distributor as a dependent agent and PE under the U.S.-Canada Treaty, the Canadian individual was liable for U.S. income tax on its U.S. profit.[32]

## EXAMPLE

Ujwala, a foreign national residing in Australia, sells handcrafted boomerangs to U.S. customers through Charlie, a full-time sales representative in Los Angeles. During the year, Ujwala's U.S. profit attributable to Charlie amounts to $48,000. If Charlie frequently concludes sales for Ujwala, he is a dependent agent, and Article 7(1) of the U.S.-Australia Treaty does not preclude the United States from taxing Ujwala's profit. However, if Charlie just takes orders and sends them to Ujwala for approval, Charlie's activities do not constitute a U.S. PE, and the $48,000 profit escapes U.S. taxation.

## KEY CASE

Four Japanese property and casualty insurance companies contract separately with a U.S. reinsurance underwriting manager. Under the contract, the U.S. manager possesses complete authority to underwrite insurance for its Japanese clients; the Japanese clients exercise no external control over the U.S. manager beyond the contractual terms. Either the U.S. manager or its Japanese clients can terminate their respective contracts with six months' notice. The U.S. manager can conclude underwriting contracts with other clients, which it does. At no time do the Japanese clients hold equity interests in the U.S. manager. The court held that the U.S. reinsurer was an independent agent since it was legally and economically independent of the Japanese companies. Thus, the U.S. manager did not constitute a PE of the four Japanese companies under the U.S.-Japan Treaty, and the Japanese companies were not subject to U.S. taxation on income under their respective contracts.[33]

---

[32]*Handfield v. Comm.*, 23 TC 633 (1955).
[33]*Taisei Fire & Marine Insurance Co. v. Comm.* 104 TC 535 (1995), *acq.*

Most countries do not treat foreign subsidiaries as PEs of their parent companies merely because the parents own the subsidiaries' shares. However, in some cases, subsidiaries may qualify as their parents' dependent agents and, thus, constitute PEs.[34] Regardless of the parent company tax implications, most countries can directly tax subsidiaries conducting business within their borders. Thus, countries often tax the business income of domestically incorporated subsidiaries even though treaties prevent the countries from taxing the subsidiaries' parent corporations incorporated and operating abroad.

---

**EXAMPLE**

Galaxy, Inc. (a domestic corporation) manufactures and sells telescopes, equatorials, and other astronomical equipment in the United Kingdom, resulting in $165,000 of profit. If Galaxy does not incorporate its U.K. operations, the $165,000 profit belongs to a U.K. branch. Since branches are PEs, Article 7(1) of the U.S.-U.K. Treaty allows the United Kingdom to tax Galaxy on its $165,000 branch profit. However, if Galaxy incorporates its foreign activities and the U.K. subsidiary does not act as a dependent agent, Galaxy has no U.K. PE, and the United Kingdom cannot tax Galaxy on the $165,000 profit attributable to the U.K. subsidiary. Of course, the United Kingdom can tax Galaxy's U.K. subsidiary directly.

---

Finally, PEs include building, construction, drilling, and installation projects when the related business activity lasts beyond a specified period. Twelve months is the typical period for determining whether a PE exists. Under this provision, drilling rigs or ships used to explore for or exploit natural resources can be PEs even though movable.[35]

Income tax treaties carve out some special exceptions from the three types of PEs just discussed. Facilities used solely to purchase, store, display, or deliver goods are not PEs since, by themselves, they do not produce income. Also, treaties do not treat facilities used solely to collect information (e.g., market data) as PEs. Once the taxpayer uses a facility in sales or production activities, however, it has crossed the PE line. Similar to facilities, agents limiting their activities to purchasing, storing, displaying, or delivering goods or collecting information do not qualify as PEs.[36]

---

[34]For the U.S. position, see Rev. Rul. 76-322, 1976-2 CB 487.
[35]U.S. Model Treaty, Article 5(3).
[36]U.S. Model Treaty, Article 5(4).

## FLASHBACK

The host country may tax a foreign company conducting business through a PE while exempting the company's foreign employees under the rules applicable to personal service income (as discussed earlier in this chapter). Conversely, the host country may exempt a foreign company conducting business without a PE while taxing the company's foreign workers. The jurisdictional disparity results from differences in criteria for taxing personal service income and business profit.

A special rule applies to international shipping and air transportation companies. Often, these companies maintain PEs in the host country (e.g., service counters and ticket offices). Nonetheless, most treaties provide that, whether involved in shipping cargo or transporting people, only the home company can tax cross-border transportation profit.[37] However, the host country can tax business profit from coastwise transportation and cruises to nowhere. Coastwise transportation occurs when both the departure and termination points lie within the host country. Cruises to nowhere are cruises departing from and terminating in the host country with no foreign port calls.[38]

## EXAMPLE

Jackrabbit Parcel Service, Inc. is a U.S. company guaranteeing three-day deliveries between any two major cities worldwide. During the year, Jackrabbit earns $128,000 from parcel deliveries between the United States and Italy and $42,000 from deliveries between major cities within Italy where Jackrabbit has offices. Under Article 8(1) of the U.S.-Italy Treaty, Italy can tax only the $42,000 from coastwise deliveries. Without the treaty, Italy could tax the $42,000 and, depending on its source of income rules, some portion of the $128,000 profit.

In contrast to the treatment of transportation income, most treaties allow the host country to tax income from real property located in the host country. Having no PE in the host country does not matter. Since treaties usually allow home countries to tax the real property income also, unilateral

---

[37]U.S. Model Treaty, Article 8.
[38]U.S. Model Treaty, Article 3(1)(d); U.S. Model Treaty Explanation, Article 3.

provisions (e.g., the home country's foreign tax credit) provide double tax relief. Real property income includes profit from agricultural activities, forestry, natural resource extraction, and leasing agreements.[39]

---

### EXAMPLE

Manchester Realty, Inc., a domestic corporation, owns agricultural land in the Philippines that it leases to a local farming cooperative for $35,000. Even if Manchester has no Philippines PE, Article 7(2) of the U.S.-Philippines Treaty allows the Philippines to tax the $35,000 since Manchester earns it from leasing real property.

---

## INVESTMENT INCOME

Treaties often provide for lower-than-normal tax rates when residents of one treaty country derive investment income from the host country or when multinational companies receive their foreign subsidiaries' business profit as dividends, interest, or royalties. For instance, the United States taxes foreign persons on investment income received from U.S. sources at 30 percent.[40] However, the applicable rate typically ranges between 0 and 15 percent if the foreign person resides in a treaty country.

Withholding rates determine the respective portions of tax revenue the home and host countries receive on cross-border investments. Thus, countries often negotiate over the level of treaty withholding rates. If the capital flowing between the two treaty countries is about the same, the treaty negotiators may set the withholding rates fairly low. The lower the withholding rates, the greater the efficiency of resource allocations and the simpler compliance becomes. However, zero or very low withholding rates sometimes encourage treaty shopping, a practice explained later. But if one country is a capital exporter (developed nation) and the other is a capital importer (developing nation), the latter often prefers high withholding rates. With low withholding rates, capital importers receive a relatively small share of tax revenue.

> **COMPLIANCE POINTER:**   The host country cannot readily verify a foreign taxpayer's deductions properly allocable against investment income. Thus, the country imposes the tax on gross investment income before deductions. To assure collection, the host country requires the payor to withhold tax from the investment income.

---

[39]U.S. Model Treaty, Article 6.
[40]IRC §§871(a)(1)(A), 881(a)(1).

Separate rates may apply to different types of investment income. For instance, treaties might tax interest income at 10 percent while exempting royalty income. Also, lower rates sometimes apply when the taxpayer owns a substantial portion of the payor. Foreign investment holdings above 10 percent represent **direct investments abroad**, while lesser holdings are **portfolio investments**.[41] For corporate recipients, most U.S. treaties require 15 percent withholding on dividends from portfolio investments and 5 percent for dividends from direct investments abroad. A few U.S. treaties set the ownership threshold to obtain the lower withholding rate at 25, 50, or 95 rather than 10 percent. Unlike corporate distributees with direct investments abroad, treaties impose the higher withholding rate applicable to portfolio investments on individual recipients regardless of their percentage holdings.

---

## EXAMPLE

Multi-Optics AB is a Finnish corporation. During the year, Multi-Optics derives $40,000 dividends from U.S. companies. Half of the dividends come from companies in which Multi-Optics owns a portfolio interest (i.e., less than 10 percent of the shares). Under Article 10(2) of the U.S. Finland Treaty, the United States taxes $20,000 of the dividends (the portfolio portion) at 15 percent and $20,000 at 5 percent.[42] Rather than the $12,000 ($40,000 × .30) tax applicable to residents from nontreaty countries, Multi-Optics pays a U.S. tax of only $4,000 [($20,000 × .15) + ($20,000 × .05)].

---

**PLANNING POINTER:** Pushing portfolio investments beyond the 10 percent (or, under some treaties, higher) threshold can result in a much lower dividend withholding tax rate.

Treaties provide substantial tax savings to those qualifying as residents. Unfortunately, this potential savings has led to many abuses. For instance, some investors from nontreaty countries set up **shell corporations** in a treaty country so lower tax rates apply to their investments. This strategy involves identifying a country that has favorable tax treaties with both the home and host countries, a process known as **treaty shopping.** The treaties bridge the "tax gap" between the two countries.

---

[41]Based on market value, U.S. direct investment abroad totaled $2.5 trillion in 2000. See Jeffrey H. Lowe, "U.S. Direct Investment Abroad: Detail for Historical-Cost Position and Related Capital and Income Flows, 2000," *Survey of Current Business*, 81 (September 2001), pp. 80–110.

[42]U.S. Model Treaty, Article 10(2).

**EXAMPLE**

A U.S. corporation has a wholly owned Taiwanese subsidiary that pays a $1,000 dividend. Since no treaty exists between the United States and Taiwan, the latter withholds $250, and the subsidiary remits $750 to the U.S. parent. The left side of Exhibit 3.1 summarizes the transaction. Suppose the U.S. company interposes a Malaysian holding company between it and the Taiwanese subsidiary. Article 10(3) of the Malaysia-Taiwan Treaty provides for a 12.5 percent dividend withholding tax. Though the United States has no treaty with Malaysia, the latter imposes no dividend withholding tax.[43] Thus, treaty shopping reduces the withheld taxes from $250 to $125, which the right side of Exhibit 3.1 illustrates.

**COMPLIANCE POINTER:** The IRS will not rule in advance on whether a corporate structure constitutes abusive treaty shopping and, thus, whether the persons involved are entitled to treaty benefits.[44]

**EXHIBIT 3.1**   Treaty Shopping Comparison

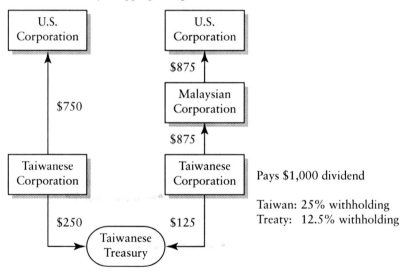

Pays $1,000 dividend

Taiwan: 25% withholding
Treaty:  12.5% withholding

---

[43]PricewaterhouseCoopers, *Corporate Taxes: Worldwide Summaries 2002–2003* (Hoboken, NJ: John Wiley & Sons, Inc., 2002), p. 497.
[44]Rev. Proc. 2003-7, §3.01(2), 2003-1 IRB 233.

Many treaties prohibit treaty shopping and deny benefits to companies that treaty country residents do not beneficially own. For instance, the U.S. Model Treaty denies benefits to any company established in a treaty country unless individual residents of the treaty country beneficially own, directly or indirectly, more than 75 percent of the company.[45] However, even when treaties do not explicitly prohibit treaty shopping, the IRS may question the existence of a business purpose and raise other form-over-substance arguments to deny treaty benefits.

## KEY CASE

ECL (a Bahamian corporation) owns two subsidiaries, CCN (an Ecuadorian corporation) and Aiken (a U.S. corporation). Aiken, in turn, owns MPI (a U.S. corporation). CCN loans funds to MPI, taking back a promissory note. However, since no income tax treaty exists between Ecuador and the United States, a 30 percent U.S. withholding tax applies to the interest CCN receives. To avoid the 30 percent withholding tax, CCN forms Industrias (a Honduran corporation), to which it transfers the promissory note. The corporate structure and interest payment appear as follows:

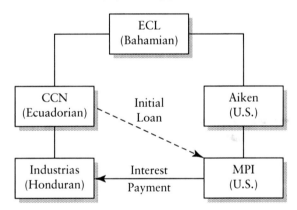

Under the then-existing U.S.-Honduras income tax treaty, the taxpayer asserts that the interest withholding tax is zero. The Tax Court disagrees, holding that the interest income really belongs to CCN (the Ecuadorian corporation), and upholds the 30 percent withholding. Though the events in this case occurred before U.S. treaties included antishopping provisions, the

---

[45] U.S. Model Treaty, Article 16. Treaty articles that curb treaty shopping often are titled "Limitation on Benefits" or "Holding Companies."

outcome is consistent with current-day treaty shopping restrictions. Since Honduran residents did not beneficially own Industrias's stock, the court denied Industrias the benefit of the U.S.-Honduras Treaty (i.e., zero withholding for interest received).[46]

> **PLANNING POINTER:** Most U.S. treaties prevent foreign persons from reducing U.S. withholding taxes through treaty shopping. However, U.S. persons can use other treaties to reduce foreign withholding taxes since non-U.S. agreements often do not deny benefits when the beneficial owners of a company reside elsewhere (i.e., they permit treaty shopping). For instance, U.S. multinationals with Asian-Pacific operations may find that a Malaysian or Barbados holding company can reduce overall withholding taxes, while European operations might rely on a Dutch holding company. In addition to reducing withholding taxes, treaties with favorable capital gain rates can diminish the tax cost of eventually winding down foreign operations.

Contractual agreements and corporate capital structures often play significant roles in international tax planning. U.S. multinationals wishing to return their foreign subsidiaries' earnings to the United States while minimizing foreign tax may conclude contracts for using intangible property rights with their foreign affiliates or capitalize a substantial portion of foreign operations with debt. To avoid income reallocations and possible penalties, the royalty or interest charge should fall within acceptable arm's-length standards. Also, the taxpayer should assure that total debt does not exceed ceilings that thin capitalization rules specify. Many countries set maximum debt-to-equity ratios to limit the amount of debt in corporate capital structures and, thus, the amount of business profit foreign businesses can siphon out of the country as interest.

> **PLANNING POINTER:** In contrast to dividends, which are mere distributions of after-tax profit, most countries treat interest and royalty payments as expenses of earning profit and permit their deduction.

---

[46]*Aiken Industries, Inc. v. Comm.*, 56 TC 925 (1971). Similarly, the IRS examines the substance of **back-to-back loans** in determining whether to give them separate effect. Such arrangements involve two loans of similar terms in which the same person, often a bank, acts as the borrower under one loan contract and the creditor in the second loan. For an analogous situation that involves **cascading royalties** (i.e., back-to-back licensing contracts), see Rev. Rul. 80-362, 1980-2 CB 208.

Thus, foreign earnings remitted as interest and royalties avoid foreign income tax. They also may qualify for treaty withholding rates lower than those applying to dividends.[47]

## EXAMPLE

Delphic Designs, Inc. is the U.S. parent company of a wholly owned Austrian subsidiary. The subsidiary earns $100,000 of before-tax business profit during the year. Austria taxes business profit at 34 percent.[48] If remitted to the parent as a dividend, the $66,000 after-tax profit [$100,000 × (1 − .34)] is subject to a dividend withholding tax of 5 percent under the U.S.-Austria Treaty. Thus, Delphic receives only $62,700 [$66,000 × (1 − .05)] of the $100,000 before-tax profit. An alternative strategy might be to include debt in the subsidiary's capital structure and return the business profit as interest. For the sake of illustration, assume that the interest payment on the debt is $100,000 each year. Interest is not subject to a withholding tax under the treaty. Thus, the interest deduction reduces before-tax business profit to zero, and no Austrian income tax results. Delphic receives $100,000 when remitting profit as interest.

## GAIN FROM DISPOSITIONS

Treaties normally allow host countries to tax gain from selling or otherwise disposing of real estate. This treatment extends to direct holdings in real estate as well as certain indirect holdings through domestic corporations. Similarly, host countries can tax gain from disposing of personal property if attributable to PEs or, when related to independent personal services, fixed places of business within host countries.[49]

Only home countries can tax gain from disposing of personal assets that taxpayers use in international transportation activities. Also, only home

---

[47]For empirical evidence that U.S. multinationals choose remittance policies that reduce taxes, see Julie H. Collins and Douglas A. Shackelford, "Global Organizations and Taxes: An Analysis of the Dividend, Interest, Royalty, and Management Fee Payments Between U.S. Multinationals' Foreign Affiliates, 24 *Journal of Accounting and Economics* (December 1998), pp. 151–173.

[48]PricewaterhouseCoopers, *Corporate Taxes: Worldwide Summaries 2002–2003* (Hoboken, NJ: John Wiley & Sons, Inc., 2002), p. 29.

[49]U.S. Model Treaty, Article 13(1)-(3).

countries can tax gain from disposing of personal assets not mentioned previously.[50] Thus, host countries usually cannot tax gain from selling securities and other investment assets. Finally, contingent gain from selling intangible assets, if not attributable to a host country PE, often escapes income taxation in host countries.[51]

---

**EXAMPLE**

Finesse SA, a French resident, sells U.S. securities through a U.S. broker and realizes a $173,000 capital gain. The security holdings do not represent indirect interests in U.S. real estate. If Finesse does not maintain a PE in the United States, article 13(6) of the U.S.-France Treaty prevents the United States from taxing the $173,000 gain.

---

## SPECIAL CLAUSES

Nearly all U.S. income tax treaties contain four special provisions: the savings, nondiscrimination, statutory allowance, and competent authority clauses. These provisions assure that treaties operate as intended. Without these provisions, some taxpayers might take advantage of unintended loopholes, while others might lose intended benefits.

The **savings clause** maintains the right of a treaty country to tax its own citizens or residents as if the treaty did not exist.[52] Income tax treaties reduce taxes of the host country, not the home country. Thus, U.S. citizens, U.S. residents, and domestic corporations can use treaties to reduce their foreign tax base but not to reduce U.S. taxable income. With only a few exceptions, the savings clause prevents home country residents from using treaties to reduce home country taxes.

---

**EXAMPLE**

Stanley, a U.S. citizen, resides permanently in Norway and receives U.S. source interest income of $32,000 from corporate bonds. Article 9(1) of the U.S.-Norway Treaty exempts the interest income a Norwegian resident receives from U.S. sources. Absent some exception, this provision

---

[50]U.S. Model Treaty, Article 13(4), (5).
[51]U.S. Model Treaty, Article 12(1), (2).
[52]U.S. Model Treaty, Article 1(4).

bars the United States from taxing Stanley's $32,000 even though he is a U.S. citizen. However, the savings clause in Article 22(3) allows the United States to tax the $32,000 as though the treaty does not exist. In effect, the savings clause overrides the treaty article exempting interest income and reinstates the United States' right to tax Stanley's worldwide income. As discussed in Chapter 11, the foreign tax credit mitigates the effect of the double tax when both countries tax the same income.

The nondiscrimination clause provides that a country cannot place a greater tax burden on a treaty partner's individuals and entities than it places on its own taxpayers.[53] This clause provides no guarantee against the host country raising tax rates or otherwise increasing tax burdens. However, it does guarantee that tax burdens of foreign persons will not increase unless they also increase for domestic persons. It also assures that a country extends to treaty country residents any tax breaks it gives to its own individuals and entities.

Signatory nations intend for income tax treaties to confer tax benefits. Treaties confer these benefits through measures limiting the host country's jurisdiction to tax. If through unintended language, a treaty's article reduces deductions, credits, exemptions, or other tax benefits a country's internal laws allow, the preservation clause (or statutory allowance clause) acts to preserve these benefits.[54] In effect, the preservation clause nullifies any treaty provision inadvertently taking away benefits that domestic laws otherwise permit.

## EXAMPLE

Until recently, Hostia (a hypothetical country) imposed a 30 percent withholding tax on Hostian source interest paid to nonresidents. However, to attract foreign capital, a new statutory provision eliminates withholding on all interest income that nonresidents earn. The U.S.-Hostia Treaty specifies a 5 percent withholding tax when U.S. persons receive interest from Hostian sources. Despite this treaty rate, the preservation clause overrides the 5 percent tax and preserves the exemption benefit under Hostian tax law. Hostia exempts interest income that U.S. persons receive.

---

[53]U.S. Model Treaty, Article 24.
[54]U.S. Model Treaty, Article 1(2).

To assure fairness, U.S. treaties contain procedures for resolving issues not otherwise addressed. The need for these procedures often arises when two treaty nations assert jurisdiction to tax the same income stream under differing treaty interpretations. The individual or entity subject to double taxation can invoke the treaty's competent authority procedures to resolve the conflicting interpretations. In the United States, the Secretary of the Treasury acts as **competent authority**. Sometimes, the U.S. competent authority seeks a mutual agreement with its counterpart in the other treaty country to resolve conflicts.

# CHAPTER 4

# Source of Income

Most international tax planning and research projects involve questions of source. In fact, the **source of income rules** so pervade most areas of international tax law that some understanding of their implications is indispensable. Novices to the international tax area often assume source rules impose U.S. tax or, at least, distinguish between taxable and exempt income. That is, they mistakenly believe the United States taxes U.S. source income while exempting foreign source income. Such is not always the case. As Chapter 2 explains, U.S. persons are taxable on all income, whether it is from U.S. or foreign sources. As Chapters 7 and 8 explain, the United States taxes foreign persons on some foreign source income and exempts some types of U.S. source income. So, rather than imposing tax or determining what income to tax, the source rules merely categorize income as either **U.S. source income** or **foreign source income**.

When sourcing an individual's or entity's income, the **United States** includes the 50 states, District of Columbia, airspace (other than outer space) overland masses, and the waters extending 12 nautical miles from the low watermark of U.S. shores.[1] The United States also includes the **U.S. continental shelf** area, but only when exploring for or exploiting natural resources offshore (e.g., drilling for oil).[2] The United States normally does not include **U.S. possessions**.[3] Thus, income from a U.S. possession is foreign source income.

## FUNDAMENTAL IMPORTANCE

Among the international tax provisions drawing from the source rules, two stand out as most important:

---

[1] IRC §7701(a)(9); PLR 9012023.
[2] IRC §638(1); Reg. §1.638-1(a)(1).
[3] IRC §7701(a)(9). U.S. possessions include Guam, the Northern Mariana Islands, Puerto Rico, and the U.S. Virgin Islands.

■ Calculating the foreign tax credit, which primarily is a concern for U.S. persons, and

■ Determining U.S. tax liability for foreign persons.

Chapter 11 discusses the foreign tax credit in more detail, but, a brief presentation is in order at this point to explain why the source of income rules are so vital. Section 901 allows U.S. taxpayers to take a credit on their federal tax returns for any foreign income taxes they pay or accrue. However, Section 904 limits the credit to the result of equation 4.1:

$$\text{Limit} = \frac{\text{Foreign source taxable income}}{\text{Worldwide taxable income}} \times \text{U.S. tax before the credit} \qquad (4.1)$$

The ratio's numerator requires knowledge of the income sourcing rules. Since the equation acts as a ceiling on the foreign tax credit, U.S. taxpayers prefer the result to be high. Thus, as a general rule, U.S. taxpayers prefer foreign source income over U.S. source income.

The United States taxes foreign persons (i.e., nonresident aliens and foreign corporations) on two types of income: U.S. source investment income and income effectively connected with a U.S. trade or business (which is usually U.S. source income also). Thus, foreign persons cannot determine their U.S. tax liabilities without considering the source rules. As with U.S. persons, foreign persons prefer foreign source income since such income usually, but not always, avoids U.S. income tax.

> **RESEARCH POINTER:**   Source rules appearing in some U.S. income tax treaties differ from those found in the Code. If more favorable than the Code, the "due regard" rule of IRC §894(a)(1) often permits foreign persons to follow the treaty. If less favorable than the Code, the treaty's preservation clause (discussed in Chapter 3) allows the taxpayer involved to follow the Code. However, the person cannot selectively apply the Code in some cases and the treaty in similar situations.[4]

## GENERAL SOURCE RULES

Most source of income rules appear in Sections 861 through 863 and 865. They vary according to types of income. Though exceptions exist, as discussed in "Interest Income" and "Dividend Income," Exhibit 4.1 summarizes some of the basic source rules.

---

[4]U.S. Model Treaty Explanation, Article 1.

**EXHIBIT 4.1**   Basic Source Rules

| Type of Income | Sourced Where |
| --- | --- |
| Interest | Noncorporate debtor resides or corporate debtor incorporates. |
| Dividends | Corporate payor incorporates. |
| Personal services | Person renders services. |
| Rent | Property exists. |
| Gain on realty | Property exists. |
| Royalty | Intangible property used. |
| Inventory profit | Title passes if person purchases inventory for resale. |

The first step in sourcing income is to determine the type of income. The type of income usually is obvious. In other situations, it is unclear. Many of the difficulties in identifying the type of income involve personal services.

## KEY CASE

As an orchestral conductor, a foreign individual records musical arrangements while in the United States. As compensation, the conductor receives a percentage of the recording's sales. The contract refers to his compensation as a royalty. However, since the contract never conveys property rights to the conductor, the Tax Court holds that he could not exchange property rights for royalties. Thus, the payments represent personal service income.[5]

## INTEREST INCOME

In keeping with the idea that "source" means "origin," the Code sources interest according to the residence of noncorporate debtors (i.e., payors) and incorporation site of corporate debtors. The underlying theory seems to be that debtors use borrowed capital primarily where they reside or incorporate, and interest income emanates from economic activities the borrowed

---

[5]*Boulez v. Comm.*, 83 TC 584 (1984). Also, see *Bank of America v. U.S.*, 680 F.2d 142 (Ct. Cl. 1982), which distinguished between interest and personal service income; and *Ingram v. Bowers*, 57 F.2d 65 (CA-2, 1932), which determined that Enrico Caruso's payment for voice recordings was personal service income rather than royalties.

capital funds. Similarly, interest the United States government pays on its obligations (e.g., T-bills and savings bonds) is U.S. source income to the recipient.[6] Under these rules, the creditor's (or recipient's) residence or place of incorporation is irrelevant.

---

### EXAMPLE

Fine Jewelry, Inc., a U.S. corporation, conducts most of its business in the United States. During the year, it pays $4,000 interest to Paragon SA, a Luxembourg corporation. The interest Paragon receives is U.S. source income.

---

Interest a resident alien or domestic corporation pays is U.S. source income to the recipient under the general rule just cited. The main exception takes the form of a look-through rule called the **active foreign business test**. This test partially addresses the questionable theory that interest income always relates to economic activity occurring at the place of residency or incorporation. The exception applies whenever a resident alien or domestic corporation derives at least 80 percent of its gross income from active foreign businesses. Tax professionals refer to domestic corporations meeting the test as **80-20 companies**. In determining whether the payor (or debtor) attains the 80 percent threshold, one must examine the gross income for the three-year period preceding the taxable year the resident alien or domestic corporation pays the interest (hereafter, the **testing period**). Equation 4.2 summarizes the test.[7]

$$\frac{\text{Foreign source business gross income of payor}}{\text{Worldwide gross income of payor}} \geq 80\% \qquad (4.2)$$

If the debtor attains this 80 percent threshold, the interest the resident alien or domestic corporation (i.e., 80-20 company) pays is entirely foreign source income to an unrelated recipient. If the debtor reaches the 80 percent threshold and pays the interest to a related person, a proportionate amount of interest income is from foreign sources.[8] In effect, the recipient looks through to the underlying income of the resident alien or 80-20 company in

---

[6]IRC §§861(a)(1), 862(a)(1).
[7]IRC §§861(a)(1)(A), (c).
[8]For this purpose, a related person is one owning 10 percent of either the voting power or stock value of the other party. IRC §861(c)(2)(B).

**EXHIBIT 4.2**   Sourcing Interest Income from Resident Aliens and Domestic Corporations

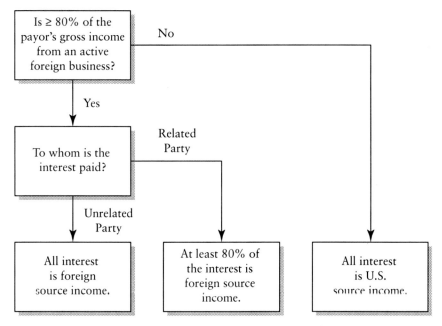

determining the interest income's source. Exhibit 4.2 summarizes these source rules for interest income.

> **PLANNING POINTER:**   Resident aliens and domestic corporations below the 80 percent threshold might consider engaging in more transactions generating foreign business income and fewer transactions yielding other income. If such efforts allow these persons to surpass the 80 percent threshold and meet the active foreign business test, they convert U.S. source interest creditors receive to foreign source income. The creditor's more favorable characterization of the interest income might permit the debtor to negotiate more favorable financing terms.

To determine the foreign source interest to the related recipient, the resident alien or domestic corporation uses its gross income for the three-year testing period in the ratio of equation 4.3.

$$\frac{\text{Foreign source gross income of payor}}{\text{Worldwide gross income of payor}} \times \text{Interest}$$

$$= \text{Foreign source interest} \tag{4.3}$$

Compare the ratio in this formula to the ratio used in the active foreign business test. The denominators are the same, but the numerator is broader here since it includes more than just business income. Thus, if the debtor meets the active foreign business test and pays interest to a related person, 80 to 100 percent of the interest is foreign source income to the recipient.

---

**EXAMPLE**

The Above Average Angler Company (AAA) is a domestic corporation with extensive branch operations abroad. AAA derives 90 percent of its gross income from foreign business sales over the three prior taxable years. Another 5 percent of its gross income comes from foreign investments. The remaining 5 percent is from U.S. sources. During the year, AAA pays $15,000 interest to Verna, an unrelated U.S. citizen, and $25,000 interest to Fly Fisherman Fanatic, Ltd. (FFF), a related U.K. subsidiary. The entire $15,000 interest to Verna is foreign source income since at least 80 percent of AAA's gross income is from foreign business activities (90 percent, to be precise) and Verna is unrelated to AAA. Only $23,750 (95% × $25,000) of the $25,000 interest income FFF receives is from foreign sources. The remaining $1,250 is U.S. source interest to FFF.

---

Special sourcing rules apply to interest income in the following situations. Each rule represents a departure from the general decree that sources interest income based on the payor's residency or incorporation site.

- Interest from deposits with foreign branches of U.S. companies is foreign source income if the branches engage in commercial banking.[9]
- Interest received from the U.S. trade or business of a foreign corporation (i.e., U.S. branch) is U.S. source income.[10]
- If 10 percent or more of a **U.S.-owned foreign corporation's** current **earnings and profits** (E&P) are attributable to U.S. sources, interest a U.S. shareholder receives from the corporation is proportionally from U.S. sources.[11] This look-through exception prevents a U.S. shareholder

---

[9]IRC §861(a)(1)(B).
[10]IRC §884(f)(1)(A). Chapter 10 discusses the branch interest tax resulting from this source rule.
[11]IRC §904(g). For this purpose, a "U.S. shareholder" is a U.S. person owning at least 10 percent of the foreign corporation's voting power. Under IRC §904(g)(6), a "U.S.-owned foreign corporation" is a foreign corporation in which U.S. persons directly or indirectly own 50 percent or more of the voting power or stock value.

from increasing the numerator of its foreign tax credit limitation when receiving interest income from a related foreign entity if the interest income is indirectly derived from U.S. sources.

## DIVIDEND INCOME

Under the general rule, dividends received from domestic corporations are U.S. source income, and dividends received from foreign corporations are foreign source income.[12] Like sourcing interest income, the underlying theory relates dividends' source to economic activity occurring where the distributor incorporates. Also like the interest sourcing rules, a look-through exception applies when the economic activity makes the general theory insupportable. The exception applies whenever at least 25 percent of a foreign corporation's gross income is effectively connected with a U.S. trade or business, per equation 4.4.[13]

$$\frac{\text{Effectively connected income of payor}}{\text{Worldwide gross income of payor}} \geq 25\% \qquad (4.4)$$

Similar to the active foreign business test for interest income, the foreign corporation tests for the 25 percent threshold using its income data for the three-year period preceding the taxable year during which it declares the dividend. If the ratio exceeds 25 percent, shareholders treat a proportionate amount of the dividends as U.S. source income, according to equation 4.5 in which the ratio uses gross income for the three-year testing period.

$$\frac{\text{Effectively connected income of payor}}{\text{Worldwide gross income of payor}} \times \text{Dividend}$$

$$= \text{U.S. source dividend} \qquad (4.5)$$

---

### EXAMPLE

Fly by Night Transport SA, a Brazilian corporation, declares and pays $12,000 dividends during 2004. If 20 percent of Fly by Night's gross income is effectively connected with a U.S. trade or business during 2001 through 2003, shareholders treat all dividends as foreign source income. If, instead, the ratio is 60 percent, the dividend recipients treat $7,200 as U.S. source income ($12,000 × 60%) and the remaining $4,800 as foreign source income.

---

[12]IRC §§861(a)(2), 862(a)(2).
[13]IRC §861(a)(2)(B).

## EXAMPLE

Flea Bag Resorts, Inc., a domestic corporation, owns 30 percent of a French corporation. The latter derives substantial income from U.S. business activities. For the past few years, the French company's world-wide gross income breaks down as follows:

|      | Effectively Connected | Not Effectively Connected |
|------|-----------------------|---------------------------|
| 2001 | $70,000               | $10,000                   |
| 2002 | 80,000                | 40,000                    |
| 2003 | 30,000                | 70,000                    |
| 2004 | 90,000                | 20,000                    |

In 2004, the French company declares and pays a $14,000 dividend to its shareholders. Flea Bag's U.S. source portion of its dividend is:

$$\frac{\$70,000 + \$80,000 + \$30,000}{\$80,000 + \$120,000 + \$100,000} \times (\$14,000 \times 30\%) = \$2,520$$

## FLASHBACK

As explained in "Interest Income," interest income received from 80-20 U.S. companies is primarily or entirely foreign source income. No sim-ilar exception applies for dividend income received from 80-20 compa-nies, so such dividends are U.S. source income. This disparity exists because the 80-20 company often deducts its interest payments against taxable income in the foreign country where the company conducts business. As deductible payments, interest reduces foreign income taxes and, thus, the foreign tax credit that the United States must allow. Therefore, interest payments conserve U.S. revenue through reducing foreign tax credits. In contrast, most countries do not permit distribu-tors to deduct dividend payments, so the 80-20 company's dividends do not affect the U.S. foreign tax credit. Since interest payments conserve U.S. revenue, interest from an 80-20 company receives favorable treat-ment (i.e., foreign source income), while dividends do not.

## EXAMPLE

Rackets Areus, Inc., a U.S. company, derives 88 percent of its gross in-come from foreign business activities in 2001 through 2003, and its remaining income from U.S. sources. In 2004, Rackets Areus declares a $40,000 dividend and pays $30,000 interest to its sole shareholder. Under the general sourcing rule, the shareholder treats the entire $40,000 dividend as U.S. source income. However, the shareholder receives $26,400 interest from foreign sources ($30,000 × 88%) since Rackets Areus is an 80-20 company.

The Code transforms some dividends U.S.-owned foreign corporations pay into U.S. source income.[14] However, companies can pay dividends from E&P attributable to multiple years.[15] Under a look-through rule, dividends paid from a given year's E&P are transformed into U.S. source income in the same proportion as that year's U.S. source E&P bears to the same year's total E&P.[16] However, if the proportion is less than 10 percent, dividends paid from that year's E&P are all foreign source income (i.e., no look-through).[17] This exception to the general dividend sourcing rule applies only when calculating the numerator of the foreign tax credit limitation and, thus, does not affect most foreign shareholders receiving dividends.

## EXAMPLE

Bambinelli Designs SA is a U.S.-owned foreign corporation since U.S. persons own at least 50 percent of its voting power. Its E&P for the current and two preceding years are:

|  | *2003* | *2002* | *2001* |
|---|---|---|---|
| E&P from U.S. sources | $ 18,000 | $ 9,000 | $ 25,000 |
| E&P from foreign sources | 82,000 | 91,000 | 75,000 |
| Total E&P | $100,000 | $100,000 | $100,000 |

*(continues)*

---

[14]IRC §904(g)(1)(C). This sourcing rule does not apply to dividends already treated as foreign source income under the 25 percent exception discussed earlier in this section. Section 904(g)(1) clarifies that the provision applies only to dividends "which would be treated as derived from sources outside the United States without regard to this subsection. . . ."
[15]Section 316(a) states that corporations pay dividends from current E&P first, and afterwards from the most recently accumulated E&P.
[16]IRC §904(g)(4).
[17]IRC §904(g)(5).

During 2003, Bambinelli declares and distributes $240,000 of dividends. Thus, under Subchapter C's dividend ordering rules, $100,000 comes from 2003, $100,000 from 2002, and $40,000 from 2001. For foreign tax credit purposes, U.S. shareholders treat $18,000 of dividends from 2003 E&P and $10,000 of dividends from 2001 E&P ($40,000 × 25%) as U.S. source income and the remaining $212,000 dividends as foreign source income. For most other purposes (e.g., determining a foreign person's U.S. tax liability), the entire $240,000 dividends are foreign source income.

As Chapters 12 and 13 discuss, U.S. persons report constructive dividends as gross income under the controlled foreign corporation, foreign personal holding company, and qualified electing fund regimes. If the distributor is a U.S.-owned foreign corporation, such constructive dividends are U.S. source income to the extent attributable to U.S. sources. Like actual dividends, this special rule applies only when determining the limitation for foreign tax credits.

## EXAMPLE

Planet International, Ltd. is a controlled foreign corporation and a U.S.-owned foreign corporation. During the current year, Planet derives 20 percent of its profits from U.S. sources. Under the controlled foreign corporation rules, Planet's U.S. shareholders must report a $220,000 constructive dividend, all from current E&P. For foreign tax credit purposes, the U.S. shareholders receive $44,000 ($220,000 × 20%) of the constructive dividend as U.S. source income even though derived from a foreign entity.

Other look-through rules apply to dividend income in the following situations. Each rule represents a departure from the general sourcing rule that recipients source dividends according to the distributor's place of incorporation.

■ When domestic corporations with a Section 936 election (i.e., **possession corporations**) distribute earnings, a look-through rule treats the dividends as foreign source income.[18]

---

[18]The IRC §936 election provides a tax credit to qualifying domestic corporations conducting business in Puerto Rico or the U.S. Virgin Islands. Under IRC §936(j), the credit benefit phases out entirely for taxable years beginning after 2004.

- When foreign corporations distribute earnings accumulated as domestic corporations, the dividends are U.S. source income.[19] For instance, when a domestic corporation reorganizes as a foreign corporation and distributes its prereorganization earnings, the shareholders receive U.S. source income.
- Dividends shareholders receive from domestic international sales corporations (DISCs) are foreign source income to the extent attributable to qualified export receipts.[20] Chapter 14 discusses DISCs.

## PERSONAL SERVICE INCOME

The Code sources personal service income according to where the individual or entity renders services.[21] Like other source rules, the premise is that persons should source personal source income where the related economic activity (i.e., performance of services) occurs. This general rule applies to both current and deferred compensation, such as bonuses and retirement income. However, the Code always treats U.S. Social Security benefits as U.S. source income.[22]

### EXAMPLE

Mia, a U.S. citizen, travels to Japan to teach a two-week course in American folklore and traditions. She receives an $8,000 fee for teaching the course. The $8,000 is foreign source income since the teaching occurs abroad. However, Mia treats any postretirement Social Security benefits attributable to these services as U.S. source income.

As mentioned earlier, distinguishing between personal service income and other types of income, such as interest and royalties, is sometimes difficult. Another thorny issue arises when the taxpayer renders some services in the United States and some abroad. When entities render services, classifying fees as U.S. or foreign source income often depends on both the time and value of services. For individuals, employment contracts may be inconsistent with actual practice or unclear about the services for which the employer pays compensation.

---

[19] IRC §861(a)(2)(C).
[20] IRC §861(A)(2)(D).
[21] IRC §§861(a)(3), 862(a)(3).
[22] IRC §861(a)(8).

---

**EXAMPLE**

Ambueh Lance Chaser & Associates (ALC), a U.S. law firm specializing in personal injuries, handles mostly domestic claims. However, an employment-related injury in Norway results in a $4.2 million professional fee. The company renders all of its clerical services ($100,000 of the total) and 90 percent of its legal services in the United States. Thus, ALC receives $410,000 [($4,200,000 – $100,000) × 10%] as foreign source income. A simple allocation of the professional fee based on hours would have been inappropriate since the company bills an hour of professional work at a higher rate than it bills clerical services.

---

**KEY CASE**

A Canadian national and resident plays professional hockey. The hockey season consists of four periods: (1) training and exhibition play, (2) the regular season, (3) playoff games, and (4) the off-season. During the off-season and the period of training, the taxpayer stays in Canada. He lives in the United States the remainder of the year, spending only a few days of the regular season and playoff period in Canada. The court held that the player's basic compensation covers the period of training, regular season, and playoff games, but not the off-season. The court indicated that the standard player's contract, which docks the salary of suspended or striking players by dividing basic salary by only the regular-season days, does not control.[23]

---

A **de minimis** exception affects the source of compensation a nonresident alien receives for U.S. services, either as an employee or independent contractor. The exception applies if the individual:

- Limits U.S. visits during the taxable year to an aggregate of 90 or fewer days,
- Receives no more than $3,000 compensation for U.S. services during the taxable year, and
- Renders services for either (1) a foreign person not engaged in a U.S. trade or business or (2) a foreign business of a U.S. person (e.g., the overseas branch of a domestic corporation).[24]

---

[23]*Stemkowski v. Comm.*, 690 F.2d 40 (CA-2, 1982). Also, see Rev. Rul. 87-38, 1987-1 CB 176.
[24]IRC §861(a)(3). U.S. law has never adjusted the $3,000 for inflation. Thus, the $3,000 threshold often disqualifies foreign professionals from qualifying under this de minimis exception even though their U.S. visit falls far short of the 90-day threshold.

If the nonresident alien meets all three conditions, the compensation is foreign source income even though the individual renders services in the United States. This exception applies only to inbound services. Thus, a U.S. person working only a few days abroad for a small amount of pay receives foreign source income under U.S. law, an application of the general sourcing rule.

---

### EXAMPLE

Geriatrics, Ltd. employs Senitra, a nonresident alien, as a marketing specialist. During the year, Senitra tours and lectures in the United States for two months. Geriatrics, Ltd. is a foreign corporation not currently engaged in business within the United States. Senitra's compensation for the two months she visits the United States is all foreign source if it does not exceed $3,000.

---

### FLASHBACK

Through the commercial traveler articles explained in Chapter 3, U.S. income tax treaties often provide more favorable de minimis rules than the Code. For instance, most commercial traveler articles allow employees to remain in the host country up to 183 days and permit nonresident employers to conduct business in the host country.

---

### EXAMPLE

Garrick, a nonresident alien, is an employee of a German company with sales branches in several countries including the United States. During the year, Garrick visits the United States for 45 days and receives compensation of $2,000 for his U.S. work. Under the Code, the $2,000 is U.S. source income since the employer conducts a U.S. business. However, depending on additional facts, Article 15(2) of the U.S.-Germany Treaty may exempt the income despite its U.S. source.

---

Special rules apply to other types of income related to personal services. Some of these rules extend the general sourcing rule for personal services to special situations, while others bear no relation to the general rule. The following list provides interesting applications:

■ Alimony is a splitting of personal service income between ex-spouses. When ex-spouses live in different countries, the payor's residence determines the alimony's source.[25]

■ Covenants not to compete prohibit the rendering of services in specified geographical areas. The location where the taxpayer cannot render services establishes the source of income from such covenants.[26]

■ The source of damages received for failure to perform services, whether judicial or out-of-court settlements, depends on the source of income if the defendant had rendered the services.[27]

■ Recipients treat scholarships, fellowships, prizes, and awards as U.S. source income if a U.S. person makes the award, and foreign source income otherwise. However, nonresident aliens treat grants to study or research abroad, and achievement awards for activities previously conducted abroad, as foreign source income, even if a U.S. person presents the award.[28]

## RENT AND ROYALTY INCOME

The source of rent and leasing income depends on the property's location or where the lessee uses the property.[29] The rule presumes that the economic activity producing the income occurs where the property exists or where the lessee uses property. Thus, the rental of property situated or used in the United States yields U.S. source income. Renting property located (or that the lessee uses) on foreign soil results in foreign source income. Special allocation rules often apply to movable property, such as railroad rolling stock, that crosses national borders.[30]

---

### EXAMPLE

Capital Realty, Inc., a U.S. company, owns and leases luxury condos in the United States and Caribbean. The company signs all leasing agreements in its Chicago office. Leasing income from its Aspen, Colorado, properties yields U.S. source income. Capital Realty treats leasing income from its Nassau, Bahamas, condos as foreign source income.

---

[25]Rev. Rul. 69-108, 1969-1 CB 192; *Manning v. Comm.*, 614 F2d 815 (CA-1, 1980).
[26]Rev. Rul. 74-108, 1974-1 CB 248.
[27]Rev. Rul. 83-177, 1982-2 CB 112.
[28]Reg. §1.863-1(d).
[29]IRC §§861(a)(4), 862(a)(4).
[30]IRC §861(e).

> **EXAMPLE**
>
> Tuxs for Bucks, Ltd. is a foreign corporation that rents formal wear for all occasions. The company operates through rental offices in major U.S. and foreign cities. Tuxedos rented for use outside the United States produce foreign source income. Rental income for tuxedos worn in the United States is U.S. source income.

The Code sources royalty income according to where the licensee uses or has the privilege of using intangible assets. This rule treats the geographical area where the licensee uses (or can use) intangible assets as the place of economic activity giving rise to the income. Intangible assets include manufacturing intangibles, such as patents, secret formulas, secret processes, and copyrights, and marketing intangibles, such as trademarks, brand names, franchises, and goodwill.[31]

> **EXAMPLE**
>
> Margaret, a U.S. citizen, owns the worldwide rights to a secret formula for root beer. She licenses the European rights to a U.S. company planning to manufacture and distribute root beer in Europe. Since the rights extend only to the European market, all royalties Margaret receives under the license contract are foreign source income.

> **EXAMPLE**
>
> Clematis, a nonresident alien, licenses the right to publish and market her book, *Life in a Stove Pipe*. Under the royalty contract, she receives $3 per book sold. The publisher sells 60,000 books, one-third in the U.S. market. Clematis receives $60,000 U.S. source income and $120,000 foreign source income.

## GAIN FROM SELLING PROPERTY

Before the Tax Reform Act of 1986, the tax law sourced gains from disposing of all personal property—including noninventory items—according to

---

[31]IRC §§861(a)(4), 862(a)(4).

where sales took place. Usually, sales occur where title passes. Since persons effectively managed title passage through clear statements in sales contracts, they easily controlled the source of gains from a variety of transactions. Stocks, bonds, and other investment assets were particularly easy to sell abroad. The resulting foreign source income allowed U.S. taxpayers to increase foreign tax credits and permitted foreign persons to avoid U.S. taxation. To establish some consistency between a transaction's economic realities and the source rules, Congress drastically restricted application of the title passage rule after 1986. The changes curtailed the practice of artificially generating foreign source income when disposing of personal property.

Now, the source rules for gain vary according to the type of property and depend on myriad factors. Separate rules apply to gain from the sale or exchange of realty, inventory, depreciable property, and investment assets. Depending on the type of property, the transferor's residency, how the transferor acquired the asset, which offices participate in the sale, the direction of the transfer (inbound versus outbound), and whether the transferor pays foreign income tax may affect the gain's source.

Notwithstanding any of the rules discussed later in this section, a nonresident's sale of personal property through a U.S. office or other fixed place of business yields U.S. source income unless two conditions exist. First, the property must be inventory the final customer uses, consumes, or disposes of outside the United States. Second, the seller must have another office or fixed place of business abroad that materially participates in the sale.[32] If both conditions exist, the nonresident sources income under the inventory rules discussed here (which often depend on title passage), even though sales occur through a U.S. office or fixed place of business.

> **PLANNING POINTER:** Foreign manufacturers selling in the U.S. market must proceed with caution. Selling production through a U.S. office exposes the entire profit, including the portion attributable to manufacturing, to U.S. taxation. At least four possible solutions exist. First, the foreign manufacturer can market its production in the United States through catalogue mailings or other forms of advertisement not requiring a physical presence. Passing title outside the United States prevents any portion of the profit from becoming U.S. source income. Second, selling through independent U.S. distributors or brokers may provide a reasonable solution since the manufacturer does not sell through its own U.S. office or fixed location. Third, the foreign manufacturer can establish a U.S. subsidiary to

---

[32] IRC §865(e)(2). For this purpose, the term "nonresident" is defined later in this section.

act as distributor in the U.S. market. The foreign manufacturer sells its production to the U.S. subsidiary, passing title outside the United States. Thus, profit attributable to foreign production activities (but not U.S. marketing activities) avoids U.S. taxation. Fourth, if a U.S. treaty exists with the home country, the foreign manufacturer can structure its U.S. place of business so it does not become a permanent establishment and, thus, avoid U.S. taxes.

## Real Estate Gain

The Code sources gain from the sale or exchange of real property according to the property's location.[33] If situated in the United States, the gain is U.S. source income. Otherwise, it is foreign source income.

### EXAMPLE

Global Resorts SpA, is an Italian corporation that rents vacation properties. During the year, the company receives rental income of $138,000 from renting Montana cottages to U.S. and foreign individuals. This rental income is from U.S. sources (under rules discussed in the prior section). At year end, Global Resorts sells its Montana property at a $670,000 gain to a Saudi investor. The gain also is U.S. source income.

Gain from disposing of a U.S. real property interest (discussed in Chapter 9) is U.S. source income also. A foreign person's direct ownership of U.S. real estate or indirect ownership through a U.S. corporation is a U.S. real property interest. For instance, a nonresident alien selling shares in a domestic corporation owning primarily U.S. realty has U.S. source income. Exhibit 4.3 recaps the sourcing rules discussed so far regarding gain from property dispositions and, in some cases, directs the reader to later exhibits.

## Investment Gain

The source of gain from the sale or exchange of stocks, bonds, commodities, and other investment properties (other than real estate) depends on the transferor's residency. Gain a U.S. resident realizes is U.S. source income, while a nonresident treats the gain as foreign source income.[34]

---

[33]IRC §§861(a)(5), 862(a)(5), (8).
[34]IRC §865(a).

**EXHIBIT 4.3** Sourcing Gain from Property Dispositions

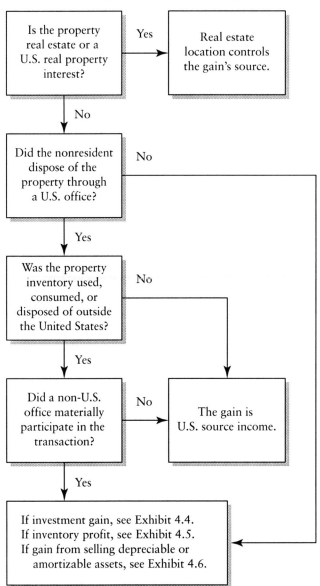

---

**EXAMPLE**

---

Anywhere Cellular, Inc. is a U.S. resident (as defined following). During the year, the company sells a portfolio interest in a French corporation for a $275,000 gain. The broker executing the sale resides in Australia, and the sale occurs on the Australian Stock Exchange. The entire gain is U.S. source income since the transferor is a U.S. resident.

---

When selling investment assets, the source rules define U.S. residents and nonresidents differently from treaties (see Chapter 3) and other parts of the Code (see Chapters 6 and 15). Thus, U.S. law can treat a person as a nonresident when sourcing gain on investment assets, but a resident for other tax purposes, and vice versa. If sourcing investment gains, U.S. residents include:

- U.S. citizens and residents without foreign tax homes,[35]
- U.S. citizens and residents with foreign tax homes paying at least a 10 percent foreign income tax on the gain,[36]
- Nonresident aliens with U.S. tax homes,
- U.S. corporations,
- U.S. estates, and
- U.S. trusts.[37]

All other individuals and entities (except partnerships) are nonresidents. Partnership gain passes through to owners where the status of each partner (i.e., U.S. resident or nonresident) determines the source of allocable gain.[38]

---

**EXAMPLE**

---

Roxanne is a U.S. resident and Peruvian national. She works in Chicago as an interior designer. During her recent visit to Peru, she sold stock in a Peruvian company and realized gain of $125,000. She paid no income tax in Peru on the gain. The entire gain is U.S. source income since Roxanne is a U.S. resident with a U.S. tax home.

---

[35]Tax homes generally exist at the location of one's principal place of business. Rev. Rul. 93-86, 1993-2 CB 71, provides more definitive guidance.

[36]The 10 percent requirement prevents U.S. citizens and residents working abroad from treating investment gain as foreign source income (and, thus, obtaining foreign tax credit benefits that shield other income) when the host country does not treat the gain similarly and tax it.

[37]IRC §865(g).

[38]IRC §865(i)(5).

When U.S. residents maintain foreign offices or other fixed places of business abroad, investment gain attributable to such offices or business locations is foreign source income if the seller pays at least a 10 percent foreign income tax. This favorable provision also applies to manufacturing and marketing intangibles U.S. residents sell when the sales price does not depend on future productivity, use, or disposition of the intangible asset.[39]

Under the rules just itemized, a U.S. corporation's gain from selling stock normally results in U.S. source income. However, gain is foreign source income when a domestic corporation sells stock in an 80-percent-owned foreign corporation and the sale occurs in a foreign country meeting two conditions. First, the affiliate must be actively conducting business in such country. Second, the affiliate must have derived more than half its gross income from business activities within such country over the prior three taxable years.[40] Exhibit 4.4 portrays general source rules for gain that individuals and entities derive from selling or exchanging investment assets.

---

## EXAMPLE

United Pixels, Inc., a domestic corporation, owns all shares of UPX, Ltd., a Belizean corporation. Over the previous three taxable years, UPX conducted business in Belize and derived 75 percent of its gross income from Belizean business activities. During the current year, United Pixels sold 5 percent of its UPX stock at a $338,000 gain. If sold in Belize, the gain is foreign source income. If sold in any other foreign country or the United States, the gain is U.S. source income since United Pixels is a U.S. resident.

---

### Inventory Profit

The Code sources inventory profits differently depending on how the seller acquired the inventory. Different source rules apply to inventory a business purchases and then resells and inventory the seller produces or manufactures. The former involves only one economic activity (i.e., selling, whether retail or wholesale distribution); the latter involves two (i.e., producing and selling). Also, special source rules apply to natural resources exported from the United States.

Taxpayers source gain from selling purchased inventory (other than real property) where sales occur.[41] As noted earlier, sales occur where inventory

---

[39]IRC §865(e)(1).
[40]IRC §865(f).
[41]IRC §§861(a)(6), 862(a)(6).

**EXHIBIT 4.4**   Sourcing Investment Gain[a]

```
┌──────────────────┐  No
│ Did a U.S. resident├──────────────────────────────────────────────────────┐
│   dispose of the │                                                          │
│  investment asset?│                                                         │
└────────┬─────────┘                                                          │
         │                                                                    │
        Yes                                                                   │
         │                                                                    │
         ▼                                                                    │
┌──────────────┐  Yes ┌──────────────────┐  Yes                              │
│ Is the gain  ├─────►│   Did the U.S.   ├──────────────────────────────────►│
│attributable to a│   │resident pay at least│                                │
│foreign office?│     │  a 10% foreign   │                                    │
└──────┬───────┘      │  income tax on   │                                    │
       │              │    the gain?     │                                    │
      No              └────────┬─────────┘                                    │
       │                      No                                              │
       ◄───────────────────────┘                                             │
       │                                                                      │
       ▼                                                                      │
┌──────────────┐ Yes ┌──────────────────┐ Yes ┌──────────────────┐ Yes       │
│ Is the U.S.  ├────►│ Is the investment ├────►│ Did the foreign  ├──────────►│
│resident a domestic│ │asset stock in an │     │ affiliate do business│       │
│ corporation? │     │80-percent-owned  │     │  in and derive   │           │
└──────┬───────┘     │    foreign       │     │   > 50% of its   │           │
       │             │  corporation?    │     │ income from the  │           │
      No             └────────┬─────────┘     │ country of sale? │           │
       │                     No               └────────┬─────────┘           │
       ▼                      ▼                        No                     │
┌──────────────┐                              ┌──────────────────┐           │
│ The gain is  │                              │   The gain is    │◄──────────┘
│ U.S. source  │                              │  foreign source  │◄──────────
│   income.    │                              │      income.     │
└──────────────┘                              └──────────────────┘
```

[a]For investment gain a foreign person derives through a U.S. office, see Exhibit 4.3.

title changes hands, which is the ~~title passage rule.~~ Shipping terms rarely determine the source of income.

## KEY CASE

A U.S. corporation purchases and resells goods to various foreign customers. Since its sales contracts specifically state that title passes abroad, the taxpayer contends that such language controls the source of profits. The government argues that, in contrast to the stated intent, shipping terms (i.e., CIF or cost, insurance, and freight) imply the seller intends to pass title within the United States; thus, the profit should be U.S. source income. The U.S. Claims Court held that a clear statement of title passage controls; resorting to presumptions based on shipping terms is unnecessary. An intent to avoid taxes is not important if the seller has a valid business purpose for passing title abroad. Business reasons might include avoiding unexpected trade embargoes, expropriations, or national strikes. Further, the taxpayer might prefer to retain title until after delivery so it can insure goods in the United States and, in the event of damage in transit, expedite and denominate a later recovery in U.S. dollars.[42]

---

### EXAMPLE

Flagrant Fowl, Inc., a U.S. distributor of frozen foods, sells 2,000 frozen turkeys to a South American food service business. Title to the frozen turkeys passes in South America. All profit from the sale is foreign source income.

---

**PLANNING POINTER:** All contracts should state explicitly where persons intend to transfer inventory title on cross-border sales. Otherwise, the IRS may assert that shipping terms control. U.S. taxpayers prefer to pass title abroad since this procedure increases the foreign tax credit limit. However, passing title abroad sometimes involves trade-offs, such as bearing the risk of delivery.

---

### EXAMPLE

Penguin Pools, Inc., a U.S. distributor, exports pool equipment, always transferring title in the United States. This year, Penguin Pools earns $700,000 export profit and $1,100,000 profit on domestic sales. Further, the company pays $100,000 foreign taxes on $200,000 of foreign branch profit (i.e., the effective foreign tax rate is 50 percent). At a 34 percent U.S. rate, the U.S. income tax before credits is $680,000 ($2,000,000 × 34%). The company's foreign tax credit limit is:

$$\frac{\$200,000}{\$700,000 + \$1,100,000 + \$200,000} \times \$680,000 = \$68,000$$

---

[42]*A.P. Green Export Co. v. U.S.*, 284 F2d 383 (Ct. Cl., 1960).

Thus, Penguin Pools cannot use excess credit of $32,000 this year ($100,000 − $68,000). If the company had reworded its export sales contracts so title always transferred abroad, it could have converted $700,000 of U.S. source income to foreign source income. Then the limitation would have been large enough to permit Penguin to credit all $100,000 of the foreign taxes on its U.S. return. Specifically, the limitation would have been:

$$\frac{\$700,000 + \$200,000}{\$700,000 + \$1,100,000 + \$200,000} \times \$680,000 = \$306,000$$

Sourcing gain is a bit more problematic when the taxpayer manufactures or produces inventory items in the United States and sells them abroad, or vice versa. Under the 50-50 method, the seller allocates half the income based on where production assets exist and half according to where sales occur.[43] Thus, if production occurs in the United States and title passes abroad, this method splits inventory profit evenly between U.S. and foreign sources. The 50-50 method applies similarly to inbound and outbound transactions.

## EXAMPLE

Big Beast Taxidermist, Ltd., an African enterprise, sells stuffed animals to museums and similar establishments. For nonnative animals, the company purchases the stuffed animals it sells from taxidermists in other African regions. For the rest of its inventory, Big Beast pays big game hunters for recent kills and performs the taxidermy work itself. During the year, Big Beast sells a large rhinoceros to the Wild Side Museum in the United States at a $16,000 profit. Since the U.S. museum refuses to assume the shipment risk, title transfers in the United States. If Big Beast purchased the stuffed rhinoceros from another taxidermist, the entire gain would be U.S. source income. If Big Beast performed the taxidermy work itself and used the 50-50 method, only $8,000 of the gain would be U.S. source income. (As Chapter 8 explains, the mere fact that Big Beast earns U.S. source income does not mean it necessarily must pay U.S. income tax.)

---

[43]Reg. §1.863-3(b)(1).

## EXAMPLE

Surf's Up USA, Inc., a domestic corporation, manufactures surfing and scuba-diving equipment. Surf's Up maintains all production assets in the United States. During the year, the company sells equipment directly to an unrelated Barbadian distributor for $90,000, passing title abroad. Surf's Up's equipment cost $66,000 to manufacture, so the transaction's gross income is $24,000. The 50-50 method attributes half the profit to production and, thus, treats $12,000 as U.S. source income based on the location of production assets. The method attributes the remaining profit to sales and, thus, treats $12,000 as foreign source income since title passes abroad.

If elected, and instead of the 50-50 method, manufacturers can source inventory profit based on a fairly established independent factory price (IFP). To establish the IFP fairly, manufacturers must make regular sales to unrelated distributors (or other selling concerns) primarily involved in marketing. That is, the purchasers must be mere middlemen who do not process items further so that the IFP is entirely attributable to production. Also, the manufacturer's sales activities related to these transfers cannot be significant in relation to other economic activities (e.g., production) involving the items sold.[44]

If established, the IFP divides inventory profit from sales to retailers (and other non-distributors) between production and sales activities. Thus, the IFP method attributes prices retailers pay up to the IFP to production activities, and sources the related income where production assets exist. The method attributes income related to any portion of sales price above the IFP to sales activities and, thus, sources such income wherever sales occur (based on title passage).[45] In lieu of both the 50-50 and the IFP methods, a manufacturer or producer receiving advance IRS consent can allocate inventory profit between production and sales activities based on its books and records.[46]

## EXAMPLE

Continuing the prior example, assume Surf's Up regularly sells to the unrelated Barbadian distributor and, thus, establishes an IFP for its en-

---

[44]Reg. §1.863-3(b)(2)(i).
[45]Reg. §1.863-3(b)(2)(ii).
[46]Reg. §1.863-3(b)(3).

tire line of products. Also, the company occasionally sells to nondistributors. On a $25,000 sale to a Barbadian retailer, the IFP is $23,000. Thus, $23,000 of the sales price is attributable to production activities and $2,000 is attributable to sales activities. If the equipment sold costs $20,000, $3,000 of the inventory gain is attributable to production activities and $2,000 of the profit relates to sales activities. As indicated in the prior example, Surf's Up maintains all its production assets in the United States. Assuming Surf's Up elects to use the IFP method and passes title abroad on sales to the Barbadian retailer, $3,000 of its inventory gain is U.S. source income and $2,000 is foreign source income. If Surf's Up does not elect the IFP method, the 50-50 method results in $2,500 U.S. and $2,500 foreign source income. In this case, the 50-50 method provides a better result than the IFP.

**PLANNING POINTER:** If trying to maximize foreign source income from outbound sales, U.S. manufacturers should elect the IFP method when the IFP is closer to cost of goods sold than it is to prices charged retailers and other nondistributors in the same foreign market. In some cases, U.S. manufacturers can increase foreign source income even further through relying on their books and records to attribute inventory gain to production and sales activities.

A special export terminal rule applies to inbound and outbound sales of natural resources. For individuals or entities owning or operating farms, mines, gas or oil wells, and other business operations involving natural deposits or timber, the source of income from export sales depends on the property's fair market value at the export terminal point. The seller derives export receipts sourced in the home country up to the export terminal value. Any portion of export receipts above the export terminal value is attributable to other sources. The seller subtracts the cost of natural resources to determine U.S. and foreign source income. Notwithstanding the rules just described, the entire profit from selling unprocessed softwood timber (e.g., pine logs or cants) grown in the United States is U.S. source income; where the sale occurs or title passes is irrelevant.[47] However, the export terminal rule applies to hardwood (e.g., oak) and processed timber (e.g., board lumber). Exhibit 4.5 summarizes source rules applicable to inventory profit.

---

[47]IRC §865(b).

**EXHIBIT 4.5** Sourcing Inventory Profit

```
┌─────────────────┐         ┌─────────────────┐
│  Did the seller │   Yes   │ The title passage│
│  purchase the   │ ──────► │ rule controls the│
│   inventory?    │         │  profit's source.│
└─────────────────┘         └─────────────────┘
         │ No
         ▼
┌─────────────────┐  Yes  ┌──────────────────┐  No  ┌─────────────────┐
│ Is the inventory│ ────► │  Is the inventory│ ───► │The export terminal│
│ a natural       │       │ unprocessed soft-│      │ rule controls the│
│ resource?       │       │ wood timber cut  │      │  gain's source.  │
└─────────────────┘       │ in the United    │      └─────────────────┘
         │ No             │ States?          │
         │                └──────────────────┘
         │                       │ Yes
         ▼                       └────────────────────────┐
┌─────────────────┐  Yes  ┌──────────────────┐            ▼
│ Has the seller  │ ────► │ The seller's books│    ┌─────────────────┐
│ obtained IRS    │       │ and records control│   │  The gain is    │
│ consent to base │       │  the gain's source.│   │ U.S. source     │
│ sourcing on     │       └──────────────────┘    │  income.        │
│ books and       │                                └─────────────────┘
│ records?        │
└─────────────────┘
         │ No
         ▼
┌─────────────────┐  Yes  ┌──────────────────┐
│ Has the seller  │ ────► │ The independent  │
│ elected to use  │       │ factory price    │
│ the independent │       │ method controls  │
│ factory price   │       │ the gain's source.│
│ method?         │       └──────────────────┘
└─────────────────┘
         │ No
         ▼
┌─────────────────┐
│ The 50-50 method│
│ controls the    │
│ gain's source.  │
└─────────────────┘
```

## EXAMPLE

The Anthracite Mining Company (AMC) mines hard coal in East Tennessee. During the current year, AMC sells $200,000 of its coal to a Latin American business. It cost AMC $150,000 to mine the coal, resulting in gross income of $50,000. At the export terminal point in

Norfolk, Virginia, the coal's fair market value is $180,000. Under the export terminal rule, AMC derives $180,000 export receipts (90 percent of the total) from U.S. sources and $20,000 export receipts from foreign sources. Thus, AMC earns $45,000 U.S. source income ($50,000 × 90%) and $5,000 foreign source income.

## Depreciable Property Gain

When a person disposes of personal property, past depreciation or amortization deductions related to the property affect the source of any gain. To the extent of prior deductions, the rules source gain according to whether the seller apportioned prior depreciation or amortization against U.S. or foreign source income.[48] (Chapter 5 discusses apportionment.) For tangible assets, the seller sources any remaining gain under the title passage rule (discussed earlier in relation to inventory profit).[49] For intangible property, how the seller sources any remaining gain depends on whether it is contingent on future productivity, use, or disposition of the property. The seller sources contingent gain exceeding prior amortization according to where the purchaser uses or can use the intangible (i.e., the same rule applicable to royalty income).[50] Sourcing contingent gain from intangibles the same as royalty income prevents taxpayers from wrapping royalty income in the mantle of a sales contract and, thus, camouflaging royalties as sales income. The seller sources noncontingent gain exceeding prior amortization according to the special residency rule for investment gain (discussed earlier).[51]

## EXAMPLE

Patrick, a Canadian citizen, uses a heavy-duty flatbed truck to transport timber in both the United States and Canada. Over the years, he fully depreciated the truck from its original $20,000 cost. He apportioned 40 percent of the prior depreciation deductions against U.S. source income. This year, Patrick sells the truck for $22,000, passing title in Detroit. Of the total gain, $12,000 ($20,000 × 60%) is foreign source income. The remaining $10,000 gain is U.S. source income—$8,000 per the depreciation rule ($20,000 × 40%) and $2,000 per the title passage rule.

---

[48]IRC §865(c), (d)(4)(A).
[49]IRC §865(c)(2).
[50]IRC §865(d)(1)(B).
[51]IRC §865(d)(1)(A).

**EXAMPLE**

Vivacious Vowels, Ltd., a London publisher of educational materials, sells the copyright to print and distribute its award-winning program, *Sonic Phonics*, within the United States. Vivacious originally acquired the copyright for $330,000, though its current adjusted basis is $300,000. The company apportioned prior amortization deductions of $30,000 entirely against U.S. source income. Vivacious sells its copyright to a U.S. publisher, passing title in New York. If the company sells the copyright for $480,000, $30,000 of the gain is U.S. source income, based on prior deductions, and $450,000 is foreign source income, based on the residency rules. If the company sells the copyright for a contractual percentage of later sales, the first $30,000 of the gain is U.S. source income, based on prior deductions, and any remaining gain is U.S. source income, based on the geographical rights transferred.

Exhibit 4.6 summarizes the provisions for sourcing gain when disposing of depreciable personal property. These rules do not apply to depreciable real estate.

As mentioned previously, U.S. persons prefer to source income abroad. Foreign source income increases the foreign tax credit limit, which can result in lower U.S. taxes. Many strategies exist to convert U.S. source income into foreign, some as simple as rethinking sales contracts so the source rule changes.

**EXAMPLE**

Pheasant Hunter, Inc., a domestic corporation, wants to sell the rights to manufacture its patented shotgun shells for one year to a British company. It is considering two alternative contracts, which have equal expected values. One contract transfers the rights for a lump-sum payment of $300,000. The other contract transfers the rights for $30 per carton of shotgun shells manufactured. The lump-sum payment results in $300,000 of U.S. source income since Pheasant Hunter is a U.S. resident. The contingent contract, in contrast, sources the entire income according to where the intangible rights can be used. Thus, the latter contract is expected to generate $300,000 of foreign source income.

**EXHIBIT 4.6** Sourcing Gain from Disposing of Depreciable Personal Property

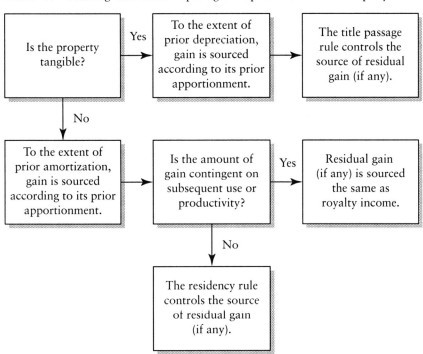

U.S. residents realizing gain from selling foreign corporate stock or intangible assets often treat the gain as U.S. source income. However, if a treaty regards the same gain as foreign source income, U.S. residents can choose to follow the treaty. This choice, in effect, may override the later-in-time rule discussed in Chapter 3.[52]

## OTHER SOURCE RULES

The Code sources underwriting income from selling annuity and insurance contracts based on the residence of annuitants and the location of insured risks.[53] Risks related to liability insurance exist where insured activities occur. Property risks exist at the site of insured property. Life and health risks exist where insured persons reside.

---

[52]IRC §865(h)(2)(A).
[53]IRC §§861(a)(7), 862(a)(7).

---

### EXAMPLE

Long Life and Health Insurance Company receives $12.25 million premiums from individuals residing in the United States and $1.4 million premiums from individuals residing abroad. The company has $12.25 million of U.S. source and $1.4 million of foreign source income.

---

Transportation income includes revenue from using or leasing vessels or aircraft to transport cargo or people. The Code considers income from coastwise transportation, transports beginning and ending in the United States, as entirely U.S. source income.[54] If transportation starts or ends (but not both) in the United States, half of the transportation income is U.S. and half is foreign source income.[55] Transportation beginning and ending abroad produces foreign source income.[56]

---

### EXAMPLE

Security Airlines, Inc. flies passengers within and between the United States and Europe. For the current year, the airline receives $8.6 million in fares for flights between U.S. cities, $5.2 million in fares for flights between the United States and Europe, and $1.6 million in fares for flights between European cities. Security Airlines has $11.2 million ($8.6 million and half of $5.2 million) U.S. source and $4.2 million ($1.6 million and half of $5.2 million) foreign source income.

---

### FLASHBACK

As Chapter 3 explained, treaties often exempt transportation income from host country taxation. Even though the Code might treat some portion of a foreign person's transportation income as derived from U.S. sources, a treaty can exempt the income.

---

[54]IRC §863(c)(1).
[55]IRC §863(c)(2)(A).
[56]U.S. law treats compensation that individuals receive for performing transportation-related services (e.g., the salary of an airline pilot) sometimes as transportation in-

International communication income is income derived from the transmission of communications (e.g., television or radio programs) or data (e.g., Internet images) between the United States and a foreign country or U.S. possession. For U.S. persons, the Code treats half of international communication income as U.S. source and half as foreign source income. For foreign persons, U.S. law considers all international communication income to be foreign source income if not attributable to a fixed U.S. place of business, and U.S. source income if so attributable.[57] Proposed regulations provide two antiabuse rules applicable to foreign persons. First, if a foreign person engages in a U.S. trade or business, the IRS presumes such person derives all international communication income from U.S. sources. To avoid U.S. source income, the foreign person must rebut the presumption.[58] Second, international communication income that foreign corporations derive is U.S. source income if U.S. persons own at least 50 percent of the corporation or the corporation is a controlled foreign corporation.[59]

---

## EXAMPLE

Fiber Optic Technocrats (FOT) derives $30 million gross income from international communications, of which $8 million is attributable to a U.S. office. If FOT is a U.S. person, half of the $30 million is U.S. source income and half is foreign source income. Generally, if FOT is a foreign person, $8 million is U.S. source income and $22 million is foreign source income. However, the entire $30 million is U.S. source income if the foreign person engages in a U.S. business and cannot establish that the income's source is foreign. Also, if FOT is a foreign corporation in which U.S. persons own at least 50 percent or which otherwise qualifies as a controlled foreign corporation, the entire $30 million is U.S. source income.

---

come and sometimes as personal service income. For instance, Section 863(c)(2)(B) sources compensation related to transportation beginning (ending) in the United States and ending (beginning) in a foreign country as personal service income, which is sourced under rules discussed earlier in this chapter. However, the flush language of Section 861(a)(3) treats most compensation of nonresident alien crewmen aboard foreign vessels as foreign source income, even if attributable to services rendered while the vessel is docked in the United States.

[57] IRC §863(e).
[58] Prop. Reg. §1.863-9(b)(2)(ii)(D).
[59] Prop. Reg. §1.863-9(b)(2)(ii)(B).

The source of income derived from space, ocean, and Antarctica activities (areas over which no nation exercises sole jurisdiction) depends primarily on the person deriving the income. The income is from U.S. sources when a U.S. person earns it. Foreign source income results when a foreign person earns the income, with two exceptions. First, if the foreign person engages in a U.S. trade or business, proposed regulations presume the person derives space or ocean income from U.S. sources.[60] Foreign source income results only if the foreign person rebuts the presumption. Second, space, ocean, and Antarctica income a foreign corporation derives is U.S. source income if U.S. persons own at least 50 percent of the corporation; but the entity nonetheless avoids controlled foreign corporation status.[61] Income from space, ocean, and Antarctica activity does not include transportation, international communication, or natural resource income; that is, if sourcing rules overlap, those relating to transportation, international communication, and natural resource income prevail over those relating to space, ocean, and Antarctica income.[62]

---

### EXAMPLE

Galactic Links leases equipment for conducting experiments beyond the Earth's atmosphere where the gravitational pull is virtually zero. The company's leasing income is from U.S. sources if Galactic is a U.S. person, Galactic is a foreign person engaged in a U.S. business (and the presumption of U.S. source is not rebutted), or Galactic is a foreign corporation (but not a controlled foreign corporation) in which U.S. persons own at least 50 percent. Otherwise, the leasing income is from foreign sources.

---

[60]Prop. Reg. §1.863-8(b)(3).
[61]Prop. Reg. §1.863-3(b)(2). This exception applies to many 50-50 joint ventures with one U.S. and one foreign owner. However, it does not apply to controlled foreign corporations in which U.S. shareholders own more than 50 percent since such shareholders report their share of Subpart F income as constructive dividends. As Chapter 12 explains, Subpart F income includes income derived from ocean and space activities (part of foreign base company shipping income).
[62]IRC §863(d).

# CHAPTER 5

# Allocation and Apportionment

As Chapter 4 indicated, sourcing income requires two distinct steps. First, the individual or entity identifies the type of gross income (e.g., personal service income versus royalty). Second, the individual or entity applies the proper sourcing rule to the income. Sourcing rules dichotomize the income between U.S. and foreign source gross income. However, many Code provisions require income amounts after subtracting deductible expenses (i.e., taxable income measures). Similar to sourcing rules, determining which deductions reduce which gross income measures involves two steps. First, taxpayers must allocate deductible expenses to gross income classes, which is analogous to identifying the type of gross income. Second, they must apportion the deductible expenses in each gross income class, which is analogous to applying source rules.

> **COMPLIANCE POINTER:** Once taxpayers adopt an **allocation** or **apportionment** method, they must apply it consistently from one year to the next.[1] Also, individuals and entities should clearly document their bases for allocation and apportionment procedures. On request, taxpayers must furnish the District Director with their documentation.[2] Failure of taxpayers to support the allocation and apportionment procedures they use can lead to audit adjustments.

While U.S. law sources income, it allocates and apportions deductible expenses. Like the sourcing rules, several Code sections require allocation and apportionment procedures. Two of the more important involve calculating the **foreign tax credit limit** and determining a foreign person's U.S. tax liability, the same provisions mentioned in Chapter 4 in relation to the sourcing rules. These and other provisions requiring allocation and apportionment procedures are **operative sections**.[3]

---

[1] Reg. §1.861-8(g).
[2] Reg. §1.861-8(f)(5).
[3] Reg. §1.861-8(f)(1).

U.S. and foreign persons desire to apportion deductions against U.S. source income. For U.S. persons, one can express the Section 904 foreign tax credit limit, which Chapter 11 discusses in more detail, as shown in equation 5.1:

$$\text{Limit} = \frac{\text{Foreign source taxable income}}{\text{Worldwide taxable income}} \times \text{U.S. tax before the credit} \quad (5.1)$$

An increase in the numerator increases the limit, which may lead to a greater foreign tax credit. Thus, all other things being equal, foreign source income is more desirable than U.S. source income. Apportioning deductions to foreign source income decreases both the numerator and denominator, which may limit the foreign tax credit and, thus, increase U.S. tax liability. In contrast, apportioning deductions to U.S. source income reduces only the denominator, which increases the foreign tax credit limit and may decrease U.S. tax.

> **PLANNING POINTER:** To minimize double taxation risks, U.S. persons should match expenses apportioned to foreign source income with deductions in a foreign jurisdiction. That is, to the extent possible, they should avoid situations in which foreign countries deny deductions for expenses U.S. law apportions against foreign source income. The U.S. apportionment rules for interest and research and experimentation deductions, in particular, can result in such mismatching.

The United States taxes foreign persons on income effectively connected with a U.S. trade or business. Deductible expenses apportioned to effectively connected income reduce these taxpayers' U.S. tax base to which regular U.S. tax rates apply. Thus, foreign persons often prefer to apportion deductions against effectively connected income rather than income not effectively connected with a U.S. trade or business. Chapters 7 and 8 discuss the U.S. taxation of foreign persons in more detail.

## ALLOCATION TO CLASSES

The allocation process precedes apportionment. Taxpayers initially allocate deductible expenses to classes of gross income based on relationships to each class. Examples of gross income classes include gross profit from sales (i.e., net sales less cost of goods sold), compensation, rent, royalties, dividends, interest, and property gains. This list is not exhaustive. Also, one can subdivide these classes.[4] For instance, if a company receives royalties from two distinct product lines, it might choose to define each royalty stream as a separate class of gross income. For administrative simplicity when calculating the foreign tax credit limit, U.S. persons should select gross income classes fitting neatly into (i.e., not overlapping) the various foreign source income baskets discussed in Chapter 11.

Taxpayers allocate deductions definitely related to a specific gross income class to that class.[5] For instance, a company might allocate depreciation on rental property to the class of rental income. Taxpayers allocate deductible expenses definitely related to all classes among all classes on the basis of gross income in each class.[6] For instance, legal and accounting fees and miscellaneous administrative deductions might relate to all classes. An important corollary is that taxpayers should allocate deductible expenses related to more than one, but not all, gross income classes to such classes. Taxpayers do not allocate deductions unrelated to any class. Examples include most personal itemized deductions, such as home mortgage interest, and the standard deduction. Individuals do not allocate personal and dependency exemptions.[7]

---

## EXAMPLE

Pedal to the Metal Auto Products, Inc., a domestic corporation, identifies two income classes: gross profit from sales of $300,000 and royalty income of $100,000. Pedal to the Metal must allocate two deductible expenses to these classes of gross income: selling expenses of $120,000 and miscellaneous administrative expenses of $40,000. The selling expenses definitely relate to the gross profit from sales and, thus, are entirely allocated to that class. The miscellaneous administrative expenses definitely relate to both classes; thus, Pedal allocates the $40,000 based on gross income in each class. Of the $40,000 miscellaneous administrative expenses, Pedal allocates $30,000 to gross profit on sales ($40,000 × 75%) and $10,000 to royalty income. The total allocation to gross profit on sales is $150,000 ($120,000 + $30,000).

---

[4]Reg. §1.861-8(a)(3).
[5]Reg. §1.861-8(b)(4).
[6]Reg. §1.861-8(b)(5).
[7]Reg. §1.861-8(e)(11).

## APPORTIONMENT TO GROUPINGS

After allocating deductible expenses to classes of gross income, taxpayers apportion such expenses between **statutory** and **residual groupings**. The two groupings consist of gross income from a particular source or activity. The source or activity depends on the operative section.[8]

If calculating the foreign tax credit limitation (i.e., when Section 904 is the operative section), foreign source income becomes the statutory grouping and U.S. source income forms the residual grouping. Section 904 bases the two groupings on source and identifies the statutory grouping as foreign source income. That is, to calculate the foreign tax credit limit, the taxpayer must know foreign source taxable income (i.e., the numerator of the limitation equation).

If determining the U.S. tax liability of a foreign person (i.e., when Section 871 or 882 is the operative section), income effectively connected with a U.S. trade or business becomes the statutory grouping and all noneffectively connected income forms the residual grouping. In this case, Section 871 or 882 bases the two groupings on the activities from which the taxpayer derives gross income. Once again, the operative section identifies the statutory grouping since, as Chapter 8 discusses, the United States taxes foreign persons at regular rates on income effectively connected with a U.S. trade or business.

After allocating deductions between statutory and residual groupings, taxpayers apportion such deductions on a factual relationship basis.[9] For instance, assume rent is the class of gross income and the statutory grouping is foreign source income. Rent deductions a company has allocated to rent income might be apportioned between foreign source and U.S. source income based on the value of rental property outside versus within the United States. In this case, the value of rental property is the factual relationship basis the taxpayer uses to apportion rental expenses. In other cases, taxpayers might choose adjusted basis or square footage as their factual relationship basis for apportionment.

---

### EXAMPLE

Tenderfoot Western Wear, a domestic corporation, must determine its foreign tax credit limitation and, thus, must know its foreign source tax-

---

[8]Reg. §1.861-8(a)(4).
[9]Reg. §1.861-8(c)(1).

able income. It allocates $20,000 of lease and miscellaneous deductions to real estate earnings, one of its gross income classes, and must apportion the $20,000 between foreign source and U.S. source income. Tenderfoot decides to apportion the $20,000 based on square footage of real estate. By square footage, one-fourth of Tenderfoot's real estate exists outside the United States. Thus, the company apportions $5,000 lease deductions ($20,000 × 25%) to foreign source income.

As mentioned before, taxpayers do not allocate expenses unrelated to any class of gross income. However, they do apportion such expenses between statutory and residual groupings based on each grouping's gross income.[10] Individuals do not allocate or apportion personal and dependency exemptions.[11]

Exhibit 5.1 summarizes the basic allocation and apportionment rules. The ability to summarize these rules in such a small space makes them appear deceivingly simple; in fact, allocation and apportionment procedures often are very difficult to apply to actual deductions not fitting a prescribed mold. Determining how to allocate and apportion some deductions has caused even seasoned cost accountants to perspire heavily. But the vagueness of the regulatory provisions also provides opportunities since the tax amounts at stake often are large, making careful analysis worthwhile.

**EXHIBIT 5.1** Allocation and Apportionment Principles

| Deductible Expense | Allocate | Apportion |
|---|---|---|
| Definitely related to specific class | To specific class | Based on factual relationship |
| Definitely related to all classes | Among all classes based on gross income | Based on factual relationship |
| Unrelated to any class | Not allocated | Based on gross income |
| Personal and dependency exemptions | Not allocated | Not apportioned |

---

[10]Reg. §1.861-8(c)(3).
[11]Reg. §1.861-8(e)(11).

### EXAMPLE

Finicky Feline, Inc., a U.S. corporation, manufactures cat food. During the year, the company derives gross profit from sales of $120,000 and rent income of $30,000 (80 and 20 percent of total income, respectively). Finicky incurs deductible selling expenses of $80,000, rent expenses of $20,000, and miscellaneous administrative expenses of $40,000. The company apportions selling expenses on the basis of sales volume and rent expenses on the basis of the real estate's fair market value. Sixty percent of Finicky's sales occur abroad, and 25 percent of the value of its real estate holdings are outside the United States. Finicky has two gross income classes—gross profit from sales and rent income—and the allocation provides the following results:

Allocation to gross profit class:

$$\$80,000 + (\$40,000 \times 80\%) = \$112,000$$

Allocation to rent income class:

$$\$20,000 + (\$40,000 \times 20\%) = \$28,000$$

Finicky apportions the $112,000 allocated to the gross profit class as follows:

Apportionment to U.S. source income:

$$\$112,000 \times 40\% = \$44,800$$

Apportionment to foreign source income:

$$\$112,000 \times 60\% = \$67,200$$

Next, the company apportions the $28,000 allocated to the rent income class as follows:

Apportionment to U.S. source income:

$$\$28,000 \times 75\% = \$21,000$$

Apportionment to foreign source income:

$$\$28,000 \times 25\% = \$7,000$$

Thus, of the $140,000 total expenses, Finicky apportions $65,800 ($44,800 + $21,000) to U.S. source income and $74,200 ($67,200 +

> $7,000) to foreign source income. As discussed in Chapter 11, both sales profit and rent income (if business related and received from unrelated persons) fall into the same foreign tax credit basket.

## INTEREST DEDUCTIONS

The general allocation and apportionment rules, as just discussed, allow much flexibility in identifying factual relationships and, thus, determining the basis for apportionment. However, U.S. law requires more specific procedures for deductible interest, which often involves very large dollar amounts. The fungible nature of money supports the theory underlying the allocation and apportionment rules for interest.

Though businesses identify the separate sources and uses of their funds, they often can only speculate about where they use specific funds from a given source. Borrowed funds commingle with other funds in bank accounts and other repositories, making it impossible to know for sure which exact dollars a company uses to acquire which specific assets. In essence, borrowing provides funds for all of a company's needs. When a company spends borrowed funds to meet needs for one project, it frees remaining funds for uses in other areas. Similarly, creditors often loan funds based on debtors' general credit and aggregate business activities; in effect, many loans represent claims against all the debtor's assets. Based on money's fungible nature, U.S. tax law associates debt with all of a company's assets. Like debt, the interest a company pays on its borrowed funds relates to all assets.

### U.S. Persons

For outbound purposes, apportionment rules affect only interest deductions of U.S. persons; they do not apply to interest expense of other persons such as foreign subsidiaries. Even though beyond the scope of U.S. apportionment rules, 100 percent of interest expense that foreign subsidiaries deduct in host countries reduce *foreign* source income. That is, foreign deductions reduce foreign subsidiaries' E&P that U.S. parent companies eventually recognize as foreign source dividend income. In contrast, U.S. companies apportion some interest expense their foreign branches and partnerships incur against *U.S.* source income.

> **PLANNING POINTER:** All other things being equal, U.S. multinationals should obtain offshore financing through foreign branches and partnerships instead of foreign subsidiaries since the former channel

allows the taxpayer to apportion some interest against U.S. source income. Also, U.S. multinationals should arrange offshore financing in high-tax jurisdictions where interest deductions reduce foreign income tax that otherwise might not receive a full foreign tax credit (due to the Section 904 limit Chapter 11 discusses).

U.S. taxpayers allocate and apportion interest deductions related to business and investment activities, including original interest discount and other interest equivalent amounts, based on asset value.[12] For U.S. persons allocating and apportioning interest between U.S. and foreign source income when calculating the foreign tax credit limit, domestic (foreign) assets consist of properties yielding domestic (foreign) source income.[13] Therefore, interest allocation and apportionment does not directly depend on property location but on the source of income that assets generate and the value of those assets. Since the basis for allocating and apportioning interest deductions is the same (i.e., asset value), the result often is mathematically equivalent to skipping the allocation process and just apportioning interest on an overall basis. However, when gross income classes fall into separate foreign tax credit baskets (as discussed in Chapter 11), U.S. persons cannot skip the allocation process.

---

### EXAMPLE

Barnacle Boats, Inc., a domestic corporation with foreign branch operations in several countries, incurs $24,000 deductible interest expense. Seventy percent of Barnacle's assets exist in the United States. The company derives $190,000 gross income from sales and $10,000 bareboat leasing income; sales and leasing are its only two gross income classes. Assets relating to sales generate $114,000 U.S. and $76,000 foreign source income and are worth $1,300,000 and $400,000, respectively. Assets relating to leasing generate $8,500 U.S. and $1,500 foreign source income and are worth $200,000 and $100,000, respectively. To summarize, the value of sales and leasing assets are $1,700,000 and $300,000, respectively.

---

[12]IRC §864(e)(2). In contrast to the general rules summarized in Exhibit 5.1, taxpayers cannot allocate business and investment interest on the basis of gross income in each class.

[13]Empirical evidence confirms that U.S. multinationals obtained relatively less (more) capital through debt (stock) following enactment of the interest apportionment rules, suggesting that the restrictive apportionment procedure increased the cost of capital for such companies. See Julie H. Collins and Douglas A. Shackelford, "Foreign Tax

Allocation of deductible interest between gross income classes:

$$\text{Selling: } \$24,000 \times \frac{\$1,700,000}{\$2,000,000} = \$20,400$$

$$\text{Leasing: } \$24,000 \times \frac{\$300,000}{\$2,000,000} = \$3,600$$

Apportionment of deductible interest to statutory groupings:

$$\text{Foreign selling: } \$20,400 \times \frac{\$400,000}{\$1,700,000} = \$4,800$$

$$\text{Foreign leasing: } \$3,600 \times \frac{\$100,000}{\$300,000} = \underline{\$1,200}$$

$$\text{Apportioned to foreign source income} \quad \underline{\underline{\$6,000}}$$

As discussed in Chapter 11, if both selling and leasing income fall in the general limitation basket, Barnacle can skip the formal allocation process and directly apportion the interest expense to foreign source income, as in the equivalent apportionment shown next. Stated differently, the purpose for apportioning deductions (i.e., calculating the foreign tax credit limit) does not require the company to segregate selling and leasing activities into two gross income classes (as long as the company operates the leasing activity as a business and the company receives the leasing income from unrelated persons).

$$\text{Apportioned to foreign income: } \$24,000 \times \frac{\$500,000}{\$2,000,000} = \underline{\underline{\$6,000}}$$

Thus, Barnacle apportions $6,000 of its deductible interest expense to foreign source income (the statutory grouping) and $18,000 to U.S. source income (the residual grouping).

Credit Limitations and Preferred Stock Issuances," *Journal of Accounting Research* 30 (Supplement 1992), pp. 103–124; Kaye J. Newberry, "Foreign Tax Credit Limitations and Capital Structure Decisions," *Journal of Accounting Research* 36 (Spring 1998), pp. 157–166. Also, instead of obtaining debt capital in U.S. markets, U.S. multinationals seemed to raise relatively more debt capital through their foreign subsidiaries following enactment of the interest apportionment rules. See James K. Smith, "The Effect of the Tax Reform Act of 1986 on the Capital Structure of Foreign Subsidiaries," *Journal of the American Taxation Association* 19 (Fall 1997), pp. 1–18.

With few exceptions, taxpayers base allocation and apportionment of interest deductions on asset values. To discourage tax-motivated asset transactions at year-end, taxpayers must average beginning-of-the-year and end-of-the-year asset values.[14] The regulations provide two methods for determining asset values. The **tax book value method** measures asset values as the adjusted basis of properties. Alternatively, taxpayers can adopt the **fair market value method,** which relies on generally accepted valuation procedures. Under this latter method, publicly traded corporations begin with trading prices for their shares on an established security market. Such trading prices measure equity value, so publicly traded companies add liabilities to trading prices in calculating asset values. Nonpublicly traded corporations using the fair market value method capitalize earnings to determine asset values.[15]

---

### EXAMPLE

Richland Company, a domestic corporation, incurs $360 deductible interest. The business classifies its assets according to the source of income each generates:

|                | *Tax Book Value* | *Fair Market Value* |
| -------------- | ---------------- | ------------------- |
| U.S. Assets    | $ 7,000          | $ 8,000             |
| Foreign Assets | 5,000            | 2,000               |
| Total Assets   | $12,000          | $10,000             |

If Richland uses the tax book value method, it apportions $150 of interest against foreign source income:

$$\$360 \text{ interest} \times \frac{\$\ 5,000}{\$\ 12,000} = \$150 \text{ foreign apportionment}$$

If the company adopts the fair market value method, it apportions $72 of interest to foreign source income:

$$\$360 \text{ interest} \times \frac{\$\ 2,000}{\$\ 10,000} = \$72 \text{ foreign apportionment}$$

---

[14]Temp. Reg. §1.861-9T(g)(2)(i).
[15]Temp. Reg. §1.861-9T(h).

In this situation, the fair market value method apportions less interest against foreign source income and, thus, results in a higher foreign tax credit limit. If the limit constrains the foreign tax credit Richland can claim, the fair market value method provides a more favorable outcome.

**COMPLIANCE POINTER:** Taxpayers adopting the fair market value method (and all related persons) must consistently use it unless the IRS consents to a change.[16]

For outbound transactions (i.e., when calculating the foreign tax credit limit), the Code requires each member of an affiliated group to allocate and apportion its deductible interest as if all members' assets belong to a single corporation.[17] Under this **one-taxpayer rule**, affiliated companies allocate and apportion only interest deductions paid to nonaffiliates; they do not treat interaffiliate stock holdings and debt obligations as assets. This provision prevents an affiliated group from establishing a domestic subsidiary, whose assets yield only U.S. source income, to borrow funds benefiting the entire group, including foreign operations, while apportioning none of the interest expense to foreign source income.[18] Thus, groups must allocate and apportion deductible interest each affiliated member incurs based on aggregate asset values. An affiliated group includes all U.S. corporations related through stock ownership and a common domestic parent company. The ownership threshold requires that group members aggregately own 80 percent of the stock value and voting power of each member corporation other than the parent.[19]

---

[16]Temp. Reg. §1.861-8T(c)(2).

[17]IRC §864(e)(1); Temp. Reg. §1.861-11T(b)(2), (c). In the case of affiliated corporations filing a consolidated return, Temp. Reg. §1.861-11T(c) clarifies that group members compute the foreign tax credit limit on a consolidated basis.

[18]Once a domestic finance subsidiary secures debt capital, the affiliated group can share funds without triggering U.S. tax. For instance, the dividend-received deduction in Section 243(a)(3) allows the subsidiary to distribute borrowed funds to its parent company tax free.

[19]IRC §864(e)(5). Temp. Reg. §1.861-11T(d)(6)(ii) also treats *foreign* corporations meeting the stock ownership requirements as affiliated members when more than 50 percent of their gross income is effectively connected with a U.S. trade or business.

## EXAMPLE

Riff, Inc., a U.S. multinational corporation, establishes Raff Corporation, a wholly owned U.S. subsidiary, and files a consolidated return. Raff borrows funds for Riff's worldwide activities. The following data provide U.S. and foreign source taxable income (before considering the interest deduction or apportionment), Raff's deductible interest, Riff's U.S. tax before credits, and the value of assets generating U.S. and foreign income (other than interaffiliate holdings):

|  | *Riff* | *Raff* | *Combined* |
|---|---|---|---|
| Foreign Source Income | $  250 | $   0 | $  250 |
| U.S. Source Income | 750 | 300 | 1,050 |
| Deductible Interest | 0 | 300 | 300 |
| U.S. Tax before Credits | 340 | 0 | 340 |
| Foreign Asset Values | 3,000 | 0 | 3,000 |
| U.S. Asset Values | 7,000 | 2,000 | 9,000 |

Thus, if the one-taxpayer rule did not exist, Raff would apportion all of the $300 interest expense against U.S. source income:

$$\text{Apportioned to foreign income: } \$300 \times \frac{\$\ 0}{\$2,000} = \$0$$

The consolidated foreign tax credit limit would be:

$$\text{FTC limit: } \frac{\$250}{\$250 + (\$750 + \$300 - \$300)} \times \$340 = \$85$$

However, U.S. law requires interest apportionment on an affiliated basis, as follows:

$$\text{Apportioned to foreign income: } \$300 \times \frac{\$3,000}{\$9,000 + \$3,000} = \$75$$

Thus, the numerator of the consolidated foreign tax credit limit declines $75 and the limit declines $25 (from $85 to $60):

$$\text{FTC limit: } \frac{(\$250 - \$75)}{(\$250 - \$75) + (\$750 + \$300 - \$225)} \times \$340 = \$60$$

If Riff, instead of Raff, had borrowed the money, the outcome would not differ since Riff uses the same group assets to apportion interest.

In departures from the fungibility theory, some exceptions associate debt obligations with specific assets and, thus, trace interest to particular gross income classes. For instance, when taxpayers acquire property using qualified nonrecourse indebtedness, they must allocate the interest deduction directly to the gross income derived from such property. After allocation, taxpayers still apportion interest from such debt based on asset values. To be **qualified nonrecourse indebtedness**, the debt must finance the acquisition, construction, or improvement of property with a useful life exceeding one year. Also, the property must be the sole security for both principal and interest payments and consist of depreciable personal property, real estate, or amortizable intangible property.[20]

> **PLANNING POINTER:** U.S. companies judiciously financing asset acquisitions or improvements can raise their foreign tax credit limits. Using qualified nonrecourse indebtedness to finance "U.S. assets" precludes any portion of the interest deduction from apportionment against foreign source income. Further, using recourse debt to finance "foreign assets" allows taxpayers to apportion some portion of the interest deduction against U.S. source income.

## Foreign Persons

Foreign persons pay U.S. tax at regular rates on their income effectively connected with a U.S. business. To determine the portion of expenses deductible in computing U.S. business income, foreign persons apply apportionment procedures. The United States could permit foreign corporations conducting U.S. business to simply deduct whatever interest expense appears on their U.S. books and records. However, as noted, the fungible nature of borrowed funds provides, at best, a tenuous link between sources and uses of funds. The amount of debts listed in a U.S. branch's books may differ significantly from the liabilities connected with U.S. business activities. In effect, the United States views branch accounting information skeptically when it involves an expense, like interest, that foreign multinationals control and manage on a global level.

Determining the interest deduction of foreign persons requires three steps.[21] First, foreign taxpayers establish the "value" of their U.S. assets (adjusted basis or, if elected, fair market value). Assets producing income or gain effectively connected with a U.S. trade or business are U.S. assets.[22]

---

[20]Temp. Reg. §1.861-10T(b).

[21]Rather than the method discussed here, foreign persons can elect the separate currency pools method for determining interest deductions under Reg. §1.882-5(e).

[22]Reg. §1.882-5(b). Chapter 8 defines effectively connected income.

Second, foreign taxpayers must ascertain the amount of liabilities connected with their U.S. businesses. The calculation, appearing as equation 5.2, assumes the ratio of assets to liabilities is the same in the United States as elsewhere.

U.S. connected liabilities =
$$\text{Value of U.S. assets} \times \frac{\text{Worldwide liabilities}}{\text{Value of worldwide assets}} \quad (5.2)$$

Instead of the worldwide debt-to-asset ratio, foreign corporations can multiply the value of U.S. assets by a fixed ratio of 50 percent (or 93 percent in the case of banks).[23] Whichever calculation foreign corporations adopt, the result effectively ignores the branches' accounting for U.S. liabilities.

The third step involves adjusting the interest U.S. businesses actually pay. When U.S. booked liabilities exceed U.S. connected liabilities, foreign persons adjust the interest payments appearing in their U.S. records downward to determine deductible interest. Equation 5.3 shows the adjustment.

$$\text{Interest deduction} = \text{U.S. interest paid} \times \frac{\text{U.S. connected liabilities}}{\text{U.S. booked liabilities}} \quad (5.3)$$

Conversely, when U.S. connected liabilities exceed U.S. booked liabilities, foreign persons adjust the interest payments appearing in their U.S. records upward to establish deductible interest.[24] Equation 5.4 provides the calculation.

$$\text{Interest deduction} = \text{U.S. interest paid} + \left( \text{Excess U.S. connected liabilities} \times \frac{\text{Interest paid on U.S. dollar denominated liabilities outside U.S.}}{\text{U.S. dollar denominated liabilities outside U.S.}} \right) \quad (5.4)$$

As Chapter 10 explains, this upward adjustment in a foreign corporation's interest deduction can result in a **branch interest tax (BIT)**.

**PLANNING POINTER:** Foreign corporations prefer the value of U.S. assets to be as high as possible. The higher the value, the more U.S. connected liabilities, per equation 5.2, and the greater the interest deduction, per equation 5.3 or 5.4.

---

[23]Reg. §1.882-5(c).
[24]Reg. §1.882-5(d).

## EXAMPLE

Mwana Pastries, Ltd. is a Zimbabwean company with branch operations in the United States. Mwana's financial statements yield the following information at year-end:

| | Value |
|---|---|
| Assets producing U.S. business income | $40,000 |
| Assets producing U.S. investment income | 90,000 |
| Assets producing foreign income | 70,000 |

| | Debt Amount | Interest Expense |
|---|---|---|
| Liabilities booked in United States | $26,000 | $3,000 |
| Liabilities booked in home country | 10,000 | 1,200 |

Mwana's U.S. business assets total $40,000. Equation 5.2 provides Mwana's U.S. connected liabilities, as follows:

$$\text{U.S. connected liabilities} = \$40,000 \times \frac{\$\ 36,000}{\$200,000} = \$7,200$$

Since U.S. booked liabilities exceed U.S. connected liabilities, equation 5.3 determines the amount of interest Mwana deducts against gross income effectively connected with its U.S. business, as follows:

$$\text{Interest deduction} = \$3,000 \times \frac{\$\ 7,200}{\$26,000} = \$831$$

Thus, even though Mwana booked interest expense of $3,000 attributable to its U.S. branch, only $831 interest is deductible (i.e., apportioned against effectively connected income).

## RESEARCH AND EXPERIMENTAL DEDUCTIONS

Companies incur research and experimental (R&E) expenses to improve their products and processes and, thus, generate more income. However, when R&E is successful, the income may not materialize until several years later, and the resulting income may be much higher or lower than expected.

Further, R&E is sometimes unsuccessful, a sunk cost not generating income. Over time, tax policymakers struggled to devise rules associating current R&E deductions with future income that may or may not materialize and the magnitude of which may be difficult for anyone to predict. As a result, Treasury frequently changed the allocation and apportionment rules for R&E during the 1980s and early 1990s.[25]

The regulations base gross income classes, to which taxpayers allocate R&E deductions, on product categories. Each gross income class includes all forms of gross income for the relevant product category, such as sales income, royalties, and dividends. Thus, in contrast to the general allocation rules, the regulations do not base gross income classes on types of gross income (e.g., sales income versus royalties) but on product categories that may include more than one type of income. Taxpayers select product categories from the **Standard Industrial Classification (SIC)** manual. The regulations permit product categories based on three-digit SIC codes. The taxpayer can aggregate SIC codes in defining product categories but cannot divide three-digit codes; for instance, two-digit codes are acceptable, but four-digit codes are not.[26]

> **COMPLIANCE POINTER:** Once taxpayers select product categories, they must continue to use them in later years unless they obtain IRS consent to change.[27]

---

**EXAMPLE**

Guzzle Deep, Inc., a U.S. company, produces and distributes frozen fruit juices (SIC 203) and bottled water (SIC 208). The company also licenses its process for freezing fruit juices. During the current year, Guzzle Deep earns $3 million gross profit from sales on its two products

---

[25]The changes to the allocation and apportionment rules provided an opportunity to empirically examine the impact of such changes on R&E location. The evidence suggests that more restrictive apportionment rules cause U.S. multinationals to shift R&E activities offshore, particularly among those multinationals with excess foreign tax credits. Conversely, one might expect that more lenient rules would result in a shift of R&E activities to the United States. See Cynthia C. Vines and Michael L. Moore, "U.S. Tax Policy and the Location of R&D," *Journal of the American Taxation Association* 18 (Fall 1996), pp. 74–88.

[26]Reg. §1.861-17(a)(1), (2).

[27]Reg. §1.861-17(a)(2)(iii).

and receives $400,000 in royalty income from U.S. licensees. The company currently incurs and deducts R&E expenses of $840,000 to develop a more effective way to preserve the nutritional value of its fruit juices during the sealing process and $300,000 to increase the purity of its bottled water. All R&E occurs in the United States. The company allocates $840,000 of R&E deductions to its frozen fruit juices product line and $300,000 to its bottled water product line. These two product lines form Guzzle Deep's classes of gross income for R&E purposes. The company cannot allocate its R&E deductions to classes based on gross income type (i.e., gross profit from sales and royalties).

In some cases, legal requirements relate R&E expenses of a product to a specific geographic region. For instance, the Food and Drug Administration may mandate that a new medicine undergo certain testing. The mandate clearly associates the R&E with the United States. When R&E occurs solely to meet legal requirements, and the expected outcome cannot reasonably provide more than de minimis benefits outside the country imposing the requirements, the taxpayer allocates such R&E deduction to that geographic region.[28] Where the R&E occurs is irrelevant.

As with other deductions, taxpayers prefer to apportion R&E to U.S. source income, while the IRS may prefer apportionment to foreign source income. Apportionment to foreign source income reduces the foreign tax credit limitation. The regulations specify two alternative apportionment procedures: the sales method and gross income method. To differing degrees, both methods exclusively apportion a percentage of R&E to the geographic region where the taxpayer incurs more than half of its R&E expenses. The theory underlying exclusive apportionment holds that R&E primarily benefits the market where incurred.

**COMPLIANCE POINTER:** Once taxpayers select an apportionment method for R&E, they must apply that method to all product categories for five consecutive years, unless the IRS consents to an earlier change.[29]

**PLANNING POINTER:** To minimize apportionment of the R&E deduction to foreign source income, taxpayers should incur more than 50 percent of their R&E expense in the United States.

---

[28] Reg. §1.861-17(a)(4).
[29] Reg. §1.861-17(d)(1)(ii), (e).

The **sales method** exclusively apportions 50 percent of the R&E deduction to the geographic area where the taxpayer incurs more than half its R&E expenses. Exclusive apportionment does not occur if no geographic area lays claim to a majority of the taxpayer's R&E expenses for the year. The taxpayer apportions its remaining deduction based on sales for the relevant product category.[30]

## KEY CASE

A domestic corporation and its U.K. and German subsidiaries each engage in R&E activities. The domestic corporation apportions its R&E deduction based on sales. However, contrary to the regulatory sales method, the corporation does not exclusively apportion any portion of its R&E deduction and makes other apportionment adjustments based on the actual R&E each foreign entity incurs. The taxpayer argues that the interpretive regulation is unreasonable and, thus, invalid since it fails to consider the direct R&E its foreign subsidiaries conduct. The IRS applies the regulatory sales method to the domestic corporation, which apportions more R&E to foreign source income, reducing the foreign tax credit and increasing the likelihood of double tax. In effect, the regulatory method decreases foreign source taxable income without reducing foreign income tax since neither the United Kingdom nor Germany permits deductions for apportioned deductions exceeding actual R&E expenses the subsidiaries incur in each country. While recognizing that the taxpayer's method may yield better results in some cases, the Tax Court holds the regulation to be a reasonable interpretation and, thus, valid.[31]

The **gross income method** exclusively apportions 25 percent of the R&E deduction to the geographic area where the taxpayer incurs more than half of its R&E expenses. The taxpayer apportions remaining R&E between groupings based on overall gross income rather than gross income per product category. However, the R&E apportioned to either the statutory or residual grouping under the gross income method cannot be less than 50 percent of the amount apportioned to the applicable grouping under the sales method. If the apportionment to the statutory grouping (i.e., foreign source income) falls below 50 percent of the apportionment under the sales method, the taxpayer apportions 50 percent of the results under the sales method to the statutory grouping. A similar procedure applies when the amount in the residual grouping falls below its 50 percent threshold.[32]

---

[30]Reg. §1.861-17(c)(1). The regulations treat income from leasing equipment as sales income.
[31]*Perkin-Elmer Corporation and Subsidiaries v. Comm.*, 103 TC 464 (1994).
[32]Reg. §1.861-17(d).

**EXAMPLE**

Assume the same facts as in the preceding example. In addition, Guzzle Deep uses the sales method to apportion R&E. The company does not choose to aggregate its two product categories. It generates $5 million in sales, broken down as follows:

|  | *Frozen Fruit Juices* | *Bottled Water* |
|---|---|---|
| U.S. sales | $2,500,000 | $1,000,000 |
| Foreign sales | 1,000,000 | 500,000 |
|  | $3,500,000 | $1,500,000 |

The sales method results in the following R&E apportionments:

Apportionment of $840,000 R&E for frozen fruit juices:

$$\text{To U.S. income: } \$420,000 + \$420,000\left(\frac{\$2,500,000}{\$3,500,000}\right) = \$720,000$$

$$\text{To foreign income: } \$420,000\left(\frac{\$1,000,000}{\$3,500,000}\right) = \$120,000$$

Apportionment of $300,000 R&E for bottled water:

$$\text{To U.S. income: } \$150,000 + \$150,000\left(\frac{\$1,000,000}{\$1,500,000}\right) = \$250,000$$

$$\text{To foreign income: } \$150,000\left(\frac{\$\ 500,000}{\$1,500,000}\right) = \$50,000$$

**EXAMPLE**

Assume the same facts as in the two previous examples, except that Guzzle Deep uses the gross income method for apportionment. The company summarizes its overall gross income as follows:

| U.S. gross profit | $2,600,000 |
|---|---|
| U.S. royalties | 700,000 |
| Foreign gross profit | 300,000 |
|  | $3,600,000 |

*(continues)*

The gross income method yields the following tentative apportionment of the $1,140,000 R&E:

$$\text{To U.S. income: } \$285,000 + \$855,000 \left(\frac{\$3,300,000}{\$3,600,000}\right) = \$1,068,750$$

$$\text{To foreign income: } \$855,000 \left(\frac{\$\ \ 300,000}{\$3,600,000}\right) = \$71,250$$

The gross income method initially apportions only $71,250 to foreign source income, which is less than half of the $170,000 apportioned under the sales method ($120,000 + $50,000 from the preceding example). Thus, Guzzle Deep must apportion $85,000 (half of $170,000) to foreign income and the remaining $1,055,000 ($1,140,000 – $85,000) to U.S. income.

Like interest deductions, members of affiliated groups (consisting of U.S. corporations) allocate and apportion R&E as though the group were a single corporation.[33] Also, under the sales method, a look-through rule requires the taxpayer to consider a controlled corporation's sales of the relevant product if experience creates a reasonable expectation that the corporation (whether domestic or foreign) will directly or indirectly benefit from the R&E. A reasonable expectation exists if the taxpayer expects to license, sell, or transfer intangible property or secret processes resulting from the R&E to the corporation. Controlled corporations include those related through 50 percent ownership of voting stock or stock value.[34] The taxpayer also must consider an uncontrolled corporation's sales of the relevant product if the reasonable expectation mentioned exists and the sales involve products benefiting from intangible property the taxpayer previously licensed or sold to the uncontrolled corporation. If the taxpayer cannot determine the relevant sales of uncontrolled corporations, it must estimate the sales.[35] No similar look-through rule applies when the taxpayer uses the gross income method.

## EXAMPLE

USA Jet, a U.S. corporation, manufactures and sells engines for aircraft (SIC 372) and, under government contracts, builds propulsion units for

---

[33]Reg. §1.861-17(a)(3).
[34]Reg. §1.861-17(c)(3).
[35]Reg. §1.861-17(c)(2).

guided missiles (SIC 376). USA Jet owns all the stock of Patriot, Inc., a U.S. company, and Jet Berlin GmbH, a German subsidiary. Patriot manufactures and sells propulsion units. Jet Berlin manufactures and sells aircraft engines. USA Jet also owns 20 percent of Avion SA, a French corporation, that in prior years concluded a licensing contract with USA Jet to receive its propulsion technology. During the current year, USA Jet deducts $700,000 R&E expenses related to its aircraft engines and $1,400,000 R&E expenses related to its propulsion technology. It conducts all research in the United States and apportions R&E based on sales. The sales for each company are:

|  | *Aircraft Engine Sales* | *Propulsion Unit Sales* |
|---|---|---|
| USA Jet (U.S. parent) | $25,000,000 | $19,000,000 |
| Patriot, Inc. (U.S., wholly owned) | 0 | 5,000,000 |
| Jet Berlin (German, wholly owned) | 10,000,000 | 0 |
| Avion SA (French, 20% owned) | 0 | 20,000,000 |

All sales of USA Jet and Patriot yield U.S. source income. Jet Berlin and Avion sell their production to non-U.S. interests. Jet Berlin expects to improve the aircraft engines it manufactures through the research USA Jet undertakes. Avion expects to negotiate a new licensing agreement with USA Jet to take advantage of the latter's technology breakthroughs. In apportioning its R&E deductions, USA Jet considers sales of Patriot, an affiliated company. USA Jet also considers the sales of Jet Berlin since the latter can reasonably expect to benefit from USA Jet's research. Finally, USA Jet considers the sales of Avion based on their prior licensing contract and a reasonable expectation that Avion will benefit from the USA Jet's current research. Accordingly, the apportionment results for the two product lines are:

Apportionment of $700,000 R&E for aircraft engines:

To U.S. income: $350,000 + $350,000 \left( \dfrac{\$25,000,000}{\$35,000,000} \right) = \$600,000$

To foreign income: $\$350,000 \left( \dfrac{\$10,000,000}{\$35,000,000} \right) = \$100,000$

*(continues)*

Apportionment of $1,400,000 R&E for missile propulsion units:

To U.S. income: $700,000 + $700,000 \left( \dfrac{\$24,000,000}{\$28,000,000} \right) = \$1,300,000$

To foreign income: $700,000 \left( \dfrac{\$4,000,000}{\$28,000,000} \right) = \$100,000$

The R&E apportionment formulae for propulsion units consider only 20 percent of Avion's $20,000,000 sales, the percentage of Avion that USA Jet owns.

## OTHER DEDUCTIONS

When a corporation renders services for a related corporation in return for a fee, the former company allocates its service-related deductions directly to the service fee it receives. The regulations treat stewardship services differently. Stewardship services benefit the provider rather than the recipient and fulfill an oversight function. Such services often duplicate those the recipient corporation already renders for itself. A corporation allocates deductions related to stewardship functions against dividend income it receives from the supervised company. The taxpayer apportions deductions on a factual relationship basis such as employee time (e.g., billing hours times applicable billing rates).[36]

### EXAMPLE

Based on its own market analysis, NorSub, a Norwegian corporation, concludes that it should begin a major advertising campaign. NorSub's U.S. parent, DomCo uses its own staff to evaluate the market analysis before authorizing its implementation. Employees from DomCo's Chicago and Nassau offices participate in the evaluation, requiring 25 hours of Chicago staff time and 5 hours of Nassau staff time. For non-stewardship services, the company normally would bill the 30 hours at $90 per hour. DomCo performs the stewardship function to protect its

---

[36]Reg. §1.861-8(e)(4).

> stock investment and, thus, does not charge NorSub a service fee. The parent allocates its $2,700 stewardship-related deductions (30 × $90) to dividends it receives from NorSub. It apportions the $2,700 on the basis of time—$2,250 ($2,700 × 25/30) to U.S. income and $450 ($2,700 × 5/30) to foreign income.

Depending on the services received, taxpayers usually treat legal and accounting fees as definitely related, and thus allocable, to either specific or all gross income classes. When the billing statement for legal or accounting services does not identify the specific services rendered, fails to allocate the fee among services provided, or allocates the fee improperly, the taxpayer, nonetheless, must follow the preceding allocation rule. After allocation, taxpayers apportion deductions for legal and accounting services based on factual relationships (i.e., the general apportionment rules discussed earlier in this chapter).[37]

### EXAMPLE

Smartnex, Inc., a U.S. multinational, hires Inkwell & Codehead LLP to: (1) perform a cost analysis for a product line Smartnex is thinking about adding, (2) conduct a transfer pricing study to determine whether the company can save taxes on its international transactions, and (3) prepare its federal tax return. Inkwell & Codehead bills Smartnex $30,000 for the product cost analysis, $140,000 for the transfer pricing study, and $35,000 for the tax return; and this fee allocation appears reasonable. Smartnex allocates $30,000 to the gross income expected from the proposed product line (e.g., gross profit from sales), $140,000 according to the gross income expected from the international transactions studied, and $35,000 to all gross income classes reflected on the tax return.[38] Apportionment of each amount follows the general rules.

Taxpayers allocate deductions for state and local income tax to the gross income on which the state and local jurisdictions impose tax. The rules treat deductible franchise tax similarly if based on income. If no foreign source income appears in the state or local income tax base, the regulations

---

[37]Reg. §1.861-8(e)(5).
[38]The $35,000 allocation is consistent with TAM 9833001.

ultimately apportion the entire deduction against U.S. income. Beyond these basic principles, the allocation and apportionment of state and local income tax deductions depend on the apportionment formulae, unitary principles, and specified exemptions under each state's law.[39]

Companies allocate deductible losses from selling, exchanging, or otherwise disposing of capital or Section 1231 assets to those types of gross income the assets ordinarily generate. When the type of gross income has varied over the last several years, the taxpayer looks to the immediately preceding years. The regulations indicate that taxpayers must base apportionment on gross income from the statutory and residual groupings.[40] Taxpayers allocate and apportion net operating loss deductions in the same way they allocate and apportion the deductions giving rise to the net operating loss.[41]

---

### EXAMPLE

Earth Mover, a Boston-based company, sells heavy-duty construction equipment. The company maintains a small fleet of BMWs for its top executives' local travel, primarily consisting of sales visits with existing and potential clients. After three years of use, the company normally exchanges each BMW for a new one. However, four years ago, a retiring executive leased one of Earth Mover's three-year-old BMWs and, one year later, moved to Canada. This year, the company sells the now-seven-year-old BMW (previously leased) to a dealership and a three-year-old BMW (used in the business) to a client. These sales result in deductible losses of $6,000 and $10,000, respectively. Earth Mover allocates the $6,000 deduction to leasing income and the $10,000 deduction to gross profit from sales. Based on the retired executive's use, the company apportions the $6,000 deduction as follows: $1,500 to U.S. income and $4,500 to foreign income. If Earth Mover sells its equipment only to domestic buyers, it apportions the entire $10,000 deduction to U.S. income.

---

[39]Reg. §1.861-8(e)(6).
[40]Reg. §1.861-8(e)(7).
[41]Reg. §1.861-8T(e)(8).

# Inbound Transactions

# CHAPTER 6

# Foreign Persons

The United States taxes foreign persons on only two types of income. First, a statutory 30 percent or lower treaty rate applies to U.S. source income not effectively connected with a U.S. trade or business, which primarily consists of U.S. investment income like dividends and interest.[1] The Code disallows deductions apportioned to such income, so the 30 percent or lower treaty rate applies to gross rather than taxable income. Second, unless a treaty exempts it, U.S. law taxes income effectively connected with a U.S. trade or business at regular rates.[2] Deductions apportioned to effectively connected income reduce the taxable base before the taxpayer applies the regular rates.[3] Chapters 7 and 8 discuss these rules in more detail.

Thus, foreign persons pay U.S. tax only on U.S. source income and effectively connected income. In contrast, U.S. persons pay U.S. tax on worldwide income, whether from domestic or foreign sources. These tax regime differences underscore the importance of distinguishing between U.S. and foreign persons.

Foreign persons include foreign corporations and nonresident aliens. Corporations organized in foreign countries or U.S. possessions are foreign corporations.[4] U.S. law does not define nonresident aliens so succinctly. Thus, the next section distinguishes between resident and nonresident aliens.

## FLASHBACK

The check-the-box procedure discussed in Chapter 1 allows many foreign business entities to elect treatment as foreign corporations under U.S. law even though host countries may treat the same entities as branches or partnerships.

---

[1] IRC §§871(a), 881(a).
[2] IRC §§871(b), 882(a).
[3] IRC §§873(a), 882(c)(1)(A).
[4] IRC §7701(a)(4), (5).

## RESIDENCY TESTS

The Code refers to individuals without U.S. citizenship as **aliens**. Aliens come in two varieties: either they reside in the United States or they do not. Those without U.S. residence are nonresident aliens and those residing in the United States are **resident aliens** (or U.S. residents).[5] U.S. law provides two tests for determining residency: the lawful permanent residence test and the substantial presence test. An individual meeting either test is a U.S. resident. By default, the tax law treats all other individuals without U.S. citizenship as nonresident aliens.

> **CULTURAL POINTER:**  Tax advisers may wish to avoid the term "alien" when communicating with their foreign clients. Though statutorily correct, some individuals may associate the term with little green men from Mars or, worse, to two well-known horror flicks.

Individuals become **lawful permanent residents** when the U.S. government grants them the privilege of indefinitely residing in the United States.[6] Permanent residents receive immigration identification cards. Though now white, cards issued years ago were green. Thus, some professionals refer to permanent residency as the **green card test**.

Aliens meet the **substantial presence test** if their U.S. presence during the current year meets two criteria: First, they must spend at least 31 days in the United States during the current year; second, their U.S. presence must equal or exceed 183 "weighted" days for the two preceding and current years together. The weighting procedure counts days in the second preceding year as one-sixth of a day, days in the first preceding year as one-third of a day, and days in the current year as full days.[7]

---

### EXAMPLE

Johann, an alien individual, had not visited the United States prior to 2001. He lived in the United States 150 days in 2001, 90 days in 2002, and 120 days in 2003. He does not meet the substantial presence test

---

[5]IRC §7701(b)(1)(B). For most purposes, U.S. law treats resident aliens as U.S. citizens (e.g., their worldwide income is taxable).
[6]IRC §7701(b)(6).
[7]IRC §7701(b)(3)(A).

since his weighted days total 175 [(150 ÷ 6) + (90 ÷ 3) + 120]. Unless Johann qualifies as a lawful permanent resident, the United States taxes him as a nonresident alien in 2003.

**PLANNING POINTER:** Alien individuals whose U.S. presence is near the 31- or 183-day thresholds can change their U.S. tax liabilities through carefully limiting or increasing their U.S. presence, depending on whether they desire U.S. residency.

## FLASHBACK:

As mentioned in Chapter 3, when the domestic laws of two countries treat an individual as their own resident, dual residency results. Tie-breaker rules in U.S. tax treaties determine the residency of such individuals. Thus, meeting either the lawful permanent resident or substantial presence test does not necessarily assure treatment as a U.S. resident when a treaty exists.[8]

The substantial presence test provides an objective means for distinguishing between resident and nonresident aliens based on days of U.S. presence. However, Congress carved out a **closer connection exception** to guard against treating alien individuals as U.S. residents when they have closer affinity with their home countries. This exception overrides the substantial presence test and treats individuals as nonresident aliens when they:

- Stay in the United States fewer than 183 days during the current year,
- Maintain a foreign tax home (regular or principal place of business),
- Keep a closer connection to a foreign country than to the United States, and
- Take no action to become U.S. residents (e.g., by applying for permanent immigrant status).[9]

Exhibit 6.1 summarizes the rules for determining whether U.S. law treats an alien individual as a U.S. resident or nonresident.

---

[8]Reg. §301.7701(b)-7(a)(1).
[9]IRC §7701(b)(3)(B), (C).

**EXHIBIT 6.1**   Determining an Alien Individual's Residency Status

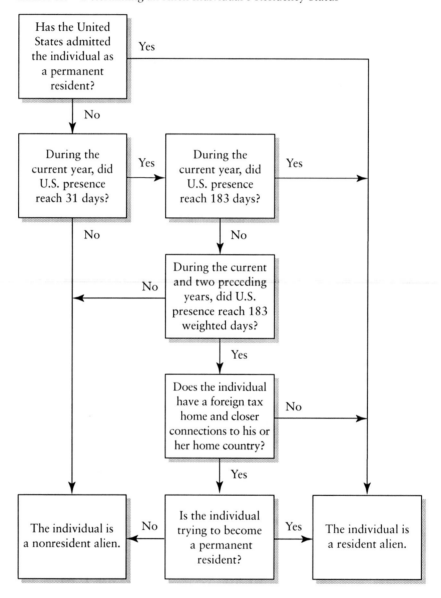

## EXAMPLE

Omar, a Saudi national, works as a civil engineer in Riyadh. His employer temporarily transferred him to a Boston affiliate on November 29, 2002. Omar's family remains in Riyadh since they know his U.S. visit ends on June 25, 2003. Omar maintains his banking account, club memberships, and driver's license in Riyadh. While in Boston, he lives in temporary quarters and uses public transportation. At all times, he intends to return permanently to Saudi Arabia. Omar meets the substantial presence test in 2003 since his weighted days total 187 [(33 ÷ 3) + 176]. Nonetheless, U.S. law treats him as a nonresident alien since he meets the closer connection exception.

## COUNTING DAYS

Unlike the closer connection exception, the three provisions in this section do not automatically override the substantial presence test. Instead, they ignore certain days of U.S. presence and, thus, may change the outcome of the substantial presence test. So, even when alien individuals otherwise meet the 31- and 183-day requirements, one of these day-counting provisions might prevent them from becoming U.S. residents.

The exempt person rule ignores days of U.S. presence when individuals engage in specified activities or professions. Individuals may qualify as exempt persons on some days of the calendar year but not others. Days on which they qualify do not count toward the 31- and 183-day thresholds. **Exempt persons** include the following individuals:

- Foreign government-related individuals (e.g., diplomats and ambassadors) and immediate family members,
- Students temporarily in the United States on F, J, M, or Q visas and immediate family members,
- Teachers and trainees temporarily in the United States on J or Q visas and immediate family members, and
- Professional athletes competing in certain charitable sports events.[10]

---

[10]IRC §7701(b)(3)(D)(i), (5); Reg. §301.7701(b)-3(b). Characterization as an "exempt person" does not mean that the United States exempts the individual from U.S. income tax. As a nonresident alien, the individual still may owe U.S. tax.

The **medical emergency** provision applies to alien individuals becoming ill or receiving injury while visiting the United States. If the illness prevents them from leaving, the recovery days do not count toward the 31- and 183-day thresholds of the substantial presence test. This provision does not apply to alien individuals traveling to the United States specifically for medical treatment.[11]

The **transient exception** applies to days of U.S. presence in three situations. This provision ignores the U.S. presence of alien individuals on days when:

- Canadian and Mexican residents regularly commute to work in the United States,
- Travelers experience brief layovers in the United States (i.e., less than 24 hours) while traveling between two foreign locations, and
- Regular crew members work aboard foreign vessels that temporarily dock at U.S. ports or sail U.S. waters but otherwise engage in international transportation.[12]

## DUAL STATUS ALIENS

The tax law bases residency status on the calendar year.[13] Unless U.S. residency starts on January 1, individuals become **dual status aliens** during their initial year. For the days preceding residency, the United States treats them as nonresident aliens. For the other days, they are resident aliens. Similarly, individuals are dual status aliens during the last year of U.S. residency unless residency ends on December 31. During the last year, the tax law treats alien individuals as U.S. residents until the residency termination date, and as nonresident aliens thereafter. Individuals can be dual status aliens under either the lawful permanent resident or substantial presence test.

Alien individuals qualifying as U.S. residents in the prior and current years begin U.S. residency in the current year on January 1. Similarly, U.S. residency extends through December 31 each year for individuals qualifying as U.S. residents in the following year.[14] These **continuum rules** avoid awkward breaks in U.S. residency status that complicate tax liability calculations and other tax issues.

If not a U.S. resident in the prior year, residency under the lawful permanent resident test begins on the first day of U.S. presence following the

---

[11]IRC §7701(b)(3)(D)(ii); Reg. §301.7701(b)-3(c).
[12]IRC §7701(b)(7).
[13]Reg. §301.7701(b)-1(b)(1), (c)(3).
[14]Reg. §301.7701(b)-4(e).

grant of permanent residency.[15] Similarly, aliens satisfying the substantial presence test start U.S. residency on the first day of U.S. presence. However, under the substantial presence test, alien individuals ignore up to 10 days of nominal U.S. presence. Nominal presence occurs when individuals maintain closer connections to a foreign country during short visits to the United States (e.g., to look for lodging).[16]

---

**EXAMPLE**

The United States grants Romola the right to permanent residency on September 2, 2003. She moves to the United States on October 18, 2003, which is her first U.S. presence in several years. From January 1 to October 17, Romola is a nonresident alien. For the remainder of the year, she is a U.S. resident. Thus, the United States combines her worldwide income after October 17 with her effectively connected income before October 18 and taxes the aggregate amount at regular rates. A 30 percent or lower treaty rate applies to her U.S. source investment income received before October 18.[17]

---

**EXAMPLE**

Under the substantial presence test, Saleitha qualifies as a U.S. resident in 2003 since her U.S. presence in 2003 is 150 days and her weighted days of U.S. presence for 2001 through 2003 equal 190. Her 2003 U.S. presence consists of a job interview for nine days in February and the 141 days from August 13 to December 31. Her U.S. residency begins on August 13. The nine days in February count toward the 183 weighted days establishing U.S. residency but do not determine the residency starting date. If she had qualified as a U.S. resident in 2002, her residency starting date in 2003 would have been January 1 under the continuum rule.

---

During the last residency year, individuals are dual status aliens unless residency terminates on December 31. For permanent immigrants, U.S. residency ends after they establish a closer connection with a foreign country than with

---

[15]IRC §7701(b)(2)(A)(ii).
[16]IRC §7701(b)(2)(A)(iii), (C). Reg. §301.7701(b)-2(d) lists several personal, business, and social factors that assist in resolving the closer connection issue.
[17]See Reg. §1.871-13 for specific rules dual status aliens must follow when calculating their U.S. tax liabilities.

the United States, and either the United States revokes their residency status or they abandon such status. For those meeting the substantial presence test, residency ceases after they establish a closer connection with a foreign country than with the United States and leave the United States for the remainder of the year. As in determining the residency starting date, up to 10 days of nominal U.S. presence are ignored when identifying the last day of residency.[18]

## IMPORTANT ELECTIONS

The United States taxes U.S. persons on worldwide income. In contrast, U.S. law taxes foreign persons at 30 percent (or a lower treaty rate) on U.S. source investment income and at regular rates on effectively connected income. Differences in how the Code treats U.S. and foreign persons provide many tax planning opportunities around residency starting and termination dates.

> **PLANNING POINTER:** Foreign individuals expecting to become U.S. residents can reduce their worldwide taxes by arranging to have their incomes taxed wherever rates are lower. If their home country tax rates are higher than U.S. tax rates, they can defer income and accelerate deductions prior to moving to the United States. Conversely, if their home country rates are lower, they can accelerate income and defer deductions before moving. Similar strategies apply when resident aliens revert to nonresidents.

## EXAMPLE

Christopher, a resident and national of New Zealand, will move permanently to the United States early next year. He owns corporate stock he purchased as an investment for $100,000 10 years ago. Today, it is worth $325,000. With few exceptions, New Zealand exempts capital gains.[19] Thus, the stock's sale before becoming a U.S. resident results in no tax anywhere. However, if he sells the stock after becoming a U.S. resident, the United States taxes the $225,000 capital gain.

Three special elections provide individuals with even more planning flexibility in the transition from nonresident alien to U.S. resident status. Each election shifts the residency starting date and may provide other tax benefits

---

[18]IRC §7701(b)(2), (6)(B).

[19]PricewaterhouseCoopers, *Corporate Taxes: Worldwide Summaries 2002–2003* (Hoboken, NJ: John Wiley & Sons, Inc., 2002), p. 596.

also. The ability to move the residency starting date when combined with an acceleration and deferral strategy can produce significant tax savings.

Alien individuals making a **first-year election** become dual status aliens in the election year. Without the election, U.S. law treats such individuals as nonresident aliens for the entire year (e.g., because they arrive too late in the calendar year to meet the substantial presence test). In effect, making the election moves the residency starting date backward from the postelection year into the election year. To qualify for the first-year election, an alien individual must:

- Not be a U.S. resident under either the lawful permanent resident or substantial presence tests during the election or prior year,
- Meet the substantial presence test in the first postelection year,
- Be present in the United States at least 31 consecutive days in the election year, and
- Be present in the United States at least 75 percent of a testing period during the election year.

The testing period begins on the first day of the earliest 31-consecutive-day period and ends on December 31 of the election year. In testing for the 75 percent threshold, the procedure arbitrarily treats five days of U.S. absence as five days of U.S. presence. Alien individuals making the first-year election become U.S. residents on the first day of the testing period.[20]

## EXAMPLE

Dugald, a Scottish national, is not a U.S. resident in either 2002 or 2003. During 2003, he stays in the United States from September 23 to November 6 and from December 5 to December 31. The diagram depicts the relevant days.

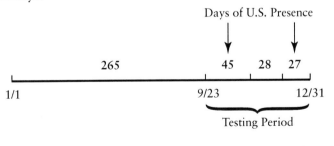

*(continues)*

---

[20]IRC §7701(b)(4).

The first day of the earliest 31-consecutive-day period is September 23. Thus, the testing period runs from September 23 to December 31. The equation indicates Dugald meets the 75 percent requirement:

$$\frac{45 + 5 + 27}{45 + 28 + 27} = 77\%$$

Assuming he meets the substantial presence test in 2004, he can make the first year election, and his U.S. residency starts September 23, 2003. Without the election, Dugald's U.S. residency begins during 2004.

**COMPLIANCE POINTER:** The IRS will not rule on whether an alien individual is a nonresident, especially when the characterization depends on facts it cannot determine until after year-end (e.g., whether the individual meets the substantial presence test in the following year).[21] Thus, those filing as dual status aliens under the first year election often extend their U.S. returns until they meet the postelection substantial presence test.[22]

The **new resident election** accelerates the residency starting date for dual status aliens to January 1, so the Code treats them as U.S. residents for the entire year. To qualify for the election, alien individuals must be:

- Nonresident aliens on January 1 and resident aliens on December 31 (i.e., dual status aliens) and
- Married to a U.S. person on December 31.

Each spouse must make the election. Once made, the spouses cannot make the election again (i.e., at the beginning of a future residency period). In addition to moving the residency starting date, the new resident election allows the married couple to file jointly.[23] Further, the election permits couples to claim the standard deduction, itemized deductions (beyond those available to nonresident aliens), and additional personal and dependency exemptions.[24]

---

[21] Rev. Proc. 2003-7, §3.01(5), 2003-1 IRB 233.
[22] Reg. §301.7701(b)-4(c)(3)(v).
[23] IRC §6013(h). Per IRC §6013(a)(1), married couples cannot file jointly if either is a nonresident alien at any time during the year.
[24] See IRC §§63(c)(6)(B), 873(b).

---

**EXAMPLE**

---

Pablo, a Panamanian national and lifelong resident, owns common stock in Home Depot and receives a $10,000 dividend on March 22, 2003. As a territorial country, Panama does not tax the U.S. source dividend.[25] Pablo and his wife move to the United States on April 15, 2003, where he expects to work for the next two years. During this time, he will not travel abroad. Pablo meets the substantial presence test and becomes a U.S. resident on April 15. He files as a dual status alien unless he makes the new resident election. As a dual status alien, he receives the $10,000 dividend as a nonresident alien (i.e., before April 15). The United States imposes a $3,000 withholding tax ($10,000 × 30%). However, if Pablo and his wife (a U.S. citizen) make the new resident election, they receive the $10,000 dividend as U.S. residents. Assuming Pablo pays $500 investment expenses allocable to the dividends, and his marginal U.S. tax rate when filing jointly is 15 percent, his U.S. income tax on the dividend income falls to $1,425 [($10,000 − $500) × 15%].

---

The **nonresident election** allows a nonresident alien to be treated as a U.S. resident for the entire year. To qualify, individuals must be:

- Nonresident aliens on December 31 and
- Married to a U.S. person on December 31.

Like the new resident election, each spouse must join in the election, and electing couples can file joint U.S. returns, claim more than one personal and dependency exemption, take the standard deduction, and claim itemized deductions beyond those normally allowed nonresident aliens. An election continues in effect until either spouse revokes it or it is terminated through the death of either spouse or the couple's legal separation. If revoked or terminated, neither spouse can ever make the election again.[26]

Exhibit 6.2 summarizes the effects of the three elections available to alien individuals.

---

[25]PricewaterhouseCoopers, *Corporate Taxes: Worldwide Summaries 2002–2003* (Hoboken, NJ: John Wiley & Sons, Inc., 2002), p. 641.
[26]IRC §6013(g).

**EXHIBIT 6.2**   Comparing Elections Available to Alien Individuals

|                | Without Election   | With Election      | Effect of Election                                                                                                          |
|----------------|--------------------|--------------------|---------------------------------------------------------------------------------------------------------------------------|
| First year     | Nonresident alien  | Dual status alien  | Accelerates starting date                                                                                                   |
| New resident   | Dual status alien  | Resident alien     | Accelerates starting date and allows joint return, standard deduction, itemized deductions, and more than one exemption     |
| Nonresident    | Nonresident alien  | Resident alien     | Accelerates starting date and allows joint return, standard deduction, itemized deductions, and more than one exemption     |

# CHAPTER 7

# Nonbusiness Income

The Code taxes foreign corporations and nonresident aliens on two types of income: Regular U.S. tax rates apply to income effectively connected with a U.S. trade or business; a 30 percent tax applies to U.S. source income not effectively connected with a U.S. trade or business. Chapter 8 covers effectively connected income, and this chapter addresses taxation of nonbusiness income from U.S. sources.

## FIXED OR DETERMINABLE, ANNUAL OR PERIODICAL INCOME

U.S. law taxes foreign persons on their U.S. source income, if not effectively connected with a U.S. trade or business, at a flat 30 percent. Taxpayers cannot subtract deductions apportioned to this income, so the 30 percent rate applies to the gross income amount. The United States collects the tax on this income through withholding procedures.

### FLASHBACK

Chapter 4 discussed the meaning of U.S. source income, and Chapter 6 identified foreign persons. Also, as Chapter 3 explained, income tax treaties often reduce the statutory 30 percent rate applicable to U.S. source investment income to between 15 percent and zero.

### EXAMPLE

Bizarre Bazaar SA, a foreign corporation not conducting U.S. business, receives $4,000 U.S. source dividends from a portfolio interest (i.e., less than 10 percent) and $3,000 U.S. source royalties. Brokerage fees of

*(continues)*

$250 relate to the dividends. If the company resides in the Ivory Coast, a country with which the United States does not have an income tax treaty, the U.S. withholding tax is $2,100 [($4,000 + $3,000) × 30%]. However, if Bizarre Bazaar resides in France, Articles 10(2)(b) and 12(2) of the U.S.-France Treaty reduce the dividend and royalty withholding taxes to $600 ($4,000 × 15%) and $150 ($3,000 × 5%), respectively.

The U.S. source income the Code taxes at 30 percent consists primarily of investment earnings—interest, dividends, rents, royalties, premiums, the income portion of annuities, and other **fixed or determinable, annual or periodical (FDAP)** income. However, the 30 percent tax also reaches the following gains and income items if not effectively connected with a U.S. trade or business:

- Gain on disposal of timber, coal, and domestic iron ore when the seller retains an economic interest;
- Accrued original issue discount when selling or exchanging a debt obligation;
- Gain from sale or exchange of manufacturing and marketing intangibles to the extent proceeds depend on later productivity, use, or disposition;[1]
- Eighty-five percent of U.S. Social Security benefits received;[2] and
- Prizes, awards, alimony, and gambling income.[3]

For convenience, this text refers to all U.S. source income not effectively connected with a U.S. trade or business (i.e., gross income taxable at 30 percent or a lower treaty rate) as FDAP income.

---

[1]IRC §§871(a)(1), 881(a). These statutory provisions also list salaries, wages, compensation, remuneration, and emoluments among the income items that U.S. law taxes at 30 percent. These inclusions relate to a bygone era when such compensatory receipts might have escaped taxation if deferred to a later taxable year. Now, their inclusions among FDAP items is mostly deadwood language since IRC §864(c)(6) taxes them at regular rates.

[2]IRC §871(a)(3). U.S. individuals do not pay tax on U.S. Social Security benefits they receive if their modified adjusted gross income does not exceed certain thresholds. However, when nonresident aliens receive U.S. Social Security benefits, the statute treats the maximum amount (i.e., 85 percent) as taxable.

[3]Rev. Rul. 58-479, 1958-2 CB 60; *Howkins vs. Comm.*, 49 TC 689 (1968); and *Barba v. U.S.*, 2 Cl.Ct. 674 (1983). However, unless future regulations otherwise specify, IRC §871(j) excludes nonresident aliens' winnings from blackjack, baccarat, craps, roulette, and big-6 wheel. This exclusion exists because U.S. collection of the tax due is not administratively feasible.

## EXAMPLE

Ali, a Liberian national and resident, buys a five-year, $10,000 U.S. government savings bond for $7,600 (i.e., the original issue discount equals $2,400). Before maturity, Ali sells the bond for $8,600. A 30 percent withholding tax applies to the portion of the $1,000 gain that is original issue discount. If Ali instead holds the bond until maturity, a 30 percent withholding tax applies to the $2,400 profit.

## EXAMPLE

Antoine, a French citizen and resident, receives a $2,000 U.S. Social Security benefit based on prior years he worked in the United States. The Social Security Administration withholds $510 ($2,000 × 85% × 30%). The U.S.-France Treaty does not change the result. However, if Antoine had been a German resident, Article 19(2) of the U.S.-German Treaty would have exempted the income.

Controversies often arise over the meaning and scope of FDAP income. For instance, if receiving an income amount periodically over time qualifies as FDAP income, should the same income received as a lump-sum amount also qualify?

## KEY CASE

A nonresident alien receives a lump-sum payment for the U.S. copyright to his literary work. He views the transaction as the sale of intangible property rights and, thus, its income as exempt from U.S. tax. However, the government contends the payment is FDAP income, and the Supreme Court agrees. The receipt clearly would have been FDAP if received over the 28 years of the copyright. The receipt's characterization should not differ merely because the taxpayer receives it as a lump-sum amount.[4]

---

[4]*Comm. v. Wodehouse*, 337 US 369 (1949). Whether current law would have taxed this lump-sum amount depends on the FDAP income's source under IRC §865 (enacted in 1986).

**COMPLIANCE POINTER:** A withholding tax of 30 percent (or lower treaty rate) applies to FDAP income. The last U.S. person with custody and control over the payment usually withholds and remits the tax. Any withholding agent failing to withhold is liable for the tax, interest, and penalties.[5]

## MARGINAL TAX RATES

Foreign corporations often conduct U.S. business through domestic subsidiaries and receive business profits as FDAP income such as dividends. When making investment or financing decisions about U.S. operations, foreign corporations may view U.S. business profits as incremental income and focus on the marginal tax rate from such profits. The **marginal tax rate** **(MTR)** equals the present value of all taxes applicable to incremental income divided by such income.[6] In the present context, U.S. business profits are the incremental income of the affiliated group, and the applicable taxes include the U.S. income tax and dividend withholding tax. Equation 7.1 yields the MTR when a foreign corporation receives all after-tax business profits as current dividends and incurs no foreign income tax on the dividend income:

$$MTR = t_{us} + t_{div}(1 - t_{us}) \tag{7.1}$$

where:

$t_{us}$ = effective U.S. income tax rate[7] and
$t_{div}$ = U.S. dividend withholding tax rate

---

[5]IRC §§1441, 1442, 1461, 1463, 6672.

[6]Multinational companies and their advisors often focus on **effective tax rates** (ETRs), total tax liability divided by total incomes, and benchmark against ETRs of similar companies. However, this text emphasizes MTRs because accounting and tax professionals can use them to quickly estimate the overall tax impact of an international transaction, an important analytical skill that considers the impact of U.S. tax law, foreign tax law, and treaties. If a company determines that a transaction's MTR is lower than the existing ETR, the transaction will lower the company's ETR.

[7]The effective U.S. income tax rate equals the U.S. and state income tax on U.S. business profits divided by the U.S. business profits. Domestic corporations with taxable incomes between $335,000 and $10 million have effective U.S. income tax rates of 34 percent, assuming no state income tax. Similarly, domestic corporations with taxable incomes above $18,333,333 have effective U.S. income tax rates of 35 percent, assuming no state income tax.

---

**EXAMPLE**

Tea Time, Ltd., an Australian corporation, owns all the stock in Bright Fawn Coffee, Inc., a U.S. company. Bright Fawn earns $1 million U.S. business profits during the year, on which it pays $340,000 U.S. income tax, a 34 percent effective U.S. income tax rate. It remits the remaining $660,000 to Tea Time, less a dividend withholding tax of 15 percent, per Article 10(2) of the U.S.-Australia Treaty. Thus, Tea Time's after-tax profit on its $1 million before-tax income is $561,000 ($660,000 × 85%). Since the total tax on its $1 million before-tax income is $439,000 [$1 million − $561,000, or $340,000 + ($660,000 × 15%)], Tea Time's MTR is 43.9 percent ($439,000 ÷ $1 million). Alternatively, Tea Time can derive its MTR using equation 7.1, as follows:

$$MTR = 0.34 + 0.15 (1 - 0.34) = 43.9\%$$

---

When foreign corporations do not receive U.S. business profits in the current year from U.S. subsidiaries, the delayed remittance defers the dividend withholding tax. The longer the deferral, the smaller the present value of the dividend withholding tax and the lower the MTR. Equation 7.2 provides a more accurate MTR estimate than equation 7.1 when foreign corporations cause their U.S. subsidiaries to defer dividend remittances of U.S. business profits to a future year:

$$MTR = t_{us} + \frac{t_{div}(1 - t_{us})}{(1 + d)^y} \tag{7.2}$$

where:

$d$ = discount rate and
$y$ = deferral period in years

---

**EXAMPLE**

Assume the same facts as in the previous example except that Bright Fawn does not expect to remit its $660,000 after-tax profits for eight years. Also, assume a 9 percent discount rate. Under these facts, the estimated MTR for the $1 million U.S. business profits declines nearly five percentage points:

$$MTR = 0.34 + \frac{0.15(1 - 0.34)}{(1 + 0.09)^8} = 39.0\%$$

---

Dividends represent a division of earnings rather than an expense of doing business. In other words, paying dividends does not directly enable a business to earn higher profits. Thus, corporations cannot deduct dividends they pay as ordinary and necessary business expenses. In contrast, businesses usually can deduct interest and royalty payments. To the extent a foreign corporation adds debt to the capital structure of its U.S. subsidiary or concludes licensing agreements with its U.S. subsidiary, it can extract U.S. business profits in deductible form. In effect, some portion of U.S. business profits avoids U.S. income tax, though that portion may be subject to interest or royalty withholding taxes. Equation 7.3 shows the MTR calculation for the portion of U.S. business profits remitted to foreign corporations in deductible form.

$$MTR = t_{int} \text{ or } t_{roy} \tag{7.3}$$

where:

$t_{int}$ = U.S. interest withholding tax rate and
$t_{roy}$ = U.S. royalty withholding tax rate

**PLANNING POINTER:**    Since deductible remittances avoid the host country's income tax, they usually reduce the MTR, often dramatically. The key is to assure deductibility. Among other things, the interest-stripping provisions this chapter discusses later may disallow some deductions.

---

### EXAMPLE

Assume the same facts as in the first Tea Time example, except that Tea Time loans capital to Bright Fawn and, as a result, receives $1 million interest from Bright Fawn during the year. If fully deductible, the interest reduces Bright Fawn's taxable income to zero. In effect, Tea Time receives its U.S. business profits without reduction for U.S. income tax. However, Article 11(2) of the U.S.-Australia Treaty imposes a 10 percent withholding tax. Thus, the MTR on $1 million U.S. business profits equals 10 percent, per equation 7.3.

---

Equations 7.1 through 7.3 and the related examples presume foreign parent companies receive all business profits from their U.S. subsidiaries in one of three forms: current dividends, future dividends, or deductible payments. When foreign corporations receive U.S. business profits in a combination of these forms, they can derive a reasonable MTR estimate through appropriately weighting and summing the results of equations 7.1 through 7.3.

---

**EXAMPLE**

---

Assume the same facts as in the prior example except Tea Time's loan results in only $400,000 interest, which eliminates 40 percent of Bright Fawn's taxable income. Tea Time receives U.S. business profits remaining after interest and income taxes as a current-year dividend. Appropriately weighting the results of equations 7.1 and 7.3 yields the following MTR estimate for the $1 million of preinterest, pretax business profits:

$$MTR = (60\% \times 43.9\%) + (40\% \times 10\%) = 30.3\%$$

---

Equations 7.1 through 7.3 provide reasonable MTR estimates in many situations, especially when the foreign parent company resides in a country using a territorial system. However, a residual foreign income tax may result under a worldwide tax system when the effective tax rate in the foreign country exceeds the effective U.S. tax rate. In those cases, the equations in this section may understate the actual MTR.[8]

## NONBUSINESS EXEMPTIONS

Most exclusions available to U.S. persons (e.g., gifts and municipal bond interest) apply equally to foreign corporations and nonresident aliens. Also, foreign persons exclude certain income items U.S. persons must include in gross income. The Code allows these additional exclusions for economic, cultural, and administrative reasons.

If not effectively connected with a U.S. trade or business, foreign persons exclude interest income derived from deposits with U.S. banks and savings institutions. Similarly, interest insurance companies pay to foreign persons (e.g., on investment annuities or life insurance proceeds) is exempt if not effectively connected.[9] These interest exclusions attract foreign capital to the United States and, thus, bolster the U.S. economy.

Before 1984, U.S. **multinationals** tapped the **Eurobond market** (i.e., sources of financing in Europe) indirectly through finance subsidiaries in the Netherlands Antilles and favorable income tax treaties. Absent this circuitous route, the relatively high U.S. interest withholding tax effectively

---

[8]From an outbound investment perspective, Chapter 11 discusses the residual U.S. tax that may result from remitting foreign profits.
[9]IRC §§871(i)(2)(A), 881(d).

shut many U.S. companies out of the Eurobond market. In 1984, Congress excluded interest income of foreign persons, allowing Europeans to loan capital to U.S. persons on more favorable terms and granting U.S. borrowers direct and competitive access to the Eurobond market. Now, foreign persons exclude **portfolio interest,** which is U.S. source interest received from a corporation (or partnership) in which the foreign person owns less than 10 percent voting power (or capital or profit interest). To be excludable, the foreign recipient must receive the interest from either:

- Registered securities (i.e., debt instruments transferred through book entries) or
- Nonregistered securities (i.e., bearer bonds) marketed exclusively to foreign persons.[10]

---

### EXAMPLE

Exquisite Beauty SA, a French corporation not engaged in a U.S. trade or business, receives $20,000 interest from U.S. certificates of deposit and $6,000 interest from registered General Electric bonds. The company owns no equity interest in General Electric. Even though Exquisite Beauty derives the $20,000 and $6,000 from U.S. sources, the Code excludes both amounts.

---

Most dividends from U.S. corporations are U.S. source income to the recipients and, thus, subject to dividend withholding tax. However, the Code exempts a proportionate amount of dividends foreign persons receive from U.S. corporations deriving at least 80 percent of their gross income from active foreign business activities (i.e., 80-20 companies).[11] This look-through rule excludes 80 to 100 percent of dividends foreign persons receive, depending on the outcome of the active foreign business test.

---

[10]IRC §§871(h), 881(c). U.S. issuers must take precautions to assure that U.S. persons do not beneficially receive exempt interest income under this provision. For registered securities, the U.S. withholding agent must receive a written statement from the beneficial owner (or financial intermediary) that the beneficial owner is a foreign person. For nonregistered securities, the interest must be payable abroad and the U.S. issuer must include on the security's face a statement that income tax limitations apply to U.S. persons holding such obligations.
[11]IRC §§871(i)(2)(B), 881(d).

**FLASHBACK**

Chapter 4 stated that interest a person receives from an 80-20 company is at least 80 percent foreign source income. However, no comparable source rule applies to dividends someone receives from an 80-20 company. Thus, such dividends are entirely U.S. source income.

**EXAMPLE**

Lowell, an Irish citizen and resident, receives a $1,000 dividend from a U.S. corporation. Over the three preceding taxable years, the corporation derives 82 percent of its gross income from business conducted abroad and the residual from U.S. sources. Though Lowell derives the entire $1,000 dividend from U.S. sources, U.S. law exempts $820. Thus, the U.S. corporation withholds U.S. tax on only $180 of the dividend.

With few exceptions, foreign persons exclude U.S. source capital gain if not effectively connected with a U.S. trade or business. The exclusion does not extend to Section 1231 gain, which the Code taxes as effectively connected income. U.S. law permits the capital gain exclusion, at least partially, because of the difficulty in otherwise collecting the U.S. tax. For instance, the IRS may not know when foreign persons sell stocks and bonds of U.S. companies, particularly if such sales occur abroad, and may be unable to verify the adjusted basis of disposed assets. Foreign corporations exclude all U.S. source capital gain not effectively connected. Nonresident aliens must be present in the United States less than 183 days during the year capital gain is realized to exclude it.[12] Exhibit 7.1 summarizes these provisions.

**FLASHBACK**

Chapter 4 explained that the source of capital gain from selling investment assets (e.g., corporate stock) depends on the seller's residence. Thus, capital gain of most nonresident aliens is foreign source income.

*(continues)*

---

[12]IRC §871(a)(2). No comparable provision permits the United States to tax U.S. source capital gain of foreign corporations. Thus, unless effectively connected, foreign corporations exclude such gain.

However, nonresident aliens with U.S. tax homes (i.e., treated as U.S. residents under the source rules) derive capital gain from U.S. sources when selling investment assets. The present rule applies to capital gain from these types of foreign individuals. Nonetheless, the requirement of U.S. presence for 183 days narrows the rule's application even further. As Chapter 6 explained, most alien individuals present in the United States for 183 days qualify as U.S. residents and find no refuge under the closer connection exception. However, alien individuals commuting to work in the United States from Canada or Mexico and qualifying as exempt persons (e.g., foreign ambassadors to the United States) can aggregate 183 or more days of U.S. presence without becoming U.S. residents. Finally, as Chapter 3 mentioned, U.S. tax treaties often exempt the U.S. source capital gain of foreign persons. Thus, very few nonresident aliens pay U.S. income tax on capital gain not effectively connected with a U.S. trade or business. Taxation occurs only when a nonresident alien has a U.S. tax home, remains in the United States for 183 days without becoming a U.S. resident, and receives no treaty protection.

## EXAMPLE

José, a nonresident alien, is the sole owner of José Fiesta SA, a foreign corporation. During the year, the company sells personal property yielding a $4,000 capital gain from U.S. sources. Also, José sells personal property yielding an $18,000 capital gain from U.S. sources. Assuming neither gain is effectively connected with a U.S. trade or business, the

**EXHIBIT 7.1**    Taxing Foreign Persons on U.S. Source Capital Gain

|  | Is the income effectively connected? | |
| --- | --- | --- |
|  | Yes | No |
| *Foreign Corporations* | Regular tax rates | Exempt from tax |
| *Nonresident Aliens with U.S. Presence < 183 Days* | Regular tax rates | Exempt from tax |
| *Nonresident Aliens with U.S. Presence ≥ 183 Days* | Regular tax rates | 30% or lower treaty rates |

company's $4,000 gain escapes U.S. taxation. Similarly, José excludes his $18,000 gain if he spends fewer than 183 days in the United States during the year, has a foreign tax home, or enjoys treaty protection.

## INTEREST STRIPPING

If not effectively connected, a 30 percent withholding tax applies to interest income a foreign person receives from U.S. sources. Most U.S. treaties reduce the withholding rate below 30 percent, some to zero. When U.S. persons pay interest to foreign persons, low or zero withholding rates create incentives to increase debt so earnings can be "stripped" as deductible interest from the U.S. economy without paying U.S. tax. This tax avoidance technique is **interest stripping.**[13]

## EXAMPLE

Fortap AB, a Swedish corporation, owns all the stock of Usiphon, a U.S. corporation. No loans or debt arrangements currently exist between the two companies. Usiphon expects taxable income of $20 million next year. Without capital structure changes, Usiphon will pay $7 million of U.S. income tax on its earnings, a 35 percent effective rate. However, Fortap can reduce this U.S. tax liability with debt financing. An extreme case illustrates the point: If Usiphon pays $20 million deductible interest to Fortap, Usiphon's expected taxable income falls to zero, eliminating the $7 million U.S. tax. In effect, a loan from Fortap to Usiphon requiring interest payments of $20 million allows Fortap to strip U.S. earnings. Article 11(1) of the U.S.-Sweden Treaty exempts Fortap's interest income from U.S. withholding tax. Thus, the debt financing allows Fortap to avoid U.S. income and withholding taxes on the $20 million U.S. earnings.

---

[13]In addition to interest stripping, companies can siphon off profits through royalties and other deductible payments. Collectively, these methods for reducing income tax are known as **earnings stripping.** Many countries restrict earnings stripping through thin capitalization provisions and other rules disallowing deductions, but the antiabuse techniques vary. For instance, Latin American countries often keep interest and royalty withholding taxes high to discourage earnings stripping that enforcement efforts otherwise might not detect.

Congressional response to abusive stripping focuses on the deductibility of interest payments between related persons. U.S. law disallows interest deductions when the following conditions exist:

- A corporation pays interest to a related person (under a 50 percent ownership rule),[14]
- U.S. treaties partially or entirely exempt the interest from U.S. withholding tax,[15]
- The debtor's debt-to-equity ratio exceeds 1.5 to 1 at year-end (i.e., debt is more than 60 percent of assets),[16] and
- The debtor has excess interest expense (defined next).[17]

The absence of one or more conditions precludes the loss of interest deductions.

> **PLANNING POINTER:** U.S. companies can lease some assets for operations rather than relying entirely on debt financing. Leasing operational assets keeps the debt-to-equity ratio from increasing. To the extent the resulting debt-to-equity ratio stays below 1.5 to 1, the foreign creditor can strip interest without forfeiting interest deductions.

Under the fourth condition just given, **excess interest expense** measures the extent to which the debtor pays too much of its earnings out as interest, which suggests stripping. If interest expense is more than half of taxable income (after adjustments for items not affecting cash flow), excess interest expense often results.[18] However, results from prior years when a company had no excess interest expense can reduce the current-year's excess interest expense. Specifically, if a company's net interest expense in a year is less than 50 percent of adjusted taxable income, the difference carries forward to reduce excess interest expense in the next three years.[19] Exhibit 7.2 defines excess interest expense in more detail.

The disallowed portion of interest expense is the lesser of excess interest expense or the portion of interest income on which the related recipient is exempt.[20] Thus, debtors lose no interest deductions if excess interest ex-

---

[14]IRC §163(j)(3)(A), (4).
[15]IRC §163(j)(3)(A), (5).
[16]IRC §163(j)(2)(A).
[17]IRC §163(j)(1)(A).
[18]IRC §163(j)(2)(B)(i); Prop. Reg. §1.163(j)-1(f).
[19]IRC §163(j)(2)(B)(ii), (iii).
[20]IRC §163(j)(1)(A), (3). Prop. Reg. §1.163(j)-1(c) allows taxpayers to carry forward disallowed interest deductions.

**EXHIBIT 7.2**  Calculating Excess Interest Expense

|  | | |
|---|---|---|
| | Interest paid or accrued | |
| − | Interest included in gross income | Net interest expense* |
| | Taxable income | |
| + | Net interest expense | |
| + | Net operating loss deduction | |
| + | Depreciation, amortization, depletion | |
| + | Charitable carryover deduction | |
| + | Tax-exempt interest | |
| + | Dividend received deduction | |
| + | Capital loss carryover deduction | |
| − | Charitable contribution disallowed | |
| − | Net capital loss | |
| +/− | Similar items not affecting cash flow | |
| | Adjusted taxable income | |
| × | 50% | − Half of adjusted taxable income* |
| | Based on data from prior three years: | |
| | Half of adjusted taxable income | |
| − | Net interest expense | |
| − | Excess previously absorbed | − Excess limitation carryforward* |
| | | Excess interest expense |

*If less than zero, zero is substituted in calculation.

pense is zero. Similarly, they do not lose deductions if the creditor pays U.S. tax on the interest income at the full 30 percent statutory rate. If a U.S. treaty reduces the interest withholding tax rate below 30 percent, equation 7.4 determines the amount of interest income considered exempt:[21]

$$\text{Exempt interest income} = \text{Interest} \times \frac{30\% - \text{Treaty withholding rate}}{30\%} \qquad (7.4)$$

[21]IRC §163(j)(5).

## EXAMPLE

Oslo Pulp ASA, a Norwegian corporation, organizes Paper Supply, Inc. as a wholly owned U.S. corporation. On the first day of its first taxable year, Paper Supply borrows $1 million from its parent company at a 10 percent annual interest rate. Article 9(1) of the U.S.-Norway Treaty exempts Oslo's interest income from U.S. withholding tax. After the loan, Paper Supply's debt-to-equity ratio is 2 to 1. For its first year, Paper Supply's net interest expense is $150,000 (including interest paid to Oslo) and its adjusted taxable income is $180,000. Thus, excess interest expense is $60,000 [$150,000 – (50% × $180,000)]. Since Paper Supply meets the four conditions under the interest stripping rules, it can deduct only $40,000 of the $100,000 interest it pays to Oslo the first year ($100,000 related person interest minus the lesser of $100,000 related person exempt interest or $60,000 excess interest expense).

## EXAMPLE

Global Management, Inc. has excess interest expense of $68,000. Global pays its Canadian parent company $900,000 interest, on which Global withholds $90,000. Thus, its related person exempt interest income is $60,000 ($90,000 × 20%/30%). Assuming Global's debt-to-equity ratio exceeds 1.5 to 1, U.S. law disallows a deduction for $60,000 of Global's $90,000 interest expense (lesser of $68,000 or $60,000).

# CHAPTER 8

# Business Income

As Chapter 7 explained, the United States taxes nonresident aliens and foreign corporation at a statutory 30 percent rate on U.S. source income not effectively connected with a U.S. trade or business. U.S. law applies the 30 percent rate to gross income; apportioned deductions do not reduce the tax base. If a U.S. treaty with the foreign person's home country provides for a withholding tax lower than 30 percent, the lower rate applies. The U.S. Treasury collects the tax through withholding. Unless effectively connected, the Code exempts most capital gain.

U.S. law taxes foreign persons on business income effectively connected with a U.S. trade or business and allows foreign taxpayers to apportion deductions against such income. The United States imposes regular rates (corporate or individual) on effectively connected taxable income. Exhibit 8.1 summarizes the types of ordinary income subject to U.S. taxation.

## EXAMPLE

Tamara, a Nigerian citizen and resident, earns $50,000 U.S. business profit and $20,000 U.S. source dividends from nonbusiness investments. She apportions $15,000 expenses to the business profit and $1,000 expenses to the dividends. The Code taxes her $35,000 ($50,000 – $15,000) net business profit at the normal rates applicable to U.S. individuals and her $20,000 gross dividends at 30 percent.

PLANNING POINTER: Multinational companies can incorporate abroad even if they establish headquarters and conduct operations in the United States. For instance, publicly traded companies can incorporate in a tax haven, such as Bermuda, even though listed on a U.S. exchange. In effect, offshore incorporations protect most foreign source business income from U.S. taxation, resulting in quasiterritorial taxation. To be successful, share holdings must be dispersed

**EXHIBIT 8.1**   U.S. Taxation of Foreign Persons' Ordinary Income

|  |  | Is the income effectively connected? | |
|---|---|---|---|
|  |  | Yes | No |
| What is the source of the income? | U.S. | Regular rates apply to taxable income. | 30% or treaty rates apply to gross income. |
|  | Foreign | Regular rates apply to taxable income. | Exempt. |

so the company avoids controlled foreign corporation (CFC) status. As Chapter 12 explains, CFC status cannot occur if all U.S. persons own less than 10 percent voting power. Even when some U.S. persons reach the 10 percent threshold, CFC status does not result if aggregate holdings of these U.S. persons do not exceed 50 percent.

This chapter deals primarily with the U.S. taxation of foreign persons' business income. After defining U.S. trade or business and **effectively connected income (ECI)**, the text discusses situations in which the Code exempts business profit. The last section presents the general approach to calculating foreign persons' U.S. tax liabilities, which summarizes much of the material from this chapter and Chapter 7.

## U.S. TRADE OR BUSINESS

Neither the Code nor regulations define the phrase, "trade or business," despite its frequent appearance in the tax law. With few exceptions (mentioned later), foreign person do not realize effectively connected income unless engaged in a U.S. trade or business.[1] Thus, a U.S. trade or business acts as a prerequisite to a finding of ECI. Avoiding U.S. trade or business status is the first line of defense against U.S. taxation of business profit.

All U.S. profit-seeking activities are not U.S. trades or businesses. In addition to seeking a profit, the activity must occur on a continuous and regular basis.[2] Most investment activities do not qualify. Also, U.S. law does not treat isolated transactions and noncontinuous activities as U.S. trades or businesses.

---

[1] IRC §864(c)(1)(B).
[2] *Comm. v. Groetzinger*, 480 US 23 (1987).

**KEY CASE**

During World War II, a Swedish count assigns broad powers over his U.S. real estate and security holdings to a U.S. real estate broker in case Germany cuts off Europe from the United States and freezes assets of Swedish nationals. The U.S. agent spends half his time leasing property, supervising repairs, issuing options, making mortgage and tax payments, maintaining books and records, and acquiring insurance for the count. However, the agent understands he must consult the count before buying and selling real estate. The count grants permission to sell improved real estate he previously leased on a "net" basis (i.e., the lessee pays all expenses and the lessor merely collects the rent). The sale produces long-term capital gain. Based on the agent's considerable, continuous, and regular activities on his client's behalf, the court holds that the count conducts a U.S. trade or business.[3]

**KEY CASE**

A U.S. shipbuilding corporation acquires two war surplus landing ships (LSTs). Afterward, the company's poor financial condition forces it to seek a loan for a portion of the cost. A Mexican national and resident loans the company two-thirds of the purchase price. In return for the loan, the U.S. corporation agrees to split equally any profit from resale with the Mexican individual. Also, the company verbally assures the individual that he will not suffer any loss and, at a minimum, will realize a 25 percent return. Later, the company sells the ships to the Argentine government. The U.S. company returns the individual's original investment within two months of the loan, plus a 75 percent profit. However, the company withholds 30 percent of the profit as U.S. income tax. After repaying the loan, the U.S. corporation assists the Argentine government to convert the LSTs to peacetime use. The Mexican individual considers the loan and repayment as an investment activity and contends that he did not engage in a U.S. trade or business. The court agrees, noting that business involves continued activities, not isolated transactions.[4]

---

[3]*Lewenhaupt v. Comm.*, 20 TC 151 (1953) *aff'd* per curiam in 221 F.2d 227 (CA-9, 1955).
[4]*Pasquel v. Comm.*, 12 TCM 1431 (1954). The very high tax rates during the years at issue (up to 86.45 percent) motivated the IRS to treat the "interest" received as business income.

Often, foreign parties do not wish to treat their activities as U.S. trades or businesses. However, when apportioned deductions are large vis-à-vis the income from a profit-seeking activity, foreign parties may desire U.S. business status. In the next case, the Ninth Circuit did not explicitly state why the foreign corporation tried to become a U.S. business. Presumably, the corporation wanted to claim the dividend-received deduction that otherwise it lost.

## KEY CASE

A Panamanian corporation's principal U.S. activities consist of collecting dividends, securing loans, making principal and interest payments on outstanding loans, and selling stock. It derives most of its income from dividends on two U.S. stock holdings. The company has no employees and keeps no books of account in the United States. In short, the company primarily manages its investments. In addition to its investment pursuits, the taxpayer purchases tin milk cans on numerous occasions and immediately resells them at a nominal markup to a related company. The Panamanian corporation keeps no inventory of milk cans. The company maintains that it engages in a U.S. trade or business through the milk can transactions. However, the Ninth Circuit holds that the mere management of one's own investments, coupled with incidental businesslike activities (no matter how extensive), is not a trade or business. The milk can transactions are "isolated and non-continuous" and, rather than having a business objective, are tax-motivated.[5]

Notwithstanding the preceding decision, the IRS may assert that single events within the United States (e.g., entering a horse in the Kentucky Derby) give rise to a U.S. trade or business, especially for high-profile cases involving large profits.[6]

The performance of personal services for compensation usually is a trade or business. However, a nonresident alien rendering services in the United States does not conduct a U.S. trade or business if:

- The compensation for the U.S. services does not exceed $3,000,
- The individual's U.S. presence during the taxable year does not exceed 90 days, and

---

[5] *Continental Trading, Inc. v. Comm.*, 265 F.2d 40 (CA-9, 1959).
[6] Rev. Rul. 58-63, 1958-1 CB 624; Rev. Rul. 67-321, 1967-2 CB 470; and Rev. Rul. 70-543, 1970-2 CB 172.

■ The individual renders the U.S. services for either a foreign person not engaged in a U.S. business or a U.S. person's foreign place of business.[7]

## FLASHBACK

Meeting the three conditions listed means the nonresident alien does not engage in a U.S. trade or business and, thus, has no ECI. Chapter 4 indicated that foreign source income results when a nonresident alien meets the identical three conditions. Combining these two de minimis provisions causes the income to avoid U.S. taxation (see Exhibit 8.1). Nonresident aliens from a treaty country often find that the treaty provides an even more favorable de minimis rule. As Chapter 3 explained, most income tax treaties exempt personal service income if the individual spends no more than 183 days in the United States and meets certain other requirements. Also, the treaty exemption allows the payor to engage in a U.S. trade or business as long as the compensation is not deductible for U.S. tax purposes.

An estate or trust conducting a U.S. trade or business causes each of its beneficiaries to engage in U.S. business.[8] If a partnership engages in a U.S. trade or business, the Code also treats each of its partners as though conducting a U.S. trade or business. Conversely, partners engaging in a U.S. trade or business on their partnership's behalf cause the partnership to conduct U.S. business as well.[9]

Foreign persons do not conduct a U.S. trade or business merely as a result of the following activities:

■ Exporting to or importing from the U.S. market without using a U.S. office or dependent agent;[10]
■ Collecting passive income;[11]
■ Trading stocks, securities, or commodities through a resident broker, commission agent, custodian, or other independent agent unless the

---

[7]IRC §864(b)(1).
[8]IRC §875.
[9]*U.S. v. Balanovski*, 236 F.2d 298 (CA-2, 1956).
[10]*Amalgamated Dental, Ltd. v. Comm.*, 6 TC 1009 (1946); *European Naval Stores Co., S.A. v. Comm.*, 11 TC 127 (1948).
[11]*Neill v. Comm.*, 46 BTA 197 (1942).

foreign person maintains a fixed U.S. place of business that facilitates or directs such trades;[12]

- Engaging in other investment activities on one's own account;[13]
- Owning real estate;[14] or
- Investigating U.S. business opportunities.[15]

Nonetheless, other business activities occurring with those just listed may cause the pursuit to become a U.S. trade or business. For instance, a company earning income through regular and continuous management of its U.S. real estate holdings engages in a U.S. business.

---

### EXAMPLE

Retread SA, a Brazilian corporation, sells refurbished tires to U.S. retailers at discounted prices. Retread does not maintain a U.S. office, nor does it have employees or other dependent agents selling its tires in the United States. Retread receives all orders in, and ships all tires from, its Rio de Janeiro office. Its export sales to U.S. retailers do not constitute a U.S. trade or business. Thus, Retread's business profit is not ECI.

---

**COMPLIANCE POINTER:**  Foreign persons engaged in a U.S. trade or business at any time during the taxable year must file U.S. income tax returns by the fifteenth day of the sixth month following their taxable year-end (i.e., June 15 if using calendar year). Nonresident aliens file Form 1040-NR, U.S. Nonresident Alien Income Tax Return, and foreign corporations file Form 1120-F, U.S. Income Tax Return of a Foreign Corporation.[16] Also, foreign corporations must attach Form 5472, which provides the IRS with related person information, and maintain permanent records sufficient to determine their U.S. tax liability.[17]

---

[12]IRC §864(b)(2).
[13]*Higgins v. Comm.*, 312 US 212 (1941).
[14]GCM 18835 (1937).
[15]*Abegg v. Comm.*, 50 TC 145 (1968).
[16]IRC §6072(c); Reg. §§1.6012-1(b), 1.6012-2(g).
[17]IRC §6038C(a).

## EFFECTIVELY CONNECTED INCOME

Foreign persons engaging in a U.S. trade or business may earn income effectively connected with such activity. After subtracting apportioned deductions, the Code taxes ECI at regular rates.[18] However, U.S. treaties may alter this result.

### FLASHBACK

From Chapter 3, treaties normally exempt ECI of foreign persons not maintaining a U.S. PE. Even when a U.S. PE exists, income continues to be exempt if not attributable to the PE. The definition of a PE varies somewhat among treaties.

To determine whether income qualifies as effectively connected, foreign persons first ascertain the income's source, based on provisions explained in Chapter 4. Criteria for identifying ECI differ for U.S. and foreign source income. Whether taxpayers earn ECI often is clear (e.g., profit from U.S. office's sales to U.S. customers). However, for income categories taxpayers often consider passive, the principles and rules defined next provide guidance.

**COMPLIANCE POINTER:** The IRS ordinarily will not rule on whether a foreign person engages in a U.S. trade or business or whether a U.S. trade or business earns ECI.[19]

The tax law treats U.S. source income as ECI if it meets either the asset use test or the business activities test. Under both tests, one must give due regard to whether the asset or income appears in separate books and records of a U.S. business, though this factor alone does not control whether ECI

---

[18]Under IRC §245, domestic corporations owning at least 10 percent of a foreign corporation earning ECI may be entitled to a dividend received deduction (DRD). Without the DRD, the United States taxes a foreign corporation's ECI. When the foreign corporation distributes the after-tax ECI to its domestic parent company, the latter pays U.S. tax again on the same income stream. Allowing the parent company to claim a DRD eliminates or mitigates the extent of double U.S. taxation. Compare and contrast the intent of IRC §245 with that of the foreign tax credit that Chapter 11 discusses. Both provisions address double taxation concerns. However, the DRD reduces or eliminates instances in which *U.S.* tax and *foreign* tax apply to the same income.

[19]Rev. Proc. 2003-7, §4.01(3), 2003-1 IRB 233.

exists. Similarly, whether foreign persons follow generally accepted accounting principles, and the consistency of its accounting for assets and income over time are important factors.[20]

## U.S. Source Income

The asset use test characterizes U.S. source income as ECI when the foreign person derives income from assets it uses or holds for use in a U.S. trade or business.[21] Such assets include properties the foreign person:

- Holds primarily to conduct current business in the United States (e.g., production machinery),
- Acquires and holds in the ordinary course of U.S. business (e.g., trade receivables), or
- Holds directly in relationship to the U.S. business (e.g., working capital).[22]

The asset use test applies primarily to foreign persons manufacturing or selling goods in the United States.[23] Under the test, interest and gain from temporary investments in debt obligations are ECI since the business holds the surplus funds to meet current business needs. Further, the IRS presumes assets directly relate to a U.S. business; thus, investment earnings are ECI when foreign persons acquire investment assets with the U.S. business's earnings, retain or reinvest the investment earnings in the U.S. business, and significantly manage and control the investment assets with U.S. personnel actively involved in the U.S. business. Nonetheless, interest and gain from long-term investments that a business earmarks for future uses such as plant replacement, business contingencies, product-line diversifications, or foreign expansions do not represent ECI.[24] In contrast to the treatment of fixed-return investments, the asset use test usually does not treat dividends and gain from corporate stock as ECI.[25]

---

## EXAMPLE

Rhinestone Sparkler, Ltd. sells its jewelry through several U.S. retail outlets. When its U.S. customers do not pay on time, Rhinestone charges

---

[20]IRC §864(c)(2); Reg. §1.864-4(c)(4).
[21]IRC §864(c)(2)(A).
[22]Reg. §1.864-4(c)(2)(ii).
[23]Reg. §1.864-4(c)(2)(i).
[24]Reg. §1.864-4(c)(2)(iv).
[25]Reg. §1.864-4(c)(2)(iii).

them interest. During the year, the company earns $21,000 interest on its customers' account and note receivables. Rhinestone invests some of its surplus cash in U.S. T-bills and money market accounts until needed in the business during its slow season. These investments return $6,000 interest income. Rhinestone invests its surplus cash in shares of Fortune 500 companies and earns $4,000 dividends. When Rhinestone sells some of its stock, it realizes a $3,000 gain. All income and gain mentioned relates to its U.S. business activities and qualifies as U.S. source income. Rhinestone's $21,000 and $6,000 interest income is ECI. Its $4,000 dividend income and $3,000 gain are not ECI.

The **business activities test** classifies foreign persons' U.S. source income as ECI when the activities of a U.S. trade or business are a material factor in realizing the income or gain.[26] Income arises directly from U.S. business activities (thus, the activities are a material factor) in the following situations:

- Dealers in stock and securities earn interest and dividends,
- Investment companies realize gain from selling and exchanging capital asscts,
- Businesses licensing patents and similar intangibles earn royalties, and
- Service firms derive fees.[27]

Special rules applying to banking, financing, and similar businesses treat most U.S. source interest, dividends, and gain attributable to such a business' U.S. office as ECI.[28]

## EXAMPLE

Patent Depot SARL, a French company, purchases patent rights from European inventors and licenses them to manufacturers around the world. During the year, Patent Depot earns $219,000 royalties from licensing patents for use in the United States. If Patent Depot's licensing activities cause it to engage in a U.S. trade or business, the Code treats the U.S. source royalties as ECI under the business activities test. Otherwise, the royalties are FDAP income.

---

[26]IRC §864(c)(2)(B).
[27]Reg. §1.864-4(c)(3).
[28]Reg. §1.864-4(c)(5).

Before 1966, the United States taxed all U.S. source income of foreign persons engaged in U.S. business at regular rates. At that time, the Code lumped U.S. source business and nonbusiness income of foreign persons together and taxed the sum at regular U.S. rates when such persons conducted a U.S. trade or business. In a sense, U.S. businesses magnetically drew all U.S. source income to them, even income not attributable to U.S. business activities. In the Foreign Investors Tax Act of 1966, Congress abandoned this **force of attraction** principle with one exception. What remains of the force of attraction rule today operates as a stopgap measure. When foreign parties engage in U.S. business, the Code draws U.S. source income (other than FDAP earnings, capital gain, and income the Code specifically exempts) to the U.S. business activities and, thus, taxes such ECI at regular rates.[29] This residual force of attraction rule assures that no U.S. source income, other those amounts Congress intends to exempt, inadvertently slips through the cracks and escapes U.S. taxation. The rule primarily applies to inventory profit, service fees, and other business income not attributable to a U.S. trade or business.

---

### EXAMPLE

Wizard Electronics, a Taiwanese business, distributes consumer electronics, which it markets through several retail outlets in the Northeastern United States. A customer in California places an order directly with Wizard's home office in Taiwan. None of Wizard's U.S. retail outlets participate in this sale, and title to the electronic products pass in California. Thus, the sale results in U.S. source income. The asset use and business activities tests do not apply to this transaction since a U.S. trade or business does not participate. However, the existence of a U.S. trade or business and the force of attraction rule cause the income from this sale to be ECI. In this case, Wizard could have avoided the force of attraction result if it had transferred title in Taiwan, producing foreign source income.

---

### EXAMPLE

Biohazard Experts SA, a Uruguayan corporation, specializes in removing and safely disposing of toxic and infectious materials. Its U.S. busi-

---

[29]IRC §864(c)(3).

ness operates from offices in New Jersey. During the year, the Uruguayan home office contracts directly with a U.S. firm in Arizona and performs the removal and disposal services without involving the New Jersey business. Biohazard Experts renders these services in Arizona, so all the income qualifies as U.S. source income. The company may contend that this isolated, irregular transaction is not a separate U.S. trade or business. If the argument is successful, neither the asset use test nor the business activities test brings the income from this contract within the sphere of U.S. taxation since the transaction does not involve assets or activities of the New Jersey business. Nonetheless, the force of attraction rule draws the income to the U.S. business in New Jersey and taxes it as ECI.

**FLASHBACK**

Chapter 3 indicated that treaties exempt business profits from tax in the host country when not attributable to a PE. Thus, U.S. tax treaties often override the residual force of attraction rule.

### Foreign Source Income

The asset use test and business activities test apply only in determining whether a foreign person's U.S. source income is ECI. Similarly, the force of attraction principle applies only to U.S. source income. Ordinarily, foreign source income does not qualify as ECI. However, before 1966, some foreign companies exploited the United States as a tax haven base. In brief, they set up U.S. offices through which they sold goods to other countries. If title to their goods passed abroad, the foreign companies did not earn U.S. source income and U.S. tax did not result. Also, the customer's country usually exempted the income if the seller did not maintain a PE there.

To discourage such **tax haven** activities, Congress decided to treat some foreign source income as ECI if attributable to a foreign person's U.S. office or other fixed place of business. The foreign person must use the U.S. office regularly to derive foreign source income, and the office must be a material factor in deriving foreign source income. When a foreign person operates through a dependent agent with a U.S. office, the Code attributes the agent's office to the foreign principal.[30] Notwithstanding these broad

---

[30]IRC §864(c)(5).

provisions, U.S. law treats only the two types of foreign source income listed here as ECI:

- Royalties for the privilege of using intangible assets abroad and
- Dividends and interest an investment company (trading stocks and securities for its own account), bank, finance company, or similar business derives.[31]

RESEARCH POINTER: The Code also indicates that selling inventory through a U.S. office and passing title abroad results in foreign source ECI unless the foreign person sells the inventory for consumption, use, or disposition abroad and a foreign office materially participates in the sale.[32] However, this provision relates to a bygone era and no longer applies. Today, the sale of inventory through a U.S. office usually results in U.S. source ECI.[33] However, if a foreign office materially participates, and the foreign person sells the inventory for consumption, use, or disposition abroad, foreign source income that is not ECI results.[34] Thus, inventory sales through a U.S. office result in U.S. source ECI or foreign source non-ECI, but not foreign source ECI.

## EXAMPLE

Citifund Finance SA, a Colombian corporation, maintains a U.S. office through which it regularly loans funds to U.S. and Latin American businesses. Based on these activities, the company engages in a U.S. trade or business. The United States taxes Citifund's foreign source interest income from Latin American loans as ECI.

Exhibit 8.2 summarizes many of the points addressed so far in this chapter about ECI. It also incorporates the treaty impact on some of these rules.

### No U.S. Business

As mentioned earlier, foreign persons not engaged in a U.S. trade or business usually do not derive ECI. However, several transactions yield ECI even

[31]IRC §864(c)(4).
[32]IRC §864(c)(4)(B)(iii).
[33]IRC §§864(c)(2), 865(e)(2).
[34]IRC §§864(c)(4)(B)(iii), 865(e)(2)(B).

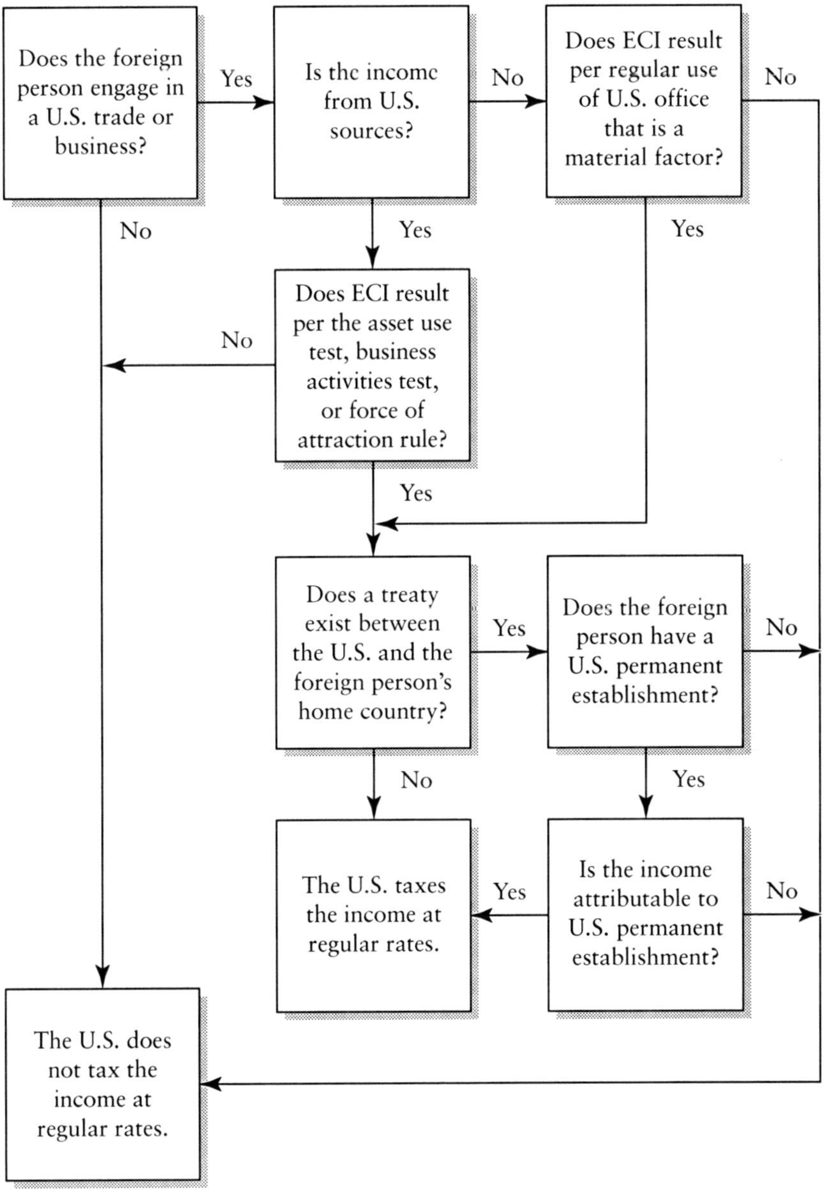

**EXHIBIT 8.2**  U.S. Taxation of Foreign Persons' Business Profits

when a U.S. trade or business does not exist during the taxable year at issue. That is, the Code sometimes treats foreign persons as if engaged in U.S. business during the current year (though they are not) and treats the income as if connected with the hypothetical business. These special cases require foreign persons to treat:

- Gain from disposing of U.S. real property interests (direct and indirect real estate holdings, which Chapter 9 discusses) as ECI,[35]
- Deferred income from an installment sale or the performance of services as ECI if the foreign persons engaged in a U.S. trade or business during an earlier year when the installment sale or the performance of services occurred,[36]
- Gain from selling or exchanging property used in a U.S. trade or business within the past 10 years as ECI,[37] and
- Investment income derived from real estate, if elected, as ECI.[38]

**PLANNING POINTER:** Without the election mentioned in the last point, U.S. law taxes real estate income at 30 percent or a lower treaty rate on a gross basis (i.e., with no allowed deductions). The election permits the real estate income to be taxable at regular rates on a net basis. Thus, this election often preserves sizeable real estate deductions (e.g., depreciation and property tax) for foreign persons. If the deductions cause a foreign corporation to realize a net operating loss, it can carry the loss back 2 years and forward 20 years.[39]

---

**EXAMPLE**

Hunky-Dory, Ltd., a Malaysian corporation, conducts a U.S. trade or business in 2003 but not in 2004. During 2003, the corporation sells inventory on the installment basis. Hunky-Dory collects some of the installment notes during 2004, resulting in a $34,000 gain. U.S. law treats the gain as ECI and taxes it at regular U.S. corporate rates.

---

[35]IRC §897(a).
[36]IRC §864(c)(6).
[37]IRC §864(c)(7).
[38]IRC §§871(d), 882(d).
[39]Rev. Rul. 92-74, 1992-2 CB 156; IRC §172(b)(1)(A).

## BUSINESS EXEMPTIONS

Like the nonbusiness exemptions defined in Chapter 7, foreign persons can exclude most business income U.S. persons can exclude. U.S. tax treaties often permit additional exclusion benefits. Further, the Code allows foreign persons to exclude some business amounts U.S. persons cannot. Two such statutory exclusions follow.

The United States excludes foreign persons' income from the international operation of ships and aircraft if the foreign person's home country provides an equivalent exemption to U.S. persons.[40] This exclusion extends to rental income, whether from a full or bareboat charter. **Bareboat charters** occur when the lessee provides the crew rather than using the lessor's crew. This exclusion may overlap with benefits treaties already provide.

Nonresident aliens exclude compensation they receive from foreign persons or foreign offices of U.S. persons when temporarily present in the United States under certain training or exchange programs. This exclusion applies primarily to trainees, teachers, and students.[41] The cultural exchange increases feelings of goodwill between countries.

## INCOME TAX CALCULATIONS

This section synthesizes many of the provisions described in Chapter 7 and earlier in this chapter about the U.S. tax liabilities of nonresident aliens and foreign corporations. It also covers some materials affecting a nonresident alien's U.S. tax that the text does not address elsewhere.

As Chapter 5 explained, the Code allows foreign persons to deduct only those expenses apportioned to ECI. U.S. law disallows deductions apportioned to FDAP and exempt income. However, nonresident aliens can claim three types of itemized deductions in full without apportionment:

- Nonbusiness casualty or theft losses for property located in the United States,
- Charitable contributions, and
- One personal exemption.[42]

---

[40]IRC §§872(b), 883(a). If not exempt and not effectively connected with a U.S. trade or business, IRC §887 may impose a 4 percent excise tax on U.S. source gross transportation income.
[41]IRC §872(b)(3).
[42]IRC §873(b). Similarly, IRC §882(c)(1)(B) allows foreign corporations to deduct charitable contributions even if unrelated to effectively connected income.

The Code permits only one personal exemption unless the individual resides in Canada or Mexico or unless a U.S. tax treaty permits more, which few do. Nonresident aliens cannot claim the standard deduction.[43] Thus, those with few itemized deductions pay tax at higher effective rates than similarly situated U.S. individuals.

> **COMPLIANCE POINTER:** Foreign persons can be denied all deductions and credits on their U.S. income tax return if they do not file "true and accurate" returns.[44] Thus, failing to file a timely return or filing an inaccurate return can cause taxation of ECI on a gross basis.

Unmarried nonresident aliens must file as single taxpayers. Foreign individuals married to other nonresident aliens file separate returns; the Code permits joint returns only when both spouses are U.S. citizens or residents.[45]

**EXHIBIT 8.3**  Tax Calculation for Nonresident Aliens

|   |   |
|---|---|
| | U.S. source FDAP income (no deductions allowed) |
| × | 30% or lower treaty rate |
| | Withholding tax on FDAP income |
| | Effectively connected gross income |
| − | Deductions for AGI apportioned to ECI |
| | Adjusted gross income |
| − | Deductions from AGI apportioned to ECI (e.g., employees) |
| − | Personal casualty and theft losses on U.S. property |
| − | Charitable contributions |
| − | One personal exemption (a few nationalities allowed more) |
| | Effectively connected taxable income |
| × | U.S. regular tax rates |
| | Tax on ECI |
| | Tax on FDAP income |
| + | Tax on ECI |
| | U.S. tax liability before credits |
| − | Withheld tax (e.g., on FDAP income) and allowable credits |
| | U.S. tax liability |

[43]IRC §63(c)(6)(B).
[44]IRC §§874(a), 882(c)(2).
[45]IRC §6013(a)(1).

However, as Chapter 6 explained, nonresident spouses making either the new resident or nonresident election can file jointly and claim the standard deduction and more than one personal exemption. Exhibit 8.3 summarizes the tax calculation for nonresident aliens.

---

### EXAMPLE

Jeongjae, a nonresident alien from Taiwan, receives $30,000 dividends from U.S. companies during 2001. He also earns $15,000 from his U.S. employment. Deductions apportioned to his employment income equal $3,000. The U.S. withholding tax on the dividends is $9,000 ($30,000 × .30). His U.S. tax from ECI is $1,365 [.15 tax rate × ($15,000 ECI − $3,000 deductions − $2,900 exemption)]. Thus, Jeongjae's 2001 U.S. tax liability is $10,365 ($9,000 + $1,365).

---

Except itemized deductions, personal exemptions, and differences in tax rates, foreign corporations determine their U.S. tax liabilities in a similar manner. Exhibit 8.4 illustrates the tax calculation for foreign corporations.

**EXHIBIT 8.4**   Tax Calculation for Foreign Corporations

|   | U.S. source FDAP income (no deductions allowed) |
|---|---|
| × | 30% or lower treaty rate |
|   | Withholding tax on FDAP income |
|   | Effectively connected gross income |
| − | Deductions |
|   | Effectively connected taxable income |
| × | U.S. regular corporate rates |
|   | Tax on ECI |
|   | Tax on FDAP income |
| + | Tax on ECI |
|   | U.S. tax liability before credits |
| − | Withheld tax (e.g., on FDAP income) and allowable credits |
|   | U.S. tax liability |

# CHAPTER 9

# Real Property Gains

**C**hapter 7 explained that foreign persons incur a 30 percent (or lower treaty rate) withholding tax on U.S. source income not effectively connected with a U.S. trade or business. The withholding tax applies primarily to U.S. source investment income. Chapter 8 indicated that nonresident aliens and foreign corporations must pay U.S. tax at regular rates on ECI. This chapter discusses the treatment of real estate gains resulting when foreign persons dispose of direct and indirect holdings in U.S. real estate. Even when foreign persons hold U.S. real estate as investments (rather than as business assets), the Code characterizes the gain from disposing of the U.S. real estate as ECI.

Before 1980, a variety of techniques existed allowing foreign persons to dispose of U.S. real estate without U.S. tax consequences. For investment properties, nonresident aliens simply limited their U.S. presence to 183 days or less during the taxable year of disposition. Foreign persons also avoided U.S. tax with U.S. holding companies and other loopholes Congress has since closed.[1] As a result, foreign investors in U.S. real estate enjoyed a competitive advantage over similarly situated U.S. investors. Both foreign and U.S. investors paid U.S. tax on income they derived from U.S. real estate. However, only U.S. investors paid U.S. tax on gain they realized from the real estate's disposition. This competitive advantage led to concerns during the 1970s that foreign investors had acquired too much U.S. property, which caused national economic concerns.[2]

In response to these concerns, Congress passed the **Foreign Investment in Real Property Tax Act of 1980 (FIRPTA)**. Under this legislation, foreign persons treat the gain from disposing of a U.S. real property interest (USRPI) as ECI. For this purpose, real property includes land, buildings, inherently permanent structures (e.g., bridges and grain storage silos), unharvested crops, uncut timber, natural deposits before extraction, and any personal

---

[1]U.S. Department of the Treasury, *Taxation of Foreign Investment in U.S. Real Estate* (May 8, 1979).

[2]Hearings before the Committee on Ways and Means, *Taxation of Foreign Investor Direct and Indirect Ownership of Property in the United States*, 96th Cong., 1st Sess. (October 25, 1979).

property associated with real property. Associated property includes machinery and equipment the foreign person uses to construct or improve real estate, harvest crops, cut timber, cultivate soil, or extract natural deposits the foreign person or a related person owns. It also includes furnishings for offices and lodging facilities when the foreign or related person owns such facilities.[3]

## U.S. REAL PROPERTY INTERESTS

When foreign persons realize gain or loss from disposing of a USRPI, the Code treats them as if engaged in a U.S. trade or business and considers the gain or loss as effectively connected with the trade or business.[4] Thus, the tax law treats gain from disposing of USRPIs as ECI and allows the deduction of effectively connected losses only against ECI.[5] This treatment prevents foreign persons from disposing of direct and indirect holdings of U.S. real estate at a profit, treating the profit as capital gain from nonbusiness investments, and avoiding U.S. taxation. As discussed later, the transferee collects U.S. tax on FIRPTA gains through withholding procedures.

### FLASHBACK

Chapter 7 explained that, except ECI, U.S. law does not tax the U.S. source capital gain of foreign corporations or nonresident aliens present in the United States less than 183 days during the realization year.

**COMPLIANCE POINTER:** Foreign persons disposing of USRPIs subject to withholding must file Forms 8288 and 8288-A by the twentieth day following the disposition.[6]

---

[3]Reg. §1.897-1(b).
[4]IRC §897(a)(1).
[5]If the loss also qualifies as a capital loss, the foreign person can deduct it only to the extent of capital gain. For example, see Rev. Rul. 92-74, 1992-2 CB 156. Similarly, if the loss is a passive activity loss, the foreign person can deduct it only to the extent of passive activity gain. Thus, FIRPTA acts as an additional hurdle to deductibility (i.e., beyond the capital loss and passive activity loss provisions).
[6]Reg. §1.1445-1(c).

U.S. real property interests come in two varieties: direct and indirect. Direct USRPIs include fee ownership, co-ownership, options to purchase, time-sharing arrangements, rights of first refusal, leaseholds, rights to appreciation or future profits, life estates, remainder interests, and reversionary interests in U.S. real estate.[7] Indirect USRPIs comprise interests (e.g., stock ownership) in domestic corporations qualifying as U.S. real property holding corporations (defined in the next section).

---

### EXAMPLE

Matanmi, a Nigerian national and resident, owns a beach condo in southern California and a time-sharing interest in a Wyoming villa. She normally lives in Nigeria 10 months a year and the United States the other two. During the current year, Matanmi sells her beach condo and time-sharing interest, realizing $75,000 and $90,000 gains, respectively. FIRPTA treats both gains as ECI. Before FIRPTA, the gains would have escaped U.S. taxation.

---

For both direct and indirect holdings, the identity of the interest's owner does not affect whether the interest qualifies as a USRPI, so the owner of a USRPI can be a U.S. or foreign person.[8] However, as noted earlier, a foreign person must dispose of a USRPI to trigger effectively connected gain or loss. Exhibit 9.1 portrays direct and indirect USRPIs and the ownership structures producing ECI on disposition.

Several exceptions apply to the general definition of USRPIs just given:

- Interests persons hold solely as creditors, whether direct or indirect holdings, are not USRPIs.[9] Loans with equity kickers (i.e., return based partially on profitability of underlying property) usually do not meet the "solely" criterion.[10]
- A de minimis provision does not consider classes of stock regularly traded on established securities markets to be USRPIs when shareholders directly or constructively own no more than 5 percent of the stock at all times during their holding period (maximum lookback of five

---

[7]Reg. §1.897-1(d)(2).

[8]For instance, a domestic corporation can hold a USRPI. Similarly, the upcoming equation defines a U.S. real property holding corporation so that it can be either a U.S. or foreign entity.

[9]IRC §897(c)(1)(A)(ii); Reg. §1.897-1(d)(1).

[10]Reg. §1.897-1(d)(3)(i)(D).

**EXHIBIT 9.1**    Gain from Disposing of USRPIs Treated as ECI

*Panel A: Direct Holding*

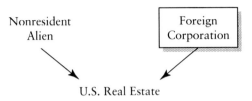

*Panel B: Indirect Holding*

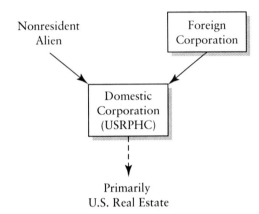

years).[11] Thus, before investing in nonpublicly traded domestic corporations or positions in publicly traded domestic corporations exceeding
5 percent, foreign persons should know enough about the corporations'
plans to judge whether such companies are likely to become USRPHCs
in the future.

- Interests in domestic corporations are not USRPIs when such corporations purge themselves through disposing of all their USRPIs, whether
direct or indirect holdings, in transactions in which they recognize all
gain.[12] However, given the broad definition of USRPIs, domestic corporations with numerous assets or extensive operations may find this
purging difficult to achieve.
- Stock held in real estate investment trusts (REITs) U.S. persons control
at all times during the year is not a USRPI.[13]

---

[11]IRC §897(c)(3). This de minimis rule also applies to interests in publicly traded
partnerships and trusts under Reg. §1.897-1(c)(2)(iv).
[12]IRC §897(c)(1)(B).
[13]IRC §897(h)(2). REITs include corporations and trusts investing primarily in real
estate equity and debt instruments and meeting the requirements of IRC §856.

**EXAMPLE**

For the past six years, Anwyn and Booth have owned 4 and 96 percent of Evergreen Resorts, Inc., respectively. Clayborne owns Evergreen bonds. Anwyn, Booth, and Clayborne are unrelated nonresident aliens who rarely visit the United States and hold their Evergreen interests as investments. Evergreen is a domestic U.S. real property holding corporation whose shares trade regularly on the New York Stock Exchange. Booth holds a USRPI; the Code treats any gain Booth realizes from selling his shares as ECI. Anwyn does not own a USRPI since her equity ownership falls below the de minimis threshold. Clayborne does not own a USRPI since he holds his interest solely as a creditor. Thus, FIRPTA does not apply to Anwyn and Clayborne; any gains they realize from selling their interests are not ECI.

**FLASHBACK**

In addition to excluding the gain from disposing of real estate investments individuals or entities hold solely as creditors, Chapter 7 explained that creditors can exclude interest they receive from such loans if it qualifies as portfolio interest. Further, the U.S. estate tax does not apply to debt instruments yielding exempt portfolio interest.[14] Chapter 3 also discussed ways treaties may eliminate or reduce withholding taxes on interest income.

**EXAMPLE**

Hollywood Hills, Inc. is a domestic U.S. real property holding corporation owning the following assets and liabilities:

|                            | *Fair Market Value* *(millions)* | *Adjusted Basis* *(millions)* |
|----------------------------|:----------------:|:--------------:|
| U.S. real estate (USRPIs)  | $70              | $60            |
| Other business assets      | 30               | 10             |
| Liabilities                | 20               |                |

---

[14]IRC §§2104(c), 2105(b).

> Orli, a nonresident alien, owns all of Hollywood's shares. Her shares are worth $80 million and her adjusted basis is $50 million. If she sells her shares, she realizes a $30 million gain, which the United States taxes as ECI. However, suppose Hollywood sells all its U.S. real estate first, realizing a $10 million gain ($70 – $60 million) on which it pays U.S. tax of $3.4 million. The sale purges Hollywood of all USRPIs. Then Orli can sell her Hollywood stock and avoid U.S. tax on her gain.

## U.S. REAL PROPERTY HOLDING CORPORATIONS

To be a USRPI, an indirect holding must involve ownership in a domestic corporation qualifying as a U.S. real property holding corporation. This section explains which corporations qualify and suggests some means for avoiding such status. Also, this section clarifies when corporations must test for such status.

### How to Test

A **U.S. real property holding corporation (USRPHC)** is any corporation whose USRPIs equal or exceed 50 percent of its aggregate USRPIs, foreign real estate, and business assets at any time during the owner's holding period.[15] In testing the 50 percent threshold, the corporation measures each asset based on its fair market value. Equation 9.1 summarizes the calculation on any given day:

$$\text{USRPHC if } \frac{\text{USRPI}_{fmv}}{\text{USRPI}_{fmv} + \text{Foreign realty}_{fmv} + \text{Business assets}_{fmv}} \geq 50\%$$

$$(9.1)$$

USRPHCs can be domestic or foreign corporations. Thus, the "US" portion of the term refers to the underlying assets, not the place of organization.

> **COMPLIANCE POINTER:** Fair market value means the going concern, rather than the liquidation, value. USRPHC rules do not require independent professional appraisals. Usually, the IRS accepts other valuation methods if consistently applied and likely to reflect fair market value.[16] For instance, the IRS might accept insurance valuations or earlier appraisals adjusted through indices from one year to the next.

---

[15] IRC §897(c)(2).
[16] Reg. §1.897-1(o).

An alternative test measures the items in the 50 percent test just described in terms of book value. One can use the alternative book value test only when a reasonable presumption exists that the fair market value test will not result in USRPHC status. When taxpayers choose the alternative test, the threshold drops from 50 to 25 percent, as in equation 9.2:[17]

$$\text{USRPHC if } \frac{\text{USRPI}_{bv}}{\text{USRPI}_{bv} + \text{Foreign realty}_{bv} + \text{Business assets}_{bv}} \geq 25\% \quad (9.2)$$

Debt that secures property reduces the fair market or book values included in the respective 50 and 25 percent tests, but only when the borrower uses the loan proceeds to acquire, improve, or maintain the secured property. Thus, second mortgages do not reduce asset values unless the debtor spends proceeds to improve or maintain the secured property. In addition to financing arrangements, other debts the owner assumes in direct connection with property reduce the values appearing in the two calculations (e.g., tax liens on real estate).[18]

> **PLANNING POINTER:** Acquiring USRPIs with debt financing and using the USRPIs as security can assist a corporation in avoiding USRPHC status (i.e., it reduces the numerator in equations 9.1 and 9.2). Similarly, cash financing of foreign real estate and business asset acquisitions or debt financing without using the acquired assets as security can reduce the chances of USRPHC status. However, an antiabuse rule requires corporations to reduce the acquisition price of foreign real estate and business assets when they borrow funds that allow them to obtain the assets but separate the two transactions for the principal purpose of avoiding USRPHC status.[19]

To avoid USRPHC status, one must establish that the corporation has not met the 50 percent test (or alternative 25 percent test) at any time during the owner's holding period. The holding period begins on the more recent of the owner's acquisition (e.g., purchase of corporate stock) or the day five years before the interest's disposition. It ends with the owner's disposition (e.g., sale of corporate stock).[20] The holding period is specific to the interest's owner, not the corporation in which the owner invests; thus, the relevant holding period may vary from one investor to the next for the same corporation.

---

[17]Reg. §1.897-2(b)(2).
[18]Reg. §1.897-1(o)(2).
[19]Reg. §1.897-1(o)(2)(iv).
[20]IRC §897(c)(1).

## EXAMPLE

Forpar SA, a Paraguayan corporation, owns 80 percent of Domsub, Inc., a U.S. corporation. Chang, a Taiwanese national and resident, owns the other 20 percent. Both Forpar and Chang hold Domsub shares as an investment. On July 1, 2003, Forpar and Chang sell all their shares in Domsub to a single buyer at a gain. On the date of sale, Domsub is not a USRPHC. However, Domsub was a USRPHC from the beginning of 1997 through the end of 2000. Forpar purchased its Domsub shares on July 1, 2001, so its holding period runs from July 1, 2001, to July 1, 2003. Since Domsub was not a USRPHC at any time during Forpar's holding period, U.S. law does not treat Forpar's gain as ECI. In contrast, Chang bought Domsub shares at the beginning of 1999, so his holding period begins on January 1, 1999, and ends on July 1, 2003. Since Domsub qualified as a USRPHC during some portion of Chang's holding period (i.e., 1999 and 2000), the Code treats Chang's gain as ECI. The diagram accentuates the relationships between relevant periods.

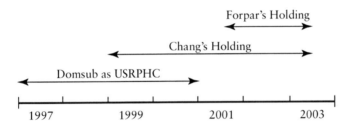

## EXAMPLE

Ananth, an Indian national and resident, sells all the stock of Foxfire, Inc. (adjusted basis $110,000), a domestic corporation, for $200,000. Before the sale, Ananth owned the Foxfire stock for six years. On the date of sale, Foxfire owns business assets worth $30,000, foreign realty valued at $50,000, and U.S. real estate worth $70,000. Foxfire is not a USRPHC on the sale date since its USRPIs do not equal or exceed 50 percent of its real estate and business assets ($70,000 ÷ $150,000 < 50%). If Foxfire has not been a USRPHC at any time during the five years preceding the sale, the Foxfire stock Ananth owns is not a USRPI. Ananth can limit his presence in the United States to 182 or fewer days during the year, sell his Foxfire stock for a $90,000 capital gain ($200,000 − $110,000), and avoid U.S. tax on the gain. FIRPTA does not apply.

---

**EXAMPLE**

In the prior example, assume the same facts, except that the U.S. real estate's value is $100,000. Now Foxfire *is* a USRPHC ($100,000 ÷ $180,000 ≥ 50%), so Ananth must treat his $90,000 capital gain as ECI. Article 13 of the U.S.-India Treaty allows the United States to tax capital gain under its domestic law, so FIRPTA applies.

---

In testing for USRPHC status, equations 9.1 and 9.2 do not require corporations to include all assets they own in the denominator. Corporations omit some investment assets from the computation (but not real estate holdings). However, special rules apply to investment interests testing corporations hold in other corporations and flow-through entities:

- Corporations look through interests they own in partnerships, estates, and trusts and treat each flow-through entity's underlying assets as though held proportionately.[21]
- A similar look-through rule applies to controlling interests (at least 50 percent of value directly or constructively owned) in corporations, whether domestic or foreign.[22]
- Corporations treat noncontrolling interests in USRPHCs, whether foreign or domestic, as entirely USRPIs.[23]

The USRPHC tests ignore noncontrolling interests in corporations not qualifying as USRPHCs themselves.[24] Such interests appear in neither the numerator nor denominator of equations 9.1 and 9.2.

---

**EXAMPLE**

A nonresident alien owns 20 percent of the stock in Frock Wear, Inc., a domestic corporation, as an investment. He wishes to sell the stock and wants to know whether his holding is a USRPI. It depends on whether Frock is a USRPHC (see Exhibit 9.1). Frock owns the following assets:

---

[21]IRC §897(c)(4)(B).
[22]IRC §897(c)(5).
[23]IRC §897(c)(4)(A). Look-through rules do not apply to noncontrolled interests since the company testing for USRPHC status may not have access to the underlying financial information.
[24]Reg. §1.897-2(e)(1).

|  | Percent Owned | Fair Market Value |
|---|---|---|
| Interest in Alpine Wear (partnership) | 40% | $ 40,000 |
| Stock in Bundle Wear (foreign non-USRPHC) | 70% | 30,000 |
| Stock in Cool Wear (domestic USRPHC) | 20% | 60,000 |
| Stock in Debonair Wear (foreign non-USRPHC) | 30% | 50,000 |
| Stock in Everyday Wear (domestic USRPHC) | 60% | 10,000 |
| Business assets and foreign realty |  | 70,000 |
| Total value of Frock Wear's assets |  | $260,000 |

When testing whether Frock Wear is a USRPHC, Frock's Cool stock is a USRPI since Cool is a USRPHC Frock does not control. Thus, Frock includes $60,000 (i.e., the value of its Cool stock) in the numerator and denominator of equation 9.1. The Debonair stock does not affect Frock's USRPHC status since Debonair is not a USRPHC and Frock does not control it. Frock looks through Alpine and its controlling interests in Bundle and Everyday to each company's underlying assets. The underlying financial data for these three companies follows:

|  | Fair Market Value |
|---|---|
| Assets of Alpine Wear (40%-owned partnership): |  |
| U.S. real estate | $ 60,000 |
| Business assets and foreign realty | 40,000 |
| Total assets | $100,000 |
| Assets of Bundle Wear (70%-owned foreign corporation): |  |
| U.S. real estate | $ 10,000 |
| Business assets and foreign realty | 40,000 |
| Total assets | $ 50,000 |
| Assets of Everyday Wear (60%-owned domestic USRPHC): |  |
| U.S. real estate | $ 20,000 |
| Business assets and foreign realty | 0 |
| Total assets | $ 20,000 |

*(continues)*

<br>

As the equation 9.1 calculation shows, Frock Wear is not a USR-PHC on this date since the test result falls below 50 percent:

$$\frac{.4(\$60,000) + .7(\$10,000) + \$60,000 + .6(\$20,000)}{.4(\$100,000) + .7(\$50,000) + \$60,000 + .6(\$20,000) + \$70,000}$$
$$= 47.5\%$$

Assuming Frock Wear has not been a USRPHC at any other time during the nonresident alien's holding period, U.S. law does not treat the nonresident alien's gain as ECI when selling Frock stock.

## When to Test

As defined earlier, a USRPHC is any corporation whose USRPIs equal or exceed 50 percent of its aggregate USRPIs, foreign real estate, and business assets *at any time* during the owner's holding period. The relevant holding period requires that the owner look back at the corporation's status for up to five years. Thus, one might wonder how often corporations must test whether they exceed the 50 percent threshold. Annual computations might not be often enough; daily computations would be impractical. As a compromise solution, the regulations require corporations to test the 50 percent threshold (and, thus, their USRPHC status) at least once a year but also on dates when the test results (using equation 9.1 or 9.2) increase. These **applicable determination dates** include the:

- Last day of each taxable year;
- Day cumulative acquisitions of USRPIs exceed a specified limitation amount;
- Day the corporation disposes of foreign real estate; and
- Day cumulative dispositions of business assets exceed a second limitation amount.[25]

Except determinations on the taxable year's last day, corporations can assume the fair market value of each asset equals its fair market value on the last day of the preceding year or the day during the current year when the corporation acquired the asset.[26]

[25]Reg. §1.897-2(c)(1)(i)-(iii).
[26]Reg. §1.897-2(c)(4)(ii).

**COMPLIANCE POINTER:** The IRS does not require a domestic corporation to report its test results on applicable determination dates, though the corporation can voluntarily attach a statement to its return if it wishes. However, if foreign persons require the test results to determine whether they hold USRPIs, the domestic corporation must provide such information within a reasonable period. Also, the corporation must notify the IRS following such a request.[27]

The two **limitation amounts** (second and fourth dates in the preceding list) are functions of the test results from the immediately preceding determination date. When corporations use the fair market value test (equation 9.1), and the results on the preceding determination date fall below 25 percent, the limitation amount for either cumulative acquisitions of USRPIs or cumulative dispositions of business assets equals 10 percent of the USRPIs or business assets (whichever applies) on the preceding determination date. When the test results on the preceding determination date fall below 35 percent but equal or exceed 25 percent, the limitation amount for either cumulative acquisitions of USRPIs or cumulative dispositions of business assets equals 5 percent of the USRPIs or business assets (whichever applies) on the preceding determination date. If the test results on the preceding determination date equal or exceed 35 percent, the limitation amount equals 2 percent of USRPIs or business assets (whichever applies) on the preceding determination date. If instead of the 50 percent fair market value test the corporation uses the 25 percent alternative book value test (equation 9.2), the limitation amount for either cumulative acquisitions of USRPIs or cumulative dispositions of business assets equals 10 percent of the USRPIs or business assets (whichever applies) on the preceding determination date. Once cumulative acquisitions or dispositions trigger a determination date, the corporation resets them to zero.[28] Exhibit 9.2 summarizes these limitation rules.

**EXHIBIT 9.2** Limitation Amount Triggering New Determination Date

| Preceding Determination Date | | |
|---|---|---|
| Test | Result | Limitation Amount |
| 50% FMV | < 25% | 10% of FMV[a] on preceding determination date |
| 50% FMV | ≥ 25% and < 35% | 5% of FMV on preceding determination date |
| 50% FMV | ≥ 35% | 2% of FMV on preceding determination date |
| 25% BV | < 25% | 10% of BV[b] on preceding determination date |

[a]Fair market value
[b]Book value

[27]Reg. §1.897-2(h).
[28]Reg. §1.897-2(c)(2)(iii).

## EXAMPLE

Orangetta, a U.K. national and resident, owns Lemon Squeeze Products, Inc., a calendar-year U.S. corporation whose stock does not trade on an established securities market. On December 31, 2002, Lemon Squeeze owns USRPIs valued at $2.6 million and foreign real estate worth $7.9 million. The corporation is not a USRPHC on this date since equation 9.1 yields a test result of 24.8 percent. Thus, the limitation amount for cumulative acquisitions of USRPIs becomes $260,000 (10 percent of $2.6 million). During 2003, Lemon Squeeze engages in the following transactions:

- Sold foreign real estate for $500,000 (January 15)
- Bought USRPI for $100,000 (April 2)
- Bought USRPI for $50,000 (August 13)
- Bought USRPI for $4,750,000 (November 8)

Disposing of foreign real estate, no matter how small the transaction, triggers a determination date. Thus, the January 15 sale of foreign realty requires the corporation to test for USRPHC status. The test result of 26 percent decreases the limitation amount for cumulative acquisitions of USRPIs to $130,000 (5 percent of $2.6 million). The $100,000 USRPI acquired on April 2 does not trigger a new determination date since it falls below the $130,000 limitation amount established on January 15. However, the $50,000 USRPI purchase on August 13, when added to the $100,000 USRPI acquired on April 2, exceeds

**COMPLIANCE POINTER:** To avoid the complexities involved in identifying applicable determination dates and determining limitation amounts, corporations can elect end-of-every-month determination dates using either equation 9.1 or 9.2. However, USRPI acquisitions or dispositions of foreign real estate or business assets still trigger within-month determination dates if the fair market value of assets in a single transaction exceeds 5 percent of aggregate USRPIs, foreign real estate, and business assets.[29]

Notwithstanding these provisions, the regulations do not require corporations to check for USRPHC status during the 120 days following the

---

[29]Reg. §1.897-2(c)(3).

the $130,000 limitation amount. The test on August 13 yields a result of 27.1 percent, so the new limitation amount changes to $137,500 (5 percent of $2,750,000). The $4.75 million USRPI acquisition on November 8 triggers a new determination date since it exceeds the $137,500 limitation amount. The November 8 test result is 50.3 percent, meaning that Lemon Squeeze becomes a USRPHC on this date. Its limitation amount changes to $150,000 (2 percent of $7.5 million), and Lemon Squeeze resets its cumulative acquisitions to zero. The following schedule summarizes these transactions, determination dates, test results, and limitation amounts:

| Dates | USRPIs | Foreign Real Estate | Test Results | Limitation Amounts for USRPIs |
|---|---|---|---|---|
| Dec. 31 | $2,600,000 | $7,900,000 | 24.8% | 10% of $2,600,000 |
| Jan. 15 | 0 | – 500,000 | | |
| | $2,600,000 | $7,400,000 | 26.0% | 5% of $2,600,000 |
| April 2 | + 100,000 | 0 | | |
| | $2,700,000 | $7,400,000 | | |
| Aug. 13 | + 50,000 | 0 | | |
| | $2,750,000 | $7,400,000 | 27.1% | 5% of $2,750,000 |
| Nov. 8 | +4,750,000 | 0 | | |
| | $7,500,000 | $7,400,000 | 50.3% | 2% of $7,500,000 |

later of incorporation or date they obtain the first shareholder. Neither must corporations check to determine whether they become a USRPHC during a 12-month period of complete liquidation.[30] Thus, a liquidating corporation can sell foreign real estate and business assets before USRPIs without triggering USRPHC status. Also, corporations can ignore routine dispositions of business assets, such as selling inventory or collecting receivables, since these transactions do not trigger determination dates.[31]

---

[30] Reg. §1.897-2(c)(1)(iv), (3)(iv).
[31] Reg. §1.897-2(c)(2).

## WITHHOLDING PROCEDURES

To assure at least partial collection, U.S. law requires the transferee to withhold and remit tax equal to 10 percent of the foreign person's amount realized from disposing of a USRPI, even if the foreign seller realizes a loss.[32] Unlike the 30 percent withholding tax on FDAP income, this 10 percent withholding is an estimate of the tax due. The actual U.S. tax liability for any FIRPTA gain might be greater or less than the amount withheld.[33] If 10 percent of the amount realized exceeds the actual U.S. tax liability, the foreign transferor or the transferee can ask the IRS to determine the maximum tax liability (i.e., estimate the actual U.S. tax liability, erring on the high side). In this situation, the transferee withholds only the maximum tax liability.[34]

---

### EXAMPLE

Garrison, Ltd., a foreign corporation, sells a U.S. strip mall for $4 million. Since its adjusted basis is $3.5 million, Garrison realizes a $500,000 gain. Unless Garrison negotiates a lower amount with the IRS, the purchaser must withhold $400,000 on the sale ($4 million × 10%) and pays only $3.6 million to Garrison. If the IRS agrees that $175,000 ($500,000 gain × 35%) reasonably approximates Garrison's maximum tax liability, the purchaser withholds this lesser amount.

---

### EXAMPLE

Rhubarb SA, a foreign corporation, sells a wholly owned domestic corporation for $10 million, realizing a $6 million gain. The purchaser withholds $1 million ($10 million × 10%) even though the actual U.S. tax liability from the sale is closer to $2.1 million ($6 million × 35%). Rhubarb pays the additional $1.1 million it owes with its U.S. tax return.

---

[32]IRC §1445(a).
[33]Reg. §1.1445-1(f).
[34]IRC §1445(c). Per Reg. §1.1445-3, the IRS issues a withholding certificate as evidence of any adjustment it allows to the amount withheld. Rev. Proc. 2000-35, 2000-2 CB 211, provides the detailed guidance for obtaining withholding certificates.

To reduce administrative burdens, U.S. law exempts dispositions of US-RPIs from withholding when:

- The transferor provides an affidavit certifying that it is not a foreign person or, if transferring an interest in a domestic corporation, that such interest is not a USRPHC;
- The USRPI consists of a domestic USRPHC's stock regularly trading on an established security market;
- The transferor provides evidence that it posted security with the IRS covering the U.S. tax liability (which might equal zero when the transferor realizes a loss); or
- The buyer acquires the USRPI as a residence, and the foreign transferor's amount realized does not exceed $300,000.[35]

These exemptions apply only to withholding requirements and, thus, may relieve the transferee from collecting and remitting U.S. tax. The exemptions do not affect the U.S. tax liabilities of foreign transferors disposing of USRPIs.

> **COMPLIANCE POINTER:** Failure to withhold when required or to withhold the correct amount subjects the transferee to any U.S. tax, penalties, and interest due.[36] Thus, U.S. persons acquiring direct and indirect interests in U.S. real estate must be familiar with withholding requirements and exemptions to avoid liability for a foreign transferor's noncompliance with FIRPTA.

## STRUCTURES FOR HOLDING U.S. REAL ESTATE

Foreign persons can own U.S. real estate in several ways. They may hold a direct interest or they may own U.S. real estate through a domestic or foreign entity. Each ownership structure has its own advantages and disadvantages.

### Direct Ownership

Holding U.S. real estate directly entails several advantages. The structure is simple and the realty's disposition results in only one level of tax. Nonresident aliens and foreign corporations disposing of direct holdings treat realized gain as effectively connected with a U.S. trade or business. Often, the

---

[35]IRC §1445(b).
[36]IRC §1461.

ECI qualifies as long-term capital gain. Nonresident aliens experience relatively low tax rates (usually 20 percent) rather than the higher rates often applicable to capital gains corporations realize.[37] However, foreign persons cannot avoid U.S. taxation by exchanging U.S. real estate for foreign real estate and then selling the latter.[38]

Directly holding U.S. real estate also involves the following drawbacks:

- If the foreign investor later wishes to transfer its directly held U.S. real estate to a foreign corporation, the investor normally must recognize any gain from the restructuring.[39] U.S. law also taxes transfers to domestic corporations when the stock received does not qualify as a USRPI; or, if it does qualify, when no U.S. tax results on its later disposition (e.g., because of a treaty exemption).[40]
- Direct holdings do not provide the foreign investor with legal liability protection. However, owning the U.S. real estate through a limited liability company (LLC) might eliminate such exposure.
- Holding U.S. real estate directly exposes foreign individuals to the possibility of U.S. estate taxes if they die.[41] Also, U.S. gift taxes may apply to inter vivos gifts of U.S. real estate.[42]
- Direct ownership does not provide foreign persons with the anonymity they sometimes desire. Many legal and business dealings require disclosure of information about the foreign investor (e.g., name, address, and identification number).

When nonresident aliens dispose of USRPIs, the alternative minimum tax may apply.[43] The calculation parallels that applicable to U.S. persons, with one exception: After subtracting the exemption amount from alternative minimum taxable income (AMTI), the taxable excess of foreign persons cannot be less than the smaller of AMTI or net U.S. real property gain (i.e., the excess of aggregate FIRPTA gains over losses for the year).[44] Thus, if net U.S. real property gain exceeds AMTI, the taxable excess equals AMTI. The

---

[37]Cf., IRC §1(h) with IRC §1201(a).
[38]IRC §897(e)(1), 1031(h)(1).
[39]IRC §897(e)(1), (j) override the non-recognition provisions of IRC §351. But see exceptions in Temp. Reg. §1.897-6T(b).
[40]IRC §897(e)(1); Temp. Reg. §1.897-6T(a)(1), (c)(2).
[41]IRC §2103; Reg. §20.2104-1(a)(1).
[42]IRC §2511(a); Reg. §25.2511-1(b).
[43]IRC §55.
[44]IRC §897(a)(2).

calculation, in effect, adds back the exemption amount, denying this exemption benefit to nonresident aliens. Presumably, Congress included this procedure to rectify a perceived inequity in marginal tax rates under the apparent assumption that nonresident aliens possess foreign income that, if taxed in the United States, would phase out their exemption amount. Thus, denying the exemption amount achieves a rough parity with U.S. individuals subject to the alternative minimum tax. The pertinent portion of the calculation appears in Exhibit 9.3.

---

**EXAMPLE**

Sundeep, an unmarried citizen and resident of Pakistan, realizes a $100,000 short-term gain from selling his Floridian vacation home and $5,000 of ECI from U.S. consulting activities. His net U.S. real property gain equals $100,000. Assuming no adjustments or tax preferences, his alternative minimum taxable income is $105,000 less one personal exemption. (Exhibit 8.3 showed the calculation of a nonresident alien's taxable income.) Thus, Sundeep's "taxable excess" equals $100,000 and his tentative minimum tax is $26,000 ($100,000 × 26%). If his regular tax liability is $24,900, Sundeep's alternative minimum tax is $1,100 ($26,000 − $24,900).

---

**EXHIBIT 9.3**   Nonresident Alien's Alternative Minimum Tax

|   | |
|---|---|
| | Alternative minimum taxable income (AMTI) |
| − | Exemption amount (i.e., $58,000, $40,250, or $24,500, as phased out)[a] |
| | Taxable excess (cannot be < smaller of AMTI or net U.S. real property gain) |
| × | 26% of taxable excess up to $175,000 ($87,500 if married filing separately) |
| × | 28% of taxable excess over $175,000 ($87,500 if married filing separately) |
| | Tentative minimum tax[b] |
| − | Regular tax liability |
| | Alternative minimum tax |

[a]Beginning in 2005, these exemption amounts revert back to their pre-2001 levels.
[b]In calculating the tentative minimum tax, the lower tax rates in IRC §55(b)(3) apply to net capital gain.

## Domestic Corporation

In contrast to direct holdings, foreign persons owning U.S. real estate through domestic corporations protect their foreign assets from legal liability relating to their U.S. investment. Also, the indirect ownership provides some anonymity, even though domestic corporations still must identify foreign persons with majority interests on Schedule K (Other Information) of Form 1120, U.S. Corporation Income Tax Return. Similar to direct holdings, the corporation's stock is includable in the U.S. gross estate of a deceased nonresident alien.[45] However, the U.S. gift tax does not apply to a foreign individual's gratuitous lifetime transfer of corporate stock.[46]

As explained earlier, a noncreditor interest in a domestic corporation is a USRPI if the corporation qualifies as a USRPHC. Foreign persons owning stock in domestic corporations should carefully monitor corporate assets so USRPIs stay below the 50 (or 25) percent threshold, avoiding USRPHC status. Changes in market values over time, such as increasing real estate values and decreasing business asset values, may push some corporations over the brink even when acquisitions and dispositions do not occur. Also, corporations near the threshold should consider the timing of acquisitions and dispositions. These entities should acquire (dispose of) foreign realty and business assets before (after) USRPIs when practical. Once corporations reach the threshold and become USRPHCs, foreign shareholders avoid ECI treatment on appreciated shares only if they retain their interests: (1.) for five years beyond the time USRPHCs lose such status or (2.) until the corporations purge themselves of all USRPIs in taxable transactions.

> **PLANNING POINTER:**  Corporations wanting to reduce their chances of becoming USRPHCs might lease rather than buy business-use real estate in the United States. Though leasehold interests qualify as US-RPIs, the regulations value such interests at their assignment or sublet prices, which often are zero or negligible.[47] Another strategy requires isolating USRPIs in a separate corporation from the corporation owning foreign realty and business assets, keeping the stock in the latter corporation untainted.

## Foreign Corporation

Equity interests in foreign corporations are not USRPIs, even for corporations possessing only U.S. real estate. Thus, FIRPTA does not apply to foreign persons disposing of foreign shares. However, foreign corporations'

---

[45]IRC §2104(a).
[46]IRC §§2501(a)(2), 2511(b).
[47]IRC §897(c)(6)(A); Reg. §1.897-1(o)(3).

underlying U.S. real estate is a USRPI, and its sale or exchange results in ECI (see Exhibit 9.1). Also, foreign corporations must recognize ECI when they distribute appreciated USRPIs to shareholders as dividends or in redemptions and liquidations.[48]

Like ownership through domestic corporations, using foreign corporations to hold U.S. real estate limits the legal liability of shareholders. Also, foreign individuals can transfer equity interests in foreign corporations without U.S. gift tax consequences.[49] Unlike holdings through domestic corporations, nonresident aliens do not include the stock of foreign corporations in their U.S. gross estates.[50]

Foreign corporations provide partial anonymity for the beneficial owner. If the beneficial owner holds 50 percent or more of the foreign corporation's voting stock, the corporation must disclose the name and identification number of such owner on Form 1120-F, U.S. Income Tax Return of a Foreign Corporation (Section I). However, many business and legal dealings do not require disclosures about beneficial owners. To obtain more anonymity, the beneficial owner can establish a domestic corporation as the foreign corporation's subsidiary and allow the domestic corporation to hold the U.S. real estate. The domestic corporation must disclose information about the foreign corporation on its Form 1120, but the foreign corporation need not file a U.S. tax return if it does not engage in U.S. business or earn ECI. Thus, the foreign corporation does not disclose information about its beneficial owner.

Foreign USRPHCs eligible for protection against discrimination under a U.S. treaty can elect treatment as domestic corporations. This election is the exclusive remedy for discriminatory claims, and, once made, the corporation cannot revoke it without IRS consent. With two exceptions, all persons holding interests in such corporations must consent to the election. Persons holding interests solely as creditors need not consent. Also, when a corporation's stock regularly trades on an established security market, the corporation does not need consent from its de minimis shareholders (i.e., those owning 5 percent or less). If elected, the treatment as a domestic corporation applies only for FIRPTA purposes.[51] For instance, foreign source income that is not ECI continues beyond the reach of U.S. jurisdiction (i.e., the United States cannot tax the corporation's worldwide income). However, interests in electing foreign corporations, which already qualify as USRPHCs per election prerequisites, become USRPIs. Avoiding the withholding requirements applicable to foreign corporations is one election advantage.

---

[48]IRC §897(d). Cf., IRC §311(b)(1).
[49]IRC §2501(a)(2); Reg. §25.2511-3(b)(3)(ii).
[50]IRC §2104(a).
[51]IRC §897(i); Temp. Reg. §1.897-8T(b).

### Flow-Through Entity

As structures for holding USRPIs, partnerships do not provide the limited liability protection of corporations. Also, partnerships provide only partial anonymity. Each partner's Schedule K-1, Partner's Share of Income, Credits, Deductions, etc., discloses information some foreign persons prefer to keep private.

When foreign persons sell partnership, estate, or trust interests, the realized gain is ECI to the extent attributable to underlying USRPIs.[52] Nonetheless, for withholding purposes, the tax law treats the entire interest as a USRPI when the following 50/90 conditions exist:

- USRPIs comprise at least 50 percent of the flow-through entity's gross assets and
- USRPIs plus cash and cash equivalents comprise at least 90 percent of the flow-through entity's gross assets.[53]

Thus, U.S. law might partially tax the realized gain of foreign persons disposing of flow-through interests while requiring the purchaser to with-

**EXHIBIT 9.4**    Structures for Holding U.S. Real Estate: Pros and Cons

|  | Direct Holding | Domestic Corporation | Foreign Corporation | Flowthrough |
|---|---|---|---|---|
| Subject to: |  |  |  |  |
| ECI on disposition | Yes | Yes[a] | No[b] | Yes[c] |
| Double levels of tax | No[d] | Yes | No | No |
| Estate taxation | Yes | Yes | No | Yes[e] |
| Gift taxation | Yes | No | No | No |
| Legal liability | Yes[f] | No | No | Yes[f] |
| Disclosure | Yes | No[g] | No[g] | No[g] |

[a]ECI results only if corporation qualifies as a USRPHC.
[b]However, ECI does result if foreign corporation makes IRC §897(i) election.
[c]ECI results only to the extent attributable to underlying USRPIs.
[d]However, a branch profits tax might apply if a foreign corporation is the direct holder.
[e]The interest may be includable in the gross estate, per Rev. Rul. 55-701.
[f]Owning interest through a limited liability company (LLC) can eliminate exposure.
[g]The IRS requires some disclosure on income tax filings.

---

[52]IRC §897(g).
[53]IRC §1445(e)(5); Temp. Reg. §§1.897-7T(a), 1.1445-11T(d).

hold as though the United States taxes the entire gain. Unless otherwise arranged, transferees of partnership, estate, or trust interests must withhold 10 percent of the transaction's amount realized when the entity meets the 50/90 conditions.

The U.S. gift tax does not apply to inter vivos transfers of interests in flow-through entities, even when they hold USRPIs.[54] Applying U.S. estate tax law to flow-through entities holding USRPIs is less clear. The Code includes interests qualifying as U.S.-situs property in a foreign decedent's gross estate.[55] However, little guidance exists about the situs of a foreign partnership interest managed abroad but holding only USRPIs.[56] Exhibit 9.4 summarizes the advantages and disadvantages of investing in U.S. real estate through alternative structures.

---

[54] IRC §§2501(a)(2).
[55] IRC §§2103.
[56] Rev. Rul. 55-701, 1955-2 CB 836, suggests that the situs corresponds with where the entity conducts business.

# CHAPTER 10

# Branch Taxes

**B**ranch operations are extensions of corporate business activities that may take a variety of forms. U.S. branches often consist of foreign corporations' offices, divisions, retail outlets, or other unincorporated places of business in the United States. Branches remit profits to their **home office** or the place of corporate residence.

As extended business endeavors, U.S. law does not view U.S. branches as separate taxable entities but as corporate activities reaching across national borders. Nonetheless, branch activities can lead to or affect corporate taxes that depend on branch profits or other branch characteristics. This chapter deals with two such taxes the United States imposes on foreign corporations: the **branch profits tax (BPT)** and the **branch interest tax (BIT)**.

## BRANCH PROFITS TAX

Foreign corporations can conduct U.S. business through either U.S. branches or domestic subsidiaries. The United States taxes both structures on their business profits at regular corporate rates, the former since such profits are ECI to foreign persons and the latter since the United States taxes the worldwide income of domestic persons. However, before 1987, the Code taxed foreign corporations on their receipt of U.S. business profits differently depending on the structure. U.S. law imposed a 30 percent withholding tax on foreign corporations for dividends (FDAP income) they received from U.S. subsidiaries. The Code required withholding even when a U.S. subsidiary's business gross income was only a small part (e.g., less than 25 percent) of the parent-subsidiary's aggregate gross income. In contrast, the United States did not tax profit remittances foreign home offices received from U.S. branches, viewing them as intrafirm, nontaxable transfers.

Thus, the Code requires many foreign corporations with U.S. branches to withhold tax on U.S. source dividends the foreign corporations pay to their shareholders. However, pre-1987 U.S. law characterized foreign corporate distributions as U.S. source dividends only when 50 percent (not the 25 percent under current law) or more of the distributor's gross income was ECI over a three-year period. To avoid U.S. source dividends (and, thus, the second-level shareholder tax), some foreign corporations carefully monitored U.S. branch profits to assure they stayed below the 50-percent ceiling. Foreign corporations whose U.S. branch activities caused them to reach the 50-percent threshold often deferred dividends until U.S. business activities ceased. After their percentage of ECI dropped below the 50-percent ceiling, future dividends required no U.S. withholding since they all were foreign source income. Other foreign corporations simply neglected to withhold and remit the required dividend withholding tax. The IRS found it difficult to detect and enforce the failure to withhold among such foreign corporations.

Congress enacted the BPT in 1986 to reduce opportunities for avoiding the second-level remittance tax and remove the incentive for foreign corporations to conduct U.S. business through branches. The BPT applies regardless of foreign corporations' ratio of ECI to total gross income (i.e., even if the ratio falls below 25 percent). Thus, the BPT achieves parity between foreign corporations engaged in business through a U.S. subsidiary and foreign corporations conducting business through a U.S. branch. Since the BPT substitutes for the second-level dividend withholding tax, the latter does not apply to E&P already subject to the BPT.[1] Exhibit 10.1 emphasizes the pre-1987 disparity between conducting business through either a U.S. branch or domestic subsidiary and the post-1986 parity the BPT creates.

The Code taxes dividends from U.S. subsidiaries to their foreign parents as FDAP income (i.e., at 30 percent or a lower treaty rate).[2] To achieve

---

[1] IRC §884(e)(3)(A).
[2] IRC §881(a).

**EXHIBIT 10.1**    Comparisons Before and After Branch Profits Tax Legislation

*Panel A: Pre-1987 Disparity*

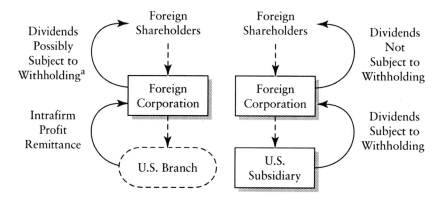

*Panel B: Post-1986 Parity*

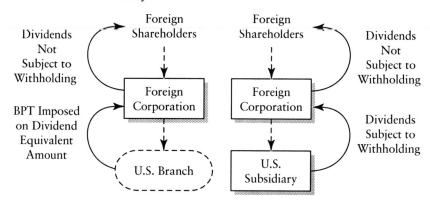

[a]U.S. withholding tax applied only if foreign corporation's ECI (primarily from U.S. branch) comprised at least 50 percent of its gross income over three-year testing period. Even when applicable, some foreign corporations did not collect and remit the dividend tax.

parity, U.S. law imposes a BPT equal to 30 percent (or lower treaty rate) of a foreign corporation's **dividend equivalent amount (DEA)**, which approximates the dividends the U.S. branch could pay if it operated as a U.S. subsidiary.[3] Specifically, the DEA equals the foreign corporation's effectively connected E&P (i.e., U.S. branch's after-tax business profits) adjusted for changes in its U.S. investment. Increases in U.S. net equity (a proxy for re-

---

[3]IRC §884(a).

**EXHIBIT 10.2** Calculating Foreign Corporation's Branch Profits Tax

|   | Foreign corporation's effectively connected E&P |
| --- | --- |
| − | Increases in foreign corporation's U.S. net equity |
| + | Decreases in foreign corporation's U.S. net equity |

|   | Dividend equivalent amount |
| --- | --- |
| × | 30% or lower treaty rate |

|   | Branch profits tax |
| --- | --- |

taining current branch profits) reduce the DEA, while decreases in U.S. net equity (a proxy for remittance of past branch profits) increase the DEA.[4] Exhibit 10.2 summarizes the BPT calculation.

---

**EXAMPLE**

Bouquet Delivery NV, a Suriname corporation, conducts business in the United States through a retail store in New Orleans. During 2003, Bouquet's effectively connected taxable income (after apportioned deductions but before U.S. income tax) equals $400,000 and its U.S. tax equals $140,000 ($400,000 × 35%). Thus, Bouquet's effectively connected E&P for 2003 is $260,000 ($400,000 − $140,000). Assuming Bouquet's U.S. net equity increases $110,000 (i.e., Bouquet acquires branch assets or liquidates branch debts during 2003), the BPT applies only to the DEA of $150,000 ($260,000 − $110,000). Thus, Bouquet's BPT for 2003 equals $45,000 ($150,000 × 30%). When Bouquet distributes 2003 E&P to foreign shareholders in 2004, no U.S. dividend withholding tax applies.

---

Under the Code, the BPT equals 30 percent of a foreign corporation's DEA. Most U.S. income tax treaties signed or renegotiated since 1986 explicitly recognize the BPT and allow the United States to impose it on a DEA. However, nondiscrimination clauses in some pre-1987 treaties can preclude the United States from imposing the BPT since such treaties do not specifically provide for the tax. U.S. law recognizes these nondiscrimination

---

[4]IRC §884(b).

arguments only for **qualified residents** of the treaty country.[5] The following are qualified residents:

- Foreign corporations whose shares primarily and regularly trade on an established securities market in the treaty country and wholly owned foreign subsidiaries of such corporations, and
- Wholly owned foreign subsidiaries of U.S. corporations, where the latter's shares primarily and regularly trade on an established U.S. securities market.[6]

Any other foreign corporation residing in the treaty country also is a qualified resident, unless:

- Individuals other than treaty country residents, U.S. resident aliens, and U.S. citizens directly or indirectly own 50 percent or more of the corporation's share value (stock ownership test), or
- The company uses 50 percent or more of its income to pay creditors other than treaty country residents, U.S. resident aliens, and U.S. citizens (base erosion test).[7]

Under pre-1987 treaties not specifically allowing a BPT, the treaty's dividend withholding rate applicable between foreign corporations and their wholly owned domestic subsidiaries substitutes for the BPT rate.[8] However, as noted, qualified residents can invoke nondiscrimination protection under these treaties to avoid the BPT.

---

### EXAMPLE

Assume the same facts as in the prior example except that Bouquet Delivery is a Mexican corporation. Article 11A of the U.S.-Mexico Treaty (signed in 1992) allows the United States to impose a BPT equal to 5 percent on the DEA of Mexican residents. Thus, Bouquet's BPT equals $7,500 ($150,000 × 5%). Demonstrating it is a qualified resident does not allow Bouquet to avoid the BPT since the treaty specifically authorizes the tax.

---

[5]IRC §884(e)(1).
[6]IRC §884(e)(4)(B), (C).
[7]IRC §884(e)(4)(A). The first restriction denies treaty protection when the beneficial owners reside outside the treaty countries and, thus, precludes treaty shopping. The second restriction prevents base erosion.
[8]IRC §884(e)(2).

---

**EXAMPLE**

Assume the same facts as in the prior example except the Bouquet Delivery is an Egyptian corporation. Signed in 1980, the U.S.-Egyptian Treaty does not mention the BPT or DEA. Under Article 26(2), the United States cannot impose more burdensome taxes on Egyptian residents with U.S. PEs than U.S. residents engaged in similar activities. However, to invoke this nondiscrimination protection and avoid the BPT, an Egyptian entity must demonstrate it meets the statutory definition of a qualified resident. If the Egyptian entity is not a qualified resident, the United States can impose a BPT of 5 percent, the withholding rate under Article 11(2)(b) applicable to dividends that wholly owned subsidiaries pay.

---

## MARGINAL TAX RATES

Unless U.S. net equity changes, foreign corporations do not adjust effectively connected E&P in computing the DEA, and the BPT applies to all current business profits. In fact, the marginal tax rate (MTR) calculation is similar to the one in equation 7.1, which assumed U.S. subsidiaries remit all E&P as dividends during the current year. Equation 10.1 provides the MTR formula when the BPT applies to all effectively connected E&P:

$$MTR = 1_{us} + t_{bp}(1 - t_{us}) \qquad (10.1)$$

where

$t_{us}$ = effective U.S. income tax rate
$t_{bp}$ = BPT rate

---

**EXAMPLE**

Quidesco SA, a Panamanian corporation, conducts a U.S. business through its Houston sales office. Its effective U.S. income tax rate is 35 percent. Since a treaty does not exist between the United States and Panama, the BPT rate equals 30 percent. Assuming no change in U.S. net equity, equation 10.1 determines the following MTR applicable to the U.S. business profits:

$$MTR = 0.35 + 0.30 \ (1 - 0.35) = 54.5\%$$

---

Retaining branch profits (i.e., increasing U.S. net equity) reduces the present value of the second term in equation 10.1 and, thus, the MTR. Similar to equation 7.2, equation 10.2 shows the MTR calculation when reinvestment of U.S. business profits causes deferral of the BPT:

$$MTR = t_{us} + \frac{t_{bp}(1 - t_{us})}{(1 + d)^y} \qquad (10.2)$$

where

$d$ = discount rate

$y$ = years branch profits invested in U.S. net equity

---

**EXAMPLE**

Assume the same facts as in the previous example, except that Quidesco does not expect to remit its after-tax branch profits for five years (increasing its U.S. net equity in an amount equal to its effectively connected E&P) and the applicable discount rate is 10 percent. Under these facts, the estimated MTR declines more than seven percentage points:

$$MTR = 0.35 + \frac{0.30(1 - 0.35)}{(1 + 0.10)^5} = 47.1\%$$

---

When foreign corporations reinvest only part of their U.S. branch profits, appropriately weighting the results of equations 10.1 and 10.2 provides a reasonable MTR estimate.

---

**EXAMPLE**

Assume the same facts as in the first Quidesco example, except that Quidesco retains 25 percent of its after-tax U.S. business profits (increasing its U.S. net equity) and remits the rest to Panama. Quidesco expects it will remit the reinvested E&P to its Panama office (decreasing its U.S. net equity) in about five years. Appropriately weighting the results of equations 10.1 and 10.2 results in the following MTR estimate:

$$MTR = (75\% \times 54.5\%) + (25\% \times 47.1\%) = 52.7\%$$

Any incremental foreign income tax the foreign corporation pays attributable to U.S. branch profits increases the MTR estimates from equations 10.1 and 10.2. If the foreign jurisdiction relies on a territorial system, no foreign income tax applies to the U.S. branch profits. However, under a worldwide system and foreign tax credit relief, an additional tax may be due when the effective foreign income tax rate exceeds the effective U.S. income tax rate.[9]

## BRANCH INTEREST TAX

For most purposes, U.S. law does not distinguish between corporations and their branches since the latter are not separate legal entities. Thus, conventional wisdom attributes branch activities to the corporation of which the branch is a part. However, before 1987, this traditional view of branches as nonentities created two inconsistencies when U.S. branches of foreign corporations paid interest. The BIT attempts to rectify these inconsistencies. First, the BIT seeks similar treatment for foreign corporations conducting U.S. business through U.S. subsidiaries and those conducting U.S. business through branches. Second, the BIT assures that the interest subject to a withholding tax equals the amount foreign corporations deduct as interest.

As with the BPT, the BIT achieves parity between foreign corporations conducting U.S. business through either U.S. subsidiaries or U.S. branches. When U.S. subsidiaries pay interest to foreign creditors, they withhold U.S. tax unless the interest income qualifies for exemption (e.g., under the portfolio interest rules or pursuant to a treaty). However, before 1987, interest U.S. branches paid to foreign creditors avoided U.S. withholding tax since the recipients derived the interest from foreign corporations and, thus, foreign sources. To rectify this disparity, Congress amended the Code in 1986 to treat U.S. branches as domestic corporations when they pay interest.[10] This treatment causes the interest to be U.S. source income to the recipient. Thus, when recipients are foreign persons, foreign corporations must withhold U.S. tax on interest their U.S. branches pay (unless the interest is otherwise exempt).

Theoretically, a foreign corporation's interest payment (on which recipients are subject to U.S. tax) should equal the foreign corporation's U.S. deduction for interest. However, the foreign corporation's interest deduction under apportionment procedures usually differs from the recipient's interest income subject to U.S. tax.

---

[9]From an outbound investment perspective, Chapter 11 discusses the residual U.S. tax that may result from remitting foreign profits.
[10]IRC §884(f)(1)(A).

**COMPLIANCE POINTER:**   Collecting the branch-level information necessary to determine the interest deduction can be a prodigious task. The collection effort is one factor that encourages foreign corporations to incorporate U.S. business activities.

Before 1987, U.S. withholding procedures did not apply to interest income received from foreign corporations since recipients derived such income from foreign sources. As a result, foreign corporations often deducted interest against ECI on which the recipient was not subject to U.S. income tax. To remedy this inconsistency between payors and payees, the Code treats excess interest of foreign corporations as FDAP income. Equation 10.3 indicates how foreign corporations calculate **excess interest:**

Excess interest =
   Interest foreign corporation deducts − Interest branch pays     (10.3)

In effect, the Code treats excess interest as interest income foreign corporations receive from hypothetical, wholly owned domestic subsidiaries on **notional loans** (i.e., from U.S. sources).[11] Thus, unless treaties otherwise exempt it, foreign corporations pay U.S. tax on excess interest.

**EXAMPLE**

Kabelenga Ltd., a Zambian corporation, conducts business in the United States through an Atlanta office. Following U.S. apportionment procedures, Kabelenga deducts $9,800 interest against its ECI. The Atlanta office pays interest to the creditors listed here:

---

[11]IRC §884(f)(1)(B).

| | |
|---|---:|
| J.R. Uswing (U.S. citizen) | $3,000 |
| Peter Smirnov (Russian national and resident) | 1,000 |
| Banco Vista SA (Brazilian bank) | 5,000 |
| Total interest Atlanta office paid during year | $9,000 |

Peter owns no stock in Kabelenga, so his interest income qualifies as exempt portfolio interest. Banco Vista owns 22 percent of Kabelenga, so its interest income is not exempt as portfolio interest. Kabelenga does not withhold BIT on the interest it pays to J.R. and Peter. Kabelenga withholds $1,500 ($5,000 × 30%) on the interest the Atlanta office pays to Banco Vista. Also, Kabelenga must pay $240 U.S. tax on its excess interest [($9,800 – $9,000) × 30%].

**COMPLIANCE POINTER:** Foreign corporations withhold BIT on branch interest they pay to foreign persons (unless exempt as portfolio interest or under a treaty). However, foreign corporations pay BIT on excess interest (at 30 percent or lower treaty rate) with their U.S. returns since excess interest involves hypothetical payments.[12]

Like the BPT, U.S. income tax treaties can override the statutory BIT. Foreign corporations meeting a treaty's post-1986 limitation on benefit requirement (i.e., antitreaty shopping requirements discussed in Chapter 3) can claim treaty benefits reducing or eliminating the BIT. For pre-1987 treaties, foreign corporations must be qualified residents (as defined earlier for BPT purposes) and satisfy the limitation on benefits article, if any, to claim treaty benefits.[13]

---

[12]Reg. §1.884-4(a)(2)(iv).
[13]IRC §884(f)(3); Reg. §1.884-4(b)(8), (c)(3).

# PART Three

## Outbound Transactions

# CHAPTER 11

# Foreign Tax Credit

**B**eginning with this chapter, the text shifts its focus to foreign investment and business activities of U.S. persons. Outbound transactions raise the specter of double taxation, a major concern to both U.S. policymakers and U.S. taxpayers investing or conducting business abroad. Double taxation occurs when individuals or entities pay tax on the same income stream to both the home country where they reside and the host country where they derive the income.

The tax systems of most countries provide means to mitigate the effect of double taxation. Territorial systems usually exempt income a resident earns abroad, while global systems tax residents' worldwide income but grant a foreign tax credit (FTC) for foreign income taxes.[1] Some countries, like Australia and Canada, allow an exemption in some situations but depend on the FTC in others. Regardless of the approach, tax policies must deal with double taxation concerns or risk discouraging foreign direct investment and impeding economic growth.

Like many global systems, U.S. tax law relies primarily on the FTC to reduce the debilitating effects of double taxation.[2] Since the FTC causes more similar taxation of U.S. persons' foreign and domestic income, it promotes capital export neutrality.[3] For each taxable year, U.S. persons claim

---

[1]Territorial systems tend to be capital-import-neutral and provide competitive advantages in low-tax countries. Residents of territorial systems reduce (increase) their effective worldwide tax rates when conducting business in relatively low-tax (high-tax) countries. Global systems place more emphasis on capital export neutrality. Residents of global systems maintain (increase) their effective worldwide tax rates when conducting business in low-tax (high-tax) countries. For a more detailed explanation, see Ernest R. Larkins, "Double Tax Relief for Foreign Income: A Comparative Study of Advanced Economies," *Virginia Tax Review*, 21 (Fall 2001): pp. 233–75.

[2]*Burnet v. Chicago Portrait Co.*, 285 US 1 (1932).

[3]The FTC mitigates the effect of double taxation for U.S. persons and, thus, affects mostly outbound investments. Nonetheless, in some situations, IRC §§901(b)(4) and 906 allow foreign persons to claim the U.S. FTC for foreign income tax paid on ECI.

the FTC only if they so elect.[4] Each partner in a partnership must separately elect the FTC.[5]

> **COMPLIANCE POINTER:**   U.S. individuals file Form 1116, and domestic corporations file Form 1118, to elect the FTC on their U.S. tax returns. Form 1118 contains several complex schedules. For each taxable year, U.S. individuals and domestic corporations can change their initial decision to elect (or not elect) the FTC at any time during the period for filing claims for tax refunds.[6]

U.S. persons not electing the FTC can deduct foreign income taxes.[7] Of course, deductions provide smaller tax benefits than similar-size credits. Exhibit 11.1 provides an example of this tax benefit difference. The corporation in the illustration loses $195 of U.S. tax benefits if it forgoes the FTC and deducts foreign income taxes, increasing its worldwide marginal tax rate on foreign earnings by 19.5 percentage points.

Since FTC benefits usually exceed tax benefits from deducting foreign income taxes, U.S. taxpayers generally should elect the FTC. However, forgoing the FTC and claiming a deduction results in greater tax benefits in a few situations.

> **PLANNING POINTER:**   Taxpayers not benefiting from the FTC due to the formula limitation (discussed later in this chapter) might settle for the tax benefits of deducting their foreign levies. When U.S. taxpayers have domestic losses, deducting foreign taxes causes such losses to grow. Nonetheless, the carryover period for net operating losses covers more years than the FTC carryover period.[8] Thus, deducting foreign taxes allows a longer period for deriving some tax benefits than electing the FTC. In deciding between these alternative strategies, tax planners should consider the likelihood of absorbing their FTC before the end of the carryover period and the present

---

[4]IRC §901(a).

[5]IRC §703(b)(3).

[6]IRC §901(a).

[7]In addition to foreign income taxes, IRC §164(a) allows U.S. taxpayers to deduct foreign property taxes, and IRC §§162(a) and 212 allow deductions for any other foreign taxes related to business or investment activities (e.g., capital-based and value-added taxes).

[8]Under IRC §172(b)(1)(A), taxpayers can carry net operating losses back 2 and forward 20 years. In contrast, IRC §904(c) allows taxpayers to carry an unused FTC back 2 and forward 5 years. Legislative bills have proposed increasing the FTC carryforward period.

**EXHIBIT 11.1**   Tax Benefit Difference: Foreign Tax Credit versus Deduction

|  | FTC | Deduct | Difference |
|---|---|---|---|
| a. Foreign source income | $1,000 | $1,000 | |
| b. Foreign tax rate | × .30 | × .30 | |
| c. Foreign income tax | $ 300 | $ 300 | |
| d. Foreign source income (same as line a) | $1,000 | $1,000 | |
| e. Deduction of foreign income tax (from line c) | 0 | − 300 | |
| f. Foreign source income taxable in United States | $1,000 | $ 700 | |
| g. U.S. effective tax rate for corporations | × .35 | × .35 | |
| h. U.S. tax before the FTC | $ 350 | $ 245 | |
| i. Foreign tax credit | 300 | 0 | |
| j. U.S. tax liability | $ 50 | $ 245 | |
| k. Worldwide tax liability (sum of lines c and j) | $ 350 | $ 545 | $195 |
| l. U.S. tax benefit (line i or line e times line g) | $ 300 | $ 105 | $195 |
| m. Marginal tax rate (line k divided by line a) | 35.0% | 54.5% | 19.5 points |

value of any anticipated tax benefits. Instances in which deduction benefits exceed FTC benefits are atypical; thus, the remainder of this chapter deals only with the FTC benefit.[9]

For accrual-basis taxpayers, foreign income taxes accrue on the last day of the foreign jurisdiction's tax year. Thus, accrual-basis taxpayers recognize such taxes during the U.S. taxable year with or within which the foreign tax year ends.[10] In contrast, cash basis taxpayers recognize foreign income taxes after paying them. To avoid mismatching taxes with related foreign source

---

[9]State tax treatment of creditable foreign taxes differs significantly from the federal tax treatment. Many states prohibit deductions for creditable taxes. In those states permitting a deduction, the U.S. taxpayer usually must deduct creditable taxes on the federal return before the state allows a deduction.

[10]Rev. Rul. 61-93, 1961-1 CB 390. However, Rev. Rul. 84-125, 1984-2 CB 125, and Reg. §1.905-1(b) clarify that contested taxes and taxes related to income that the taxpayer does not yet recognize as gross income due to exchange controls or similar restrictions do not accrue until the foreign country makes a final determination of tax liability or lifts the exchange controls or restrictions, respectively.

income, cash-basis taxpayers often elect to recognize foreign income taxes when they accrue. Once made, the election applies to all future years and precludes the taxpayer from deducting such taxes.[11]

U.S. persons usually pay their foreign tax liabilities in the foreign jurisdiction's currency. However, to determine the FTC, they must translate the foreign tax into U.S. dollars. Cash-basis taxpayers use the exchange rate in effect on the date they pay their foreign taxes. Accrual basis taxpayers usually rely on the year's average exchange rate to translate their foreign tax liabilities. However, accrual basis taxpayers use the exchange rate on the payment date when they pay foreign taxes:

- Before the applicable taxable year begins,
- More than two years after the taxable year ends, or
- In an inflationary currency.[12]

The FTC allows U.S. persons to credit foreign income taxes they directly pay or incur against their U.S. tax liabilities. Thus, income tax a U.S. corporation's foreign branch pays or incurs entitles the corporation to an FTC. Also, domestic corporations can claim indirect or deemed paid credits for foreign income taxes that foreign subsidiaries pay or incur. Limitation formulae assure that taxpayers use the FTC only to reduce U.S. taxes imposed on foreign source income. U.S. persons can carry excess credits that the limitation formula disallows to other taxable years.

## CREDITABLE TAXES

Foreign government levies qualify for the FTC only if they are income taxes or taxes imposed in lieu of income taxes. To be **creditable** as an income tax, levies must be taxes a foreign country, U.S. possession, or political subdivision of either (e.g., a state, city, or province) imposes on income.[13] Further, levies are creditable as income taxes only if they qualify as income taxes under U.S. law; foreign statutes or decisions are not determinative.[14] Thus, a foreign levy is a creditable income tax only if:

- It qualifies as a tax and
- Its predominant character is that of an income tax in the U.S. sense.[15]

---

[11]IRC §905(a).
[12]IRC §986(a).
[13]*Burnet v. Chicago Portrait Co.*, 285 US 1 (1932); Reg. §1.901-2(g)(2).
[14]See dicta in *Biddle v. Comm.*, 302 US 573 (1938), which became the basis for the predominant character requirement.
[15]Reg. §1.901-2(a)(1).

Foreign levies not based on income are creditable if imposed in lieu of income taxes. Such taxes often apply to particular industries (e.g., banking or petroleum) or taxpayers (e.g., nonresidents). A foreign levy imposed in lieu of an income tax is creditable only if:

- It qualifies as a tax and
- It substitutes for a generally imposed income tax.[16]

> **RESEARCH POINTER:** Tax professionals need not evaluate every foreign levy under the two regulatory standards just listed. Covered taxes that U.S. income tax treaties specifically identify as creditable qualify for the FTC.[17] Also, IRS rulings and judicial decisions sometimes examine specific foreign levies to determine their eligibility for the FTC. In effect, these taxes are "precertified" if evaluated according to the two regulatory criteria and if the underlying foreign tax law has not changed substantially since the ruling or judicial decision evaluated them.

> **COMPLIANCE POINTER:** The IRS indicates that it no longer will ordinarily rule on whether a particular foreign levy is creditable.[18]

## Tax Requirement

Foreign government levies must be **taxes** to be creditable. Only compulsory expenditures qualify as taxes.[19] Voluntary payments, even if the foreign law refers to such outlays as taxes, do not qualify. Also, to the extent payments exceed a person's tax liability under foreign law or applicable treaties, they are noncompulsory and, thus, are not taxes. To be compulsory, the amount paid must be consistent with a reasonable interpretation and application of foreign law and applicable treaties. Further, taxpayers must exhaust all effective and practical remedies for reducing their foreign tax liabilities, including the use of competent authority procedures. Whether a remedy is effective and practical depends on the cost to pursue the remedy, the tax amount involved, and the chances of success.[20]

---

[16]Reg. §1.903-1(a).
[17]U.S. Treasury Department Technical Explanation of the United States Model Income Tax Convention (September 20, 1996), Article 23.
[18]Rev. Proc. 2003-7, §4.01(16), 2003-1 IRB 233.
[19]Reg. §1.901-2(a)(2)(i).
[20]Reg. §1.901-2(e)(5)(i).

## EXAMPLE

Winter Veggies, Inc., a U.S. corporation, designs and constructs a new greenhouse farm for a Lithuanian company. Its compensatory fee, less deductible expenses, results in taxable profit of $1 million. At Lithuania's 29 percent tax rate, Winter Veggies owes $290,000 foreign income tax. However, Lithuania mistakenly omits some of Winter Veggies' deductions, resulting in $340,000 Lithuanian income tax. Winter Veggies can correct the mistake with a small amount of time and expense. However, Winter Veggies' CFO decides to "just let it go since we can claim a foreign tax credit for the additional $50,000, so it won't cost us anything." However, the United States can disallow an FTC for the additional $50,000 since it represents a payment exceeding Winter Veggies' legal liability for Lithuanian income tax. Winter Veggies did not exhaust all effective and practical remedies to reduce the tax to the correct amount. Thus, the additional $50,000 is noncompulsory, not a tax, and not creditable. Contrary to the CFO's conclusion, the FTC disallowance means the mistaken omission costs Winter Veggies $50,000 unless the company can recover the overpayment from Lithuania.

Payments not pursuant to a government's taxing authority do not qualify as taxes. A government's assertion that it collects an amount under its authority to raise taxes is not determinative since such an assertion may be self-serving. U.S. principles apply in determining the authority behind a foreign levy. Thus, fines, penalties, interest, custom duties, and compulsory loans that persons pay a foreign government do not qualify as taxes and, thus, are not creditable.[21]

Governments do not impose foreign levies entitling payers to specific economic benefits pursuant to their taxing authority; thus, such levies are not taxes.[22] A **specific economic benefit** is one that is unavailable on essentially the same terms to substantially all other taxpayers or the general public. Specific economic benefits include services, property, contractual rights, and discharges of legal obligations the foreign government provides or grants; they do not include the right to conduct business within the host country or to conduct business in a particular form.[23]

---

[21]Reg. §1.901-2(a)(2)(i).

[22]Id.

[23]Reg. §1.901-2(a)(2)(ii)(B). Similarly, IRC §901(i) denies a credit for foreign income tax entitling the taxpayer or a related person to a subsidy that depends on the magnitude of the tax base or tax.

When foreign levies contain elements of both payments for specific economic benefits and taxes, payers are **dual capacity taxpayers** and must establish the portion qualifying as taxes. Only the latter payments, if they otherwise qualify, are creditable.[24] Taxpayers can use the safe harbor formula in equation 11.1 to determine the creditable portion of a foreign levy:[25]

$$(A - B - C) \times \frac{D}{1 - D} \qquad (11.1)$$

where:

A = Gross receipts subject to the levy
B = Cost and expenses
C = Levy taxpayer actually paid
D = General income tax rate

---

**EXAMPLE**

---

Gasohol Supreme, Inc., a domestic corporation, earns $10 million profit from its foreign oil business, on which it pays 85 percent "petroleum profit tax" to Nigeria. In contrast, the general income tax, which Gasohol does not pay, applies at a 30 percent rate.[26] Paying the oil tax entitles Gasohol to extract crude oil from government-owned land, a specific economic benefit not available to other taxpayers. Thus, Gasohol is a dual capacity taxpayer. Initially, $3 million might appear to be the foreign tax under U.S. law [30/85 × ($10,000,000 × .85)]. However, this conclusion fails to consider that royalties (i.e., the noncreditable portion paid for a specific economic benefit) are deductible under general income tax principles. The safe harbor formula considers this deductibility issue and isolates the portion of the petroleum tax the United States treats as a tax:

$$(\$10,000,000 - \$8,500,000) \times \frac{.30}{1 - .30} = \$642,857$$

---

[24]Reg. §1.901-2(a)(2)(i).
[25]Reg. §1.901-2A(e)(1).
[26]PricewaterhouseCoopers, *Corporate Taxes: Worldwide Summaries 2002–2003* (Hoboken, NJ: John Wiley & Sons, Inc., 2002), pp. 606–607.

The $642,857 portion of Gasohol's petroleum tax is a tax under U.S. law and might be creditable, depending on other criteria (e.g., the levy's predominant character). The bulk of the petroleum tax Gasohol pays ($8,500,000 − $642,857 or $7,857,143) does not qualify as a tax under U.S. law and, thus, is not creditable despite its characterization as a tax under Nigerian law. It more closely resembles a royalty since it purchases the right to extract the government's crude oil. As a check on the result, one can determine the amount of income tax Gasohol would have paid if it had been subject to the Nigerian income tax rather than the petroleum profit tax:

| | |
|---|---|
| Foreign profits before royalty | $10,000,000 |
| Deductible royalty | 7,857,143 |
| Taxable profits | $ 2,142,857 |
| General income tax rate | × .30 |
| Foreign income tax | $ 642,857 |

### Predominant Character

If U.S. law determines that a foreign government levy qualifies as a tax, it is creditable as an income tax only if its predominant character is that of an income tax in the U.S. sense. To meet this standard, a foreign tax must:

- Be likely to reach net gain under normal circumstances and
- Not be dependent on the availability of a U.S. FTC.[27]

A tax is likely to reach net gain under normal circumstances only if its predominant character satisfies tripartite criteria known as the *realization, gross receipts,* and *net income tests.*[28] Thus, U.S. law may treat a tax as creditable for all persons subject to it even though the tax does not reach net gain for some taxpayers. The relevant criteria involve the overall characteristics of a tax and its application under normal circumstances, not whether it reaches the net gain of every taxpayer. If a tax meets the criteria, it is creditable for all taxpayers, even those for whom it fails to reach net gain.

---

[27]Reg. §1.901-2(a)(3).
[28]Reg. §1.901-2(b)(1). A tax that is unlikely to reach net gain still is creditable if it qualifies as a tax imposed in lieu of an income tax. Thus, failure to meet all three tests does not necessarily mean that the tax is noncreditable.

The **realization test** focuses on the timing of a tax's assessment rather than its base. Taxpayers meet the realization test if the foreign government assesses its tax after a sale, exchange, or other realization event occurs. In addition, a tax assessed before a realization event (i.e., at the time of a prerealization event) satisfies the test if the foreign government:

- Imposes the prerealization tax to recapture a previously allowed deduction, credit, or other tax benefit;
- Exempts the same income stream when a later realization event occurs;
- Taxes the same income stream when a later realization event occurs but allows a tax credit for the earlier prerealization tax or some comparable double tax relief; or
- Imposes the prerealization tax on a deemed distribution from a corporation and protects the same income stream from double taxation on a later actual distribution (i.e., realization event) with an exemption, basis adjustment, credit, or similar relief mechanism.[29]

## EXAMPLE

Hedgehog, Inc., a U.S. corporation, conducts business in Spain through a branch and earns $5 million subject to the 35 percent Spanish income tax. Thus, Hedgehog's Spanish income tax is $1.75 million ($5 million × 35%), and its after-tax profits equal $3.25 million ($5 million – $1.75 million). The branch remits $1 million to its U.S. home office and, under Article 14(2) of the U.S.-Spain Treaty, pays a 10 percent "additional tax on permanent establishments" of $100,000.[30] Spain imposes its income tax after Hedgehog realizes its profit, so the income tax meets the realization test. Similarly, since Spain imposes its branch profits tax after Hedgehog realizes the related profit, that tax satisfies the realization test, too.

---

[29]Reg. §1.901-2(b)(2). In the itemized list's third situation, prerealization events include the physical transfer, processing, or export of readily marketable inventory or the determination of property value changes between the beginning and end of the taxable period. The most common example occurs when fully integrated U.S. petroleum companies export crude oil from host countries for further processing and ultimate sale to U.S. motorists. Host countries dare not await a realization event that is difficult for them to monitor or verify before imposing a tax.

[30]PricewaterhouseCoopers, *Corporate Taxes: Worldwide Summaries 2002–2003* (Hoboken, NJ: John Wiley & Sons, Inc., 2002), pp. 772, 774.

**EXAMPLE**

Hostia (a hypothetical country) imposes a 20 percent income tax and a 20 percent stock appreciation tax on increases in local stock values that nonresident companies hold as portfolio investments. The assessment of the stock appreciation tax represents a prerealization event. Opulenox, Inc., a U.S. company, owns a portfolio interest in a Hostian company worth $1 million and $1.3 million at the beginning and end of 2003, respectively. Thus, Hostia imposes a $60,000 stock appreciation tax on Opulenox [($1.3 million – $1 million) × 20%]. Opulenox sells its portfolio holding in 2004 for $1.4 million. If Hostia imposes a 2004 income tax on Opulenox's $400,000 capital gain ($1.4 million – $1 million), the 2003 stock appreciation tax fails the realization test and, thus, is not creditable as an income tax. However, if Hostia taxes Opulenox on only $100,000 of its capital gain, or taxes Opulenox on $400,000 of capital gain but provides a $60,000 credit against Opulenox's income tax, the stock appreciation tax meets the realization test and, depending on other criteria, may be creditable.[31]

Appreciation of stock, land, or other assets is not the only prerealization event meeting the realization test. Some foreign governments specify means of estimating gross receipts when taxpayers extract natural resources or export products. These prerealization events may be the most efficient time to measure income tax, especially if the government cannot determine when and to whom taxpayers ultimately sell natural resources or other products, making later tax collections difficult.

A foreign levy satisfies the **gross receipts test** if the starting point for determining its tax base is actual gross receipts. Alternatively, taxpayers can estimate gross receipts under a method likely to result in a starting point not greater than fair market value (i.e., arm's-length or actual gross receipts).[32] Allowing an amount greater than fair market value increases foreign income tax, potentially increasing the FTC under U.S. law and, thus, decreasing U.S. tax revenues. Underestimating gross receipts is acceptable since it cannot result in less U.S. tax revenues. Foreign governments might require tax-

---

[31]Most countries imposing a "stock appreciation tax" or "land appreciation tax" do not assess such tax until a realization event occurs. Thus, examples of foreign countries taxing increases in security or land values are rare.
[32]Reg. §1.901-2(b)(3)(i).

payers to estimate gross receipts when determining actual gross receipts is administratively difficult, particularly if transactions producing gross receipts occur with related persons.

---

### EXAMPLE

France provides a special tax regime for French corporations organized solely to administer, manage, and coordinate functions for affiliated nonresident companies. Given the difficulty in determining arm's-length fees for such services, France allows headquarters corporations to estimate gross receipts using a cost-plus formula. The percentage markup is negotiable but usually ranges between 5 and 10 percent.[33] For instance, a French headquarters corporation that incurs operating expenses of $500,000 and negotiates a markup of 8 percent estimates its gross receipts as $540,000 ($500,000 × 108%). If formula-based gross receipts are likely not to exceed arm's-length gross receipts for affiliate transactions, the predominant character of the headquarters company tax satisfies the gross receipts test. The fact that the markup for a particular headquarters company causes the formula-based gross receipts to exceed its arm's-length gross receipts is irrelevant if the predominant character of the headquarters tax is unlikely to result in an excess under normal circumstances.[34]

---

Some Latin American countries impose **asset taxes** on the value of property at fairly low rates of 2 percent or less. Based on the presumption that businesses expect to earn a minimum return on assets, host countries impose these taxes to reduce the loss of tax revenues from illegal or aggressive conduct depleting the income tax base (e.g., inflating deductible royalties paid to related persons in the home country or manipulating transfer prices). Asset taxes do not meet the gross receipts test since they depend on asset values. Thus, the interaction between a country's asset tax and income tax determines the extent to which a person's foreign tax payments

---

[33]Marcellin N. Mbwa-Mboma, "French Tax Review: New Ruling Requirements for Multinationals' Headquarters, Logistics Centers," *Worldwide Tax Daily* (November 12, 2003), LEXIS 2002 WTD 218-5.
[34]See Reg. §1.901-2(b)(3)(ii)Ex.(1)-(2).

are creditable. In some countries, the interaction converts creditable income taxes into noncreditable asset taxes under U.S. multiple levy rules explaining how to characterize taxes when one levy partially or entirely offsets a second levy.[35]

---

**EXAMPLE**

Mexico imposes a 1.8 percent tax on a business's average assets. Taxpayers can credit any Mexican income tax they pay against their asset tax.[36] Consider a U.S. company incurring a $70 asset tax (before credit) and a $100 income tax. The latter offsets the former, so the taxpayer pays a $100 income tax and no asset tax. This offset procedure results in creditable taxes of $100.

---

**EXAMPLE**

Colombia imposes its 35 percent corporate tax on the larger of taxable income or "presumptive income" (i.e., 6 percent of net equity).[37] Consider a U.S. company with taxable income of $90 and presumptive income of $100. The resulting $35 tax is based on net equity, not income. Thus, it is not creditable.

---

The **net income test** focuses on a foreign levy's tax base. To meet the test, a tax must allow for the recovery of significant costs and expenses (including capital expenditures). That is, the tax must permit these amounts to reduce actual (or estimated) gross receipts in determining the tax base. Instead of actual costs and expenses, taxes allowing recovery through methods unlikely to underestimate these amounts meet the net income test.[38] Underestimating actual costs and expenses increases foreign income tax, potentially increasing the FTC under U.S. law and, thus, decreasing U.S. tax

---

[35]See Reg. §1.901-2(e)(4).
[36]PricewaterhouseCoopers, *Corporate Taxes: Worldwide Summaries 2002–2003* (Hoboken, NJ: John Wiley & Sons, Inc., 2002), p. 520.
[37]Ibid., p. 153.
[38]Reg. §1.901-2(b)(4)(i)(A), (B).

revenues. Overestimating actual costs and expenses is acceptable since it does not result in lower U.S. tax revenues.

## KEY CASE

A U.S. parent company owns a Canadian subsidiary that mines and processes copper, zinc, lead, and silver deposits in Ontario. The subsidiary pays the Ontario mining tax (OMT) on its "profit," which the relevant statute defines as gross receipts (or actual market or appraised value) less an "allowance for profit in respect of processing," less salaries, depreciation, research and development, and most other operating expenses. However, the statute does not permit deductions for nonrecoverable expenses, including investment interest, cost depletion, and certain royalties. The U.S. government contends that the nondeductibility of these other expenses causes the OMT to be noncreditable since it does not meet the net income test. In supporting its assertion that the OMT is a creditable deemed paid tax,[39] the U.S. parent company demonstrates that its processing allowance exceeds its nonrecoverable expenses in 10 of 13 years and that its aggregate processing allowance is 91 percent greater than its aggregate nonrecoverable expenses over the same years. It also submits an industry expert's empirical data indicating that the OMT's processing allowance exceeds the nonrecoverable expenses on 84 percent of mining industry returns showing OMT liability (and 67 percent for all mining industry returns) and that aggregate processing allowances exceed aggregate nonrecoverable expenses by a 2.7 to 1 ratio for the industry. In affirming the Tax Court, the Second Circuit relies on the return-by-return industry data, noting the large and representative nature of the empirical data. It holds that the processing allowance likely exceeds the nonrecoverable expenses under normal circumstances, and, thus, the OMT meets the net income test.[40]

Recoverable costs and expenses include all operating expenses necessary to conduct business. If a tax restricts recoverable amounts to those expenses directly related to operations, it does not satisfy the net income test. Recoverable amounts must also include general and administrative expenses related to the business.[41]

---

[39]This chapter discusses deemed paid taxes later.
[40]*Texasgulf, Inc. v. Comm.*, 172 F.3d 209 (CA-2, 1999).
[41]*Keasbey & Mattison Co. v. Rothensies*, 33 F.2d 894 (CA-3, 1943).

---

**EXAMPLE**

In addition to an income tax, Australia imposes a 10 percent **goods and services tax (GST)** on the value of goods delivered or services performed in commercial transactions. Taxpayers receive "input tax credits" for acquiring goods or receiving services.[42] Thus, the GST is similar to the **value-added tax (VAT)** many countries impose on the incremental value added to transferred property. Though the GST input credits do permit companies to recover many costs, the GST does not allow for recovery of business operating expenses. Thus, it fails the net income test and is not creditable. Likewise, VATs that other countries impose are not creditable.

---

In determining whether a tax satisfies the net income test, the following broad principles apply:

- The timing of cost and expense recoveries can differ from the timing of comparable cost recoveries and deductions under U.S. law, unless the difference effectively denies the recoveries. For instance, the foreign law can allow for more or less rapid depreciation deductions than U.S. law.
- The foreign government's substitution of an allowance for actual costs and expenses does not necessarily violate the net income test. Consistent with the earlier discussion, the allowance should not underestimate actual costs and expenses under normal circumstances.
- Foreign tax law principles attributing costs and expenses to gross receipts can differ from those of U.S. law, but must be reasonable.
- A tax does not fail the net income test solely because the foreign law disallows the recovery of some costs and expenses that U.S. law permits. Thus, the foreign tax law can differ from U.S. tax law in some respects.
- Whether the foreign tax law permits another tax meeting the realization, gross receipts, and net income tests to be deductible is immaterial. For instance, a national income tax disallowing deductions for income tax (meeting the tripartite conditions) paid to states, provinces, or other political subdivisions does not fail the net income test.
- The foreign tax law should permit losses incurred in one activity of a trade or business as deductions against profits earned in a separate ac-

---

[42]Ernest R. Larkins and Matthew Wallace, "ANTS and the Shifting Sands of Tax Reform Down Under," *Journal of International Taxation* 13 (March 2002), pp. 28–39.

tivity of the same trade or business, either currently or through reasonable carryovers to other years. An example of such activities might be two North Sea contract areas of a business involving Norwegian oil exploration. Alternatively, the law should allow losses to offset profits of the same activity (e.g., same contract area) in other years through reasonable carryover procedures.

- Taxes disallowing deductions for losses in one trade or business against profits in a separate trade or business do not violate the net income test.
- Taxes that do not allow passive losses (gains) to offset business gains (losses) do not fail the net income test.
- Whether the foreign tax law requires, permits, or prohibits profit and loss consolidation for related persons is immaterial unless the law requires separate taxable entities for separate activities within the same trade or business. In this latter instance, U.S. law views the separate entities as a single entity in determining whether the tax meets the net income test.
- Except as mentioned previously, whether the foreign law allows taxpayers to carry over net losses to offset income or gains in other taxable periods is immaterial.[43]

## KEY CASE

A Delaware corporation explores for and extracts oil from the North Sea subsoil under a royalty contract with Norway. In addition to royalties, the corporation pays Norwegian national, municipal, and special levies on its income from selling the oil. The special levies apply primarily to companies engaged in subsoil exploration and exploitation. The corporation sells the oil to its U.S. parent company at the Norwegian Petroleum Price Board's "norm price," which a Royal Decree mandates as the price of petroleum sold in a free market between independent persons. Under several arguments, the U.S. government contends that all three levies are noncreditable. First, it argues that the levies represent fees for rights to extract petroleum, a specific economic benefit, payable in addition to the contractual royalties. However, the court notes that neither the special tax's enactment nor its payment results in additional rights or benefits. Also, all three levies seem to be taxes unrelated to the grant of exploration and exploitation rights. Second, the government asserts that the norm price, which substitutes for gross receipts in all three levies, does not satisfy the gross receipts test. However, the court observes that the resulting norm prices closely approximate fair market val-

---

[43]Reg. §1.901-2(b)(4)(i)-(iii).

ues. Third, the government contends that the three levies do not meet the net income test, since none of the three are deductible in computing any of the other levies; related party sales commissions are nondeductible; and certain net operating losses are not currently deductible. However, the court finds the nondeductibility of the three levies to be a nonissue since they are taxes, not royalties (i.e., not significant costs and expenses). Further, the nondeductibility of related party commissions is consistent with the use of norm prices to proxy for gross receipts (i.e., such commissions are suspect); and the net operating losses, though not currently deductible, may be deductible in carryover years (i.e., it is only a timing difference). In short, the disallowed deductions do not cause substantial deviations from net income. Thus, the court holds that all three levies are creditable taxes.[44]

In rare situations, the regulations treat a tax permitting no recovery of costs and expenses as satisfying the net income test. To meet the test, the tax must be almost certain to reach some net gain under normal circumstances. Costs and expenses must be almost never higher than gross receipts so that, if the levy had allowed recovery of such amounts, some taxable profit almost always would have resulted. Further, the rate of tax must be low enough so that gross receipts less costs and expenses (which the tax treats as nonrecoverable), less the tax, result in positive economic income. In short, a tax allowing no recovery of costs and expenses can meet the net income test if affected taxpayers almost certainly will never experience a net economic loss after paying the tax.[45]

## KEY CASE

A U.S. bank conducts business through branches in Thailand, the Philippines, and Argentina. In addition to the general income tax in each country, the bank pays additional business taxes on gross income without recovery of costs and expenses. Banks have substantial costs and expenses (e.g., salaries, rent, interest on deposits, and bad debts) and can experience net losses. Since each country imposes its additional business tax regardless of whether

---

[44]*Phillips Petroleum Company and Affiliated Subsidiaries v. Comm.*, 104 TC 256 (1995). Though this case deals with the 1981 and 1982 tax years to which the taxpayer elected to apply previously issued temporary regulations, the outcome likely would have been the same under the final regulations issued in 1983 since the taxpayer petitioned the court to apply the final regulations, but the court declined.
[45]Reg. §1.901-2(b)(4)(i).

the bank earns a profit or incurs a loss, it is not clear that such taxes are almost certain to reach net gain under normal circumstances. The general income taxes are creditable, but the additional business taxes are not creditable since they fail the net income test.[46]

---

## EXAMPLE

Mexico taxes the personal service income of U.S. individuals working as employees in Mexico but allows no deductions for related employment expenses.[47] However, since employee expenses are minimal under normal circumstances, the Mexican tax is almost certain to reach net gain. Thus, the levy meets the net income test even though it allows no deductions.

---

The predominant character of a foreign tax is not that of an income tax under U.S. principles to the extent the foreign tax depends on the availability of an FTC in the United States.[48] Known as a **soak-up tax**, foreign jurisdictions may design such levies to absorb as much tax revenue as possible without increasing the payer's tax burden. When they work as intended, soak-up taxes drain tax revenues from the home country into the host country's treasury.

---

## EXAMPLE

Under Uruguayan law, a 30 percent withholding tax applies to dividend and branch profit remittances only to the extent recipients receive an

---

[46]*Bank of America National Trust and Savings Association v. U.S.*, 459 F.2d 513 (Ct.Cl., 1972). If the bank had not been subject to the general income tax in one or more of the countries, the additional business taxes paid in such jurisdictions may have been creditable as taxes paid in lieu of the income tax. See Reg. §1.901-2(b)(4)(iv)Ex.(1), (2).

[47]PricewaterhouseCoopers, *Individual Taxes: Worldwide Summaries 2002–2003* (Hoboken, NJ: John Wiley & Sons, Inc., 2002), p. 326. See Reg. §1.901-2(b)(4)(iv)Ex.(3), (4).

[48]Reg. §1.901-2(c)(1).

FTC in their home countries.[49] Consider a U.S. corporation conducting business in Uruguay that earns and remits a $100 profit. As intended to apply, a Uruguayan withholding agent withholds $30, which the U.S. corporation claims as an FTC on its U.S. return. Assuming a 35 percent U.S. income tax rate, the U.S. corporation incurs a $35 U.S. income tax but claims a $30 FTC. Thus, the U.S. corporation pays $30 to Uruguay and $5 to the United States; the withholding tax does not affect the company's worldwide tax. It only shifts $30 of tax revenue from the United States to Uruguay. However, this is not the outcome. As a soak-up tax, the United States disallows an FTC for this levy. Since Uruguayan withholding agents collect the tax only from persons entitled to a home country credit, no withholding occurs, and the U.S. corporation pays $35 income tax to the United States.

### Substitution for Income Tax

Foreign government levies not qualifying as income taxes are still creditable if they are taxes (as previously defined) and act as substitutes for a generally imposed income tax. Unlike income taxes, substitute taxes need not meet the realization, gross receipts, or net income requirements. Thus, the taxable base of a substitute tax can be gross receipts, gross income, units extracted or exported, or anything else.[50] Substitute taxes are creditable:

- When they apply in lieu of an income tax and
- To the extent they do not act as soak-up taxes (as explained earlier).[51]

Substitute taxes often apply to specified taxpayers (e.g., nonresidents) or activities (e.g., oil extraction, construction, insurance, and banking) and often exist when circumstances make net income difficult to measure or verify. To qualify as substitute taxes, taxpayers cannot be subject to such taxes and the generally imposed income tax on the same activities. The fact that a substitute tax may represent a greater (or lesser) economic burden than the general income tax does not matter.[52] Withholding taxes on divi-

---

[49]PricewaterhouseCoopers, *Corporate Taxes: Worldwide Summaries 2002–2003* (Hoboken, NJ: John Wiley & Sons, Inc., 2002), p. 915. See Rev. Rul. 87-39, 1987-1 CB 180, and, in the case of Costa Rican withholding tax, Rev. Rul. 2003-8, 2003-3 IRB 290.

[50]Reg. §1.903-1(a).

[51]Reg. §1.903-1(b)(1), (2).

[52]Reg. §1.903-1(b)(1).

dends, royalties, and interest received are the most common types of substitute taxes.

---

**EXAMPLE**

Alicia, a U.S. citizen, receives $1,000 dividends from Shamrock Enterprises, Ltd., an Irish corporation. Irish residents pay income tax on dividends they receive.[53] However, in lieu of the Irish income tax, Article 10(2)(b) of the U.S.-Irish Treaty imposes a 15 percent withholding tax on gross dividends nonresidents, such as Alicia, receive. Arguably, the withholding amount itself is an income tax since it clearly meets the realization and gross receipts tests. In addition, the withholding tax might meet the net income test. Even though it permits no deductions against dividend income, one might contend that it almost certainly reaches some net gain under normal circumstances since costs and expenses of earning dividend income often are nominal. However, even if the withholding tax fails the net income test, it still qualifies as a substitute tax and, thus, is creditable.

---

**EXAMPLE**

Freedom & Security Life, Inc., a U.S. corporation, conducts two businesses in Barbados—consulting and life insurance. Barbados taxes Freedom & Security's consulting profits under its generally imposed income tax at 40 percent. In contrast, Barbados exempts Freedom & Security's insurance profits from the income tax but imposes a 5 percent "gross direct premium tax" instead.[54] If the gross direct premium levy qualifies as a tax (other than the soak-up variety), it is a creditable payment since it substitutes for the general income tax.

---

Substitute taxes must apply instead of, not in addition to, a generally imposed income tax to be creditable. Implicit in this requirement is the existence of an income tax. Countries not imposing an income tax cannot have a tax substituting for an income tax, by definition.

---

[53]PricewaterhouseCoopers, *Corporate Taxes: Worldwide Summaries 2002–2003* (Hoboken, NJ: John Wiley & Sons, Inc., 2002), p. 221.
[54]Ibid., p. 42.

---

**EXAMPLE**

---

Dubai does not impose a general income tax. However, it does impose a 55 percent tax on oil profits and a 20 percent tax on banking income.[55] Absent a generally imposed income tax, neither the oil tax nor the bank tax qualifies as substitute taxes. To be creditable, the oil and bank taxes must meet the realization, gross receipts, and net income tests.

---

Exhibit 11.2 summarizes the rules for determining whether a foreign government levy qualifies as a creditable tax under U.S. law.

## DEEMED PAID TAXES

The Code allows U.S. persons an FTC for creditable taxes they pay or incur directly or that others withhold. Thus, U.S. citizens and residents can elect an FTC for either their own creditable taxes or their share of creditable taxes through fiscally transparent entities, such as partnerships or S corporations, in which they hold interests. Similarly, U.S. corporations claim an FTC for creditable taxes they pay on foreign branch profits and their share of partnership profits. U.S. individuals and corporations also can credit foreign withholding taxes on dividends, royalties, and interest they receive.

In addition to direct and withholding taxes, U.S. law permits an FTC when domestic C corporations pay foreign taxes indirectly. Specifically, the Code grants domestic C corporations an FTC for creditable taxes their foreign subsidiaries pay.[56] Professionals often refer to these creditable taxes as **deemed paid taxes (DPTs)** and the resulting benefit as a **deemed paid credit (DPC)**. However, U.S. law treats DPTs the same as other creditable taxes; and the DPC is not separate from the FTC but a part of it. Thus, a domestic C corporation's creditable taxes equal the sum of foreign income taxes directly paid (e.g., through branch activities), foreign taxes paid in lieu of a generally imposed income tax (e.g., dividend withholding taxes), and DPTs.[57] Equation 11.2 highlights this point:

---

[55]Ibid., p. 888.

[56]Reg. §1.902-1(a)(1). In this section, the term "subsidiary" is used in a very broad sense. It does not necessarily refer to a foreign corporation that its domestic parent company controls. The ownership requirement discussed later makes this clear.

[57]One finds the authority for these three sources of creditable taxes in IRC §§901, 903, and 902, respectively.

$$\text{Creditable taxes} = \text{FIT} + \text{Taxes in lieu of FIT} + \text{DPT} \qquad (11.2)$$

where:

FIT = Foreign income taxes paid or incurred
DPT = Deemed paid taxes (allowed only for domestic C
corporations)

**EXHIBIT 11.2** Determining Whether a Foreign Government Levy Is Creditable

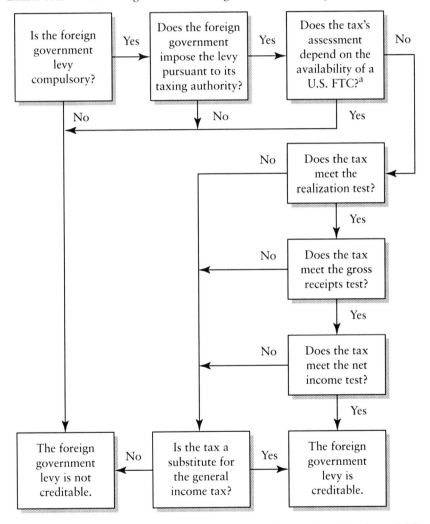

[a]If the taxpayer demonstrates that some portion of the tax does not depend on the availability of an FTC in the United States, that portion still may be creditable.

**PLANNING POINTER:** The Code does not permit U.S. shareholders other than domestic C corporations to claim foreign income taxes foreign corporations pay as DPTs. Thus, U.S. individuals, partnerships, and S corporations owning stock in a foreign corporation derive no FTC from creditable taxes the foreign entity pays. However, as Chapter 1 explained, check-the-box regulations allow many foreign corporations to elect treatment as partnerships (i.e., multiple-owner, hybrid entities) or branches (i.e., disregarded hybrid entities, or "tax nothings"). If made, the election permits U.S. individuals owning the corporation's stock to claim an FTC under flow-through procedures as though paid directly or through a fiscally transparent entity.

---

### EXAMPLE

Mercer, a U.S. citizen, owns all the stock of Rambler, Inc., an S corporation, which, in turn, owns all the stock of Duryea SARL, a French subsidiary. Neither Mercer nor Rambler can claim an FTC for foreign income tax Duryea pays since neither is a domestic C corporation.

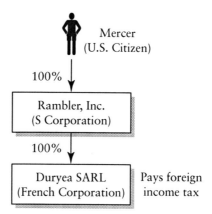

However, under check-the-box regulations, Duryea can elect treatment as a branch of Rambler for U.S. tax purposes. The election permits the flow-through of creditable taxes to Rambler, which itself is a fiscally transparent entity, and Mercer.

---

Congress enacted the DPC to provide parity between U.S. corporations operating abroad in branch form and those establishing foreign subsidiaries.

Domestic corporations can claim creditable taxes their branches pay since branches are mere extensions of the corporate identity rather than separate taxable entities. The DPC extends similar treatment to U.S. corporations with foreign subsidiaries. Absent the DPC, U.S. corporations could not claim creditable taxes their foreign subsidiaries pay and, thus, would experience some double taxation on the same income. As a result, U.S. multinationals would operate abroad with fewer foreign subsidiaries. In fact, given the legal liability exposure accompanying the use of foreign branches, fewer U.S. companies likely would conduct foreign business if the DPC did not exist. Fortunately, the DPC remedies the disparate tax treatment and double tax exposure otherwise resulting and, thus, encourages direct investment abroad and facilitates international commerce.

The DPC allows U.S. corporations to claim creditable taxes their foreign subsidiaries pay. In looking through foreign subsidiaries and attributing their foreign taxes to domestic parent companies, U.S. law treats foreign subsidiaries similarly to foreign branches. Consistent with the DPC, the Code also requires U.S. corporations to include an amount equal to their DPTs in gross income. In effect, U.S. corporations must **gross up** dividends they receive for any foreign income tax that foreign subsidiaries pay.[58] The combination of allowing DPTs to qualify for the FTC and requiring U.S. corporations to gross up dividends is economically equivalent to U.S. corporations earning foreign profits themselves and paying related foreign income taxes directly. In effect, the gross-up procedure treats a domestic parent as though it receives sufficient funds from a foreign subsidiary, in addition to actual dividends, to pay the subsidiary's taxes itself. The U.S. company includes the hypothetical receipt of funds in gross income, just like actual dividends.

---

## EXAMPLE

Grate Expectations, Inc., a U.S. corporation, wishes to expand its fireplace supply business into Hostia (a hypothetical country). To simplify the illustration, assume Hostia's income tax rates are identical to U.S. rates, the company will remit all foreign profits each year, and no dividend withholding tax or branch profits tax applies. Grate Expectations forecasts $1 million Hostian profits each year. The results for the first year appear in the following table. The first two columns show the outcomes when Grate Expectations conducts business abroad through a

---

[58]IRC §78; Reg. §1.78-1(d).

branch or subsidiary. The worldwide tax is the same for each alternative ($340,000). The last column shows the disparity resulting if the
Code does not allow a DPC or if a foreign corporation does not qualify
its U.S. parent for the DPC. In effect, the absence of a DPC causes taxation of $660,000 foreign profits twice.

### Choice of Foreign Business Entity

| | Branch | Subsidiary with DPC | Subsidiary without DPC |
|---|---|---|---|
| a. Foreign profits | $1,000,000 | $1,000,000 | $1,000,000 |
| b. Foreign tax rate | × .34 | × .34 | × .34 |
| c. Foreign income tax | $ 340,000 | $ 340,000 | $ 340,000 |
| d. Dividends (line a less line c) | | $ 660,000 | $ 660,000 |
| e. Gross up (from line c) | | 340,000 | 0 |
| f. U.S. taxable income | $1,000,000 | $1,000,000 | $ 660,000 |
| g. U.S. tax rate | × .34 | × .34 | × .34 |
| h. U.S. tax before FTC | $ 340,000 | $ 340,000 | $ 224,400 |
| i. FTC (from line c) | 340,000 | 340,000 | 0 |
| j. U.S. tax liability | $        0 | $        0 | $ 224,400 |
| k. Worldwide tax (line c plus line j) | $ 340,000 | $ 340,000 | $ 564,400 |

U.S. law allows domestic corporations to claim DPTs for foreign income
tax that first-tier through sixth-tier foreign subsidiaries pay. To qualify, the
corporate group must satisfy both ownership and dividend requirements.
The ownership requirement contains direct, indirect, and control ownership
components, as the following rules explain:

- Domestic corporations must own at least 10 percent of a first-tier foreign subsidiary's voting stock directly. To obtain DPTs for foreign income taxes its second-tier subsidiary pays, the parent company's
  first-tier entity must own at least 10 percent of the second-tier sub-

sidiary's voting stock. This direct ownership requirement applies at each level of the chain through the sixth-tier foreign subsidiary.[59] If a foreign subsidiary does not directly own the requisite 10 percent, the U.S. parent company receives no DPTs from foreign subsidiaries below the break in the chain.

- The U.S. parent company must own at least 5 percent of the voting stock of second-tier through sixth-tier foreign subsidiaries indirectly.[60] For instance, to determine whether the U.S. parent owns the requisite 5 percent of a third-tier foreign subsidiary, the parent must multiply its ownership percentage in its first-tier subsidiary by the first-tier subsidiary's ownership percentage in the second-tier subsidiary by the second-tier subsidiary's ownership percentage in the third-tier subsidiary. If the result is less than 5 percent, the U.S. parent does not meet the indirect ownership requirement and, thus, cannot obtain DPTs from its third-tier foreign subsidiary. Further, the U.S. parent cannot obtain DPTs from any other foreign subsidiary in the chain below the break.
- The control requirement applies only to fourth- through sixth-tier foreign subsidiaries. In addition to the direct and indirect ownership requirements, these lower-tier entities must qualify as controlled foreign corporations (CFCs), and U.S. parent companies must be U.S. shareholders of such CFCs.[61] As Chapter 12 explains, CFCs are foreign corporations U.S. shareholders control through direct, indirect, or constructive ownership exceeding 50 percent of either the stock's value or voting power. U.S. shareholders include U.S. persons directly, indirectly, or constructively owning at least 10 percent of the CFC's voting power.

Exhibit 11.3 summarizes the direct, indirect, and control ownership requirements a U.S. parent corporation must meet to qualify for a DPC. If the corporate group fails to meet the ownership requirement at any level, the U.S. parent cannot claim a DPC for foreign income tax of subsidiaries below the ownership break.

> **PLANNING POINTER:** As Chapter 1 explained, foreign corporations can elect treatment as hybrid entities. Since U.S. law does not permit DPCs for foreign income tax that seventh- or lower-tier foreign entities pay, such entities should elect to become hybrid entities (i.e., partnerships or branches) for U.S. tax purposes. The election treats sixth-tier entities as though they pay the lower-tier entities' foreign

---

[59]IRC §902(b)(1).
[60]IRC §902(b)(2)(B).
[61]See the flush language following IRC §902(b)(2)(B).

**EXHIBIT 11.3** Ownership Requirements for Deemed Paid Credit

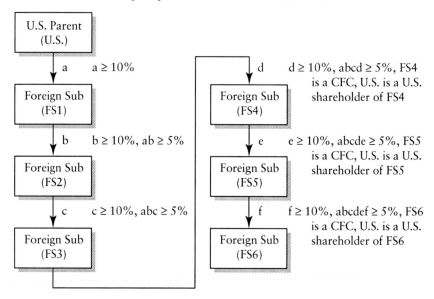

income taxes directly and, thus, preserves FTCs for the U.S. parent company.

In addition to the ownership requirements, domestic parents must receive dividends from their foreign subsidiaries to be eligible for the DPC. In effect, a proportionate amount of a subsidiary's foreign income tax accompanies each dividend. Specifically, U.S. law treats a domestic corporation as paying post-1986 foreign income taxes its foreign subsidiary actually pays in proportion to the percentage of the subsidiary's post-1986 earnings and profit it receives.[62] Equation 11.3 expresses the calculation:

$$\text{DPT} = \frac{\begin{array}{c}\text{Dividends received}\\ \text{from foreign subsidiary}\end{array}}{\begin{array}{c}\text{Post - 1986 earnings}\\ \text{of foreign subsidiary}\end{array}} \times \begin{array}{c}\text{Post - 1986}\\ \text{foreign income taxes}\end{array} \qquad (11.3)$$

A similar calculation determines the DPTs of first- through fifth-tier subsidiaries based on the foreign income tax of second- through sixth-tier

---

[62]IRC §902(a). While IRC §902 allows a DPC related to an actual dividend, IRC §960 provides for a DPC based on a constructive dividend, a topic that Chapter 12 discusses.

subsidiaries. Thus, dividends represent the mechanism through which foreign income taxes move up the ownership chain and eventually reach the U.S. parent company. As equation 11.2 indicates, the domestic corporation sums its DPT with foreign income taxes it pays directly or has withheld to arrive at total creditable taxes.

---

## EXAMPLE

A domestic corporation owns all the stock of a Finnish corporation that, in turn, owns all the stock of an Australian corporation. The Australian company earns $50,000, pays Australian income taxes of $16,000, and distributes $25,500 of its after-tax profit to the Finnish company. Thus, U.S. law treats the Finnish corporation as paying Australian income taxes of $12,000, calculated as:

$$\frac{\$25,500}{\$50,000 - \$16,000} \times \$16,000 = \$12,000$$

The Finnish corporation earns operating profits of $100,000, pays Finnish income taxes of $28,000, and distributes $58,500 of its after-tax profit to the domestic parent company. Thus, U.S. law treats the domestic parent as though it pays Finnish and Australian income taxes of $24,000, calculated as:

$$\frac{\$58,500}{\$100,000 + \$25,500 - \$28,000} \times (\$28,000 + \$12,000) = \$24,000$$

As the calculation shows, the Finnish corporation's post-1986 earnings include the $25,500 dividend from its Australian subsidiary. Also, the procedure treats the $12,000 taxes the Finnish subsidiary is deemed to pay as taxes it actually pays when computing the domestic parent's DPT. As a result of the dividends, the U.S. parent company reports the following changes:

| | |
|---|---:|
| Dividends received | $58,500 |
| Gross up of dividends | 24,000 |
| Increase in taxable income | $82,500 |
| U.S. tax rate | × 35% |
| Increase in U.S. tax before the FTC | $28,875 |
| DPC (if not limited) | 24,000 |
| Increase in U.S. tax | $ 4,875 |

## LIMITATION FORMULA

The FTC allows U.S. persons to offset creditable taxes against their U.S. tax liabilities. Thus, the credit mitigates the effect of double taxation on foreign source income that both the United States and a foreign jurisdiction otherwise might fully tax and fosters capital export neutrality. U.S. persons can claim an FTC for the lesser of: (1) creditable taxes paid or incurred, as equation 11.2 defined, or (2) the result of the limitation formula appearing below as equation 11.4:[63]

$$\text{Limitation} = \frac{\text{Foreign source taxable income}}{\text{Worldwide taxable income}} \times \begin{array}{c}\text{U.S. tax before}\\\text{the FTC}\end{array} \qquad (11.4)$$

Congress did not intend for creditable foreign taxes to offset U.S. taxes on U.S. source income since the FTC's purpose is not to shield taxes on domestic income. Though the FTC directly reduces the U.S. income tax, the limitation assures that the FTC does not reduce U.S. taxes on U.S. source income. Thus, U.S. law permits the FTC to offset only U.S. taxes imposed on foreign source income. Rearranging terms in equation 11.4 to yield equation 11.5 clarifies this purpose:

$$\text{Limitation} = \frac{\text{U.S. tax before the FTC}}{\text{Worldwide taxable income}} \times \begin{array}{c}\text{Foreign source}\\\text{taxable income}\end{array} \qquad (11.5)$$

Since the "U.S. tax before the FTC" in equation 11.4 is the product of worldwide taxable income and the U.S. tax rate, international specialists often shorten the limitation formula as in equation 11.6. The shortened version assumes the user knows the effective U.S. tax rate; progressive tax rates, phase-out rules, and other rate-altering provisions can cause the effective U.S. tax rate to differ from the top statutory tax rate. Thus, one should rely on equation 11.6 with this proviso in mind.

$$\text{Limitation} = \text{Foreign source taxable income} \times \text{U.S. tax rate} \qquad (11.6)$$

---

[63]The parenthetical language in IRC §904(a) clarifies that the formula's ratio cannot exceed 1. Though domestic losses do not cause the ratio to exceed 1, they do reduce "U.S. tax before the FTC" and, thus, the overall limitation. Also, IRC §904(b)(2) requires special adjustments to the formula for differential rates applicable to capital gains and losses. Similarly, IRC §1(h)(11)(C)(iv) requires special adjustments for dividends U.S. individuals receive taxed at capital gain rates, including those from companies incorporated in U.S. possessions and treaty countries.

## EXAMPLE

Boilerplate Docs, a domestic corporation, earns $70,000 of U.S. source income and $30,000 of foreign source income. The U.S. and foreign effective tax rates applicable to this income are 35 and 40 percent, respectively. The following table shows how Boilerplate calculates its tax liabilities:

|  | *Domestic* | *Foreign* | *Worldwide* |
|---|---|---|---|
| Taxable income | $ 70,000 | $ 30,000 | $100,000 |
| Applicable tax rates |  | × .40 | × .35 |
| Foreign income tax |  | $ 12,000 |  |
| U.S. tax before the FTC |  |  | $ 35,000 |
| FTC (see limit in the equation following) |  |  | 10,500 |
| U.S. income tax |  |  | $ 24,500 |

Boilerplate's U.S. tax before the FTC of $35,000 is actually a U.S. tax of $24,500 on the U.S. source income ($70,000 × 35%) and a U.S. tax of $10,500 on the foreign source income ($30,000 × 35%). Ignoring the limitation formula for a moment, Boilerplate takes an FTC for the $12,000 foreign income tax it pays. However, claiming the entire $12,000 allows foreign taxes it pays to offset not only the $10,500 of U.S. tax on foreign source income but also $1,500 of U.S. tax on U.S. source income ($12,000 − $10,500). To prevent unintended benefits, equation 11.4 (or 11.6) limits the FTC to U.S. taxes on foreign source income as:

$$\frac{\$30,000}{\$100,000} \times \$35,000 \text{ or } \$30,000 \times 35\% = \$10,500$$

The FTC's limitation formula uses taxable, not gross, income as defined under U.S. law. Thus, following the allocation and apportionment rules given in Chapter 5, apportioned deductions reduce foreign source gross income in the numerator while all deductible expenses reduce total gross income in the denominator. Taxpayers apportion itemized deductions and the standard deduction to foreign source income on a gross income basis.[64]

---

[64]Reg. §1.861-8(e)(11).

Individuals do not subtract personal and dependency exemptions from gross income in either the numerator or the denominator.[65]

---

### EXAMPLE

Josiah, an unmarried U.S. citizen, works 10 months in the United States and 2 months abroad. Of his $80,000 salary, he derives 10 percent from foreign services. Josiah pays no deductible expenses and receives no other income. Assuming a $4,700 standard deduction and a $3,000 personal exemption, equation 11.4 determines Josiah's FTC limit as:

$$\frac{\$8,000 - (10\% \text{ of } \$4,700)}{\$80,000 - \$4,700} \times \text{U.S. tax on } (\$80,000 - \$4,700 - \$3,000)$$

---

**PLANNING POINTER:**   To increase the FTC, U.S. persons often intermingle or **cross-credit** low-taxed foreign income with high-taxed foreign income. Cross-crediting allows taxpayers to combine foreign income and creditable taxes across countries, across years (within the carryover period explained next), and across types of income (within the baskets discussed later).

---

### EXAMPLE

Pegasean Publishers Company, a domestic corporation, earns $700,000 U.S. source income. It also earns $200,000 profit from business sales in foreign country A, on which it pays a foreign tax of $80,000 (a 40 percent rate) and $100,000 profit from business sales in foreign country B, on which it pays a foreign tax of $20,000 (a 20 percent rate). If the Code did not allow cross-crediting between countries, Pegasean would determine its tax liability as follows:

|                        | *Country A* | *Country B* | *United States* |
|------------------------|-------------|-------------|-----------------|
| Taxable income         | $200,000    | $100,000    | $1,000,000      |
| Applicable tax rates   | × .40       | × .20       | × .34           |
| Foreign income tax     | $ 80,000    | $ 20,000    |                 |

---

[65]IRC §904(b)(1).

| | | | |
|---|---|---|---|
| U.S. tax before the FTC | | | $ 340,000 |
| FTC limits (equation 11.6) | $ 68,000 | $ 34,000 | |
| FTC ($68,000 + $20,000) | | | 88,000 |
| U.S. income tax | | | $ 252,000 |

This procedure determines the FTC separately for each country and sums the amounts to obtain an overall FTC. In country A, the limitation formula prevents an FTC for $12,000 of the creditable taxes, but the country B limitation does not constrain the FTC. To lower its U.S. income tax, Pegasean can cross-credit (i.e., combine) the results from countries A and B, as follows:

| | *Countries A and B* | *United States* |
|---|---|---|
| Taxable income | $300,000 | $1,000,000 |
| U.S. tax rate | | × .34 |
| Foreign income tax | $100,000 | |
| U.S. tax before the FTC | | $ 340,000 |
| FTC limit (equation 11.6) | $102,000 | |
| FTC ($80,000 + $20,000) | | 100,000 |
| U.S. income tax | | $ 240,000 |

When cross-crediting, the equation 11.6 result exceeds creditable taxes. Thus, the FTC increases from $88,000 to $100,000, and the U.S. income tax declines from $252,000 to $240,000. In effect, cross-crediting averages high-taxed and low-taxed foreign income.

When calculating the alternative minimum tax (AMT), the taxpayer substitutes the tentative minimum tax and alternative minimum taxable income (AMTI) in the FTC limitation equation, as follows:[66]

$$\text{AMT limit} = \frac{\text{Foreign AMTI}}{\text{Worldwide AMTI}} \times \frac{\text{Tentative minimum tax}}{\text{before the FTC}} \qquad (11.7)$$

Since applying the source rules, given in Chapter 4, to AMTI can be complex, electing taxpayers replace the numerator's foreign AMTI with for-

---

[66]IRC §59(a)(1).

eign source taxable income.[67] The FTC for AMT purposes equals the lesser of creditable taxes and the AMT limitation, per equation 11.7, subject to one additional restriction. The allowable FTC cannot exceed 90 percent of the taxpayer's tentative minimum tax before the FTC.[68]

## Excess Credits and Limits

When the limitation restricts the FTC, the amount by which the creditable taxes (equation 11.2) exceed the limitation (equation 11.4) is an **excess credit**. In contrast, when the limitation exceeds creditable taxes, the result is an **excess limit**. Equations summarize these concepts.

$$\text{Excess credit} = \text{Creditable taxes} - \text{Limitation} \qquad (11.8)$$

$$\text{Excess limit} = \text{Limitation} - \text{Creditable taxes} \qquad (11.9)$$

Carryover provisions permit cross-crediting (i.e., averaging high-taxed and low-taxed income) across years. Taxpayers carry excess credits back to the two preceding taxable years and treat them as creditable taxes in those years. If excess limits exist in the prior years (before considering the carry-back), taxpayers claim the excess credits they carry back as FTCs in those earlier years, resulting in a tax refund. When taxpayers cannot claim refunds for all excess credits due to insufficient excess limits in the two previous years, they carry remaining excess credits forward as creditable taxes to the next five taxable years.[69]

Taxpayers absorb excess credits from different years on a first-incurred, first-taken basis; that is, they use excess credits from earlier years before excess credits in later years.[70] Excess credits they do not absorb by the fifth succeeding year expire unused and, thus, yield no tax benefit. Taxpayers cannot deduct excess credits about to expire.[71]

---

**EXAMPLE**

Optical Illusion, Inc., a U.S. corporation, has $130,000 creditable taxes in 2004. Its 2004 limitation, using equation 11.4, equals $80,000. Thus,

---

[67]IRC §59(a)(4).
[68]IRC §59(a)(2).
[69]IRC §904(c).
[70]Reg. §1.904-2(c)(2).
[71]Reg. §1.904-2(a).

the company has a $50,000 excess credit in 2004. Optical's FTC positions for the eight-year window applicable to 2004 (before considering carryovers) are:

|  | *Excess Credits* | *Excess Limits* |
|---|---|---|
| 2002 |  | $10,000 |
| 2003 |  | 25,000 |
| 2004 | $50,000 |  |
| 2005 | 5,000 |  |
| 2006 | 5,000 |  |
| 2007 | 15,000 |  |
| 2008 | 2,000 |  |
| 2009 |  | 12,000 |

Optical first carries its $50,000 excess credit from 2004 back to 2002 and 2003, resulting in a combined $35,000 tax refund. The remaining $15,000 excess credit from 2004 carries forward to 2009 (the next year with an excess limit) and reduces 2009 income tax by $12,000. The remaining $3,000 excess credit from 2004 expires unused; U.S. law does not permit Optical to deduct the $3,000.

The limitation formula restricts the FTC when the foreign effective tax rate exceeds the U.S. effective rate. Thus, income taxed at high foreign rates generates excess credits. Since the foreign tax on such income exceeds the U.S. tax due on a similar amount of domestic income, tax professionals view unused excess credits as a form of double taxation.[72] Persistent excess credits increase the attractiveness of investing in low-tax countries since the cross-crediting possibilities allow taxpayers to absorb excess credits and, thus, increase expected after-tax profits from the incremental income.

**PLANNING POINTER:** To use excess credits, taxpayers seek ways to generate low-taxed foreign source income. As Chapter 4 indicated, export sales result in foreign source income. Since most foreign jurisdictions do not tax such income, exporting represents one way to

---

[72]Double taxation can result for two other reasons: (1) the source of income rules, given in Chapter 4, classify income as U.S. source but the foreign host country taxes it, and (2) allocation and apportionment rules, given in Chapter 5, apportion expenses against foreign source income but the foreign host country does not allow a deduction.

absorb excess credits. Another way to generate low-taxed foreign source income is to make new foreign investments in low-tax countries or in countries offering tax holidays. However, nontax factors often dominate decisions about direct investment abroad. Though U.S. multinationals consider taxes to be significant factors in new investment decisions—and, thus, factors that should not be ignored—taxes usually do not drive such decisions.[73]

---

### EXAMPLE

For two years, Regal Regale Enterprises, Inc., a U.S. corporation, has conducted business in Belgium, a high-tax jurisdiction with a 40 percent effective rate.[74] As a result, its annual excess credits total $40,000. Regal wishes to open a branch office in Hungary, where the effective tax rate is 18 percent.[75] It projects annual profits in Hungary to be $1 million. Regal determines its worldwide tax on the $1 million incremental profits as follows:

|  | *Hungary* | *United States* |
|---|---|---|
| a. Incremental taxable income | $1,000,000 | $1,000,000 |
| b. Applicable tax rates | × .18 | × .34 |
| c. Hungarian income tax | $ 180,000 | |
| d. FTC limit (equation 11.6) | 340,000 | |
| e. Excess limit (equation 11.9) | $ 160,000 | |
| f. Increased U.S. tax before FTC | | $ 340,000 |

---

[73]For example, see Robert J. Rolfe and Richard A. White, "Investors' Assessment of the Importance of Tax Incentives in Locating Foreign Export-Oriented Investment: An Exploratory Study," *Journal of the American Taxation Association* 14 (Spring 1992), pp. 39–57; Thomas M. Porcano, "Factors Affecting the Foreign Direct Investment Decision of Firms from and into Major Industrialized Countries," *Multinational Business Review* 1 (Fall 1993), pp. 26–36; Haroldene Wunder, "The Effect of International Tax Policy on Business Location Decisions," *Tax Notes International* 24 (December 24, 2001), pp. 1331–1375.

[74]PricewaterhouseCoopers, *Corporate Taxes: Worldwide Summaries 2002–2003* (Hoboken, NJ: John Wiley & Sons, Inc., 2002), p. 50.

[75]Ibid., p. 317.

g. FTC (line c plus $80,000
   excess credit carryforward
   plus $40,000 excess credit
   anticipated from current
   Belgian operations)                          300,000

h. Addition to U.S. income tax           $   40,000
i. Increase in worldwide tax
   (line c plus line h)                  $  220,000

Without the $120,000 excess credits from the current and two pre-
ceding years, Regal's FTC would have been only $180,000 (rather than
$300,000), and worldwide tax would have risen $340,000 (rather than
$220,000). Thus, the excess credits from existing Belgian activities cre-
ated an incentive to conduct business in Hungary, a low-tax jurisdiction. Assuming profit levels remain constant, future excess limits in
Hungary will continue to absorb the annual $40,000 excess credits
Regal expects from Belgian operations.

Low-taxed foreign profits result in a **residual U.S. tax.** That is, the taxpayer pays the United States the difference between foreign and U.S. effective tax rates on foreign source income. The residual tax becomes payable
whenever the United States recognizes the foreign profits as gross income.

### EXAMPLE

Rap Recording Artists, Inc., a domestic corporation, earns $1 million
through a sales branch in Taiwan, which taxes income at a 25 percent
rate.[76] The following table summarizes the company's tax liabilities:

|                                    | *Taiwan*    | *United States* |
|------------------------------------|-------------|-----------------|
| a. Incremental taxable income      | $1,000,000  | $1,000,000      |
| b. Applicable tax rates            | × .25       | × .34           |
| c. Taiwanese income tax            | $  250,000  |                 |
| d. FTC limit (equation 11.6)       | 340,000     |                 |
| e. Excess limit (equation 11.9)    | $   90,000  |                 |

---

[76]Ibid., p. 835.

| | |
|---|---|
| f. U.S. tax on foreign income before FTC | $ 340,000 |
| g. FTC (lesser of line c or line d) | 250,000 |
| h. Residual U.S. income tax | $ 90,000 |

After paying $250,000 income tax to Taiwan, Rap pays a residual U.S. tax of $90,000 since the U.S. effective rate exceeds the Taiwanese effective rate.

The limitation formula does not restrict the FTC when the U.S. effective tax rate exceeds the foreign effective tax rate. Thus, conducting business abroad in low-tax countries yields excess limits. Tax professionals view excess limits as additional capacity to absorb creditable taxes. Thus, persistent excess limits increase the attractiveness of making new investments in or shifting existing investments to high-tax locations. As mentioned before, nontax factors often drive foreign investment decisions, but strategic plans should not ignore tax incentives.

## EXAMPLE

Assume Rap Recording Artists in the prior example has operated in Taiwan for several years and that its annual excess limit equals $90,000. The excess limit increases the attractiveness of establishing a new sales branch in Belgium, where the effective tax rate is 40 percent.[77] Based on projected Belgian profits of $10 million, the tax results are:

| | *Belgium* | *United States* |
|---|---|---|
| a. Incremental taxable income | $10,000,000 | $10,000,000 |
| b. Applicable tax rates | × .40 | × .34 |
| c. Belgian income tax | $ 4,000,000 | |
| d. FTC limit (equation 11.6 for Belgian branch plus $90,000 excess limit from Taiwanese branch) | 3,490,000 | |
| e. Excess credit (equation 11.8) | $ 510,000 | |

[77]Ibid., p. 50.

| | |
|---|---|
| f. Increased U.S. tax before FTC | $ 3,400,000 |
| g. FTC related to new Belgian branch (lesser of lines c and d) | 3,490,000 |
| h. Reduction in current U.S. income tax | $ 90,000 |
| i. Excess limit in two prior years from Taiwanese branch | $ 180,000 |
| j. U.S. tax refund (lesser of lines e and i) | $ 180,000 |
| k. Increase in worldwide tax (line c less line h less line j) | $ 3,730,000 |

Without the $270,000 excess limits from the current and two preceding years, Rap's FTC would have been only $3,400,000 (rather than $3,490,000), Rap would not have received the $180,000 U.S. tax refund, and worldwide tax would have increased $4,000,000 (rather than $3,730,000). Thus, the excess limits from existing Taiwanese activities created an incentive to conduct business in Belgium, a high-tax jurisdiction. Assuming profit levels remain constant, future excess limits in Taiwan will continue to absorb up to $90,000 of the excess credits Rap expects from Belgian operations.

## Marginal Tax Rates

U.S. persons with foreign investment or business activities may view their foreign profit as incremental income, particularly when deciding whether to make or continue a direct investment abroad. The marginal tax rate (MTR) applicable to incremental foreign profit is an important factor in the investment decision. The higher of the foreign and U.S. effective tax rates often approximates the MTR on foreign income. Ignoring the possibility of cross-crediting for the moment, conducting business in a high-tax foreign jurisdiction results in an MTR equal to the foreign rate. Conversely, doing business in low-tax countries causes the MTR to equal the U.S. tax rate. Equation 11.10 summarizes this principle for a U.S. company conducting business through a foreign branch:

$$MTR = \max{(t_{us}, t_f)} \qquad (11.10)$$

where:

$t_{us}$ = effective U.S. income tax rate
$t_f$ = effective foreign income tax rate

---

## EXAMPLE

Achilles Heel, Inc., a domestic corporation, manufactures and sells fine footwear in the United States. To expand its market, Achilles plans to establish a selling branch in either the Ukraine or Pakistan, where the effective tax rates are 30 and 45 percent, respectively.[78] The company projects taxable income of $10 million next year, 10 percent of which it expects to derive from foreign sources. Thus, $1 million is the incremental taxable income. Achilles determines its MTR on $1 million earned in the Ukraine, a low-tax country, as follows:

|  | *Ukraine* | *Worldwide* |
|---|---|---|
| Incremental income | $1,000,000 | $1,000,000 |
| Applicable tax rates | × .30 | × .34 |
| Foreign income tax | $ 300,000 | |
| U.S. tax before the FTC |  | $ 340,000 |
| FTC (equation 11.6) |  | 300,000 |
| U.S. income tax |  | $ 40,000 |
| Foreign income tax |  | 300,000 |
| Worldwide tax |  | $ 340,000 |
| MTR (worldwide tax ÷ incremental income) |  | 34% |

The company determines its MTR on $1 million earned in Pakistan, a high-tax country, as follows:

|  | *Pakistan* | *Worldwide* |
|---|---|---|
| Incremental income | $1,000,000 | $1,000,000 |
| Applicable tax rates | × .45 | × .34 |
| Foreign income tax | $ 450,000 | |
| U.S. tax before the FTC |  | $ 340,000 |
| FTC (equation 11.6) |  | 340,000 |
| U.S. income tax |  | $ 0 |

---

[78]Ibid., pp. 630, 881.

| | |
|---|---:|
| Foreign income tax | 450,000 |
| Worldwide tax | $ 450,000 |
| MTR (worldwide tax ÷ incremental income) | 45% |

Equation 11.10 yields results consistent with the 34 and 45 percent MTRs calculated.

The preceding example ignores the possibility of cross-crediting within or, through excess credit carryovers, across years. Cross-crediting allows U.S. companies to average low-taxed and high-taxed income so that the overall FTC increases and U.S. income tax declines. The resulting MTR falls between the effective tax rates in the United States and the high-tax jurisdiction.

## EXAMPLE

Assume Achilles Heel in the prior example establishes branch operations in both the Ukraine and Pakistan and expects to earn $1 million in each country. The company determines its MTR on the incremental $2 million earned abroad as follows:

| | *Ukraine* | *Pakistan* | *Worldwide* |
|---|---:|---:|---:|
| Incremental income | $1,000,000 | $1,000,000 | $2,000,000 |
| Applicable tax rates | × .30 | × .45 | × .34 |
| Foreign income tax | $ 300,000 | $ 450,000 | |
| U.S. tax before the FTC | | | $ 680,000 |
| FTC (equation 11.6) | | | 680,000 |
| U.S. income tax | | | $ 0 |
| Foreign income tax | | | 750,000 |
| Worldwide tax | | | $ 750,000 |
| MTR (worldwide tax ÷ incremental income) | | | 37.5% |

The foreign effective tax rate ($750,000 ÷ $2,000,000, or 37.5 percent) exceeds the U.S. effective tax rate of 34 percent. Thus, equation

11.10 yields a result consistent with the 37.5 percent MTR determined here. Cross-crediting results in an MTR ranging between the U.S. effective rate of 34 percent and the Pakistani effective tax rate of 45 percent. As the proportion of foreign profit derived from the high-tax jurisdiction increases, the MTR approaches 45 percent. For instance, $1 million of Ukrainian income and $3 million of Pakistani income results in an MTR of 41.25 percent.

When U.S. multinationals establish foreign subsidiaries in low-tax countries and do not currently receive dividends, the multinationals defer U.S. residual tax.[79] As a result, the present value benefit from deferring U.S. residual tax lowers the MTR. Equation 11.11 captures the impact of U.S. tax deferral for investments in low-tax jurisdictions.[80] The first term on the right-hand side is the current foreign income tax; the second term is the deferred U.S. residual income tax.

$$MTR = t_f + \frac{t_{us} - t_f}{(1 + d)^y} \qquad (11.11)$$

where:

$d$ = discount rate and

$y$ = years that company forgoes dividends and defers U.S. residual tax

Consistent with equation 11.10, currently remitting dividends (i.e., setting $y$ to 0) causes the MTR in equation 11.11 to equal the effective U.S. income tax rate.

---

[79]As Chapters 12 and 13 explain, some U.S. parent companies constructively receive dividends from certain foreign subsidiaries. As a result, they cannot defer their U.S. residual tax even though they receive no actual dividends.

[80]For this purpose, low-tax countries are those in which the effective foreign tax rate plus, on an after-tax basis, the dividend withholding tax rate does not exceed the effective U.S. tax rate. Though equation 11.11 does not explicitly consider a dividend withholding tax, the MTR result does not change since withholding taxes simply reduce U.S. residual tax. Jurisdictions in which the effective foreign tax rate plus, on an after-tax basis, the dividend withholding tax rate exceeds the effective U.S. tax rate are high-tax countries.

**EXAMPLE**

Instead of a sales branch, assume in the first Achilles Heel example that the company establishes a Ukrainian subsidiary. The subsidiary retains its first-year profits for five years before remitting them to Achilles. That example and equation 11.10 show that the MTR is 34 percent when the United States taxes the $1 million foreign profits during the year earned. However, when Achilles defers U.S. residual tax and the applicable discount rate equals 9 percent, the MTR falls to 32.6 percent on the first-year profits, per equation 11.11:

$$MTR = 0.30 + \frac{0.34 - 0.30}{(1 + 0.09)^5} = 32.6\%$$

U.S. multinationals with foreign subsidiaries in high-tax countries pay foreign income tax and dividend withholding tax, but not U.S. residual tax. When these companies defer dividend remittances, the present value of the dividend withholding tax declines. Equation 11.12 provides the MTR calculation.

$$MTR = t_f + \frac{t_{div}(1 - t_f)}{(1 + d)^y} \qquad (11.12)$$

where:

$d$ = discount rate and
$y$ = years that company forgoes dividends and defers U.S. residual tax

From a policy perspective, the closer the MTR to the U.S. effective tax rate, the more capital-export-neutral the outcome. The closer the MTR to the foreign effective tax rate, the more capital-import-neutral the result, vis-à-vis multinationals from countries where no residual home country tax results (i.e., global countries with tax rates lower than the foreign tax rate and territorial countries). Thus, the FTC mechanism tends to be capital-export-neutral for investments in low-tax countries and capital-import-neutral for investments in high-tax countries. Exhibit 11.4 summarizes the implications of conducting business in low-tax and high-tax countries.

**EXHIBIT 11.4**   Implications of Doing Business in Low- and High-Tax Jurisdictions

|  | Low-Tax Country | High-Tax Country |
| --- | --- | --- |
| Foreign ETR[a] | Below U.S. ETR | Above U.S. ETR |
| Marginal tax rate | Equals U.S. ETR | Equals foreign ETR |
| Policy tendency | Capital-export-neutral | Capital-import-neutral |
| Residual U.S. tax | When profits remitted | None |
| FTC[b] position | Excess limit | Excess credit |
| Cross-credit incentive | Seek high-tax foreign income | Seek low-tax foreign income |

[a]ETR = effective tax rate
[b]FTC = foreign tax credit

## Baskets

U.S. persons with excess credits from conducting business in high-tax jurisdictions have incentives to seek low-taxed foreign source income. The low-taxed income permits U.S. persons to absorb excess credits and, thus, shelters the existing high-taxed income through cross-crediting. The additional FTC that results decreases U.S. residual tax otherwise due from investing in the low-tax jurisdiction. Such cross-crediting strategies represent acceptable means of tax planning in many situations, particularly when the taxpayer derives the income in both jurisdictions from business activities.

However, Congress decided that unfettered opportunities for cross-crediting provided inappropriate economic incentives. Left unregulated, U.S. taxpayers might shift passive and other easily movable income from the United States to low-tax foreign jurisdictions solely for the FTC benefits. Thus, cross-crediting could result in U.S. capital flowing to low-tax jurisdictions for noneconomic reasons, hence encouraging U.S. companies to allocate global resources in suboptimal ways.

Due to these concerns, U.S. law allocates different types of foreign income among **baskets**. Each basket contains its own creditable taxes, limitation formula, and carryover periods. The Code permits taxpayers to cross-credit within, but not among, baskets. Thus, the basket approach reduces the FTC of many U.S. persons since it restricts taxpayer opportunities for cross-crediting.

U.S. law specifies separate baskets for nine types of foreign source income. Three baskets contain passive-type income, two baskets pertain to income from specific industries, and three baskets relate to export profits. Income not allocable to one of these eight baskets falls into the ninth, or **residual basket**. Unlike some countries, the United States does not require taxpayers to place income earned in different countries into separate baskets. The following listing briefly describes the nine baskets:

■ *Passive income.* This basket contains portfolio dividends, interest (other than high withholding tax interest and export financing interest), non-business rents and royalties, annuities, and certain net gains. However, U.S. persons allocate some passive income received from controlled foreign corporations based on a look-through rule discussed later. Also, the statute "kicks" passive income out of this basket if a foreign jurisdiction taxes it at more than the U.S. effective rate.[81] This **kick-out rule** prevents taxpayers from averaging high-taxed against low-taxed passive income and assures that this basket always contains an excess limit. By default, the kick-out rule consigns high-taxed passive income to the residual basket if it does not fall into another basket.

■ *High withholding tax interest.* Interest (other than export financing interest) subject to a foreign withholding rate of 5 percent or more belongs in this basket.[82] Since foreign jurisdictions apply interest withholding rates to gross interest and the United States taxes interest income on a net basis, the effective rate of foreign withholding taxes (i.e., withholding tax divided by the difference between gross interest income and apportioned deductions) usually exceeds the withholding rate applicable to gross interest received. When the effective foreign rate exceeds the U.S. effective tax rate, this basket contains an excess credit. Otherwise, an excess limit results.

■ *Noncontrolled section 902 corporation dividends.* A **noncontrolled section 902 corporation** (or **10-50 company**) is a foreign corporation in which a U.S. parent company owns at least 10 percent of the voting power but no more than 50 percent of either the voting power or stock value. For taxable years beginning after 2002, dividends received from all 10-50 companies out of pre-2003 accumulated earnings fall into a single basket. For dividends received from post-2002 earnings, a look-through rule operates to allocate dividends from 10-50 companies to appropriate baskets based on the companies' underlying income.[83] The look-through rule applies only to dividends from 10-50 companies, not to other remittance forms such as interest and royalties.

---

[81]IRC §904(d)(2)(A).

[82]IRC §904(d)(2)(B).

[83]IRC §904(d)(1)(E), (2)(E), (4). For taxable years beginning before 2003, U.S. law placed dividends from each 10-50 company into a separate basket. Thus, a U.S. corporation owning seven 10-50 companies placed the dividends from these companies in seven separate baskets. Not only did this rule entail significant record-keeping burdens for U.S. multinationals, but the lack of cross-crediting opportunities discouraged many companies from seeking or holding minority positions in foreign joint ventures. IRC §904(d)(2)(E)(iv) requires that separate baskets continue for dividends from each 10-50 company qualifying as passive foreign investment companies, which Chapter 13 discusses.

- *Financial services income.* This basket contains income financial services entities derive from banking, insurance, financing, and similar activities. Financial services entities include persons deriving 80 percent or more of their gross income from specified financing activities.[84] Thus, taxpayers not predominantly engaged in financing activities do not use this basket.
- *Shipping income.* This basket includes income derived from the use, hiring for use, or leasing for use of aircraft or vessels in foreign commerce, as well as gain from disposing of such aircraft or vessels. It also includes certain income from space or ocean activities.[85] Since many shipping activities occur on the high seas where no foreign tax results and U.S. companies often register foreign shipping activities in jurisdictions imposing little or no taxes (e.g., Lebanon), this basket usually contains an excess limit.
- *Domestic international sales corporation (DISC) dividends.* U.S. law places foreign source dividends from current and former DISCs in a separate basket.[86] Discussed in Chapter 14, DISCs rarely incur foreign income tax. Thus, this basket almost always contains an excess limit and isolates DISC dividends so taxpayers cannot cross-credit them against high-taxed income in other baskets.
- *Foreign sales corporation (FSC) income.* Income attributable to an FSC's foreign trade income falls into a separate basket.[87] Since FSCs rarely pay foreign income tax, this basket contains an excess limit. In effect, taxpayers cannot average their zero-taxed foreign trade income against high-taxed income in other baskets.
- *FSC dividends.* Like DISC dividends, the Code isolates foreign source dividends from current or former FSCs in a separate basket.[88] FSC dividends hardly ever incur a foreign tax. Thus, this basket usually contains an excess limit that taxpayers cannot use to absorb excess credit in other baskets.
- *Residual income.* Also known as the **general basket** or **overall basket**, this category includes all income the other baskets do not contain.[89] Manufacturing, marketing, and service income, as well as business rents and royalties, fall into this basket. Also, this basket contains passive

---

[84]IRC §904(d)(2)(C); Reg. §1.904-4(e).
[85]IRC §904(d)(2)(D).
[86]IRC §904(d)(1)(F).
[87]IRC §904(d)(1)(G). As Chapter 14 explains, Congress repealed the FSC program in 2000. However, transition rules allow some FSC with preexisting, binding contracts to continue.
[88]IRC §904(d)(1)(H).
[89]IRC §904(d)(1)(I).

income that is "kicked out" of the passive income basket and most export financing interest.[90]

---

## EXAMPLE

Eureka Solutions, Inc., a domestic corporation, earns profit from and pays taxes on international consulting services and portfolio investments as follows:

|  | Gross Income | Taxable Income | U.S. Tax before FTC | Creditable Foreign Tax |
|---|---|---|---|---|
| U.S. operations | $ 800,000 | $ 500,000 | $170,000 | $ 0 |
| Foreign dividends | 210,000 | 200,000 | 68,000 | 21,000 |
| Foreign operations | 900,000 | 300,000 | 102,000 | 135,000 |
| Totals | $1,910,000 | $1,000,000 | $340,000 | $156,000 |

Ignoring the separate FTC baskets, equation 11.4 yields the following limitation:

$$\text{Limitation} = \frac{\$200,000 + \$300,000}{\$1,000,000} \times \$340,000 = \$170,000$$

If all Eureka's foreign profits pertain to the same basket, the company can claim an FTC for all its creditable taxes ($156,000). However, U.S. law requires Eureka to separate its foreign activities into passive and residual income baskets. The company calculates its limitation for each basket as follows:

$$\text{Limitation}_{passive} = \frac{\$200,000}{\$1,000,000} \times \$340,000 = \$68,000$$

$$\text{Limitation}_{residual} = \frac{\$300,000}{\$1,000,000} \times \$340,000 = \$102,000$$

---

[90]Approximately 75 percent of foreign income falls into the residual basket. Some policymakers question whether U.S. law needs eight baskets to account for the remaining 25 percent of foreign income. See U.S. Department of the Treasury, *International Tax Reform: An Interim Report* (January 1993), p. 20.

Thus, the FTC for the passive basket equals $21,000 (the creditable taxes), and a $47,000 excess limitation results ($68,000 limitation less $21,000 creditable taxes). The FTC for the residual basket equals $102,000 (the limitation), and a $33,000 excess credit results ($135,000 creditable taxes less $102,000 limitation). Since they pertain to separate baskets, the $47,000 excess limitation for the passive income cannot absorb the $33,000 excess credit for the business income. Eureka's FTC for the current year equals $123,000 ($21,000 + $102,000), and the company carries over its $33,000 excess credit in the residual basket.

## EXAMPLE

Impeccable Etiquette, Inc., a domestic company, trains U.S. managers to be effective business leaders when dealing with foreign executives. The company's 49-percent-owned foreign affiliate, Savoir-Faire, Ltd., provides similar training for foreign managers conducting business with U.S. executives. Impeccable receives service fees and investment income and pays taxes as follows:

|  | Gross Income | Taxable Income | U.S. Tax before FTC | Creditable Foreign Tax |
|---|---|---|---|---|
| Interest from Savoir-Faire | $ 90,000 | $ 80,000 | $ 27,200 | $ 0 |
| Dividends from Savoir-Faire[a] | 260,000 | 200,000 | 68,000 | 13,000 |
| Other interest income | 40,000 | 30,000 | 10,200 | 12,000 |
| Portfolio dividends | 55,000 | 50,000 | 17,000 | 5,500 |
| Foreign service fees | 140,000 | 40,000 | 13,600 | 15,000 |
| U.S. service fees | 950,000 | 600,000 | 204,000 | 0 |
| Totals | $1,535,000 | $1,000,000 | $340,000 | $45,500 |

[a]Assume Savoir-Faire pays these dividends from its pre-2003 earnings.

To determine its FTC, Impeccable must consider baskets for four types of income: passive, high withholding tax interest, noncontrolled section 902 corporation dividends, and residual. The limitations in each basket appear as follows:

$$\text{Limitation}_{\text{passive}} = \frac{\$80,000 + \$50,000}{\$1,000,000} \times \$340,000 = \$44,200$$

$$\text{Limitation}_{\text{high withholding}} = \frac{\$30,000}{\$1,000,000} \times \$340,000 = \$10,200$$

$$\text{Limitation}_{\text{noncontrolled}} = \frac{\$200,000}{\$1,000,000} \times \$340,000 = \$68,000$$

$$\text{Limitation}_{\text{residual}} = \frac{\$40,000}{\$1,000,000} \times \$340,000 = \$13,600$$

Thus, Impeccable's FTC equals $42,300, or the sum of $5,500 (creditable tax in the passive basket), $10,200 (limitation in the high withholding tax interest basket), $13,000 (creditable tax in the non-controlled section 902 corporation basket), and $13,600 (limitation in the residual basket). To the extent Savoir-Faire had paid dividends from post-2002 earnings, Impeccable would have allocated such dividends among various baskets based on Savoir-Faire's underlying income, rather than using the noncontrolled section 902 corporation basket.

**PLANNING POINTER:** Many U.S. multinationals' residual income baskets contain excess credits, which yield no tax benefit if unused within the carryover period. To absorb excess credits, U.S. companies often seek foreign source income subject to little or no foreign taxes. For instance, 50 percent or more of export profits usually are foreign source income but rarely attract a foreign income tax when not attributable to a permanent establishment in the importing country. Also, many U.S. treaties allow U.S. companies to remit some foreign source income as business-related royalties at low or zero foreign withholding rates while, if deductible, avoiding foreign income tax in the host country. Other ways to absorb residual basket excess credits include minimizing apportionment of deductions against foreign source income and reducing foreign income tax liability through planning techniques appropriate in the local jurisdiction.

## EXAMPLE

Medical Tech, Inc., a U.S. corporation, has $50,000 unexpired excess credits from a recently closed Japanese sales office that operated for only two years. The excess credits provide a tax incentive for Medical Tech to begin exporting some of its products to various Asian-Pacific countries directly from the United States. During the year, the company earns export profits of $200,000, half of which is foreign source taxable income under the 50-50 method discussed in Chapter 4. No foreign jurisdiction imposes an income tax on Medical Tech's export profits since the exports occur without assistance from foreign permanent establishments. The company can calculate its incremental U.S. tax and resulting MTR on export profits as follows:

| | |
|---|---:|
| a. Export profits | $200,000 |
| b. U.S. tax rate | × .34 |
| c. Incremental U.S. tax before FTC | $ 68,000 |
| d. Incremental FTC (equation 11.6) | 34,000 |
| e. Incremental U.S. tax liability | $ 34,000 |
| f. MTR on export profits (line e ÷ line a) | 17% |

Though new export profits normally incur an MTR equal to the 34 percent U.S. tax rate, the availability of excess credits from Japanese operations cuts the MTR in half for the first year. Also, the $16,000 ($50,000 − $34,000) excess credits that remain will reduce Medical Tech's MTR on export profits next year.

Based on the nine baskets discussed earlier, the residual basket appears to include oil and gas income and related taxes. However, such is not the case. Special rules apply to oil and gas income to prevent integrated oil companies from cross-crediting foreign taxes from high-tax and low-tax activities. These special rules act much like two additional baskets—one for oil and gas extraction income (often taxed heavily) and another for oil and gas refining, transportation, marketing, and other related income (often taxed lightly).[91] Companies cannot offset excess credits in the quasi-basket pertaining to oil and gas extraction against excess limits in the nonextraction quasi-basket or excess limits in any of the nine baskets discussed earlier.

---

[91]IRC §907.

To achieve parity between U.S. companies doing business abroad through foreign subsidiaries and foreign branches, the Code requires look-through treatment when U.S. companies receive otherwise passive income from controlled foreign corporations (CFCs).[92] The look-through rules apply to actual and constructive dividends, interest, nonbusiness rent, and nonbusiness royalties. Thus, U.S. persons receiving such remittances from CFCs allocate them to baskets based on each CFC's underlying profit rather than automatically placing them in passive income baskets.[93] In effect, the look-through rules treat CFCs as foreign branches when allocating income among baskets.

## EXAMPLE

Dalliance Dating Service, Inc., a domestic corporation owns all the stock of Flirtatious Follies, Ltd. Flirtatious pays a $1,000 dividend to Dalliance. Since Dalliance controls Flirtatious (a CFC), the $1,000 income must be allocated among Dalliance's baskets based on the Flirtatious E&P, from which it paid dividends. If Flirtatious pays 30 percent of the dividends from E&P attributable to passive income and the rest from E&P attributable to business profits, Dalliance includes $300 in its passive income basket and $700 in its residual basket.

### Overall Foreign Loss

U.S. companies with losses from foreign business and investment activities can deduct such losses against U.S. source income. In effect, they avoid U.S. tax on some U.S. source income. When the foreign operations turn profitable in later years, the FTC may prevent the United States from collecting U.S. tax on the earlier year's U.S. source income. To prevent this anomaly, the Code requires that U.S. persons treat foreign source income as U.S. source income to the extent of prior-year foreign losses.[94] This re-sourcing, or recapture, rule modifies the FTC outcome and allows the United States, over time, to collect U.S. tax on all U.S. source income.

---

[92]Foreign corporations in which U.S. shareholders own more than 50 percent of either the stock value or voting power are CFCs. Chapter 12 discusses CFCs.
[93]IRC §904(d)(3).
[94]IRC §904(f)(1).

## EXAMPLE

A U.S. company operates abroad under a tax structure identical to the U.S. system. All the company's foreign source income falls into the residual basket. The operating results for two years appear as follows:

|  | U.S. Source | Foreign Source | Worldwide |
|---|---|---|---|
| Net income (or loss) in 2003 | $1,000 | $-1,000 | $ 0 |
| Net income in 2004 | 1,000 | 1,000 | 2,000 |
| Total for 2003 and 2004 | $2,000 | $ 0 | $2,000 |

In 2003, the company experiences a foreign loss and, thus, pays no foreign income tax and claims no FTC. It also pays no U.S. tax since its worldwide taxable income equals zero. As a result, $1,000 of U.S. source income avoids U.S. tax, at least temporarily. In 2004, the company's foreign taxable income is $1,000 (after any allowable net operating loss deduction), resulting in $340 of foreign income tax. U.S. tax before the FTC equals $680 ($2,000 worldwide income times 34 percent). Absent the recapture rules, the company pays U.S. tax in 2004 of $340 ($680 U.S. tax less $340 creditable foreign tax). Since the U.S. taxable income over two years is $2,000, this result allows the company to avoid U.S. tax on $1,000 of U.S. income. The recapture rules correct this result and allow the United States to collect the full U.S. tax on $2,000 of U.S. taxable income. In 2004, the company recaptures (i.e., re-sources) $1,000 foreign source income as U.S. source income, leaving zero in the numerator of the FTC limitation formula. (Under rules discussed shortly, the company in this example elects to recapture 100 percent of foreign source income rather than just 50 percent.) Thus, the taxpayer's 2004 FTC equals zero, and the 2004 U.S. tax is $680. Over the two years, the United States collects $680 U.S. tax on $2,000 of U.S. taxable income. The recapture rules prevent the company from avoiding U.S. tax on $1,000 U.S. source income. The following table summarizes the calculations just discussed.

| Results in 2004 | Without Recapture | With Recapture |
|---|---|---|
| a. Taxable income | $2,000 | $2,000 |
| b. U.S. tax rate | × .34 | × .34 |
| c. U.S. tax before FTC | $ 680 | $ 680 |
| d. Creditable tax | $340 | $340 |

e. FTC limitation
   (equation 11.4)        340                        0
f. FTC (lesser of
   lines d and e)                340                        0
g. U.S. tax liability             $  340                    $  680

With this conceptual background, the remainder of this section explains more specifically how the recapture rules work.

When apportioned deductions exceed foreign source gross income in any basket (the loss basket), U.S. taxpayers proportionately allocate that basket's net loss among baskets containing foreign source taxable income.[95] To the extent the net loss exceeds aggregate foreign source taxable income in other baskets, the excess represents an **overall foreign loss**.[96] In effect, an overall foreign loss occurs whenever foreign source gross income is less than deductions apportioned to such income for all baskets combined. U.S. companies deduct an overall foreign loss against U.S. source income and, thus, reduce their U.S. tax on U.S. source income.

## EXAMPLE

Highlander Hosier, Inc., a domestic corporation, sells Scottish attire in the United States and through foreign sales branches. The company classifies its 2003 taxable income as follows:

| | |
|---|---|
| U.S. taxable income | $1,200 |
| Foreign taxable income (passive basket) | 100 |
| Foreign net loss (residual basket) | −300 |
| Worldwide taxable income | $1,000 |

Highlander allocates $100 of the residual basket's net loss to the passive basket, reducing the latter's FTC limitation to zero and denying an FTC in 2003 for the passive basket's creditable taxes. The remaining $200 represents an overall foreign loss, which offsets U.S. taxable income. Thus, Highlander pays U.S. tax on $1,000 taxable income; in effect, $200 of U.S. taxable income escapes U.S. taxation in 2003.

[95] IRC §904(f)(5)(B).
[96] IRC §904(f)(2).

If the original loss basket contains net income in later years, taxpayers recapture any loss previously allocated against U.S. source income. The recapture occurs through treating foreign source income as U.S. source income. This re-sourcing rule reduces the numerator of the loss basket's FTC limitation (equation 11.4). The Code limits the amount of foreign source taxable income re-sourced to the smaller of:

- Unrecaptured overall foreign losses from prior years and
- Half of the current year's foreign source taxable income in the original loss basket (or any larger percentage the taxpayer elects).[97]

After applying this recapture rule, taxpayers allocate any remaining net income in the original loss basket to other baskets until they restore previously offset net income to such baskets.[98] Congress intended that these loss allocation and recapture rules maintain boundaries between income in separate FTC baskets, at least over time. Thus, the rules restore net income to baskets that net loss from the loss basket previously eliminated. Stated differently, the statutory provisions shift income among baskets to rectify a prior-year's allocation of net loss among baskets.

---

## EXAMPLE

Assume the same facts as those in the prior example. In 2004, Highlander experiences the following results before applying the recapture rules:

| | |
|---|---|
| U.S. taxable income | $1,500 |
| Foreign taxable income (passive basket) | 200 |
| Foreign taxable income (residual basket) | 300 |
| Worldwide taxable income | $2,000 |

The company's U.S. tax before FTC equals $680 ($2,000 × 34%). Highlander recaptures the overall foreign loss first. However, the recapture cannot exceed $150 unless Highlander elects a greater amount (i.e., lesser of $200 unrecaptured loss from 2003 and 50 percent of $300 foreign source income in 2004 residual basket). Next, $100 of the residual basket's income restores the $100 income to the passive

---

[97]IRC §904(f)(1); Reg. §1.904(f)-2(c)(1), (2).
[98]IRC §904(f)(5)(C).

basket. Thus, the company determines its 2004 basket limitations as follows:

$$\text{Limitation}_{\text{passive}} = \frac{\$200 + \$100}{\$2,000} \times \$680 = \$102$$

$$\text{Limitation}_{\text{residual}} = \frac{\$300 - \$150 - \$100}{\$2,000} \times \$680 = \$17$$

For 2005, Highlander's unrecaptured overall foreign loss equals $50 (i.e., $200 from 2003 less $150 recaptured in 2004).

If U.S. companies dispose of property they use predominantly abroad in business activities, the re-sourcing rule applies to any resulting foreign gain. In addition to gain normally recognized, the Code requires that U.S. taxpayers recognize gain from property sold, exchanged, distributed, or gifted up to the amount of any unrecaptured overall foreign loss, even if other portions of U.S. law normally allow such gain to go unrecognized.[99] In effect, the Code forces gain recognition for disposals of foreign business property and then requires the taxpayer to re-source the gain to the extent of unrecaptured overall foreign losses.

When taxpayers recognize gain from disposing of assets they use predominantly abroad, the amount of re-sourcing equals the lesser of:

- Unrecaptured overall foreign losses from prior years and
- Current-year's foreign source taxable income.[100]

The increase from 50 to 100 percent of foreign source taxable income reflects U.S. concern that the taxpayer may be liquidating its business abroad. Thus, the modified recapture rule often allows the recapture of overall foreign losses at an accelerated pace and, thus, lessens the chance that overall foreign losses may avoid recapture permanently. The combination of the forced gain recognition and the accelerated recapture rules makes it more difficult for U.S. companies to incorporate foreign business operations as they turn profitable and, thus, avoid recapturing overall foreign losses from prior years.

---

[99]IRC §904(f)(3)(A)(i).
[100]IRC §904(f)(3)(A)(ii).

## EXAMPLE

Assume the same facts as the previous example except that Highlander incorporates its foreign business activities at the beginning of 2005 in a transaction normally qualifying as a nontaxable exchange.[101] At the time of incorporation, the company's unrecaptured overall foreign loss equals $50. If gain from exchanging business assets for stock in the new foreign corporation equals $40, Highlander recognizes the $40 gain, and the recapture rules convert the gain to U.S. source income. Thus, the $40 gain does not appear in the numerator of the limitation formula, assuring that the FTC does not shield it from U.S. taxation. Without the acceleration provision, Highlander re-sources only $20 of the gain as U.S. income (i.e., 50 percent of the foreign source gain).

## TAX-SPARING CREDIT

Some developing countries grant tax holidays to foreign companies making direct investments in their economies. **Tax holidays** assume many forms but usually involve waiving certain taxes for specified types of investments over a stated time, such as 10 years. When the foreign investor's home country has a territorial tax system, the tax holiday provides an incentive to invest. If the tax holiday waives all income tax in the developing country, the foreign investor's worldwide effective rate for the investment is zero. However, foreign investors residing in countries with global tax systems may derive little or no benefit from the tax holiday. Whether a benefit results depends on whether the home country allows a tax-sparing credit.

Often granted through treaties, **tax-sparing credits** are similar to FTCs except taxpayers qualify without paying foreign income taxes. In effect, tax-sparing credits permit investors to offset home country tax with the host country tax otherwise due and, thus, restore the tax holiday's incentive. So, investors claim a credit for phantom taxes the host country "spares."

## EXAMPLE

Koto KK, a Japanese corporation, wishes to conduct branch operations in Vietnam. Japan taxes the worldwide income of Koto at an effective

---

[101]See IRC §351(a).

rate of 42 percent.[102] Koto negotiates a tax holiday with Vietnam that relieves the company from the 25 percent Vietnamese income tax.[103] However, absent tax sparing, the tax holiday does not benefit Koto and provides no incentive for investment. Assuming branch profits of $1,000, the worldwide tax is the same with or without the tax holiday.

|  | *No Tax Holiday* | *Tax Holiday* |
|---|---|---|
| Japanese tax before credit | $420 | $420 |
| Foreign tax credit | −250 | −0 |
| Japanese income tax | $170 | $420 |
| Vietnamese income tax | +250 | +0 |
| Worldwide tax | $420 | $420 |

Fortunately for Koto, Article 22(3) of the Japan-Vietnam Treaty allows tax sparing. Tax sparing reduces the worldwide tax to $170 as follows:

|  | *Tax Holiday* |
|---|---|
| Japanese tax before credit | $420 |
| Tax-sparing credit | −250 |
| Japanese income tax | $170 |
| Vietnamese income tax | +0 |
| Worldwide tax | $170 |

Some developed countries, such as Japan and the United Kingdom, allow tax-sparing credits through treaties with developing countries. In contrast, the United States believes tax policy encouraging investment in low-tax jurisdictions is unsound since it flouts capital export neutrality. Thus, the United States does not permit tax-sparing credits under any of its treaties.

---

[102]PricewaterhouseCoopers, *Corporate Taxes: Worldwide Summaries 2002–2003* (Hoboken, NJ: John Wiley & Sons, Inc., 2002), pp. 403–404. The effective tax rate is based on a 30 percent national income tax, 9.8 percent local enterprise tax, and 19 percent local inhabitants tax. The enterprise tax is deductible in computing the national income tax. The inhabitants tax rate applies to the national income tax. Thus, 30% (1 − 9.8%) + 9.8% + 19% (30%) (1 − 9.8%) = 42%.

[103]Ibid., p. 938.

Without tax-sparing credits, U.S. investors pay zero (or low) taxes to the developing host country. However, the residual U.S. tax eliminates (or reduces) the tax holiday's incentive effect and shifts tax revenues otherwise benefiting the host country to the U.S. Treasury.[104]

---

[104] Absent tax-sparing credits, some host countries attempt end runs and subsidize foreign investors or provide specific economic benefits in lieu of a tax holiday. As discussed earlier, IRC §901(i) and Reg. §1.901-2(a)(2)(i) deny an FTC in these situations.

# CHAPTER 12

# Controlled Foreign Corporations

The United States does not tax income of most foreign corporations or the dividends their stockholders receive. Three exceptions exist. First, as Chapters 7 and 8 explained, the United States taxes foreign corporations on U.S. source income and income effectively connected with a U.S. trade or business. Second, U.S. owners report actual dividends received from foreign corporations as gross income.[1] Third, U.S. stockholders report gross income for constructive dividends they receive from foreign personal holding companies, qualified electing funds, and controlled foreign corporations (CFCs). This chapter defines CFCs and explains when a CFC's U.S. shareholders recognize constructive dividends.[2] Chapter 13 covers foreign personal holding companies and qualified electing funds.

In 1962, Congress enacted special rules for CFCs and their U.S. shareholders that combat inappropriate long-term deferrals. The CFC legislation makes it more difficult for U.S. taxpayers to shelter foreign source income

---

[1]Added by the Jobs and Growth Tax Relief Reconciliation Act of 2003, IRC §1(h)(11) taxes dividend income U.S. individuals receive from domestic and qualified foreign corporations at capital gain rates. For lower-income individuals, the capital gain rate is 5 percent through 2007 and zero in 2003; for higher-income individuals, the applicable rate is 15 percent through 2008. Qualified foreign corporations include those incorporated in U.S. possessions, those entitled to benefits under a U.S. income tax treaty containing an exchange of information article, and those whose stock readily trades on a U.S. established securities market. However, qualified foreign corporations do not include foreign personal holding companies and passive foreign investment companies, entities discussed in Chapter 13.

[2]This chapter follows the traditional approach of referring to Subpart F inclusions as constructive dividends. This characterization is consistent with the rule that limits Subpart F inclusions to a CFC's current earnings and profits, as discussed later. However, IRC §951(a)(1) does not use this terminology, requiring that a U.S. shareholder "include in his gross income" a pro rata share of Subpart F income and earnings invested in U.S. property.

from U.S. residual tax. Without the CFC regime, many U.S. persons might establish foreign corporations in tax haven countries and shift as much income as possible to those entities. Even though the economic functions producing the income might occur elsewhere, taxpayers could arrange their affairs so they could allocate a significant portion of their income to tax haven locations.

---

### EXAMPLE

A U.S. corporation manufactures workout ergometers at a $60 cost, which it sells through a wholly owned French subsidiary to French consumers at $100 each. The two companies split the $40 profit between them, so each country taxes approximately $20. To reduce taxes, the U.S. manufacturer later establishes a wholly owned Bermudan subsidiary. Under the new structure, the U.S. company sells ergometers destined for Europe to its Bermudan subsidiary for $61, and the Bermudan entity sells the ergometers to the French company for $99. In turn, the French subsidiary sells ergometers to final consumers for $100. The corporate structure and pricing system appear as follows:

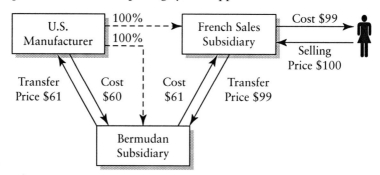

The new arrangement results in $1 profit in the United States, $38 profit in Bermuda, and $1 profit in France for each sale. In effect, it shifts $38 of the $40 profit to Bermuda, a country imposing no corporate income tax.[3] Notwithstanding the change in sales contracts, the physical flow of ergometers continues to be directly between the U.S. manufacturer and its French distributor. The Bermudan subsidiary adds no value to the ergometers and does not assist with marketing. Thus, it has no business reason for existing other than the potential tax benefits.

---

[3]PricewaterhouseCoopers, *Corporate Taxes: Worldwide Summaries 2002–2003* (Hoboken, NJ: John Wiley & Sons, Inc., 2002), p. 68.

Before 1962, U.S. persons often used arrangements such as the one just described to reap substantial tax benefits. Unless the IRS questioned the appropriateness of the transfer prices, a topic Chapter 16 explores, U.S. companies could isolate significant amounts of income in tax haven jurisdictions such as Bermuda. Theoretically, the United States eventually taxes the income. In the preceding example, the tax deferral ends when the Bermudan subsidiary remits its foreign earnings to the U.S. manufacturer as actual dividends or liquidates its foreign operations.

However, deferring income in a foreign corporation provides substantial present value benefits. Assuming a 10 percent discount rate, deferring $100 tax for five (10) years is the present value equivalent of paying $62 ($39) tax. Stated differently, deferring $100 tax for five (10) years is equivalent to reducing the present value of U.S. tax liability by 38 percent (61 percent). Longer-term deferrals approach the equivalent of complete tax exemption. Discounting cash flow at 10 percent, taxpayers deferring foreign earnings for 30 years pay only 6 percent of the U.S. tax liability in present value terms.[4]

U.S. taxpayers can reap other benefits from shifting income to tax haven countries and deferring U.S. residual tax for extended periods. During the deferral period, the tax haven subsidiary can loan foreign earnings to its U.S. parent or other affiliated entities. Thus, related companies might use the capital generated from foreign activities even though the U.S. parent company has not yet paid U.S. residual tax on the foreign earnings. Also, if the tax haven subsidiary liquidates, the foreign earnings might be taxable in the United States at more favorable capital gain rates.

The IRS has several antideferral weapons at its disposal to prevent unintended benefits from tax deferral such as those just mentioned. The next chapter examines two regimes that often thwart deferral strategies: passive foreign investment companies and foreign personal holding companies. However, the most potent antideferral weapon applies to earnings of CFCs, which this chapter discusses. When CFCs earn designated types of foreign income (defined later as Subpart F income), the Code treats the CFC's U.S. shareholders as though they receive a dividend. In effect, this constructive dividend prevents the otherwise available deferral benefit since it immediately triggers U.S. residual tax.

---

### EXAMPLE

Under the CFC regime, the Bermudan subsidiary in the previous example is a CFC and the domestic manufacturer is its sole U.S. shareholder.

---

[4]U.S. tax deferrals of foreign income can result in significant tax accrual issues under FAS 109.

Ignoring transfer pricing issues for now, the Code treats the subsidiary's $38 profit ($99 transfer price − $61 cost) as Subpart F income, which results in a $38 constructive dividend to the U.S. manufacturer during the current year. No deferral of U.S. residual tax occurs on Bermudan income.

In addition to foreign sales income (illustrated in the first example), several other types of Subpart F income result in constructive dividends to U.S. shareholders. The underlying premise for each category of Subpart F income is that U.S. shareholders establish a foreign corporation in a low-tax country primarily to defer U.S. residual tax on foreign earnings. Usually, Subpart F income results because the CFC performs no substantial economic function, such as manufacturing or marketing, in the country where the U.S. owners incorporate it. However, even when a CFC avoids Subpart F income, a constructive dividend still might result if the CFC loans foreign earnings to its U.S. shareholders or invests foreign earnings in certain other U.S. properties.

Why should Congress worry about U.S. multinationals shifting income to low-tax jurisdictions? Conducting business abroad in high-tax countries results in no U.S. tax revenues when multinationals later remit profits. In contrast, doing business abroad in low-tax jurisdictions eventually results in a U.S. residual tax equal to foreign profit times the difference between U.S. and foreign effective tax rates. The explanation for congressional concern partially lies in a desire to achieve capital-export-neutrality. Without the CFC regime, many U.S. taxpayers might shift capital and, thus, income to low-tax foreign jurisdictions, resulting in inefficient resource allocations. Perhaps congressional concern about perceived fairness plays some role also. Media accounts of U.S. multinationals escaping their fair share of taxes often create feelings of inequity and discontent among individuals and small businesses not possessing the economic means to shift income abroad.

The Code does not attribute constructive dividends to all persons holding CFC stock. Only U.S. shareholders receive constructive dividends. Further, all E&P of CFCs do not result in constructive dividends. Only earnings from Subpart F income and earnings invested in U.S. property generate constructive dividends. Thus, determining constructive dividends under the CFC regime requires the following steps:

1. Establish that foreign corporation is a CFC.
2. Identify CFC's U.S. shareholders.
3. Determine CFC's Subpart F income.
4. Ascertain CFC's earnings invested in U.S. property.
5. Calculate constructive dividends to U.S. shareholders.

## CFCS AND U.S. SHAREHOLDERS

Controlled foreign corporations are foreign corporations in which U.S. shareholders directly, indirectly, or constructively own more than 50 percent of either voting power or stock value on any day during the taxable year.[5] Only stock U.S. shareholders hold count toward the 50 percent threshold. **U.S. shareholders** are U.S. persons directly, indirectly, or constructively owning 10 percent or more of a foreign corporation's voting power.[6] U.S. persons include U.S. citizens and residents, domestic partnerships, domestic corporations, and nonforeign estates and trusts.[7]

---

### EXAMPLE

Unrelated shareholders of Nothing Ventured, Ltd. (NV), an Indian corporation, include:

|  | *Voting Power* |
|---|---|
| Nothing Gained, Inc. (domestic corporation) | 35% |
| Savindra (nonresident alien) | 40% |
| Wesley (U.S. citizen) | 12% |
| Butler (resident alien) | 7% |
| Clifton (U.S. citizen) | 6% |

All but Savindra are U.S. persons. However, only Nothing Gained and Wesley reach the 10 percent threshold and, thus, qualify as U.S. shareholders. Since the voting power of these two shareholders sum to 47 percent, NV is not a CFC unless these two persons own more than 50 percent of NV's stock value.

---

[5] IRC §957(a). Under IRC §957(b), the ownership threshold drops from 50 to 25 percent for foreign insurance companies earning more than 75 percent of gross premiums from insuring risks outside their countries of incorporation. This more liberal definition of CFCs applies only when determining how much of the foreign insurance income results in a constructive dividend.

[6] IRC §951(b). Reg. §1.957-1(b)(1)(i) clarifies that **voting power** is the authority to elect, replace, or appoint directors to a corporation's board or similar governing body. Also, Reg. §1.951-1(g)(2)(b) treats U.S. persons owning at least 20 percent of any class of voting stock as U.S. shareholders (i.e., as though they own at least 10 percent of the corporation's voting power).

[7] IRC §957(c). For foreign corporations organized in U.S. possessions other than the U.S. Virgin Islands, U.S. persons do not include certain bona fide residents of such possessions.

In testing for CFC status and whether an owner qualifies as a U.S. shareholder, direct, indirect, and constructive ownership rules apply. **Indirect ownership** exists when a person owns stock in a foreign corporation (possible CFC) through one or more foreign entities (i.e., foreign partnerships, corporations, estates, or trusts). U.S. law treats the partners, shareholders, and beneficiaries of these foreign entities as though they own a proportionate share in the underlying foreign corporation (possible CFC).[8] In a chain of ownership, indirect ownership ceases with the first U.S. person in the chain.

---

### EXAMPLE

Walkie Talkie, Ltd. is a U.K. corporation providing European cell phone services. Telesat Company, a Belgian partnership, owns 40 percent of Walkie Talkie. Cell Wide, Inc., a U.S. corporation, owns 90 percent of Telesat. Bernard, a U.S. citizen, owns 9 percent of Cell Wide. The following diagram portrays the ownership structure:

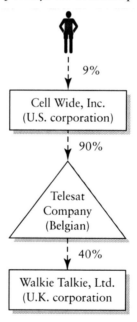

Cell Wide is a U.S. shareholder since it indirectly owns 36 percent of Walkie Talkie (.9 × .4). However, Bernard does not indirectly own stock

---

[8]IRC §958(a)(2).

of Walkie Talkie since indirect ownership exists only through foreign entities (i.e., a U.S. corporation separates Bernard from the U.K. corporation). Even if Bernard owns all of Cell Wide's stock, his indirect ownership continues to be zero (though, in this latter case, he may constructively own stock, as this chapter explains later). Unless Walkie Talkie has other U.S. shareholders, it is not a CFC since Cell Wide, its only U.S. shareholder, does not own more than 50 percent.

**Constructive ownership** rules draw heavily from Subchapter C (Code provisions applicable to domestic corporations) with modifications appropriate to the international arena. The rules fall into five categories:

- Attribution from family member
- Attribution from transparent entities
- Attribution from corporations
- Attribution to transparent entities
- Attribution to corporations

The family attribution rules ascribe to individuals any stock that parents, spouses, children, and grandchildren directly or indirectly own.[9] Nonetheless, individuals do not constructively own stock that nonresident aliens hold; so, family members must be U.S. citizens or residents for the Code to attribute their stock to someone else.[10] Also, no reattribution occurs under these rules.[11] Thus, stock ownership attributed to a woman from her mother is not reattributed to her husband. Stated differently, a man does not constructively own stock his mother-in-law holds. Exhibit 12.1 summarizes the constructive ownership rules dealing with attribution from family members.

Partners, beneficiaries, and S shareholders receive proportional attribution from their partnerships, estates, trusts, and S corporations for stock these transparent entities directly or indirectly hold.[12] When transparent entities directly or indirectly own more than 50 percent of a foreign corporation (possible CFC), partners, beneficiaries, and shareholders treat this lower-tier ownership as 100 percent when determining their proportionate holdings in the lower-tier foreign corporation.[13] The Code treats stock that partners, beneficiaries, and shareholders constructively own under this at-

---

[9]IRC §318(a)(1).
[10]IRC §958(b)(1).
[11]IRC §318(a)(5)(B).
[12]IRC §318(a)(2), (5)(E).
[13]IRC §958(b)(2).

**EXHIBIT 12.1**  Constructive Ownership: Attribution from Family Members

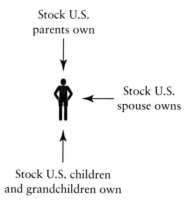

Stock U.S.
parents own

Stock U.S.
spouse owns

Stock U.S. children
and grandchildren own

tribution rule as though they actually own it (i.e., reattribution can occur).[14] Exhibit 12.2 summarizes this attribution rule.

The constructive ownership rules proportionately attribute direct and indirect corporate holdings to their 10-percent shareholders.[15] Shareholders owning less than 10 percent of a corporation's stock value do not constructively own any portion of a lower-tier foreign corporation (possible CFC). When corporations directly or indirectly own more than 50 percent of a foreign corporation, their shareholders treat this lower-tier ownership as 100 percent (the same as with attribution from transparent entities).[16] Also, once these rules attribute ownership to a shareholder, reattribution can occur.[17] Exhibit 12.3 summarizes the rules involving attribution from corporations.

The Code attributes direct and indirect ownership of partners, beneficiaries, and S shareholders in foreign corporations (possible CFCs) to the transparent entities in which they hold interests.[18] However, no attribution can pass through partners, beneficiaries, or S shareholders who are not U.S. persons.[19] Also, no reattribution can occur under this rule.[20] Exhibit 12.4 illustrates the attribution of stock ownership to transparent entities.

U.S. law attributes the direct and indirect holding in a foreign corporation (possible CFC) to any corporation in which the owner is a 50 percent

[14]IRC §318(a)(5)(A).
[15]IRC §§318(a)(2)(C), 958(b)(3). This rule does not apply to S corporations.
[16]IRC §958(b)(2).
[17]IRC §318(a)(5)(A).
[18]IRC §318(a)(3), (5)(E).
[19]IRC §958(b)(4).
[20]IRC §318(a)(5)(C).

**EXHIBIT 12.2**   Constructive Ownership: Attribution from Transparent Entities[a]

*Panel A: Lower-Tier Holding Not Exceeding 50 Percent*

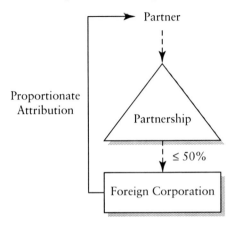

*Panel B: Lower-Tier Holding Exceeding 50 Percent*

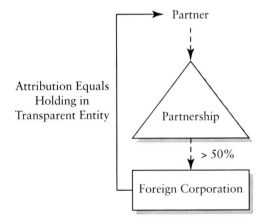

[a]Though this exhibit illustrates the attribution rule with a partnership, the application is similar to other transparent entities.

shareholder.[21] As with transparent entities, no attribution occurs unless the shareholder is a U.S. person.[22] Also, the Code prevents reattribution.[23] Exhibit 12.5 summarizes this rule.

---

[21]IRC §318(a)(3)(C). This rules does not apply to S corporations.
[22]IRC §958(b)(4).
[23]IRC §318(a)(5)(C).

**EXHIBIT 12.3**   Constructive Ownership: Attribution from Corporations

*Panel A: Lower-Tier Holding Not Exceeding 50 Percent*

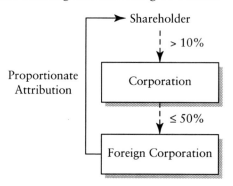

*Panel B: Lower-Tier Holding Exceeding 50 Percent*

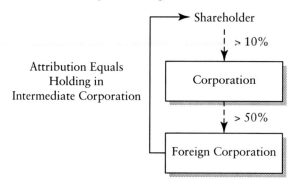

As noted earlier, the constructive ownership rules apply in determining whether a U.S. person is a U.S. shareholder and whether a foreign corporation is a CFC. However, constructive ownership is irrelevant in calculating a U.S. shareholder's constructive dividend under the CFC regime. Thus, constructive ownership rules may qualify an individual or entity as a U.S. shareholder, cause that person's stock to count toward the 50 percent CFC threshold, and trigger CFC status for the applicable foreign corporation. However, without direct or indirect ownership in the CFC, the individual or entity does not receive a constructive dividend. Odd though it may sound, constructive ownership alone does not result in a constructive dividend. In effect, U.S. shareholders through the constructive ownership rules contribute toward a foreign corporation's classification as a CFC and, thus, may result in constructive dividends to U.S. shareholders holding stock through the direct and indirect ownership rules.

**EXHIBIT 12.4**   Constructive Ownership: Attribution to Transparent Entities[a]

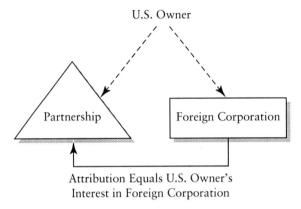

U.S. Owner

Partnership          Foreign Corporation

Attribution Equals U.S. Owner's
Interest in Foreign Corporation

[a]Though this exhibit illustrates the attribution rule with a partnership, the application is similar to other transparent entities.

**PLANNING POINTER:**   Foreign joint ventures that U.S. law treats as corporations are not CFCs when the U.S. participant owns 50 percent or less. Thus, such ventures do not generate Subpart F income and U.S. participants do not recognize constructive dividends (i.e., they defer U.S. residual tax). In short, this structure often results in substantial present value benefits for joint ventures in low-tax jurisdictions.[24]

**EXHIBIT 12.5**   Constructive Ownership: Attribution to Corporations

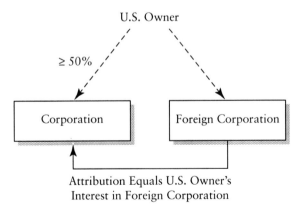

U.S. Owner

≥ 50%

Corporation          Foreign Corporation

Attribution Equals U.S. Owner's
Interest in Foreign Corporation

---

[24]As Chapter 11 explained, when a 50-50 joint venture (a 10-50 company) remits earnings as dividends, a look-through rule allocates actual dividends among the various FTC baskets.

Limiting voting power and stock value to 50 percent often allows foreign affiliates to avoid CFC status. However, the regulations clarify that staying at or below the 50 percent threshold does not assure avoidance, particularly when U.S. multinationals arrange their affairs to control foreign affiliates in other ways. In effect, the reality of control is as important as technical control when identifying CFCs. U.S. law ignores artificial arrangements to place voting shares in foreign persons' hands when, in reality, U.S. persons retain control.[25]

## KEY CASE

A family owns 100 percent of a Liechtenstein corporation. To avoid CFC status, the family issues callable 8 percent preferred stock, representing 50 percent voting power, to several unrelated persons for 10 percent of corporate value. Preferred stockholders cannot transfer shares without board approval, and the family-dominated board can deny approval for "important reasons." Later, preferred stockholders sell their shares to a foreign bank. The bank, in turn, sells 51 percent of preferred shares to a Canadian corporation and 49 percent to the family. Simultaneously, the family sells 51 percent of common shares to the Canadian corporation. The family contends that the Liechtenstein corporation is not a CFC under either corporate structure after the initial issue of preferred stock. The court disagrees, observing that the family carefully selected preferred shareholders to include close friends and business associates. In the court's opinion, it strains credibility to think the family transferred control for only 10 percent of the corporation's worth. Apparently, an 8 percent return satisfied the preferred shareholders and kept them from "rocking the corporate boat." In fact, preferred shareholders often skipped stockholder meetings. Though the family relinquished more than 50 percent of formal voting power, exercising the preferred stock's call option could resolve deadlocks. Thus, the court held that the Liechtenstein corporation is a CFC since U.S. shareholders, in reality, retained more than 50 percent of the voting power.[26]

Several factors contributed to the court's holding that the Liechtenstein corporation was a CFC. However, tweaking these factors without shifting

---

[25]Reg. §1.957-1(b)(2); *Garlock, Inc. v. Comm.*, 489 F.2d 197 (CA-2, 1973).
[26]*Kraus v. Comm.*, 490 F.2d 898 (CA-2, 1974). This decision occurred before Congress expanded the definition of CFCs to include foreign corporations in which U.S. shareholders own more than 50 percent of stock *value*.

real voting power away from U.S. shareholders does not assure a favorable judicial response.

**KEY CASE**

To avoid CFC status, the U.S. taxpayer issues preferred stock representing 55 percent voting power in its Panamanian corporation, Koehring Overseas Company (KOS), to Newton Chambers (NC), an unrelated English Corporation and foreign licensee. In contending that KOS is a CFC, the government notes that the stock transfer occurs through a cross-investment plan in which the taxpayer receives a similar interest in an NC subsidiary, the preferred stock gives NC a claim to less than 10 percent of KOS's average annual earnings, and NC representatives neglect to attend board and shareholder meetings. The taxpayer argues that since an unrelated foreign entity (NC) owns 55 percent of voting power, KOS is not a CFC. It observes that NC elected three of five members to KOS's board and twice blocked attempts to pay common stock dividends to the taxpayer. However, the court sided with the government since the voting power substantially exceeds NC's share of corporate earnings, NC does not independently exercise its voting rights, and one of the corporate structure's principal purposes seems to be the avoidance of CFC status. Also, NC did not replace existing management or market its products through KOS, an alleged joint marketing subsidiary. NC directors cannot write checks for KOS, and KOS's annual report refers to NC's investment in KOS as "nominal." Further, the court described the cross-investment plan as a formal arrangement to shift voting power away from the taxpayer. Though NC holds formal voting control, it possesses little incentive to exercise such control and jeopardize its licensing agreements with the taxpayer. The cross-investment plan further reduces NC's incentive to exercise control. Blocking the payment of common stock dividends may have been a façade to establish the appearance that NC exercises its voting power independently. In characterizing the NC directors as sham directors and NC's interest in KOS as passive, the court concludes that KOS is a CFC.[27]

---

[27]*Koehring Company v. US*, 583 F.2d 313 (CA-7, 1978). For a different result under similar circumstances, see *CCA, Inc. v. Comm.*, 64 TC 137 (1975). As in *Kraus*, these decisions precede the addition of the 50 percent stock value test to the CFC definition.

**PLANNING POINTER:**  U.S. publicly traded companies reorganizing as foreign corporations usually avoid the CFC regime. If widely held, the companies do not have U.S. shareholders or, at least, the U.S. shareholders hold insufficient shares to result in CFC status. When reorganized in low-tax foreign jurisdictions, such corporations can defer U.S. residual tax, dramatically reducing the marginal tax rate.[28]

## SUBPART F INCOME

The CFC provisions require U.S. shareholders to report constructive dividends and, thus, prevent the deferral of U.S. residual tax. U.S. law bases the constructive dividend on the CFC's Subpart F income and earnings invested in U.S. property. Subpart F income results from deriving specified types of income, earning profit in particular countries, and making certain illegal payments.

Specifically, **Subpart F income** equals the sum of foreign base company (FBC) income, certain income from insuring risks outside the CFC's country, income derived from participating in international boycotts, income from unruly countries in U.S. disfavor, and an amount equal to illegal bribes and kickbacks the CFC pays.[29] **Foreign base company (FBC) income** (one component of Subpart F income) equals the sum of FBC sales income, FBC services income, foreign personal holding company income, FBC shipping income, and FBC oil-related income.[30] Exhibit 12.6 summarizes the various elements comprising the CFC regime's constructive dividend.

**PLANNING POINTER:**  U.S. multinationals often wish to avoid Subpart F income. However, constructive dividends under the CFC regime exert both increasing and decreasing influences on a domestic parent's U.S. tax liability. Currently taxing foreign earnings through a constructive dividend precludes deferral benefits and, thus, in-

---

[28]Notwithstanding the tax benefit from reorganizing offshore (so-called corporate inversions), one study finds little empirical evidence that the securities markets value this tax benefit through increased share prices. The lack of evidence suggests that these transactions may involve political or other non-tax costs that offset the tax benefit. See C. Bryan Cloyd, Lillian F. Mills, and Connie D. Weaver, "Firm Valuation Effects of the Expatriation of U.S. Companies to Tax Haven Countries," forthcoming in *Journal of the American Taxation Association*.
[29]IRC §952(a).
[30]IRC §954(a).

**EXHIBIT 12.6** Constructive Dividend under CFC Provisions

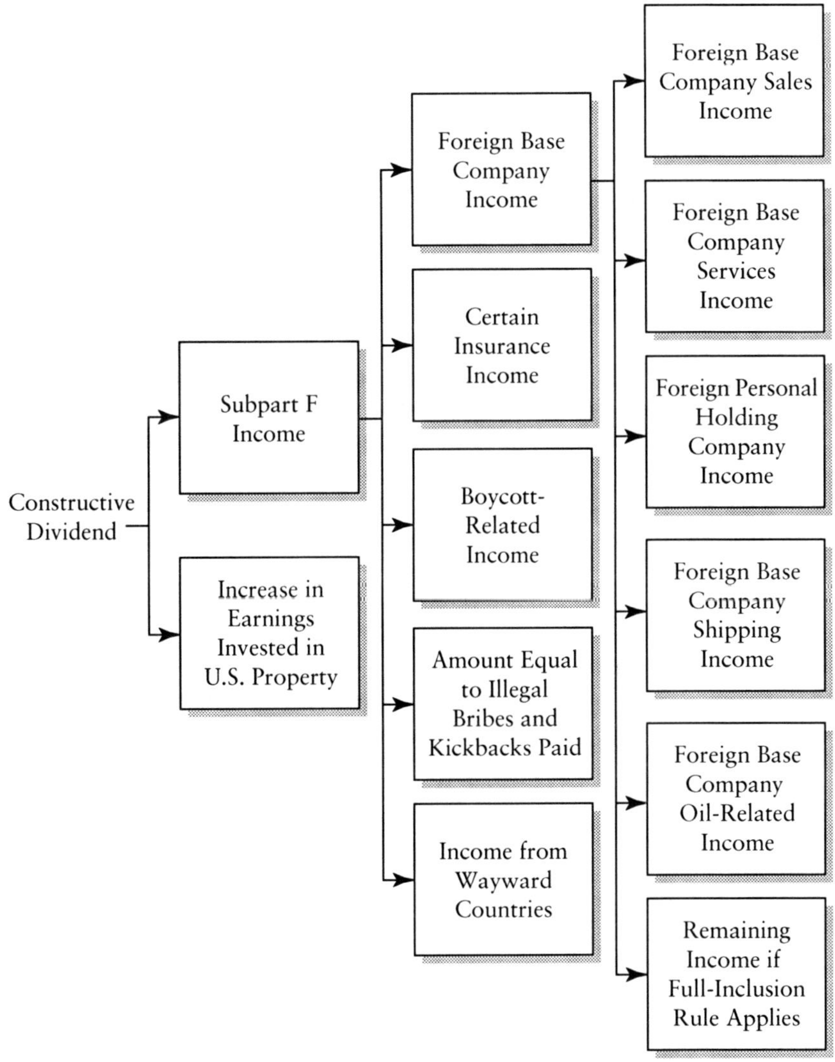

Notwithstanding the diagram, Subpart F income does not include the following:

1. Amounts exceeding current E&P (after adding back illegal payments, subtracting blocked income, and adjusting for deficits);
2. Foreign base company income and insurance income if their sum falls below the smaller of $1 million or five percent of gross income;
3. U.S. source, effectively connected income unless a treaty exempts it or taxes it at a reduced rate; and
4. Any item of foreign base company income (unless oil-related) or insurance income if the effective tax rate exceeds 90 percent of the maximum U.S. corporate tax rate.

creases the present value of U.S. residual tax (before considering the FTC). However, U.S. law allows the domestic parent to credit indirect foreign income taxes and increases its capacity to absorb excess credits from conducting business in high-tax countries.[31] Since the net effect can be favorable, some U.S. multinationals proactively seek constructive dividends.

---

### EXAMPLE

Repeat, a domestic corporation, possesses $1 million excess credits from a European branch that expire in one year if not absorbed. Repeat owns 50 percent of Echo, a Taiwanese corporation that annually earns $20 million and pays Taiwanese income tax at 25 percent.[32] If Echo qualifies as a CFC, Repeat's $10 million share is Subpart F income. However, Echo is not a CFC since Repeat owns exactly 50 percent, and a publicly traded Taiwanese corporation, Ricochet, owns the other 50 percent.

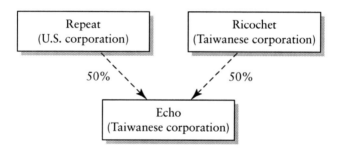

To absorb the expiring excess credit, Repeat wishes to recognize its $10 million share of Echo's earnings. However, actual dividends result in Taiwanese withholding taxes that Repeat wants to avoid, and Ricochet objects to a dividend distribution. To meet each owner's objective, Repeat buys one share in Ricochet, establishing a minute indirect ownership in Echo. Thus, Echo becomes a CFC (i.e., 50% direct interest +

---

[31]IRC §960(a)(1). This provision provides a FTC similar to the DPC in IRC §902. While IRC §902 allows a DPC related to an actual dividend, IRC §960 provides for a DPC based on a constructive dividend.

[32]PricewaterhouseCoopers, *Corporate Taxes: Worldwide Summaries 2002–2003* (Hoboken, NJ: John Wiley & Sons, Inc., 2002), p. 835.

1 share indirect interest > 50%), and Repeat recognizes a $10 million constructive dividend. Normally, dividends from low-tax jurisdictions such as Taiwan result in a U.S. residual tax. However, the excess credit about to expire shields Repeat from U.S. residual tax, as follows:

| | | |
|---|---|---:|
| Incremental U.S. taxable income | | $10,000,000 |
| U.S. corporate tax rate | | × .35 |
| Incremental U.S. tax before FTC | | $ 3,500,000 |
| Deemed paid taxes from Taiwan | $2,500,000 | |
| Excess credits about to expire | 1,000,000 | |
| FTC | | 3,500,000 |
| Incremental U.S. tax | | $ 0 |

In effect, Repeat cross-credits its high-taxed European income against its low-taxed Taiwanese income. Without tax planning, Repeat forfeits this cross-crediting opportunity and pays a $1 million U.S. residual tax when receiving Taiwanese dividends in later years.

## General Exclusions and Inclusions

Four special rules apply broadly to Subpart F income. The first provision limits Subpart F income to current earnings and profits (E&P) and, thus, excludes amounts above this limit. The second rule excludes all income from Subpart F if it falls below a de minimis amount, but includes all income as Subpart F income if the latter exceeds a threshold percentage. The third and fourth provisions apply on a transaction-by-transaction basis. Subpart F income excludes any income item that is U.S. source effectively connected income or income taxed at relatively high foreign rates. The following paragraphs discuss these four rules.

Under Subchapter C, shareholders treat distributions actually received as dividends only to the extent of the corporate distributor's E&P.[33] Similarly, a CFC's Subpart F income cannot exceed the CFC's current E&P.[34] In effect, current E&P represents the upper limit on a CFC's Subpart F income and, thus, caps the constructive dividend U.S. shareholders recognize. CFCs can elect to reduce their current E&P limits with prior E&P deficits of re-

---

[33]IRC §316(a).
[34]IRC §952(c)(1)(A).

lated corporations in the same country.[35] When illegal payments have reduced current earnings (or increased prior deficits), CFCs must add them back to E&P when determining the cap on Subpart F income.[36] Also, if foreign legal restrictions block actual dividends (e.g., preventing conversion of the local currency into dollars or mandating currency reserves), U.S. law treats constructive dividends as though blocked also. Thus, CFCs subtract **blocked income** from current E&P when determining the limit on Subpart F income.[37]

When current E&P limits recognition of Subpart F income, CFCs recharacterize future E&P as Subpart F income to the extent of any shortfall.[38] The carryforward of unrecognized Subpart F income assures that temporary E&P shortages do not allow U.S. shareholders to avoid constructive dividends indefinitely.

---

### EXAMPLE

Universal Palmtop, Inc., a U.S. corporation, establishes a wholly owned Jordanian CFC in 2003, to which the following information relates:

|                                          | 2003  | 2004  |
|------------------------------------------|-------|-------|
| Subpart F income (before E&P limit)      | $200  | $220  |
| Current E&P                              | 170   | 250   |

In 2003, the CFC pays a $10 illegal kickback, which it subtracts to compute current E&P. Thus, U.S. law limits its 2003 Subpart F income to $180 ($170 current E&P plus $10 kickback). The amount not treated as Subpart F income in 2003 due to the E&P limit carries forward. In 2004, Jordan mandates currency reserves so the CFC can distribute only $230. Subpart F income equals $230 ($220 earned in 2004 plus $20 carried from 2003, but restricted to $230). Universal Palmtop recognizes $180 and $230 constructive dividends in 2003 and 2004, respectively.

---

[35]IRC §952(c)(1)(C). Under IRC §952(c)(1)(B), prior deficits related to a qualified activity (e.g., FBC sales income) reduce U.S. shareholders' constructive dividends from the same type of activity.
[36]IRC §964(a).
[37]IRC §964(b).
[38]IRC §952(c)(2).

Subpart F income includes neither gross insurance income from insuring outside risks nor gross foreign base company income if their sum falls below the smaller of $1 million or 5 percent of total gross income. This de minimis exception allows CFCs to ignore small amounts of the more common forms of Subpart F income. At the other extreme, a **full-inclusion rule** requires CFCs to treat all gross income as Subpart F income if gross insurance income plus foreign base company income (before deductions) exceeds 70 percent of total gross income.[39] Some professionals refer to these provisions as the **5-70 rule.**

---

### EXAMPLE

Maggie, a U.S. citizen, owns all stock in Egalitarian Elite, SA, a Guatemalan corporation. Before deductions, Egalitarian earns $500,000 income from insuring property located outside Guatemala, $300,000 foreign base company services income, and $200,000 other income. Egalitarian's Subpart F income equals $1 million since gross insurance income plus foreign base company income exceeds 70 percent of total gross income ($800,000 > $700,000). If deductions equal $850,000, Maggie recognizes a $150,000 constructive dividend ($1 million Subpart F income less $850,000 deductions).

---

**PLANNING POINTER:** When more than 70 percent of a lower-tier CFC's gross income consists of gross insurance income and foreign base company income, a check-the-box election might nullify the full-inclusion rule's impact. Treating the lower-tier entity as a branch allows the U.S. parent to combine the branch income with the income of the next-higher entity in the chain, which may drop the relevant percentage below 70 percent.

---

### EXAMPLE

A U.S. corporation owns all stock in CFC1, which owns all the stock in CFC2. The diagram illustrates the corporate structure and shows the gross and taxable income amounts for both foreign corporations. Neither CFC conducts insurance activities.

---

[39]IRC §954(b)(3). Reg. §1.954-1(b)(4)(i) clarifies that the IRS can aggregate income of related CFCs in testing for the de minimis threshold when U.S. multinationals divide income among such entities principally to avoid Subpart F.

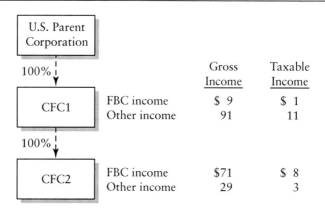

| | | Gross Income | Taxable Income |
|---|---|---|---|
| **CFC1** | FBC income | $ 9 | $ 1 |
| | Other income | 91 | 11 |
| **CFC2** | FBC income | $71 | $ 8 |
| | Other income | 29 | 3 |

The U.S. parent recognizes a constructive dividend for CFC1's $1 FBC income and, since the parent is a U.S. shareholder of CFC2 through its indirect 100 percent ownership, CFC2's $8 FBC income.[40] Also, since CFC2 derives more than 70 percent of its gross income from foreign base company activities [71 ÷ ($71 + $29)], the U.S. parent recognizes the remaining $3 of CFC2's taxable income as a constructive dividend under the full-inclusion rule. The U.S. parent could have avoided the full-inclusion rule through a check-the-box election to treat CFC2 as a hybrid entity, attributing its income to CFC1 (i.e., CFC2 becomes a branch or nonentity for U.S. tax purposes). If the U.S. parent had converted CFC2 to a hybrid entity, its constructive dividend would have been only $9 ($1 + $8). It would have avoided the full-inclusion rule since only 40 percent of CFC1's gross income would have been FBC income [($9 + $71) ÷ ($9 + $91 + $71 + $29)].

Subpart F income does not include U.S. source income effectively connected with a U.S. trade or business unless a U.S. tax treaty exempts the income or taxes it at a reduced rate.[41] As Chapter 8 explained, the United States taxes effectively connected income at the regular rates applicable to U.S. persons. Since the Code taxes such income currently, the purpose underlying the CFC regime—to force current payment of U.S. residual tax—

---

[40]The $8 inclusion occurs through the hopscotch rule, explained later in this chapter.
[41]IRC §952(b).

does not exist. Thus, Subpart F income excludes U.S. source effectively connected income.[42]

At the taxpayer's election, no item of either insurance income or foreign base company income (unless oil-related) is Subpart F income if a foreign jurisdiction taxes it at a relatively high rate.[43] Specifically, imposing a foreign tax rate exceeding 31.5 percent (i.e., more than 90 percent of the maximum 35 percent corporate tax rate) exempts the item from Subpart F classification.[44] In effect, the significant foreign tax means that U.S. residual tax, if any, is very small. Since U.S. shareholders obtain little or no benefit from deferring U.S. residual tax in this case, the rationale for attributing a constructive dividend to them does not exist.

**COMPLIANCE POINTER:** The IRS will not rule on whether a foreign effective tax rate exceeds 90 percent of the top U.S. statutory rate.[45]

## Foreign Base Company Income

Exhibit 12.6 lists five categories of foreign base company (FBC) income, one component of Subpart F income.[46] Each category contains gross income from specifically defined activities less allocable deductions.[47] These categories reflect congressional concern that U.S. multinationals might shift certain income to low-tax jurisdictions primarily for tax benefits. For instance, regarding foreign base company sales and services income, Congress wanted to discourage taxpayers from isolating sales and service functions in low-tax countries when related manufacturing activities occur in the United States or relatively high-tax jurisdictions.

---

[42]Interestingly, U.S. source income that is not effectively connected (i.e., FDAP income) does not escape classification as Subpart F income. Thus, the United States can withhold tax on a CFC's U.S. source investment income, and, in the same year, the CFC's U.S. shareholders must recognize the earnings applicable to the U.S. source investment income as a constructive dividend. Under IRC §245, no dividend received deduction relieves the double taxation since the earnings are not attributable to effective connected income. For full discussion of this paradox, see Richard L. Doernberg, "U.S. Double Corporate Taxation Under Subpart F," *Tax Notes International* 2 (May 1, 1991), pp. 503–506.

[43]Reg. §1.954-1(d)(1) clarifies that an "item" of income consists of aggregate income from specified transaction categories rather than income from a single transaction.

[44]IRC §954(b)(4). Announcement 95-107, 1995-52 IRB 37, clarifies that taxpayers do not add "bubble" tax rates (i.e., those retracting lower rate benefits over specified taxable income ranges) in determining the high-tax threshold.

[45]Rev. Proc. 2003-7, §3.01(3), 2003-1 IRB 233.

[46]IRC §954(a).

[47]IRC §954(b)(5).

Some CFCs argue that foreign business they conduct through partnerships does not result in FBC income since partnerships, as separate entities, are not CFCs and only CFCs derive FBC income.[48] However, the IRS applies the aggregate theory to CFC-owned partnerships in determining whether CFCs derive FBC income.[49] Under the aggregate theory, any income that would be FBC income in the hands of a CFC is FBC income to a CFC-owned partnership. Thus, the FBC income's nature flows through to CFC partners.

**Foreign base company sales income** results only when four conditions exist. First, the transaction must involve personal property; real estate transactions do not produce FBC sales income.[50] Second, the transaction producing the income must result from the:

- Purchase of personal property from a related person followed by its sale,
- Purchase of personal property followed by its sale to a related person,
- Purchase of personal property as agent of a related person, or
- Sale of personal property as agent of a related person.[51]

The first two transactions involve sales of property to which the CFC holds title; the latter transactions involve commission arrangements. All involve related persons (e.g., U.S. parent companies owning more than 50 percent of their CFC's voting power). When a CFC purchases property from an unrelated person and sells it to an unrelated person, FBC sales income does not

---

[48]*Brown Group, Inc. v. Comm.*, 77 F.3d 217 (CA-8, 1996), reversing 104 TC 105 (1995), supports this entity view. However, Notice 96-39, 1996-2 CB 209, announced that the IRS will not follow *Brown Group*. Also, Prop. Reg. §§1.952-1(g), 1.954-1(g), 1.954-2(a)(5), 1.954-3(a)(6), 1.954-4(b)(2)(iii), and 1.956-2(a)(3) espouse the IRS's aggregate view of partnerships in the CFC arena.

[49]Reg. §1.701-2(e)(1). Also, see Rev. Rul. 89-72, 1989-1 CB 257 for a specific application of the aggregate partnership theory to the CFC regime.

[50]IRC §954(d)(1) clarifies that selling agricultural commodities the United States does not produce in commercially marketable quantities (e.g., bananas and coffee) does not yield FBC sales income. Reg. §1.954-3(a)(1)(ii)(a) defines agricultural commodities broadly to include crops, livestock, poultry, farm-raised fish, and furbearing animals. Also, Reg. §1.954-3(a)(1)(i) exempts gain from classification as FBC sales income in two other situations. If the CFC substantially used the property within its business prior to its sale, gain is not FBC sales income. Also, if the CFC disposes of substantially all its noninventory property in a business discontinuation sale, the gain escapes characterization as FBC sales income. Finally, IRC §954(d)(4) clarifies that income from selling unprocessed softwood timber (e.g., logs and cants) cut in the United States or milling such timber abroad is FBC sales income.

[51]IRC §954(d)(1).

result. Similarly, commissions and fees received for selling or purchasing property on behalf of unrelated persons do not qualify as FBC sales income. Third, the buyer must use, consume, or further dispose of the property outside the CFC's country.[52] If sold for use within the CFC's country, no FBC sales income materializes. Where title passes does not matter. Fourth, the manufacture, production, growth, or extraction of property (hereafter, manufacture) must occur outside the CFC's country.[53] If manufactured within the CFC's country, FBC sales income does not result. These last two conditions highlight the essential point of FBC sales income: to currently collect U.S. residual tax when U.S. multinationals establish foreign operations in countries lacking economic relationships to their production or distribution functions.

**PLANNING POINTER:** To avoid FBC sales income and defer U.S. residual tax, multinationals can structure offshore operations to fail one of the four conditions just mentioned. Thus, manufacturing within the CFC's country avoids FBC sales income, as does selling products to customers within the CFC's country. However, traditional tax havens often lack the infrastructure, labor supply, or other production factors necessary for large-scale manufacturing operations, and most do not have teeming customer bases.

## EXAMPLE

Perfect Perfume, Inc., a domestic corporation, owns Aromatic Whiff, Ltd., which is organized in the Cayman Islands, a no-tax nation.[54] Thus, Aromatic Whiff is a CFC, and Perfect Perfume is a U.S. shareholder. Aromatic Whiff purchases ingredients from Perfect Perfume, produces fragrances in the Cayman Islands, and sells the finished product to U.S. customers. The income meets several conditions for treatment as FBC sales income: Aromatic Whiff purchases raw materials from a related person and sells personal property for use outside the Cayman Islands. However, the profit from these sales is not FBC sales income since manufacturing occurs in the Cayman Islands. Thus, Perfect Perfume receives no constructive dividend.

---

[52]IRC §954(d)(1)(B).
[53]IRC §954(d)(1)(A).
[54]PricewaterhouseCoopers, *Corporate Taxes: Worldwide Summaries 2002–2003* (Hoboken, NJ: John Wiley & Sons, Inc., 2002), p. 129.

Whether manufacturing occurs in the CFC's country (one of the four conditions for FBC sales income) is a question of fact on which taxpayers and the IRS often disagree. **Manufacturing** involves substantial transformation of raw materials, substantial conversion costs, or major assembly. In a subjective "eyeball" test, **substantial transformation** occurs when finished units become sufficiently distinguishable from raw materials or component parts. Transforming wood pulp into paper, steel rods into screws, tuna into canned fish, and scrap metal into steel railing for railroad tracks passes the substantial transformation test. Manufacturing also occurs when conversion costs (i.e., direct labor and overhead) equal or exceed 20 percent of total cost of goods sold. Finally, major assembly of component parts involving substantial processes that industry standards consider to be manufacturing qualifies. However, mere packaging, repackaging, labeling, and minor assembly are not manufacturing.[55]

---

### EXAMPLE

Classical Tales ASA, a Norwegian CFC, produces paper and CD copies of major literary works. It purchases all materials and supplies it needs to complete production from its U.S. parent company. The following table displays the CFC's production costs:

|                                              | *Paperback Books* | *Books on CD* |
| -------------------------------------------- | ----------------- | ------------- |
| a. Direct materials                          | $300,000          | $300,000      |
| b. Direct labor                              | 60,000            | 10,000        |
| c. Overhead charges                          | 50,000            | 40,000        |
| d. Cost of product sold                      | $410,000          | $350,000      |
| e. Conversion costs (line b + line c)        | $110,000          | $50,000       |
| f. Conversion percent (line e ÷ line d)      | 26.8%             | 14.3%         |

Producing paperback books meets the conversion cost test (26.8% > 20%) and, thus, is manufacturing. Profit from selling paperback

---

[55]Reg. §1.954-3(a)(4). When manufacturing occurs, U.S. law treats the CFC as though it sells personal property (finished goods) different from the personal property it purchases (raw materials or component parts). Thus, the manufacturing condition is intertwined with the purchase/sell condition in determining whether FBC sales income exists.

books to distributors is not FBC sales income. In contrast, conversion costs do not reach the 20 percent threshold when producing books on CD. Unless burning blank CDs is substantial transformation, the transfer of literary works to CDs is not manufacturing. Thus, sales of CDs to customers outside Norway result in FBC sales income to Classical Tales, and a constructive dividend to the CFC's U.S. parent company.

## KEY CASE

A domestic corporation sells component parts of bag-closing machines to its wholly owned Belgian CFC. The CFC assembles the parts and sells finished units to European and African distributors. The assembly of each bag-closing machine involves 58 steps, uses 283 separate parts, and requires 6 hours. The CFC has two business reasons for buying and assembling component parts rather than purchasing finished units from its U.S. parent. First, assembling the units abroad allows the CFC to obtain a Belgian origin certificate and, thus, avoid European tariffs and quotas. Second, assembling the units in Belgium reduces labor and overhead costs. The taxpayer argues that the assembly activity involves substantially transforming component parts or major assembly and, in either case, constitutes manufacturing. The government counters that the assembly is minor and does not involve manufacturing. The court noted that one cannot sufficiently distinguish the component parts from bag-closing equipment; thus, the activity does not involve substantial transformation. However, the court observed that the time-consuming, multistep activity requires trained personnel, proper equipment, and postassembly testing. As a substantial activity the industry generally considers to be manufacturing, the court held that manufacturing in Belgium occurs. Thus, no FBC sales income results from the assembly and sale of bag-closing machines.[56]

---

[56]*Dave Fischbein Manufacturing Company v. Comm.*, 59 TC 338 (1972), *acq.* Similarly, *Bausch & Lomb Inc., et al. v. Comm.*, TC Memo 1996-57, held that assembly of non-corrective sunglasses qualified as manufacturing since the process involved substantial skill and training for operators, inspectors, and managers (e.g., 13 weeks of close supervision for operators). The Tax Court downplayed the importance of physical capital investment, noting a substantial human capital investment. Also, the court dismissed the government's observation that each pair of sunglasses did not require substantial assembly time.

As mentioned earlier, either manufacturing or selling for use within the CFC's country causes resulting income to avoid classification as FBC sales income. This two-pronged geographical focus highlights Congress' primary objective when enacting the Subpart F legislation: to curb taxpayer incentives to shift sales income to low-tax foreign jurisdictions and defer U.S. residual tax. Companies can shift sales functions to other countries in various ways. U.S. manufacturers can establish sales branches abroad, but shifting sales activities to a nonentity results in no U.S. tax deferral. Alternatively, U.S. manufacturers can organize sales subsidiaries abroad (CFCs). Under these structures, sales to customers in other countries generate FBC sales income, while sales to customers within the CFCs' countries do not. A third course entails shifting part of U.S. parent companies' manufacturing operations to foreign subsidiaries (CFCs). FBC sales income does not result under this structure, regardless of where distributors or customers reside, since manufacturing occurs within CFCs' countries. To take this third approach a step further, manufacturing CFCs might sell their finished products through sales branches they establish in other foreign countries. When a CFC's country does not tax the sales branch's income, and the CFC establishes the branch in a low-tax jurisdiction, the Subpart F provisions this chapter has covered so far suggest a favorable tax outcome. Specifically, a CFC shifts foreign sales income to a low-tax jurisdiction and avoids its classification as FBC sales income since manufacturing occurs within the CFC's country. As a result, U.S. shareholders defer U.S. residual tax on sales profits allocable to the low-tax country.

---

### EXAMPLE

Eye Spy, Inc., a U.S. corporation, owns 100 percent of Spymaster SA, a French CFC. Spymaster manufactures espionage equipment in France and distributes its production through a Singaporean sales office. France taxes Spymaster's manufacturing profits at 35.3 percent but does not tax foreign branch income under its territorial system.[57] Singapore imposes a 24.5 percent tax on Spymaster's sales income.[58]

---

[57]PricewaterhouseCoopers, *Corporate Taxes: Worldwide Summaries 2002–2003* (Hoboken, NJ: John Wiley & Sons, Inc., 2002), p. 247. The effective tax rate equals the 33.33 percent corporate income tax rate plus the 3 percent surtax of the normal tax rate plus the 3.3 percent social contribution tax, which applies to the normal tax [33.33% + 3% (33.33%) + 3.3% (33.33%)].

[58]Ibid., p. 737. For 2001 and 2002, Singapore rebated 5 percent of the tax payable, reducing the effective tax rate to 19.5 percent.

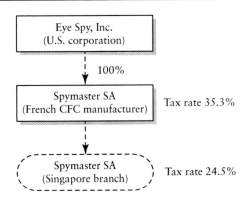

Under general rules discussed earlier, the branch profit is not FBC sales income since Spymaster manufactures the equipment it sells in France. Thus, Singapore taxes Spymaster's income attributable to its branch at a relatively low 24.5 percent and Spymaster defers U.S. residual tax on its branch income.

Special branch rules prevent the end run the preceding example illustrates. The **branch rule** applies if:

- The CFC establishes the branch outside its country of organization,
- The CFC's country does not tax foreign branch profits, and
- The branch's country imposes an effective income tax rate at least five percentage points lower than and no more than 90 percent of the effective tax rate in the CFC's country.[59]

When all three of these conditions exist, U.S. law treats the branch as a separate CFC and the branch income as FBC sales income.[60]

## EXAMPLE

In the preceding example, the branch rule applies since Spymaster establishes its sales branch outside France, France does not tax profits at-

---

[59]Reg. §1.954-3(b)(1)(i).
[60]IRC §954(d)(2). Though Congress primarily targeted sales branches, this special rule can apply to manufacturing and purchasing branches also.

tributable to the Singaporean branch under its territorial system, and Singapore's 24.5 percent rate does not exceed either 30.3 percent (35.3 − 5.0) or 31.8 percent (90% of 35.3). Thus, the CFC regime treats the branch as a separate CFC and its profit as FBC sales income. As a result, Eye Spy (as U.S. shareholder) currently pays U.S. residual tax on branch profits at the difference between U.S. and Singaporean tax rates.

## KEY CASE

Drew Chemical, a domestic corporation, owns all the stock of Drew Ameroid, a Liberian CFC. Ameroid enters into a contract manufacturing agreement with Tensia, an unrelated Belgian corporation. Under the agreement, Ameroid transfers technical information, trade secrets, know-how, and other manufacturing intangibles to Tensia that the latter uses to manufacture products Ameroid sells.

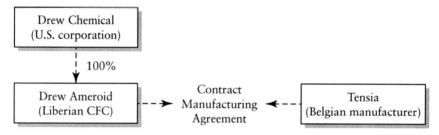

Though manufacturing occurs outside Liberia, and Ameroid sells the products to non-Liberian customers, FBC sales income does not result under the general Subpart F rules since neither the purchase nor the sale of products involves a related person. However, the government argues that the branch rule applies since Tensia is a "branch or similar establishment." The Tax Court disagrees, noting that the ordinary meaning of "branch" does not fit Tensia and that an arm's-length agreement does not cause Ameroid and Tensia to become related. Further, Ameroid possesses no right to Tensia's manufacturing income and, thus, cannot distribute such earnings to Drew Chemical, its U.S. shareholder.[61]

---

[61]*Ashland Oil, Inc. v. Comm.*, 95 TC 348 (1990). Rev. Rul. 97-48, 1997-2 CB 89, announced that the IRS would follow *Ashland Oil* but left many unanswered questions since it revoked Rev. Rul. 75-7, 1975-1 CB 244, the traditional blessing on contract manufacturing.

As Exhibit 12.6 shows, FBC income can result from CFC activities other than purchasing and selling personal property. For instance, the Code classifies income from some services as FBC income. As with FBC sales income, this provision prevents U.S. multinationals from shifting service income away from the CFC's country to low-tax jurisdictions and, thus, deferring substantial amounts of U.S. residual tax.

**Foreign base company (FBC) services income** includes compensation, commissions, and fees CFCs earn from rendering technical, managerial, engineering, architectural, scientific, skilled, industrial, commercial, or similar services if two conditions exist.[62] First, the CFC must perform such services outside its country; income from rendering services within the CFC's country is not FBC services income. Where services occur depends on the physical location of personnel performing the work. When some work occurs within, while other work occurs outside the CFC's country, service income apportionment depends on the time spent and relative value of services such personnel render.[63] The second condition exists when a CFC renders services for or on behalf of a related person (hereafter, related person services). This second condition exists when a related person substantially assists the CFC via supervision, technical staff, know-how, below-market financing (other than capital contributions), less-than-arm's-length leasing, or other means directly aiding the CFC. Performing services for which a related person compensates the CFC, to satisfy contractual or other obligations of a related person, or that represent a material portion of a related person's sales transaction (e.g., installation services related to the sale of heavy machinery) is related person services. However, when a related person merely guarantees the CFCs work, such assurance does not result in related person services.[64]

## EXAMPLE

Rose Construction Company, a U.S. corporation, owns all the stock of Desert Rose SA, a Nigerian CFC. Desert Rose contracts with an unrelated person to build an irrigation system in Botswana. To complete the contract, the CFC uses its own engineers and supervisors but relies on its U.S. parent's clerical staff. The CFC leases the needed equipment from its U.S. parent at an arm's-length rental and Rose Construction

---

[62]IRC §954(e)(1).
[63]IRC §954(e)(1)(B); Reg. §1.954-4(c).
[64]IRC §954(e)(1)(A); Reg. §1.954-4(b).

Company signs the contract as guarantor. The compensation Desert Rose receives is not FBC services income since the U.S. parent does not substantially assist the CFC. The provision of clerical services does not directly aid Desert Rose in fulfilling its contract terms and, thus, is not substantial assistance. The provision of equipment is not substantial assistance either since the CFC leases the equipment at an arm's-length rental. Finally, a mere guarantee does not qualify as substantial assistance or otherwise result in related person services.

## EXAMPLE

Disaster Recovery Services AG, a German CFC, recovers digital data from damaged computer systems following catastrophic events. Often, the CFC performs recovery services to satisfy contractual obligations of related persons and, in those cases, receives fees directly from its U.S. parent company. Disaster Recovery classifies its $700,000 service fees as follows:

|  | *Performed in Germany* | *Performed Elsewhere* |
|---|---|---|
| Related person services | $300,000 | $200,000 |
| Services on own behalf | 150,000 | 50,000 |

Disaster Recovery earns $200,000 FBC services income. If all other conditions for Subpart F income exist (e.g., effective foreign tax rate above 31.5 percent), the U.S. parent company currently recognizes the $200,000 as gross income.

Notwithstanding the two conditions just described—services outside the CFC's country and related person services—FBC services income does not result when CFCs perform services directly related to either:

- Sales or exchanges of property they manufacture when such services precede such sales or exchanges (e.g., efficiency or compatibility studies) or
- Offers or efforts to sell or exchange property they manufacture, even when the sale or exchange does not occur.[65]

---

[65]IRC §954(e)(2); Reg. §1.954-4(d).

Thus, many services directly related to and preceding sales do not produce FBC services income if the related sales do not yield FBC sales income due to the CFC manufacturing the item. Services related to sales but occurring afterward (e.g., future maintenance of equipment the owner bought from the CFC's parent company) result in FBC services income if rendered outside the CFC's country and constituting related person services.

Even more than other types of FBC income, foreign personal holding company income (FPHCI) is highly-mobile—taxpayers can easily shift this income to low-tax countries. FPHCI includes passive income such as interest (and its equivalents), dividends, annuities, rents, royalties, and net gain from investment-oriented transactions involving commodities, foreign currencies, stocks, bonds, and other investment assets.[66] However, rents and royalties CFCs derive from active businesses and receive from unrelated persons do not result in FPHCI.[67] Also, U.S. law treats most income of commodity dealers, security dealers, banks, financing companies, and insurance companies as non-FPHCI.[68]

Unlike FBC sales and services income, no blanket FPHCI exemption exists for passive income CFCs earn from within their own countries. Nonetheless, the Code carves out two specific exceptions that depend on geographical source. First, FPHCI does not include interest and dividends a CFC receives from a related corporation organized in the CFC's country if the related corporation maintains a substantial portion of its business assets in the same country. This exception recognizes that a CFC does not have FBC income if it operates a business directly and, thus, should not have FBC income from operating a business, for instance, in subsidiary form. Second, FPHCI does not include rents and royalties a CFC receives from related corporations for using property in the CFC's country.[69]

---

## EXAMPLE

Galactic Holding NV, a Dutch CFC, receives dividends from companies throughout Eurasia as follows:

|  | *Dutch Source* | *Sourced Elsewhere* |
|---|---|---|
| Dividends received from: |  |  |
| Related corporations | $10,000 | $100,000 |
| Unrelated corporations | 15,000 | 12,000 |

---

[66]IRC §954(c)(1). FPHCI does not include export financing interest.
[67]IRC §954(c)(2).
[68]IRC §954(c)(2)(C), (h), (i).
[69]IRC §954(c)(3).

Of the dividends Galactic receives from Dutch sources, it receives $10,000 from a wholly owned subsidiary that leases snow-blowing equipment and maintains all its assets in the Netherlands. Galactic has FPHCI equal to $127,000 ($100,000 + $15,000 + $12,000). The $10,000 dividend from Galactic's Dutch subsidiary avoids classification as FPHCI since Galactic receives it from a related corporation with its business assets located in the Netherlands.

**Foreign base company (FBC) shipping income** is income derived from or in connection with ocean, air, or space transportation of people or cargo. In addition to earnings from an owner's direct use of aircraft and vessels, FBC shipping income includes income from leasing or hiring aircraft and vessels for use. Income a CFC derives from or in connection with performing services directly related to using aircraft and vessels is FBC shipping income also. When the use, lease, or hire of aircraft and vessels yields FBC shipping income, gain from selling the aircraft and vessels is FBC shipping income also.[70] Notwithstanding these broad, inclusive rules, coastwise travel within the CFC's country is not FBC shipping income if the aircraft's or vessel's registration exists in the same country.[71]

**Foreign base company (FBC) oil-related income** includes foreign source income from processing, transporting, distributing, or selling minerals extracted from oil or gas wells. Foreign source income from related services and gain from disposing of related business assets (e.g., oil derricks) is FBC oil-related income also. Nonetheless, the following amounts are not FBC oil-related income:

- Income sourced within the country (including its seabed) where the oil and gas wells exist;
- Income sourced within the country where the CFC or a related person sells the oil, gas, or a primary product of either for use or consumption within the same country; and
- Income sourced within the country where an aircraft or vessel loads the oil, gas, or a primary product of either as fuel.[72]

---

[70]IRC §954(f). Rev. Rul. 87-15, 1987-1 CB 248, clarifies that even when IRC §883(a) exempts the CFC on its shipping income, Subpart F still may treat the earnings as FBC shipping income, taxable currently to U.S. shareholders.
[71]IRC §954(b)(7).
[72]IRC §954(g)(1).

Also, small corporate producers averaging fewer than 1,000 barrels daily for the current and preceding taxable year do not earn FBC oil-related income.[73] At $20 a barrel for crude oil, this limit translates into $7.3 million per year.

## Other Subpart F Components

Before the Subpart F legislation in 1962, some U.S. corporations established foreign **captive insurance companies** to self-insure their worldwide assets, activities, and personnel. U.S. corporations deducted premiums they paid to the related insurer.[74] However, when the insurance related to foreign risks, the offshore subsidiaries derived underwriting income from foreign sources and, thus, escaped U.S. taxation.[75] Domestic parent companies did not recognize the offshore earnings until they received actual dividends from their insurance subsidiaries. In effect, U.S. corporations with foreign captive arrangements often deferred U.S. residual tax for many years. In response to these self-insurance arrangements, Congress added insurance income to the Subpart F list.

Income derived from issuing or reissuing insurance or annuity contracts and attributable to risks outside a CFC's country is **insurance income**, a component of Subpart F income.[76] Thus, insurance income can result from insuring either related or unrelated persons. Whether risks lie outside a CFC's country (including within the United States) depends on the type of insurance. For property insurance, risks exist at the insured property's location. For liability insurance, risks exist where insured activity occurs. For medical and life insurance, risks exist where insured individuals reside.[77] When insurance income (attributable to outside risks) exceeds 75 percent of total premiums, the Code broadens the definition of a CFC to include foreign corporations in which U.S. shareholders hold more than 25 percent of either voting power or stock value. If U.S. shareholders hold more than 25 percent but not more than 50 percent of voting power or stock value, Sub-

---

[73]IRC §954(g)(2).

[74]In addition to the Subpart F issues, the IRS may disallow deductions when U.S. persons pay for self-insurance. See Rev. Rul. 2001-31, 2001-1 CB 1348.

[75]IRC §861(a)(7) sources underwriting income from issuing property and liability insurance according to the location of insured risks, not the insured parent company's residence. Before 1962, the United States could not tax the premiums as effectively connected income since this concept did not appear in the Code until 1966.

[76]IRC §953(a). Per IRC §953(b)(4), apportioned deductions reduce gross insurance income to determine the constructive dividend to U.S. shareholders.

[77]Reg. §1.953-2(e)-(g).

part F income includes only insurance income from outside risks (e.g., Subpart F income does not include FBC services income).[78]

---

**EXAMPLE**

The Health and Wealth Insurance Company, Ltd., a Bermudan CFC, derives $400,000 gross income from providing medical insurance; 5 percent of this income comes from Bermudan residents. The company's Subpart F income equals $380,000 ($400,000 × .95) before apportioning deductions.

---

To avoid CFC status, some U.S. multinationals pooled their resources to establish super captives in the Bahamas, Bermuda, the Cayman Islands, or similar tax haven. **Super captives** were **offshore** insurance companies with several U.S. and foreign owners with shares spread thinly so few if any U.S. owners held 10 percent or more voting power. If U.S. shareholders held no more than 25 percent of the stock, super captives were not CFCs and, thus, avoided Subpart F. In response, Congress carved out a special category of insurance income. After 1986, **related person insurance income (RPII)**, a foreign corporation's insurance income attributable to outside risks and derived from U.S. persons owning its stock and persons related to such owners, qualifies as Subpart F income if the foreign corporation receiving the income is a CFC.[79] For RPII, U.S. shareholders include all U.S. persons owning stock in the foreign corporation at issue, not just those owning 10 percent voting power. Thus, foreign corporations in which U.S. persons own more than 25 percent of either stock value or voting power are CFCs after 1986, but only for treating RPII as Subpart F income.[80]

---

**EXAMPLE**

Foreign shareholders own 73 percent of Casualty & Property Insurance, Ltd., a Bermudan corporation. Three unrelated U.S. corporations each own 9 percent. The Bermudan corporation earns income in the following categories:

---

[78]IRC §957(b).
[79]IRC §953(c)(2).
[80]IRC §953(c)(1).

| Premiums from insuring non-Bermudan risks | $400,000 |
| Foreign personal holding company income (FPHCI) | 200,000 |
| Total gross income | $600,000 |

Of the $400,000 premiums, $90,000 is RPII. For FPHCI, Casualty & Property is not a CFC since no U.S. person owns at least 10 percent voting power and, thus, U.S. shareholders do not own more than 50 percent. For the $310,000 premiums that are not RPII, Casualty & Property is not a CFC for the same reason—no U.S. shareholders—though the threshold for CFC status drops to 25 percent. However, for the $90,000 RPII, all three U.S. corporations are U.S. shareholders. Since their combined ownership exceeds the 25 percent threshold, the Bermudan corporation qualifies as a CFC and the $90,000 RPII is Subpart F income.

CFCs participating in or cooperating with **international boycotts** (other than those the United States approves) increase Subpart F income and, thus, the constructive dividend to U.S. shareholders.[81] Participation or cooperation occurs when, as a condition for doing business with any person or government, a CFC agrees not to conduct business with a particular country (e.g., Israel), U.S. persons conducting business in a boycotted country, or companies that persons with particular nationalities, races, or religions own or manage. Not selecting corporate directors or not hiring employees of particular nationalities, races, or religions may constitute participation or cooperation in a boycott when any person or government demands the practice as a condition for doing business.[82] A CFC must include the amount from equation 12.1 in Subpart F income if the CFC or any member of its controlled group participates in or cooperates with an international boycott:[83]

$$BRI = (INC - CD - ECI) \times \frac{\text{Operations related to boycotting nations}}{\text{Worldwide operations}}$$

$$(12.1)$$

---

[81]IRC §§952(a)(3); 999(b)(4)(A). Also, IRC §908 reduces the foreign tax credit, and IRC §995(b)(1)(F)(ii) increases C corporations' deemed dividends from DISCs.
[82]IRC §999(b)(3).
[83]IRC §999(b)(1), (c)(1). In lieu of the formula approach, IRC §999(c)(1) permits taxpayers to identify operations specifically related to participating or cooperating in boycotts and treat only income related to such operations as boycott-related income.

where:

BRI = CFC's boycott-related income that becomes Subpart F income

INC = Gross income less allocable deductions

CD = Constructive dividend before considering BRI

ECI = U.S. source effectively connected income less allocable deductions

> **COMPLIANCE POINTER:** The list of boycotting nations includes Bahrain, Iraq, Kuwait, Lebanon, Libya, Oman, Qatar, Saudi Arabia, Syria, United Arab Emirates, and Yemen.[84] On request, the IRS will rule on whether a particular activity constitutes participating in or co-operating with an international boycott.[85] Simply conducting business with the government or residents of these countries is not participation or cooperation.

Subpart F income results when CFCs derive income from countries:[86]

- Whose governments the Arms Export Control Act does not allow to buy U.S. defense articles or services and the United States does not recognize,
- With which the United States has severed or does not conduct diplomatic relations, or
- That repeatedly support international terrorism.[87]

The list of wayward countries includes Cuba, Iran, Iraq, Libya, North Korea, Sudan, and Syria.[88] After subtracting allocable deductions, CFCs treat all income derived from these countries as Subpart F income.[89]

CFCs include in Subpart F income amounts equal to illegal bribes, kickbacks, or other sums they pay directly or indirectly to government officials, employees, or agents. Payments are illegal under this provision if the Foreign Corrupt Practices Act of 1977 prohibits U.S. persons from making them.[90] In contrast to all other forms of Subpart F income, U.S. law bases this item on a cash outflow or expense rather than an income item. Legal bribes and kickbacks and illegal payments to persons without government ties do not produce Subpart F income.

---

[84]Notice 95-65, 1995-2 CB 342.

[85]IRC §999(d).

[86]IRC §952(a)(5).

[87]IRC §901(j)(2)(A).

[88]Rev. Rul. 95-63, 1995-2 CB 85.

[89]IRC §952(a)(5).

[90]IRC §952(a)(4). Further, IRC §964(a) clarifies that these illegal payments do not reduce E&P.

## EXAMPLE

Commercial Cargo, Ltd., a CFC, pays a $20,000 bribe to a Dubai government official to process its applications for establishing a "free zone establishment" and for obtaining a trade license in the United Arab Emirates' Jebel Ali Free Zone.[91] If a U.S. person had paid this bribe, it would have been illegal under the Foreign Corrupt Practices Act. Commercial Cargo has $20,000 Subpart F income.

## EARNINGS INVESTED IN U.S. PROPERTY

Even when CFCs earn no Subpart F income, U.S. shareholders still receive constructive dividends when CFCs increase their earnings invested in U.S. property (see Exhibit 12.6).[92] These constructive dividends result not from how CFCs derive earnings but from how they invest earnings. The presence of earnings indicates an ability to pay dividends, and U.S. law views investment of those earnings in U.S. property (e.g., loans to U.S. shareholders) as indirect repatriations. Thus, the Code precludes U.S. shareholders from using CFCs' earnings while avoiding U.S. residual tax.

> **PLANNING POINTER:** U.S. shareholders sometimes want constructive dividends because of the accompanying foreign tax credit.[93] Actual dividends may be undesirable due to high foreign withholding rates, or impossible because of foreign currency restrictions. U.S. shareholders without Subpart F income that, nonetheless, desire constructive dividends can assertively invest their earnings in U.S. property.

Only earnings CFCs directly or indirectly invest in U.S. property trigger constructive dividends. **U.S. property** includes:

- Tangible property located in the United States unless the CFC exports it to or uses it in a foreign country; uses it in transportation activities tak-

---

[91]Deloitte Touche Tohmatsu, *United Arab Emirates*, International Tax and Business Guide Series (New York: Deloitte, 1997), pp. 8–11.
[92]IRC §951(a)(1)(B).
[93]IRC §960(a). While IRC §902 permits a deemed paid credit (DPC) for actual dividends, IRC §960 allows a DPC for constructive dividends. For CFCs in low-tax jurisdictions, constructive dividends enable U.S. shareholders to absorb excess credits from other countries, especially those about to expire.

ing place predominantly abroad; or uses it to explore for, develop, remove, or transport resources from the ocean or the U.S. continental shelf's subsoil.[94]

■ Stock in and obligations of domestic corporations qualifying as U.S. shareholders or in which U.S. shareholders directly, indirectly, or constructively own at least 25 percent voting power.[95]

■ Obligations of noncorporate U.S. persons, except U.S. government instruments, currency, bank deposits, and accounts receivables from selling or processing property.[96]

■ Rights to use manufacturing intangible property in the United States.[97]

CFCs subtract their U.S. source income that is effectively connected with a U.S. trade or business from the amounts listed above.[98]

## KEY CASE

A U.S. company handles cash disbursements and receipts through a centralized cash management system. For interaffiliate transactions, the system offsets intercompany receivables against payables. The U.S. company asserts that intercompany payables it owes to two CFCs do not represent investments in U.S. properties since regulations exempt debt collected within one year and, based on a FIFO assumption, the payables turn over annually. The government counters that the balances constitute single, open account loans and, thus, represent loans to a U.S. shareholder and result in constructive dividends. The court agrees, observing that the U.S. company cannot trace

---

[94]IRC §956(c)(1)(A), (2)(B), (D), (G). Transportation assets include aircraft, vessels, motor vehicles, containers, and railroad rolling stock. Ocean-related assets include only movable properties other than aircraft and vessels (e.g., movable drilling rigs).
[95]IRC §956(c)(1)(B), (C), (2)(F). Rev. Rul. 87-89, 1987-2 CB 195, explains that indirect investments in U.S. property, such as back-to-back loans and similar multiparty financing arrangements, also produce constructive dividends.
[96]IRC §956(c)(1)(C), (2)(A), (C). However, IRC §956(c)(3) explains that U.S. property includes trade and service receivables that CFCs factor for related U.S. persons. Also, IRC §956(d) treats CFCs acting as pledgors or guarantors for U.S. obligations as though the obligations are theirs, an investment in U.S. property. *Ludwig v. Comm.*, 68 TC 979 (1977), holds that a U.S. shareholder's use of CFC stock as loan collateral does not cause the CFC to become a loan guarantor. Nonetheless, Treasury administratively limited the decision with Reg. §1.956-2(c)(2) when a U.S. shareholder pledges CFC shares representing two-thirds of the CFC's voting power and other conditions exist.
[97]IRC §956(c)(1)(D).
[98]IRC §956(c)(1)(H).

individual transactions through its clearinghouse system. Since the U.S. company can use the foreign earnings, the court holds that the CFCs invested such amounts in U.S. property, producing constructive dividends.[99]

Only increases over the prior year's investment of earnings in U.S. property trigger constructive dividends. CFCs measure investments in U.S. property as the E&P adjusted bases of assets less debts to which the assets are subject; asset appreciation and depreciation do not change a CFC's investment in U.S. property.[100] After summing the adjusted bases of U.S. properties, CFCs subtract an amount equal to their U.S. source income that is effectively connected with U.S. trades or businesses to determine their investments in U.S. property.[101] CFCs' **applicable earnings**, consisting of accumulated and current E&P, limit constructive dividends from increased investments in U.S. property.[102]

## EXAMPLE

Piratical Enterprises, a wholly owned CFC without Subpart F income, began selling nautical supplies one year ago. During the first year, its average assets include:

| | |
|---|---|
| U.S. parent company's long-term note | $20,000 |
| Balance in U.S. bank account | 50,000 |
| Mercedes for corporate officers (kept in Miami) | 70,000 |
| Stock in U.S. parent's domestic subsidiary | 30,000 |
| U.S. Treasury bills | 40,000 |
| Loan to unrelated U.S. partnership | 10,000 |
| Accounts receivable from unrelated U.S. persons | 60,000 |

Piratical's investment in U.S. property equals $130,000 ($20,000 + $70,000 + $30,000 + $10,000). If Piratical's applicable earnings equal $125,000, the U.S. parent company realizes a $125,000 constructive dividend.

---

[99]*Gulf Oil Corporation v. Comm.*, 87 TC 548 (1986). The regulations mentioned in this decision refer to former Reg. §1.956-2(d)(2).
[100]IRC §956(a).
[101]IRC §956(c)(2)(H).
[102]IRC §956(a)(2), (b)(1).

## CONSTRUCTIVE DIVIDENDS

The Code attributes constructive dividends only to U.S. shareholders of CFCs (i.e., U.S. persons owning at least 10 percent voting power). Further, U.S. shareholders receive constructive dividends only for direct and indirect holdings.[103] Under the **hopscotch rule,** constructive dividends received from indirect holdings "hop over" intermediary CFCs; that is, U.S. shareholders' gross income rises without increasing the gross income of intervening foreign corporations. Also, constructive ownership rules can treat U.S. persons as U.S. shareholders even though U.S. law does not attribute constructive dividends to the stock they constructively hold.

### EXAMPLE

United Merchant, Inc., a domestic corporation, owns 9 percent of Commercial Trading Limited, a CFC with no U.S. property, and 40 percent of Mercantile Exchange, Inc., a U.S. company. Mercantile, in turn, holds 6 percent of Commercial stock. Discount Warehouse S.A., a foreign corporation, owns the remaining 85 percent of Commercial, and Deals Are Us, Inc., a domestic company, owns all of Discount. None of these shares change hands during the taxable year.

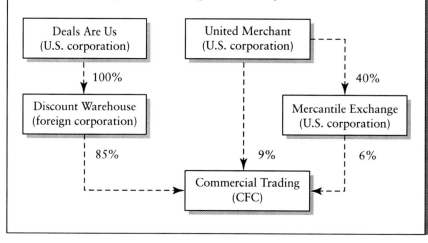

---

[103]IRC §951(a)(1). Constructive dividends occur only when a foreign corporation qualifies as a CFC for at least 30 straight days during the taxable year. Thus, momentary excursions into CFC territory for fewer than 30 days do not result in constructive dividends.

United holds 9 percent of Commercial directly, 0 indirectly, and 2.4 percent constructively (40% × 6%). Thus, United is a U.S. shareholder since its stock holdings sum to 11.4 percent. Mercantile is not a U.S. shareholder since it holds only 6 percent of Commercial directly. (Mercantile does not constructively own 9 percent through United since the latter is not a 50 percent owner of Mercantile.) However, Deals Are Us is a U.S. shareholder since it holds 85 percent of Commercial indirectly and 100 percent constructively. If Commercial's Subpart F income equals $100,000, United, Mercantile, and Deals recognize constructive dividends of $9,000, 0, and $85,000, respectively. Deals' constructive dividend from Commercial occurs under the hopscotch rule.

Each shareholder's constructive dividend equals his or her pro rata share of Subpart F income and increase in earnings invested in U.S. property.[104] To prevent double taxation, the constructive dividend increases the stock basis of U.S. shareholders.[105] In effect, the Code treats U.S. shareholders as though they receive actual dividends (involving no basis adjustment), after which they return the funds through buying additional shares (increasing their bases). Later distributions of previously taxed earnings reduce stock basis.[106] Thus, U.S. shareholders receiving distributions of amounts previously taxed treat such receipts as capital recoveries rather than earnings.

## EXAMPLE

In the preceding example, assume the adjusted basis of United Merchant's direct holding in Commercial Trading stock equals $130,000 before considering Commercial's Subpart F income. The constructive dividend increases United's basis in Commercial stock to $139,000. Later, when United actually receives a $9,000 dividend from the earnings attributable to the constructive dividend, United subtracts $9,000 from its basis in Commercial stock. Assume the adjusted basis of Deals' direct holding in Discount is $300,000 before considering Commercial's Subpart F income. The constructive dividend increases Deals' basis in Discount's stock to $385,000.

---

[104]IRC §951(a)(1).
[105]IRC §961(a). Reg. §1.961-1(a)(1)(ii) clarifies that U.S. shareholders increase the basis of stock held directly when they recognize constructive dividends attributable to indirect holdings.
[106]IRC §961(b)(1).

During each taxable year, U.S. shareholders recognize constructive dividends only for stock they directly or indirectly hold on the last day the foreign corporation is a CFC.[107] Thus, U.S. shareholders do not recognize constructive dividends when they dispose of their CFC holdings and the foreign corporation continues to qualify as a CFC. Equation 12.2 shows how U.S. shareholders calculate their constructive dividends attributable to Subpart F income (as opposed to investments in U.S. property). U.S. shareholders' pro rata shares of Subpart F income depend on their direct and indirect ownership, the portion of the year the foreign corporation is a CFC, dividends the CFC pays to prior or later owners of the relevant shares, and the portion of the year the U.S. shareholder does not own CFC stock.[108]

$$
\begin{aligned}
&\begin{array}{c}\text{Pro Rata Share}\\\text{of Subpart F}\\\text{Income}\end{array} = \left[\begin{array}{c}\text{Direct and Indirect}\\\text{Ownership on Last}\\\text{Day CFC Status}\\\text{Held}\end{array} \times \begin{array}{c}\text{Subpart}\\\text{F Income}\end{array} \times \frac{\text{Days FC Is a CFC}}{\text{Days in Year}}\right]\\[2em]
&- \left[\text{Lesser of:} \left(\begin{array}{c}\text{Dividends During}\\\text{Year to Prior or}\\\text{Later Owner}\end{array}\right) \underline{\text{or}} \left(\begin{array}{c}\text{Direct and Indirect}\\\text{Ownership on Last}\\\text{Day CFC Status Held}\end{array}\right)\right.\\[2em]
&\left.\times \begin{array}{c}\text{Subpart}\\\text{F Income}\end{array} \times \frac{\text{Days U.S. Shareholder Does Not Own Stock}}{\text{Days in Year}}\right]
\end{aligned} \qquad (12.2)
$$

For CFCs with Subpart F income, special coordination rules prevent U.S. shareholders from recognizing the same earnings as constructive dividends twice—when earned and again later when invested in U.S. property. After U.S. shareholders recognize Subpart F income as constructive dividends, CFCs can invest the same earnings (i.e., those attributable to Subpart F income) in U.S. property or distribute the earnings without burdening U.S. shareholders with further tax.[109] Also, the Code presumes that CFCs invest all their U.S. source, effectively connected income in U.S. property, so an equal amount avoids treatment as constructive dividends.[110] Equation 12.3 summarizes the calculation.

---

[107]IRC §951(a)(1).
[108]IRC §951(a)(2).
[109]IRC §959(a).
[110]IRC §956(c)(2)(H).

$$
\begin{aligned}
\begin{array}{c}\text{Pro Rata Share}\\\text{of Increase in}\\\text{Earnings Invested}\\\text{in U.S. Property}\end{array}
&= \left[
\begin{array}{c}\text{Average}\\\text{U.S.}\\\text{Property}\end{array}
\times
\begin{array}{c}\text{Direct and Indirect}\\\text{Ownership on Last}\\\text{Day CFC Status}\\\text{Held}\end{array}
\times
\begin{array}{c}\text{Days FC Is}\\\text{a CFC}\\\hline\text{Days in Year}\end{array}
\right]
\end{aligned}
$$

$$
\begin{aligned}
-\;
\begin{array}{c}\text{Pro Rata Share of}\\\text{Earnings Previously Taxed}\\\text{as Subpart F Income}\end{array}
\;-\;
\begin{array}{c}\text{Pro Rata Share of}\\\text{Earnings Previously}\\\text{Taxed Due to Investment}\\\text{in U.S. Property}\end{array}
\qquad (12.3)
\end{aligned}
$$

**PLANNING POINTER:** Deemed paid credits (DPCs) accompany constructive dividends to U.S. shareholders that are Corporations. U.S. law usually does not allow DPCs to noncorporate U.S. shareholders. However, U.S. shareholders who are individuals, trusts, or estates can elect treatment as domestic corporations. Electing individuals pay U.S. income tax at corporate rates on their constructive dividends and obtain DPCs the same as domestic corporations.[111] Elections apply only to single taxable years. Individuals, trusts, and estates can choose whether to make the election again in each future year.[112] The election often reduces U.S. taxation when the top individual tax rate exceeds the highest corporate rate since the DPC mitigates the effect of double taxation.

When investors sell or exchange stock held longer than one year for more than adjusted basis, they normally recognize long-term capital gain.[113] However, under the CFC regime, concern arose that U.S. shareholders might convert dividend income into more favorably taxed capital gain. Thus, when U.S. shareholders realize gain from disposing of foreign stock, the Code may treat some gain as a dividend. The dividend portion equals the seller's pro rata share of **Section 1248 earnings**, which are E&P that U.S. law has not previously treated as constructive dividends and the foreign corporation accumulated while a CFC and during the period the seller qualified as a U.S. shareholder.[114] Thus, this anticonversion rule applies to E&P not previously

---

[111]IRC §962(a); Reg. §1.962-2(a). The election does not allow noncorporate persons to obtain deemed paid credits when receiving actual dividends.
[112]IRC §962(b).
[113]IRC §1222(3).
[114]IRC §1248(a). Only persons who have been U.S. shareholders of CFCs (i.e., owning 10 percent or more voting power) within the past five years must treat gain as dividend income.

treated as Subpart F income and not previously treated as an increased investment in U.S. property. Conversion of long-term capital gain is not necessarily unfavorable to U.S. corporate shareholders since deemed paid credits may accompany the dividends.[115]

---

[115]IRC §960(a)(1).

# CHAPTER 13

# Other Antideferral Provisions

**U.S.** multinationals have significant economic incentives to earn profit abroad in low-tax jurisdictions and defer dividend remittances to the United States. The present value benefits of postponing U.S. residual tax on such earnings can be substantial. For instance, assuming a 10 percent discount rate, deferring U.S. tax of $1 million for 20 years saves, on a present value basis, over $850,000.

Chapter 12 explained the Code's primary obstacle to long-term deferral strategies: U.S. shareholders of controlled foreign corporations (CFCs) must report constructive dividends for their pro rata share of the CFC's Subpart F income and other earnings invested in U.S. property. However, avoiding the elongated reach of the CFC tentacles does not necessarily yield a tax deferral bonanza. Congress has added other long-range artillery to the IRS's formidable arsenal of antideferral weaponry besides the CFC legislation, namely provisions affecting passive foreign investment companies and foreign personal holding companies. These regimes often prevent foreign corporations from reaching tax deferral paradise, even if such entities avoid CFC status.

## PASSIVE FOREIGN INVESTMENT COMPANIES

Between 1962 and 1987, U.S. investors found several ways to circumvent Subpart F's constructive dividend mechanism. The most obvious means involved dispersing a foreign corporation's ownership widely so the company did not become a CFC. Passive investors found this strategy simple. Instead of investors setting up separate foreign corporations to hold stocks, bonds, and similar passive assets, investors pooled their resources into one foreign investment company or mutual fund. If no U.S. person owned 10 percent or more of the voting power, the foreign investment company did not have U.S. shareholders. Without U.S. shareholders, the company did not qualify as a CFC. If not a CFC, Subpart F's constructive dividend mechanism did not operate to end tax deferral. Even with one or more U.S. shareholders, the company still avoided CFC status if such shareholders owned no more than 50 percent of voting power and stock value.

---

### EXAMPLE

Eleven unrelated U.S. citizens invest $1 million each in a newly organized Bermudan corporation, and each receives 9.09 percent of the company's only class of stock. The Bermudan corporation invests the $11 million in high-grade U.S. corporate bonds. The corporation's interest income qualifies as portfolio interest and, thus, avoids U.S. tax.[1] Also, Bermuda imposes no corporate income tax on the interest.[2] To avoid U.S. residual tax, the corporation pays no dividends to its stockholders. The longer the corporation defers dividends, the longer the U.S. citizens defer payment of U.S. residual tax and the greater their present value benefits.

---

U.S. persons owning passive foreign investment company (PFIC, pronounced PEA-fick) stock pay an interest charge based on the present value benefits they derive from deferring U.S. residual tax. Congress had sound reasons for imposing the interest charge: to discourage U.S. persons from pooling resources in foreign mutual funds and, thus, indefinitely deferring U.S. residual tax. The PFIC legislation sought parity between the treatment of U.S. investors investing in passive assets directly and U.S. investors investing in passive assets through foreign corporations. Congress wanted to place both types of investors on an equal footing—current U.S. taxation or its equivalence.[3]

---

[1]IRC §881(c).
[2]PricewaterhouseCoopers, *Corporate Taxes: Worldwide Summaries 2002–2003* (Hoboken, NJ: John Wiley & Sons, Inc., 2002), p. 68.
[3]One might wonder why Congress did not compel U.S. investors to annually report their pro rata shares of PFIC profit. Though such an approach prevents deferral of U.S. residual tax and, thus, achieves parity, minority owners lack the clout to demand earnings information from PFICs, and the United States could not require PFICs, as foreign entities, to disclose or provide such information. Nonetheless, Congress does allow U.S. investors to treat their investments as qualified electing funds if they choose, which provides flow-through treatment. This chapter discusses qualified electing funds later.

Unfortunately, something went dreadfully wrong in the waning moments preceding the congressional vote.[4] As a result, the final version of the PFIC legislation cast a much broader net than many expected. Not only did it lessen foreign investment companies' incentives to defer U.S. tax, but it also jeopardized deferral benefits for many foreign corporations with legitimate, ongoing business activities. The loss of deferral benefits reduced capital import neutrality for many U.S. multinationals with active businesses, impairing their global competitiveness.

## PFIC Definition

Only U.S. persons owning stock in PFICs pay interest charges. PFICs are foreign corporations meeting either of the following tests, shown in equations 13.1 and 13.2, for the taxable year:[5]

$$\frac{\text{Passive gross income}}{\text{Gross income}} \geq 75\% \qquad (13.1)$$

$$\frac{\text{Passive assets}}{\text{Assets}} \geq 50\% \qquad (13.2)$$

Unlike the CFC regime, PFIC status does not depend on ownership.[6] As a result, most offshore mutual funds engaging primarily in passive investment activities meet one or both tests annually and, thus, qualify as PFICs every year. Despite the word "passive" in PFIC, foreign corporations engaged in active businesses can and often do become PFICs also. Whether engaged in passive investment activities or ongoing business activities, once a foreign corporation qualifies as a PFIC, the taint lingers. Tax professionals sometimes articulate the adage: "Once a PFIC, always a PFIC."[7]

In equation 13.1, **passive gross income** includes dividends, interest, annuities, and nonbusiness rents and royalties. The term also embraces net gain

---

[4]For in interesting historical perspective, see George F. Bernardi, "The Stealth Bombing of CFCs by the PFIC Provisions: Tax Strategies after TAMRA," *Taxes*, 67 (June 1989), pp. 351–367.

[5]IRC §1297(a).

[6]Though foreign corporations with no U.S. owners may qualify as PFICs, no tax consequences result.

[7]IRC §1298(b)(1) treats shares as PFIC stock if the foreign corporation has been a PFIC at *any* time during the U.S. investor's holding period. Thus, a U.S. person may own shares in a foreign corporation meeting the passive income test, passive asset test, or both in 2003 but meeting neither test in 2004. In this case, the Code treats the U.S. person's shares as PFIC stock in 2004 also.

from disposing of stocks, bonds, commodities, currencies, and other investment assets. However, passive income does not include dividends, interest, rents, and royalties received from related persons if allocable to their nonpassive income or sourced in the PFIC's country.[8] For instance, the passive nature of nonbusiness rental income a foreign corporation receives from its parent company depends on the parent's activities. If the parent's rental expense relates to its business, the foreign subsidiary's rental income is active and, thus, does not appear in the numerator of equation 13.1 when testing for PFIC status.

Foreign corporations meet the passive asset test in equation 13.2 only if their average percentage reaches or exceeds 50 percent. **Passive assets** include property that produces passive income (e.g., stocks and bonds a manufacturer holds) or that the foreign corporation holds to produce passive income in the reasonably foreseeable future (e.g., bank CDs a newspaper publisher holds to fund expansion in two years).[9] Publicly traded foreign corporations use the value of assets in equation 13.2. Nonpublicly traded CFCs use the earnings and profits (E&P) adjusted bases of assets. All other foreign corporations use the value of assets unless they elect to use E&P adjusted bases.[10]

> **PLANNING POINTER:** In some ways, the approach to defining PFICs is menacingly simplistic. It focuses only on aggregate income and assets, ignores ownership entirely, and applies separately to each taxable year. As a result, foreign corporations with active business operations must monitor passive income and asset levels closely and, as appropriate, strategically modify each level to avoid PFIC status. Particularly vulnerable entities include companies owning few business assets, such as service and Internet-based firms, firms experiencing shortfalls in sales or increases in expenses so business profits decline or turn into losses, enterprises raising large amounts of capital for future expansion, and companies disposing of large equity interests in operating companies.

---

[8] IRC §1297(b)(1).

[9] IRC §1297(a)(2) and Notice 88-22, 1988-1 CB 489.

[10] IRC §1297(f). For many mutual funds, the nature of their asset holdings (i.e., publicly traded stocks and bonds) facilitate the collection of asset values and computation in equation 13.2. For CFCs whose stock does not publicly trade and, thus, whose financial information might not be as readily available to minority shareholders, assets' adjusted bases provide the equation 13.2 measures.

---

## EXAMPLE

Foreign persons own 94 percent of Marathon Ltd., a foreign investment company. Owen, the only U.S. stockholder, holds a 6 percent interest. Thus, the company is not a CFC. Marathon actively conducts some business, but most of its activities involve passive investments in European stocks and bonds. During the year, Marathon classifies its gross income and average assets as follows:

|                | Passive         | Active          |
|----------------|-----------------|-----------------|
| Gross income   | $ 15,000,000    | $  6,000,000    |
| Average assets | 150,000,000     | 100,000,000     |

Marathon falls below the gross income threshold in equation 13.1 ($15,000,000 ÷ $21,000,000 < 75%). However, its passive assets exceed the asset limit in equation 13.2 ($150,000,000 ÷ $250,000,000 > 50%). Thus, Marathon qualifies as a PFIC even though only one U.S. person owns stock in Marathon and that person holds a portfolio interest. As this chapter explains later, the consequences of PFIC status fall on Owen. PFIC status does not directly affect Marathon or the foreign shareholders.

---

Even when foreign corporations meet the passive income test, passive asset test, or both, the Code identifies two situations in which such corporations still escape PFIC status. One relates to start-up years; the other relates to years in which foreign corporations sell off one or more businesses. In both situations, companies may earn more passive income than normal, increasing the possibility of reaching equation 13.1's 75 percent threshold. For instance, business income often is relatively low during a company's initial year when it has yet to establish a market for its products or services. Also, new capital may sit idly in passive investments for a while, increasing passive income, until the company buys operating assets. Nonetheless, foreign corporations escape PFIC status in start-up years—even though they may meet the passive income test, passive asset test, or both—if they avoid PFIC status in their second and third years.[11] Similarly, foreign corporations deriving substantially all their passive income from selling one or more businesses escape PFIC status if they do not meet the passive income test or the passive asset test in the following two years.[12]

---

[11]IRC §1298(b)(2).
[12]IRC §1298(b)(3).

To provide relief for foreign holding companies, Congress enacted a look-through rule. In testing for the 50 and 75 percent thresholds, foreign corporations look through 25-percent-owned subsidiaries. That is, foreign corporations ignore dividends received from such subsidiaries when applying equation 13.1, and U.S. law treats the foreign corporation as though it receives a proportionate amount of its subsidiary's income. Similarly, foreign corporations do not treat stock they hold in 25-percent-owned subsidiaries as assets when applying equation 13.2. Instead, the Code treats the foreign corporation as though it owns a proportionate interest in each asset of its 25-percent-owned subsidiary.[13]

---

## EXAMPLE

Opal SA, a foreign corporation U.S. shareholders do not control, owns 40 percent of Zircon, Inc. Zircon owns only active business assets and earns only active business income. The following table shows the income and average assets of these entities for the taxable year:

|  | *Passive* | *Active* |
|---|---|---|
| Opal (parent) | | |
| Gross income | $ 24,000,000 | $ 6,000,000 |
| Average assets | 110,000,000 | 90,000,000 |
| Zircon (subsidiary) | | |
| Gross income | $ 0 | $10,000,000 |
| Average assets | 0 | 60,000,000 |

Without the look-through rule, Opal meets the passive income and asset tests, either of which causes it to be a PFIC. Specifically, its passive income equals 80 percent of total gross income ($24 million ÷ $30 million) and its passive assets equal 55 percent of total assets ($110 million ÷ $200 million). Assume Opal's income and asset totals in the table include a $1 million dividend from Zircon and a $22 million holding in Zircon stock. Removing these passive items from Opal's totals and applying the look-through rule yields the following result for the passive income test:

$$\frac{\$24,000,000 - \$1,000,000}{\$24,000,000 + \$6,000,000 - \$1,000,000 + .4(\$10,000,000)}$$

$$= 69.7\%$$

---

[13]IRC §1297(c).

Thus, the look-through rule causes the passive income percentage to drop from 80 to 69.7 percent. Similarly, applying the look-through rule to the passive asset test yields the following result:

$$\frac{\$110,000,000 - \$22,000,000}{\$110,000,000 + \$90,000,000 - \$22,000,000 + .4(\$60,000,000)}$$
$$= 43.6\%$$

Thus, the look-through rule causes the passive asset percentage to drop from 55 to 43.6 percent. Since the passive income and asset test results fall below the respective 75 and 50 percent thresholds, Opal avoids classification as a PFIC thanks to its 40 percent interest in Zircon.

**PLANNING POINTER:** In some cases, foreign corporations holding less than 25 percent of corporations conducting active businesses can avoid PFIC status through increasing their equity ownership beyond the 25 percent threshold.

## PFIC Consequence

Unlike the CFC regime, PFIC provisions do not use constructive dividends as the mechanism for reducing deferral benefits. In fact, U.S. persons owning PFIC stock can defer U.S. residual tax for many years. However, when U.S. persons receive distributions from PFICs or dispose of PFIC stock, U.S. law recaptures the present value benefit attributable to the deferral period through an interest charge. That is, interest charges retroactively negate the benefits from deferring U.S. residual tax.

Receiving distributions from PFICs significantly exceeding distributions in prior years can result in an interest charge. U.S. persons, even those owning portfolio interests, calculate their **total excess distribution** as the aggregate distributions they receive during the year less a base amount. The base equals 125 percent of distributions the U.S. person received during the preceding three taxable years (or the person's holding period if shorter), but only to the extent the U.S. person included those distributions in gross income.[14] As a relief measure, the Code sets the total excess distribution to

---

[14]IRC §1291(b)(2)(A). Thus, the base does not include distributions a U.S. person received in the three preceding years that were allocable to earlier PFIC years and, thus, not included in gross income during those three years. The chapter explains this allocation procedure later.

zero in the first year U.S. persons hold PFIC stock.[15] Equation 13.3 summarizes the calculation for the second and succeeding years:

$$
\begin{array}{l}
\text{Total} \\
\text{Excess} \\
\text{Distribution}
\end{array}
=
\begin{array}{l}
\text{Current} \\
\text{Aggregate} \\
\text{Distributions}
\end{array}
-
\left(
125\% \times
\begin{array}{l}
\text{Average Distributions} \\
\text{Included in Gross} \\
\text{Income Over Preceding} \\
\text{Three Years}
\end{array}
\right)
\quad (13.3)
$$

The underlying premise is that significant increases in current distributions compared with recent years suggest that the PFIC curtailed dividends in prior years to defer U.S. residual tax.

For specific PFIC shares, the Code allocates the total excess distribution ratably among all distributions for the taxable year. The portion allocable to a given distribution is an **excess distribution,** which the U.S. person allocates on a daily basis over the shares' holding period. For each distribution, the U.S. person includes the nonexcess portion (i.e., distribution amount not exceeding the base) in gross income as ordinary income. Also, the U.S. person reports current gross income for any portion of the excess distribution allocable to the current taxable year, days before 1987 (i.e., preceding the PFIC legislation), and days preceding PFIC status.[16] Exhibit 13.1 captures the process of allocating PFIC distributions among years.[17]

Any portion of an excess distribution allocable to post-1986 years (other than the current year) during which the distributor company qualifies as a PFIC results in a deferred tax amount. The **deferred tax amount** consists of two parts: the aggregate increases in taxes and the aggregate amount of interest on such taxes.[18] The U.S. person's **aggregate increases in taxes** equals the portion of the excess distribution allocable to each prior PFIC year times

---

[15]IRC §1291(b)(2)(B). Without this relief, U.S. persons would include all first-year distributions in their total excess distribution since their base would equal zero.

[16]IRC §1291(a)(1). This allocation process means that the U.S. person retains deferral benefits for any amount allocable to periods preceding the PFIC legislation and periods preceding the company's PFIC status.

[17]Interestingly, the excess distribution results in gross income during the current year and, as explained later, a deferred tax amount related to prior years even if the PFIC has no earnings and profits (E&P) from which to pay dividends. The absence of E&P suggests that these distributions do not represent "income" to the recipient. If not income, Congress cannot tax the distributions under the Sixteenth Amendment to the Constitution.

[18]IRC §1291(c)(1). A bit of a misnomer, the deferred tax amount includes interest charges in addition to deferred taxes.

**EXHIBIT 13.1**   Allocating PFIC Distributions

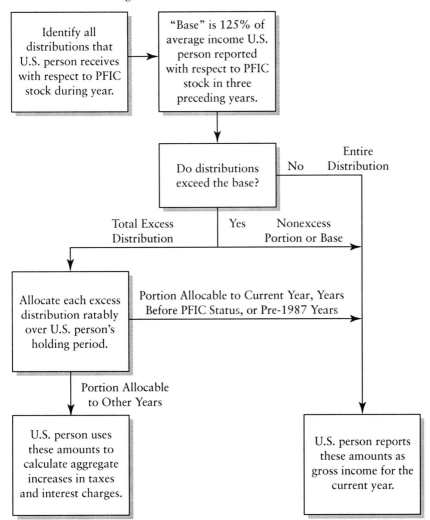

the highest U.S. statutory rate applicable to each such year and then summed together.[19] The **aggregate amount of interest** equals the summed interest

---

[19]IRC §1291(c)(2). The Code's highest statutory rate for the year applies to the allocated amount even if the U.S. taxpayer's marginal tax rate that year was lower. Further, net operating loss carryovers cannot offset income allocated to these prior years.

charges on the aggregate increases in taxes using a rate three percentage points higher than the federal short-term rate.[20]

---

## EXAMPLE

Brian, a U.S. citizen, buys stock in Starburst Investment, Ltd., a calendar-year Cayman corporation, on January 1, 2000. Starburst is a PFIC for 2002 through 2006 and distributes the following amounts to Brian with respect to his shares:

| | |
|---|---|
| December 31, 2002 | $200,000 |
| December 31, 2003 | 200,000 |
| December 31, 2004 | 200,000 |
| December 31, 2005 | 200,000 |
| December 31, 2006 | 950,000 |

No excess distributions result in 2002 through 2005. In 2006, the total excess distribution equals $700,000 ($950,000 – 125% of $200,000), and the nonexcess portion equals $250,000. Brian spreads the $700,000 over his seven-year holding period, allocating $100,000 to each year. The diagram illustrates the allocation, where GI identifies the excess distribution Brian includes in his 2006 gross income and DTA indicates the allocated amounts Brian uses to calculate his deferred tax amount:

Allocation of $700,000 Excess Distribution

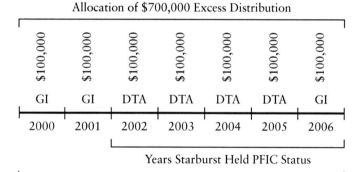

---

[20]IRC §1291(c)(3). In most cases, corporate taxpayers can deduct these interest charges. However, IRC §163(h) may preclude individuals from deducting interest.

Brian reports gross income on his 2006 tax return equal to $550,000 ($250,000 nonexcess distribution + $100,000 excess distribution allocable to 2006 + $200,000 excess distribution allocable to pre-PFIC years of 2000 and 2001). Assuming the applicable interest rate for the entire period is 10 percent, Brian calculates his deferred tax amount as follows:

|  |  |  |
|---|---|---|
| **2002** | | |
| Increase in tax ($100,000 × 38.6%) | $ 38,600 | |
| Amount of interest | | |
| ($38,600 × 10% × 4 years) | | $ 15,440 |
| **2003** | | |
| Increase in tax ($100,000 × 38.6%) | 38,600 | |
| Amount of interest | | |
| ($38,600 × 10% × 3 years) | | 11,580 |
| **2004** | | |
| Increase in tax ($100,000 × 37.6%) | 37,600 | |
| Amount of interest | | |
| ($37,600 × 10% × 2 years) | | 7,520 |
| **2005** | | |
| Increase in tax ($100,000 × 37.6%) | 37,600 | |
| Amount of interest | | |
| ($37,600 × 10% × 1 year) | | 3,760 |
| Aggregate increases in tax | $152,400 | |
| Aggregate amount of interest | | $ 38,300 |
| Deferred tax amount | | |
| ($152,400 + $38,300) | | $190,700 |

In summary, Brian receives $950,000 from Starburst in 2006, includes $550,000 in his 2006 gross income, and pays a $190,700 deferred tax amount (i.e., deferred tax plus interest charge).

A deferred tax amount also results when the U.S. owner disposes of PFIC shares at a gain. The Code treats the gain the same as an excess distribution (see the previous discussion).[21] U.S. taxpayers must include any por-

---

[21]IRC §1291(a)(2), (f). Dispositions include posting PFIC stock as security for a loan per IRC §1298(b)(6).

tion of the gain allocable to the current taxable year, pre-1987 years, and years preceding PFIC status in current gross income as ordinary gain. Thus, disposing of PFIC shares does not result in capital gain to which lower tax rates otherwise might apply.

---

### EXAMPLE

Periwinkle, Inc., a U.S. corporation, buys stock in Coquina, Ltd., a Bermudan PFIC, on January 1, 2001, for $30,000. On December 31, 2004, Periwinkle sells the PFIC stock for $70,000 and allocates the $40,000 gain over its four-year holding period. Assuming Periwinkle's 2004 marginal tax rate equals 34 percent and an applicable interest rate throughout these years of 8 percent, Periwinkle calculates its liability from selling Coquina stock as follows:

*2001*

| | | |
|---|---|---|
| Increase in tax ($10,000 × 35%) | $ 3,500 | |
| Amount of interest | | |
| ($3,500 × 8% × 3 years) | | $   840 |

*2002*

| | | |
|---|---|---|
| Increase in tax ($10,000 × 35%) | 3,500 | |
| Amount of interest | | |
| ($3,500 × 8% × 2 years) | | 560 |

*2003*

| | | |
|---|---|---|
| Increase in tax ($10,000 × 35%) | 3,500 | |
| Amount of interest | | |
| ($3,500 × 8% × 1 year) | | 280 |
| Aggregate increases in tax | $10,500 | |
| Aggregate amount of interest | | $ 1,680 |
| Deferred tax amount ($10,500 + $1,680) | | $12,180 |

*2004*

| | | |
|---|---|---|
| Tax on gross income ($10,000 × 34%) | | 3,400 |
| Liability resulting from sale assuming no FTC | | $15,580 |

---

**FLASHBACK**

As Chapter 11 explained, the Code may allow U.S. persons receiving dividends from 10-percent-owned foreign subsidiaries to claim deemed paid credits. Further, they can claim credit for any dividend withholding tax the subsidiary's jurisdiction imposes. In short, the foreign tax credit (FTC) assures that U.S. persons pay only U.S. residual tax. Special coordination rules clarify that taxpayers treat creditable taxes allocable to excess distributions includable in current gross income (i.e., amounts allocable to the current year, pre-1987 years, or pre-PFIC years) as current year FTCs. However, they treat creditable taxes allocable to other years (i.e., years resulting in deferred tax amounts) as reducing the deferred tax for the year to which allocable.[22]

---

U.S. investors can make **mark-to-market elections** to eliminate deferred tax and interest charges and, thus, sidestep the PFIC regime. However, only U.S. persons owning PFIC stock regularly trading on national exchanges or otherwise possessing a clearly established market value can make the mark-to-market election.[23] If made, this election requires U.S. investors to recognize gain or loss immediately as if they sold their PFIC shares on the first day their election takes effect.[24]

The election applies to the current and later years. Thus, electing PFIC shareholders must recognize gain or loss for market value changes each year. The election terminates only if the PFIC stock ceases to be marketable or the taxpayer revokes it with IRS consent.[25] Gain includable in gross income or deductible losses receive ordinary, rather than capital, treatment.[26] Recognizing gain requires an upward adjustment in stock basis; deductible losses reduce stock basis.[27] In short, the mark-to-market election provides one means to avoid the PFIC regime and its interest charge.

---

[22]IRC §1291(g).
[23]IRC §1296(e)(1)(A).
[24]IRC §1296(a).
[25]IRC §1296(k).
[26]IRC §1296(c)(1).
[27]IRC §1296(b)(1).

## QUALIFIED ELECTING FUNDS

Mark-to-market elections are not the only way to avoid PFIC consequences. U.S. persons wanting to avoid deferred tax and interest charges can elect to treat their PFIC shares as stock in a **qualified electing fund (QEF)**.[28] Once made, QEF elections apply to all later years, even if the foreign corporation ceases to be a PFIC. Taxpayers can revoke elections only with IRS consent.[29]

> **COMPLIANCE POINTER:** U.S. persons elect QEF status using Form 8621, Return by a Shareholder of a Passive Foreign Investment Company or Qualified Electing Fund. To become a QEF for a taxable year, they must make the election by the due date of that year's tax return, including extensions. In some situations, the IRS allows later elections if the elector reasonably thought its foreign company did not qualify as a PFIC.[30]

> **PLANNING POINTER:** Sometimes U.S. investors are uncertain whether their foreign corporation qualifies as a PFIC. In these cases, they can treat their holding as though it is not PFIC stock but, at the same time, file protective QEF elections just in case.[31]

U.S. persons owning QEF stock report their pro rata share of the corporation's net capital gain (not to exceed current E&P) and ordinary income each year.[32] In effect, QEF elections result in foreign branch treatment for income items; however, losses do not flow through. Though QEF elections ter-

---

[28]IRC §1291(d)(1). Each U.S. person decides whether to make the QEF election. One person's election does not obligate others to make the election. Thus, some U.S. persons owning PFIC stock can elect QEF treatment for their shares while other U.S. persons owning stock in the same PFIC can forgo the QEF election.
[29]IRC §1295.
[30]IRC §1295(b)(2); Reg. §1.1295-1(f).
[31]Notice 88-22, 1988-1 CB 489.
[32]IRC §1293(a)(1). If a QEF also qualifies as a CFC, IRC §951(f) clarifies that U.S. law does not tax Subpart F income a second time under the QEF regime. Also, IRC §1293(g)(1) precludes inclusion in a U.S. investor's gross income if the QEF qualifies as a CFC, the investor qualifies as a 10 percent U.S. shareholder, and either a foreign effective tax rate more than 90 percent of the maximum U.S. corporate tax rate applies to the amount in question or the amount in question constitutes U.S. source effectively connected income that a U.S. treaty taxes at a reduced rate or exempts.

minate deferral benefits, they avoid some of the inequities and complexities of the PFIC regime.

> **PLANNING POINTER:** QEF elections provide three benefits vis-à-vis PFIC treatment. First, they often avoid application of maximum statutory tax rates to U.S. persons receiving excess distributions or realizing gain from PFIC stock dispositions. Second, they permit the character of PFIC income (e.g., net capital gain) to flow through to owners. Third, they allow U.S. persons selling PFIC stock to treat the profit as capital gain. On the downside, the QEF precludes deferral of U.S. residual tax.

Like constructive dividends under the CFC regime, income inclusions and distributions under the QEF rules require U.S. persons to adjust the basis in their shares. Income U.S. persons report but do not receive increase their stock's adjusted basis. When they later receive earnings they previously reported as gross income, they reduce their adjusted basis.[33]

---

### EXAMPLE

On January 1, 2003, Sunbelt Packaging, Inc., a U.S. corporation, buys a 20 percent holding in Tech First SA, a foreign-owned PFIC, for $4.2 million. Both corporations report on a calendar-year basis. During the first two years, Tech First derives and distributes earnings as follows:

*2003*

| | |
|---|---|
| Ordinary income | $1,000,000 |
| Net capital gain | 4,000,000 |
| Distribution of earnings | 0 |

*2004*

| | |
|---|---|
| Ordinary income | $2,000,000 |
| Net capital gain | 0 |
| Distribution of earnings | 7,000,000 |

Using equation 13.3, Sunbelt has a $1,400,000 ($7 million × 20%) excess distribution in 2004. Assuming a 10 percent interest rate, Sunbelt reports $700,000 as ordinary gross income and pays a $269,500 deferred tax amount [($700,000 × 35%) + ($700,000 × 35% × 10%)].

---

[33]IRC §1293(d).

## EXAMPLE

In the prior example, suppose Sunbelt elects to treat its investment as a QEF from the start. It reports $200,000 ordinary income ($1 million × 20%) and $800,000 net capital gain ($4 million × 20%) in 2003 and increases the basis of its shares to $5.2 million ($4.2 million + $200,000 + $800,000). In 2004, Sunbelt receives $1.4 million dividends ($7 million × 20%), reports $400,000 ordinary income ($2 million × 20%), and reduces the basis of its shares to $4.2 million ($5.2 million – $1.4 million + $400,000). The following table compares the tax implications under the PFIC and QEF regimes for these facts:

|                          | PFIC Results | QEF Results |
|--------------------------|-------------:|------------:|
| **2003**                 |              |             |
| Ordinary gross income    | $      0     | $200,000    |
| Net capital gain         | 0            | 800,000     |
| Deferred tax amount      | 0            | 0           |
| **2004**                 |              |             |
| Ordinary gross income    | $700,000     | $400,000    |
| Net capital gain         | 0            | 0           |
| Deferred tax amount      | 269,500      | 0           |

Making a QEF election the first year a foreign corporation becomes a PFIC allows the electing U.S. person to avoid the PFIC regime completely. However, the PFIC rules still apply to U.S. investors holding PFIC shares during post-1986 PFIC years preceding a QEF election. In these cases, a **deemed sale election** allows U.S. investors to recognize gain (but not loss) as if they sold their shares and, thus, purge the PFIC taint.[34] Shareholders can make this special election only during the initial year when they elect to treat their interests as QEFs.[35] For a given U.S. investor, PFICs that have been QEFs for all PFIC years in the investor's holding period, or PFICs for which the investor elects to recognize all built-in gain, are **pedigreed QEFs**. All other QEFs (i.e., those still subject to the PFIC regime for some years) are **unpedigreed**.[36]

---

[34]IRC §1291(d)(2).
[35]Reg. §1.1291-10(a), (e)(1).
[36]Reg. §1.1291-9(j)(2).

**PLANNING POINTER:** Making the deemed sale election simultaneous with a QEF election avoids the complexity of dealing with both the PFIC and QEF regimes and the possibility of later ordinary income and interest charge surprises.

QEF elections can create cash flow hardships since they obligate U.S. investors to recognize gross income for amounts the foreign corporation might retain. Particularly when the electing U.S. person holds a minority interest, the U.S. tax attributable to the QEF inclusion in gross income may require cash the U.S. person does not possess and cannot acquire. As an annual relief measure, Congress allows U.S. investors, if they elect, to delay payment of U.S. tax on QEF income until they receive dividends or sell their QEF shares.[37] The IRS imposes interest on the deferred U.S. tax.[38] Also, to protect government revenues, the IRS may require U.S. investors to post bond for the deferred tax and can terminate the election when U.S. investors revoke their QEF election or when circumstances jeopardize the U.S. tax.[39]

## FOREIGN PERSONAL HOLDING COMPANIES

Avoiding application of the Code's antideferral regimes for CFCs and PFICs requires careful and continual planning. The CFC and PFIC provisions adopt different approaches to U.S. multinationals with foreign subsidiaries organized in low-tax jurisdictions. The CFC rules attribute constructive dividends to U.S. shareholders during the current year, while the PFIC rules impose interest charges on the deferred tax of U.S. owners. The combined effects make it difficult for many U.S. multinationals to defer U.S. residual tax.

However, safely navigating the CFC and PFIC regimes does not assure long-term deferral benefits, especially for closely held foreign subsidiaries with substantial passive income. Designed to thwart deferral strategies for wealthy individuals wishing to incorporate their pocketbooks, the foreign personal holding company (FPHC) rules adopt an antideferral approach similar to the CFC regime. In short, failure of a FPHC to distribute earnings results in constructive dividends to its U.S. owners.[40]

---

[37]IRC §1294(a)(1).
[38]IRC §1294(g).
[39]IRC §1294(c), (e).
[40]*Eder et al. v. Comm.*, 138 F.2d 27 (CA-2, 1943), confirms the constitutionality of the FPHC provisions even when the operation of law or contractual agreements preclude the distribution of earnings on which U.S. owners must pay tax. Lack of wherewithal to pay is not a constitutional bar to taxation when the statute is unambiguous. If both FPHC and CFC provisions result in constructive dividends, IRC §951(d) clarifies that the CFC regime prevails. Similarly, if both the FPHC and QEF provisions produce constructive dividends, IRC §551(g) clarifies that the FPHC rules control.

### FPHC Definition

FPHCs are foreign corporations, other than tax-exempt organizations and foreign banks, meeting both ownership and income tests.[41] The ownership test requires that five or fewer U.S. citizens or residents directly, indirectly, or constructively own more than 50 percent of the foreign corporation's voting power or stock value at any time during the taxable year. Foreign corporations meet the income test if at least 60 percent of their gross income is foreign personal holding company income.[42] For this purpose, gross income includes both U.S. and foreign source income.[43] Equations 13.4 and 13.5 summarize these ownership and income tests.

$$\frac{\text{Stock value (or voting power) that five or fewer U.S. individuals own}}{\text{Total stock value (or voting power)}} > 50\% \tag{13.4}$$

$$\frac{\text{Foreign personal holding company income}}{\text{Gross income}} \geq 60\% \tag{13.5}$$

These dual tests apply annually, so a foreign corporation can move into and out of FPHC status. However, after initially becoming a FPHC, the 60 percent income threshold in equation 13.5 drops to 50 percent for later years. After the equation 13.5 threshold drops to 50 percent, it reverts to 60 percent following three consecutive years in which the corporation does not meet the income test (at the 50 percent threshold) or for years during and after which it no longer meets the ownership test in equation 13.4.[44] Exhibit 13.2

**EXHIBIT 13.2**    Comparing and Contrasting Antideferral Regimes

|  | CFC | PFIC | FPHC |
|---|---|---|---|
| *Ownership test* | U.S. shareholders own > 50% | None | Five or fewer U.S. individuals own > 50% |
| *Asset test* | None | Passive assets are ≥ 50% of assets | None |
| *Income test* | None | Passive income is ≥ 75% of income | FPHCI is ≥ 60% of income |

---

[41]IRC §552(b).
[42]IRC §§552(a), 554.
[43]IRC §555(a); Reg. §1.555-1.
[44]IRC §552(a)(1).

compares and contrasts the FPHC rules with those for the CFC and PFIC regimes.

---

### EXAMPLE

Six unrelated individuals own the following percentages of voting power and share value in Delectable Delites, Ltd., a Bermudan corporation:

| | |
|---|---|
| Albert (U.S. citizen) | 15% |
| Bertha (U.S. citizen) | 15% |
| Charles (U.S. resident alien) | 15% |
| Donna (U.S. citizen) | 8% |
| Ernie (U.S. citizen) | 7% |
| Fama (nonresident alien) | 40% |

Delectable uses most of its assets each year in business activities. During the current year, its gross income consists of the following:

| | |
|---|---|
| Gross profit from gourmet food business | $30 million |
| Dividends and net gain from stock sales | 70 million |

Delectable is not a CFC since only Albert, Bertha, and Charles are U.S. shareholders, and, together, they do not own more than 50 percent (15% + 15% + 15%). Delectable is not a PFIC since less than 50 percent of its assets produce passive income and less than 75 percent of its gross income is passive ($70 million ÷ $100 million). However, Delectable does qualify as a FPHC since Albert, Bertha, Charles, Donna, and Ernie together own more than 50 percent (15% + 15% + 15% + 8% + 7%) and at least 60 percent of its gross income is FPHCI ($70 million ÷ $100 million).

---

In equation 13.5's numerator, foreign personal holding company income (FPHCI) includes passive income such as dividends, interest, and annuities.[45] However, under a look-through rule, the Code treats dividends and interest received from related persons (other than FPHCs) as FPHCI only to the extent attributable to FPHCI of the related persons. The look-through attribution applies only when related persons organize in the same country as the FPHC and use a substantial part of their assets to conduct business in

---

[45]IRC §553(a)(1). As used here, FPHCI has a similar but different meaning from the identical term under the CFC regime. Cf., IRC §954(c).

the same country.[46] Mineral, oil and gas, copyright, and patent royalties are FPHCI, but receipts for active business computer software are not.[47]

Rent qualifies as FPHCI unless it is 50 percent or more of the foreign corporation's gross income.[48] Thus, bona fide leasing operations usually avoid classification as FPHCs. Nonetheless, compensation received for using the corporation's property is FPHCI if the payment allows a 25 percent shareholder of the FPHC to lease, sublease, or otherwise use the property, and the corporation derives nonrent FPHCI exceeding 10 percent of gross income.[49]

Personal service income is FPHCI if received under a contract designating a 25 percent shareholder as the individual performing the services. Also, if the contract grants the right to designate the performer to some person other than the FPHC, and a 25 percent shareholder is a possible designee, the compensation is FPHCI.[50] These provisions combat situations in which individuals with high-value talents (e.g., professional athletes) make their services available to foreign corporations they own for modest compensatory amounts. When the corporations contract their services to others at full market value, income remains within the offshore entity, deferring substantial amounts of U.S. residual tax.

FPHCI includes income derived from estates and trusts as beneficiary and gain from disposing of interests in estates and trusts. Also, investment net gain from trading commodity futures and selling or exchanging stock and securities is FPHCI.[51]

## KEY CASE

Two family-owned U.S. corporations each hold 40 percent of Simarloo, an Australian corporation actively engaged in raising and selling fruit. Asian Food Industries, Ltd. (AFIL), a Hong Kong enterprise, owns the remaining 20 percent of Simarloo. During the year at issue, Simarloo sells shares in two

---

[46]IRC §552(c). Related persons include those who control the FPHC and whom the FPHC controls. Also, if the same person controls both the FPHC and the dividend or interest payor, the payor is a related person. Control means direct or indirect ownership of 50 percent voting power, stock value, or beneficial interest. See IRC §954(d)(3).
[47]IRC §553(a)(1); Reg. §1.553-1(b)(1).
[48]IRC §553(a)(7).
[49]IRC §553(a)(6).
[50]IRC §553(a)(5).
[51]IRC §553(a)(2)-(4), (b).

AFIL affiliates at substantial gains, amounting to 69.2 percent of its gross income, which pushes Simarloo beyond the 60 percent threshold in equation 13.5. (Without the gains, Simarloo's FPHCI amounts to only 21.9 percent of total income.) The government asserts that Simarloo qualifies as a FPHC since it meets the ownership and income tests. Thus, through the constructive ownership rules, it attributes constructive dividends to the U.S. family members of the two U.S. corporations. Among other arguments, the taxpayers insist the two U.S. corporations cannot force Simarloo to pay dividends since AFIL can block dividends under rights the articles of incorporation grant to this minority shareholder. However, the court finds no precedent for setting aside the normal application of the FPHC regime under these facts but observes that the U.S. corporations willingly transferred the dividend-blocking power to AFIL. Based on the legislative history, the taxpayers also contend that Congress never meant for the FPHC regime to apply to an operating enterprise such as Simarloo. The court rejects this argument, finding the Code's mechanical test unambiguous. Thus, the U.S. family members must report the constructive dividends as gross income.[52]

---

> **PLANNING POINTER:** Large gains from stock and security transactions can propel some taxpayers unexpectedly into the FPHC realm, even those owning foreign corporations actively engaged in business. Splitting sale transactions between contiguous years so gain realized each year is a smaller percentage of total income and using the stock or securities as collateral for loans represent alternative means of raising corporate capital that might avoid FPHC status.

## FPHC Consequence

U.S. persons owning stock in an FPHC recognize a constructive dividend for their pro rata shares of any undistributed FPHCI (as defined shortly), not to exceed current E&P.[53] Thus, U.S. law denies the deferral benefit in the same

---

[52]*Mariani Frozen Foods v. Comm.*, 81 TC 448 (1983), aff'd per curiam sub nom. in *Melinda L. Gee Trust v. Comm.*, 761 F.2d 1410 (CA-9, 1985). For a different outcome when the U.S. government blocked payment of dividends, see *Alvord v. Comm.*, 277 F.2d 713 (CA-4, 1960), rev'g 32 TC 1 (1959).

[53]IRC §551(a), (b). The major difference between FPHCs and their first cousins, personal holding companies, lies in the remedy for failing to distribute earnings. Under the personal holding company regime, the Code imposes a penalty on the company itself. However, concepts of national sovereignty deny the same remedy for foreign entities such as FPHCs. So, under the FPHC regime, the Code attributes gross income to the company's U.S. owners.

manner as with a CFC—through current recognition of gross income. Any amount included in gross income increases the stock basis of the applicable U.S. person.[54] In effect, the Code treats U.S. owners as though they receive actual dividends that, in turn, they reinvest in the FPHC. Later receipts of previously taxed income decrease stock basis.

> **COMPLIANCE POINTER:** U.S. stockholders directly or indirectly owning at least 5 percent of an FPHC's share value and reporting a constructive dividend for the year must include in their tax returns detailed information about the FPHC's gross income, deductions, credits, taxable income, FPHCI, and undistributed FPHCI.[55] Also, U.S. citizens and residents directly or indirectly owning at least 10 percent of an FPHC's share value or serving as an officer or director must file a return containing similar income data as well as shareholder information.[56]

**Undistributed FPHCI** represents the FPHC's dividend-paying ability. U.S. persons owning FPHC stock on the last day during the taxable year the corporation meets the ownership test include in gross income their pro rata share of undistributed FPHCI.[57] To determine undistributed FPHCI, begin with taxable income, make certain adjustments to more closely identify dividend-paying ability, and subtract a dividend paid deduction.[58] The **dividend paid deduction** consists of three separate components: dividends the FPHC actually pays during the taxable year, dividends the FPHC actually pays in the two and a half months following the taxable year and chooses to apply to the preceding year (not to exceed the undistributed FPHCI), and

---

[54]IRC §551(e).

[55]IRC §551(c), (f).

[56]IRC §6035.

[57]IRC §551(a), (b). One might reasonably conclude that undistributed FPHCI is simply FPHCI that the corporation does not distribute. In fact, the two concepts differ considerably and are not related. Whereas undistributed FPHCI is a measure of dividend-paying ability and, thus, must be partitioned among shareholders to determine the constructive dividend, FPHCI is an equation 13.5 component that determines whether a foreign corporation qualifies as an FPHC. Further, undistributed FPHCI is a taxable income concept (i.e., after deductions); FPHCI is a gross income measure. The calculations of these two concepts are dissimilar, and the reasons for their computation also differ.

[58]IRC §556(a).

consent dividends.[59] **Consent dividends** are earnings common shareholders agree to report as dividends though not actually received.[60] Like other constructive distributions, consent dividends increase the recipient's stock basis.[61] Exhibit 13.3 summarizes the calculation of undistributed FPHCI.

**EXHIBIT 13.3**   Calculating Undistributed FPHCI

|   | |
|---|---|
|   | Taxable income of foreign personal holding company |
| − | Nondeductible U.S. and foreign income tax |
| − | Nondeductible charitable contributions exceeding 10% of taxable income[a] |
| + | Dividend received deduction |
| + | Net operating loss deduction[b] |
| + | Certain business and depreciation deductions[c] |
| + | Deductions for taxes paid on behalf of shareholders |
| + | Deductions for pension, profit sharing, stock bonus, and annuity contributions |
| − | Dividend paid deduction[d] |

Undistributed FPHCI[e]

[a]However, charitable contributions exceeding 50 percent of taxable income do not reduce undistributed FPHCI.

[b]Nonetheless, U.S. law does allow a deduction for net operating losses from the immediately preceding year (computed without considering the dividend received deduction).

[c]The amount added back equals the excess of deductions over the rent income or similar compensation the FPHC receives for using (or the right to use) certain property unless the FPHC obtains rent or other compensation that is the highest obtainable, uses the property in a bona fide business for profit, and reasonably expects the property to produce profit or that the property is necessary for conducting the business.

[d]This amount includes dividends paid during the taxable year, consent dividends, and, if the FPHC chooses, dividends paid by the fifteenth day of the third month after the taxable year.

[e]Undistributed FPHCI cannot exceed current E&P.

---

[59]IRC §§ 561(a), 563(c)(1).
[60]IRC § 565(a).
[61]IRC § 565(c).

## EXAMPLE

Gertrude (U.S. citizen) owns 48 percent, Henrietta (U.S. citizen) owns 8 percent, and Isaac (nonresident alien) owns 44 percent of an FPHC. The three individuals are unrelated to each other. The FPHC calculates its taxable income as follows:

| | |
|---|---|
| Gross income | $800,000 |
| Dividend received deduction | −230,000 |
| Other deductible expenses | −70,000 |
| Taxable income | $500,000 |

Assuming foreign income tax of $50,000 and a dividend paid deduction of $20,000, the FPHC determines its undistributed FPHCI as shown:

| | |
|---|---|
| Taxable income | $500,000 |
| Dividend received deduction | 230,000 |
| Foreign income tax | −50,000 |
| Dividend paid deduction | −20,000 |
| Undistributed FPHCI | $660,000 |

Gertrude and Henrietta recognize constructive dividends of $316,800 ($660,000 × 48%) and $52,800 ($660,000 × 8%), respectively. Isaac does not recognize gross income since he is not a U.S. person.

# CHAPTER 14

# Export Incentives

Exporting involves a relatively low-cost, low-risk means of conducting business abroad and represents a "toe-dipping" approach for purely domestic companies wishing to go global. It requires little or no investment in foreign machinery, equipment, real estate, or other tangible assets, minimizing **expropriation** concerns in moderate- to high-risk countries.[1] Also, few, if any, exporting personnel spend time abroad, and those who do go abroad stay only for short periods to negotiate agreements or confirm export channels. Relative to offshore manufacturing and other permanent establishments, an export operation's start-up and shut-down phases involve small expenses and simple tax issues.

---

### FLASHBACK

As Chapter 3 explained, treaties protect many export sales from host country income tax. If U.S. exporters do not sell abroad through fixed places of business or dependent agents (i.e., permanent establishments or PEs), foreign income taxes do not result. Thus, selling abroad through independent brokers, commission agents, and sales representatives (i.e., businesses with multiple principals) avoids PE status. Also, exporters escape PE status when they sell abroad through dependent sales representatives or other agents not regularly concluding contracts but instead routing orders to home offices for approval.

---

Some exporting occurs between vertically integrated related or controlled entities. For instance, U.S. manufacturers may sell products to wholly owned foreign distributors; or U.S. suppliers may provide raw materials or

---

[1]Similar to the legal concept of eminent domain, expropriation occurs when a foreign government seizes a company's assets for national security or other reasons.

component parts to related manufacturers or assembly operations abroad. U.S. companies without a ready market locate foreign buyers through advertisements, Internet research, and foreign trade trips.

Export sales contribute positively to the U.S. economy, creating high-paying jobs for American workers. Thus, Congress passes much legislation encouraging export activities, some providing tax incentives. In 1971, Congress created the domestic international sales corporation (DISC) to provide exporters with long-term tax deferrals. Our major trading partners protested that the DISC was an illegal export subsidy, violating the **General Agreement on Tariffs and Trade (GATT)**. So, in 1984, Congress replaced the old DISC with two new export incentives: the **foreign sales corporation (FSC)** and a restructured DISC targeted at small exporters and subject to an interest charge. The FSC exempted 15 to 30 percent of export profits from U.S. taxation.[2] After European Union (EU) complaints, a **World Trade Organization (WTO)** dispute settlement panel pronounced the FSC illegal, and a WTO appellate body upheld the decision in 2000. Later that year, Congress replaced the FSC with a regime providing similar benefits, the extraterritorial income exclusion (EIE). Following a second round of EU protests, a WTO panel found the EIE to be illegal also, and an appellate body affirmed the holding in 2002. This latest decision may prompt Congress to repeal the EIE, but repeal is not certain. Until Congress decides how to respond to the latest WTO ruling, the EIE continues to be the law of the land, bestowing significant tax benefits on U.S. exporters.[3]

> **PLANNING POINTER:**   The EIE provides a permanent tax exemption of 15 to 30 percent. In contrast, the DISC provides a temporary deferral of 47 to 100 percent, and DISC shareholders pay interest charges on deferred tax. Small- to medium-sized exporters should compare EIE and DISCs on a present value basis to determine the best alternative.

This chapter explains tax benefits the EIE and DISCs provide. Though each regime provides attractive incentives, some exporters choose to forgo

---

[2]For empirical evidence that the DISC and FSC programs increased U.S. export volume after controlling for product categories and macroeconomic variables, see B. Anthony Billings, Gary A. McGill, and Mbodja Mougoué, "The Effect of Export Tax Incentives on Export Volume: The DISC/FSC Evidence," *Advances in Taxation*, 15 (2003), forthcoming.

[3]For a review of the WTO decision and its implications, see Ernest R. Larkins, "WTO Appellate Body Denounces ETI Exclusion: Anatomy of an Export Subsidy," *Journal of International Taxation*, 13 (May 2002), pp. 10–17.

these benefits. For instance, small exporters may perceive that the tax benefits do not exceed setup and maintenance costs. Break-even analysis can clarify this issue.[4] Also, U.S. companies with domestic losses may reduce the marginal tax rate on export income to zero without the EIE or DISC incentives. Especially when exporters expect domestic losses to expire unused, recognizing all export earnings tax-free (i.e., offsetting domestic losses against export profits for a 50 percent exemption) is better than the EIE's 15 to 30 percent exemption and, under the DISC regime, deferring earnings until later but paying U.S. tax on all such earnings.

> **PLANNING POINTER:** U.S. exporters with excess foreign tax credits (FTCs) derive substantial benefits selling to foreign customers directly and passing title abroad. As Chapter 4 explained, this approach yields foreign source income without incurring foreign income tax. In effect, exporting creates an excess limit that absorbs preexisting or current-year excess credits from business operations in high-tax jurisdictions. When U.S. law characterizes half of export profits as foreign source income, the resulting marginal tax rate equals 50 percent of the income tax rate otherwise applicable. Refer back to the example in Chapter 11 for an illustration.

## EXTRATERRITORIAL INCOME EXCLUSION

C and S corporations, foreign corporations electing treatment as domestic corporations, partnerships, limited liability companies, and individuals qualify for the EIE.[5] To prevent duplicate benefits, members of controlled corporate groups including a DISC cannot claim the EIE.[6] Thus, U.S. exporters must choose between the EIE and DISC regimes.

The EIE provides a tax exemption ranging from 15 to 30 percent of export profit.[7] For net export profit margins of 8 percent or higher (4 percent

---

[4]For guidance on identifying the relevant factors and conducting break-even analyses for export activities with DISCs, see Ernest R. Larkins, "The Tax Aspects of Exportation: A Decision Model Approach," *Journal of the American Taxation Association*, 13 (Spring 1991), pp. 92–107, and Ernest R. Larkins and Fred A. Jacobs, "Tax Incentives for Small Businesses with Export Potential: A Capital Budgeting Decision Analysis," *Accounting Horizons*, 10 (June 1996), pp. 32–50.
[5]IRC §943(a)(2).
[6]IRC §943(h).
[7]IRC §941(a)(1).

or lower), the EIE benefit equals 15 percent (30 percent). Profit margins between 4 and 8 percent result in tax savings between 15 and 30 percent. Thus, the marginal tax rates applicable to export profits depend on profit margin levels and range between 70 and 85 percent of the U.S. tax rate applicable to domestic sales.

---

**EXAMPLE**

---

During the year, International Conglomerate, Inc. earns $5 million net profit from domestic sales and $1 million net profit from export sales. The export profits represent a return of 14 percent. Normally, taxable income of $6 million results in U.S. tax of $2,040,000 ($6 million × 34%). However, International Conglomerate claims the EIE. Since export sales with profit margins of 14 percent yield a 15 percent EIE benefit, the marginal tax rate on export sales equals 28.9 percent (34% × 85%). Thus, the U.S. tax liability on the $6 million of worldwide profit is $1,989,000 (34% of $5 million + 28.9% of $1 million), a tax savings of $51,000.

---

Only **foreign trading gross receipts (FTGRs)** qualify for the EIE.[8] FTGRs are amounts received from the following transactions:

- Selling, exchanging, or disposing of qualifying foreign trade property;
- Leasing or renting qualifying foreign trade property for offshore use;
- Providing services related and subsidiary to activities in the two previous categories;
- Performing engineering or architectural services for foreign construction projects; and
- Rendering managerial services for unrelated persons that assist them in qualifying for the EIE but only when taxpayers derive at least half of their FTGRs from the first three categories.[9]

In addition to fitting into one of these five categories, transactions must meet certain economic process requirements to qualify as FTGRs.[10] Though

---

[8]IRC §114(e).
[9]IRC §942(a)(1). Nonetheless, IRC §942(a)(3) allows taxpayers to treat any gross receipts as though they do not qualify as FTGRs.
[10]IRC §942(b).

these requirements appear complex, taxpayers usually find them simple to meet. Nonetheless, to encourage small businesses exports, Congress exempted taxpayers with no more than $5 million of FTGRs from the economic process requirements.[11]

The first three categories of FTGRs (just listed) involve **qualifying foreign trade property (QFTP)**. QFTP is property:

- Manufactured, produced, grown, or extracted;
- Held primarily for sale, lease, or rental in the ordinary course of business for use, consumption, or disposition abroad; and
- Consisting of foreign direct material and labor costs not exceeding 50 percent of the property's fair market value.[12]

However, QFTP does not include property leased or rented to a related person, certain intangible assets, oil and gas (including primary oil and gas products), unprocessed softwood timber, products the export of which federal law prohibits or curtails, and property the U.S. president declares in short supply (i.e., insufficient for meeting domestic needs).[13]

## DOMESTIC INTERNATIONAL SALES CORPORATIONS

Low organization and maintenance costs characterize DISCs. Sometimes called **paper entities**, most DISCs own no tangible assets, hire no employees, fit neatly into file drawers, and appear as mere book entries. In short, they serve as alter egos to their related suppliers. U.S. law does not require DISCs to possess corporate substance or to perform substantial economic functions.[14] Targeted to small exporters, DISCs often generate significant cash flow since they can make "producer loans" of deferred earnings to related suppliers (i.e., U.S. exporters) while preserving their deferral benefits.[15]

---

[11]IRC §942(c).

[12]IRC §943(a)(1).

[13]IRC §943(a)(3), (4). For a more detailed analysis of the EIE, see Ernest R. Larkins, "Mirror Rules, Broader Spectrum: Extraterritorial Exclusion Replaces FSC Regime," *Journal of International Taxation*, 12 (May 2001), pp. 22–29.

[14]Reg. §§1.992-1(a), 1.994-1(a)(2).

[15]For an overview of the concepts and theory underlying the DISC incentive, see Robert Feinschreiber, *Domestic International Sales Corporation* (New York: Practicing Law Institute, 1978).

---

**FLASHBACK**

In contrast to DISCs, Chapter 12 explained how controlled foreign corporations lose their deferral benefits when they invest in U.S. property, such as loans to related U.S. entities.

---

## DISC Requirements

Domestic corporations become DISCs if they make timely elections and all shareholders consent.[16] Exempt entities, personal holding companies, financial institutions, insurance companies, regulated investment companies, and S corporations are ineligible.[17] Though requiring only negligible capital investments, the par, or stated, value of outstanding shares must stay at or above $2,500, and the Code limits DISCs to only one class of stock.[18] Also, DISCs must maintain separate books and records.[19]

> **COMPLIANCE POINTER:** Exporters make the DISC election and shareholders file consents on Form 4876A, Election to Be Treated as an Interest Charge DISC. DISCs report operational results and deemed distributions on Form 1120-IC-DISC, Interest Charge Domestic International Sales Corporation Return.

The two most crucial DISC requirements involve dual 95 percent thresholds. At least 95 percent of the year's gross receipts must constitute qualified export receipts, and qualified export assets must comprise 95 percent or more of total assets at year-end.[20] However, belated distributions in amounts covering any shortfalls can remedy failures to meet one or both of the dual 95 percent tests.[21]

**Qualified export receipts** include gross receipts from the following transactions:

* Selling, exchanging, or otherwise disposing of export property or other qualified export assets;

---

[16]IRC §992(a)(1)(D), (b).
[17]IRC §992(d).
[18]IRC §992(a)(1)(C).
[19]Reg. §1.992-1(a)(7).
[20]IRC §992(a)(1)(A), (B).
[21]IRC §992(c). Someone once referred to failing these tests as a "slipped DISC."

- Leasing or renting export property for use abroad;
- Providing services related and subsidiary to the two previous categories;
- Rendering engineering or architectural services for foreign construction projects; and
- Assisting other DISCs, through managerial services such as conducting export market studies or handling export delivery, to generate qualified export receipts.

In addition, interest income from obligations that are qualified export assets and certain dividends from related foreign export corporations are qualified export receipts.[22]

The bulk of qualified export receipts results from transactions involving export property. Not all inventory items qualify as export property. Specifically, **export property** includes only those items:

- Some person other than a DISC manufactures, produces, grows, or extracts in the United States;
- The DISC or its related supplier holds primarily for sale, lease, or rental in the ordinary course of business for direct use, consumption, or disposition abroad; and
- Whose fair market value consists of 50 percent or more domestic content (i.e., 50 percent or less attributable to imported articles).[23]

Notwithstanding, export property does not include assets a DISC leases or rents for a member of its controlled group to use, most types of intangible assets, property eligible for depletion deductions, items whose export the federal government prohibits or curtails to protect the U.S. economy, unprocessed softwood timber, and items the U.S. president designates as short in supply.[24]

The second percentage test requires that 95 percent or more of a DISC's assets be qualified export assets at year end. **Qualified export assets** include export property (as just defined). They also include assets the DISC uses primarily in export activities, trade receivables arising from export transactions, working capital the DISC reasonably needs for export operations, producer loans (i.e., amounts advanced to the DISC's related supplier), certain other export-related loans (e.g., obligations of the U.S. Export-Import

---

[22]IRC §993(a)(1).
[23]IRC §993(c)(1). IRC §993(g) clarifies that, for purposes of the DISC rules, the United States includes U.S. possessions. For instance, items a related supplier manufactures in Puerto Rico constitute export property if they meet all other criteria.
[24]IRC §993(c)(2).

Bank), and deposited amounts the DISC uses to acquire other qualified export assets.[25]

> **PLANNING POINTER:** DISCs find it easy to meet the asset test during their initial few years. However, as the accumulated DISC income grows, finding investments constituting qualified export assets and providing a reasonable rate of return becomes more difficult. U.S. exporters must monitor the 95 percent asset test carefully to assure continued DISC benefits.

### DISC Benefits

DISCs pay no U.S. income tax.[26] Thus, exporters defer U.S. tax on export profits allocable to DISCs that the latter do not distribute to shareholders. However, only $10 million of annual export sales yield profits qualifying for deferral, and DISC shareholders pay interest charges on deferred taxes.[27] In substance, the DISC regime provides a guaranteed, low-interest loan to small U.S. exporters.

Most DISCs operate on a commission basis rather than taking title to export property. Commission arrangements usually are simpler. For instance, they avoid the double invoicing of buy-sell relationships, and exporters can write contracts so sales not generating qualified export receipts earn no commissions, minimizing the possibility of inadvertently failing the 95 percent test. Thus, related suppliers, such as parent or sibling companies, pay commissions to DISCs for their export roles.

In allocating export profits between DISCs and their related suppliers (i.e., in computing the commission), the Code allows two special transfer pricing approaches:

- Combined taxable income (CTI) method and
- Gross receipts (GR) method.[28]

Since DISCs are tax-exempt, undistributed income allocable to DISCs escapes current U.S. taxation. Thus, the larger the DISC allocation (i.e., commission), the larger the tax benefit. The transfer pricing method maximizing

---

[25]IRC §993(b).

[26]IRC §991.

[27]IRC §995(b)(1)(E), (f).

[28]Except by coincidence, these transfer pricing methods do not result in arm's-length prices. Thus, outside the DISC regime, taxpayers must adopt methods resulting in true taxable income, a topic Chapter 16 explores.

**EXHIBIT 14.1** Treatment of Export Profit Allocable to DISCs with C Corporate Shareholders

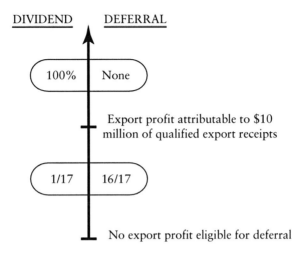

commissions depends on the export sale's **net profit margin** (i.e., an export sale's net profit divided by sales receipts). After the profit allocation, shareholders receive constructive dividends for earnings attributable to qualified export receipts exceeding $10 million.[29] Also, C corporate shareholders receive one-seventeenth of DISC commissions as deemed dividends.[30] Exhibit 14.1 clarifies the treatment of DISC commissions.

Exhibit 14.2 displays two common structures using DISCs. U.S. multinational companies with widely dispersed stockholdings often use the parent-subsidiary structure in Panel A. In contrast, closely held companies tend to use brother-sister structures similar to the one appearing in Panel B. The closely held configuration causes export profits allocable to the DISC to avoid corporate-level tax, effectively allowing tax-deductible dividends. That is, the related supplier deducts DISC commissions, bypassing the corporate income tax, and individual shareholders pay income tax on the export earnings when they receive deemed or actual dividends.

Exporters usually apply the **combined taxable income (CTI)** method to export sales with net profit margins above 8 percent, which yields a com-

[29]IRC §995(b)(1)(E). Exporters do not consider earnings attributable to nonqualified export receipts when determining DISC commissions. Thus, DISCs never receive commissions based on nonqualified receipts, removing the necessity for a deemed distribution of nonqualified earnings.
[30]IRC §995(b)(1)(F)(i).

**EXHIBIT 14.2**   Common DISC Structures

*Panel A: Structure for Widely Held Exporter*

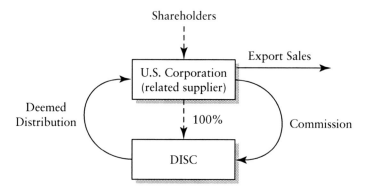

*Panel B: Structure for Closely Held Exporter*

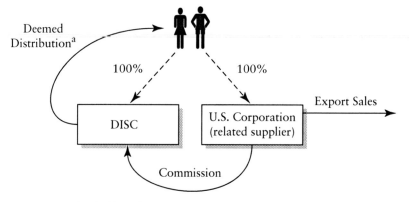

[a]For C corporate shareholders, deemed distributions include export earnings equal to one-seventeenth of DISC commissions plus export earnings attributable to qualified export receipts exceeding $10 million each year. For individual shareholders, deemed distributions only include export earnings attributable to qualified export receipts exceeding $10 million.

mission equal to 50 percent of the transaction's CTI plus 10 percent of the DISC's **export promotion expenses** related to the sale.[31] CTI is the aggre-

---

[31]IRC §994(a)(2). IRC §994(c) defines export promotion expenses as all expenses that advance the sale or distribution of export property for use, consumption, or distribution abroad, including half of transportation expenses on aircraft that U.S. persons own and operate and U.S. registered ships. Many DISCs incur no export promotion expenses. Reg. §1.994-1(a)(2) indicates that export promotion is the only substantial economic function affecting DISC commissions.

gate net profit for the DISC and its related supplier attributable to qualified export receipts. That is, CTI represents the total export profit the DISC and related supplier must divide. The portion allocable to the DISC is the commission. Under the CTI method, 47 percent of export profits attributable to qualified export receipts up to $10 million avoids current U.S. income tax when DISCs have C corporate shareholders (50 percent commission, assuming no export promotion expenses, less one-seventeenth of commission as deemed dividend). For DISCs with non-C corporate shareholders, the tax deferral applies to 50 percent of export profits since no deemed dividend occurs.

---

## EXAMPLE

Robotic Enterprises, a domestic corporation, establishes a wholly owned DISC to which it pays export sales commissions. During the DISC's first year, Robotic uses the CTI method to allocate all export profit. Its DISC incurs no export promotion expenses. Export profit from qualified export receipts total $400,000. The exporter allocates half of this profit or $200,000 to its DISC. U.S. law currently taxes Robotic Enterprises on $211,765 export profits [$200,000 + (1/17 × $200,000)] and defers the remaining $188,235 export profits (16/17 × $200,000).

---

Lower margin export sales use the GR method, which allows a commission equal to 4 percent of export receipts plus 10 percent of the DISC's export promotion expenses related to the sale.[32] Under a **no loss rule**, commissions cannot exceed CTI.[33] Without this rule, exporters could allocate income exceeding 100 percent of export profits to DISCs, providing related suppliers with deductible losses. Thus, the GR method allows DISCs with C corporate shareholders to defer up to 94 percent of export profits (100 percent commission less one-seventeenth of commission as deemed dividend) and other DISCs to defer up to 100 percent. Exporters with profit margins between 4 and 8 percent defer between 47 and 94 percent of U.S. income tax when the DISC has C corporate shareholders, and between 50 and 100 percent otherwise.

---

[32]IRC §994(a)(1). For export profit margins of 8 percent, the CTI and GR methods result in the same commission.
[33]Reg. §1.994-1(e)(1)(i).

**PLANNING POINTER:** To minimize the marginal tax rate from exporting, companies can group transactions, break down invoices to perform transaction-by-transaction analyses, and, when seeking to establish or maintain foreign markets, use marginal costing techniques.[34]

Each year, DISC shareholders pay interest on deferred U.S. tax. The interest charge starts small but mushrooms as accumulated DISC income increases. To compute the interest charge, shareholders add their pro rata share of **deferred DISC income** from prior years to their own taxable incomes, compute a hypothetical tax on this sum, and subtract their actual U.S. tax from the hypothetical tax. The Code assesses interest on the difference, or the shareholder's **DISC-related deferred tax liability,** at the average annual yield of one-year U.S. Treasury bills (T-bills). A one-year lag imposing interest causes deferred tax to be interest-free the first year.[35] Corporate shareholders deduct the interest, but individual shareholders cannot.[36]

## EXAMPLE

Assume the same facts in the prior example and that Robotic Enterprises pays U.S. tax at 35 percent, and the applicable U.S. T-bill rate is 7 percent. Robotic's DISC-related deferred tax liability equals $65,882 ($188,235 × 35%), and, after the first year and assuming no actual DISC distributions, Robotic must pay $4,612 deductible interest ($65,882 × 0.07).

### Marginal Tax Rates

The marginal tax rate (MTR) on export profits depends on the DISC's shareholders, deferral period, export profit margin, and prevailing interest

---

[34]Though dealing with the now-defunct foreign sales corporation regime, the following articles provide some guidance in using these strategies: Fred A. Jacobs and Ernest R. Larkins, "Export Tax Incentives for Establishing Foreign Markets: An Analysis of Marginal Costing Techniques." *Accounting Horizons*, 12 (December 1998), pp. 374–396; Fred A. Jacobs and Ernest R. Larkins, "Marginal Costing Can Help Exporters Gain Entry into Foreign Markets." *Journal of International Taxation*, 9 (November 1998), pp. 26–33, 46–47; and Ernest R. Larkins and Fred A. Jacobs, "Grouping for FSCs Reduces Taxable Profits." *Journal of International Taxation*, 5 (April 1994), pp. 159–167.

[35]IRC §995(f).

[36]*Tedori v. U.S.*, 211 F.3d 488 (CA-9, 2000).

rates. Three components comprise the MTR: current tax due, future tax due, and annual interest charges.[37] Equation 14.1 presents the first of these components assuming an 8 percent or higher profit margin and C corporate shareholders. Equation 14.2 shows the comparable calculation for individual shareholders (who do not receive one-seventeenth of commissions as deemed distributions). For profit margins of 4 percent or less, the DISC's share of export profit equals CTI, the related supplier's share is zero, and, in the case of C corporate shareholders, U.S. law taxes one-seventeenth of CTI under the deemed distribution rules.[38] Equations 14.3 and 14.4 show the current tax calculation under the GR method, assuming C corporate and individual shareholders, respectively.

$$CTAX_{cti,c} = t_{us}\left[0.5\ CTI - 0.1\ EPE + \frac{1}{17}(0.5\ CTI + 0.1\ EPE)\right] \quad (14.1)$$

$$= t_{us}(0.5294\ CTI - 0.0941\ EPE)$$

$$CTAX_{cti,i} = t_{us}\ (0.5\ CTI - 0.1\ EPE) \quad (14.2)$$

$$CTAX_{gr,c} = t_{us}\left(CTI \times \frac{1}{17}\right) \quad (14.3)$$

$$CTAX_{gr,i} = 0 \quad (14.4)$$

where:

$CTAX_{cti,c}$ = current U.S. income tax on export profits allocable to C corporate shareholders under the CTI method, assuming a profit margin of 8 percent or more

$CTAX_{cti,i}$ = current U.S. income tax on export profits allocable to individual shareholders under the CTI method, assuming a profit margin of 8 percent or more

$CTAX_{gr,c}$ = current U.S. income tax on export profits allocable to C corporate shareholders under the GR method, assuming a profit margin of 4 percent or less

$CTAX_{gr,i}$ = current U.S. income tax on export profits allocable to individual shareholders under the GR method, assuming a profit margin of 4 percent or less

$t_{us}$ = effective U.S. income tax rate on DISC shareholder

---

[37]For ease of exposition, this analysis treats interest charges as taxes.
[38]Profit margins between 4 and 8 percent generate U.S. income tax between these extremes.

CTI = combined taxable income of DISC and related supplier for a given year attributable to qualified export receipts not exceeding $10 million

EPE = DISC's export promotion expenses

---

## EXAMPLE

Globalite, Inc., a C corporation in the 35 percent bracket, pays a commission to its wholly owned DISC for an export sale yielding $10,000 profit. The DISC's export promotion expenses attributable to the sale equal $150. Using the CTI method, Globalite allocates $5,015 of the profit to its DISC [(0.5 × $10,000) + (0.1 × $150)] as a commission and receives a deemed distribution of $295 ($5,015 × 1/17). Thus, Globalite's currently taxable export profits equal $5,280 ($10,000 CTI − $5,015 allocable to DISC + $295 deemed distribution from DISC), and its current tax attributable to this export sale is $1,848 ($5,280 × 35%). Equation 14.1 yields the same result:

$$CTAX_{cti,c} = 0.35 \, [(0.5294 \times \$10{,}000) - (0.0941 \times \$150)] = \$1{,}848$$

---

Equations 14.5 through 14.8 show the present value of future tax due on export profits allocable to the DISC and not deemed distributed (i.e., escaping U.S. tax during the related export year). They assume DISCs distribute deferred income to their shareholders to end the deferral period.[39] The numerators of equations 14.5 through 14.7 consist of CTI less the parenthetical amounts in the corresponding equations 14.1 through 14.3. Equation 14.8 includes all CTI in its numerator since equation 14.4 taxed no portion of CTI during the export year.

$$FTAX_{cti,c} = t_{us} \frac{CTI - (0.5294 \, CTI - 0.0941 \, EPE)}{(1 + d)^y} \tag{14.5}$$

$$= t_{us} \frac{0.4706 \, CTI + 0.0941 \, EPE}{(1 + d)^y}$$

---

[39] DISC deferrals also end when shareholders revoke DISC elections or export entities fail to meet all DISC requirements. In these situations, IRC §995(b)(2) provides for deemed distributions over 10 or fewer years. Stretching out the deferral so that shareholders recognize deferred DISC income on an installment basis increases the present value benefits of deferral and, thus, decreases the MTR only slightly.

$$FTAX_{cti,i} = t_{us} \frac{CTI - (0.5\ CTI - 0.1\ EPE)}{(1 + d)^y} \qquad (14.6)$$

$$= t_{us} \frac{0.5\ CTI + 0.1\ EPE}{(1 + d)^y}$$

$$FTAX_{gr,c} = t_{us} \frac{CTI - \left(CTI \times \frac{1}{17}\right)}{(1 + d)^y} \qquad (14.7)$$

$$= t_{us} \frac{CTI \times \frac{16}{17}}{(1 + d)^y}$$

$$FTAX_{gr,i} = t_{us} \frac{CTI}{(1 + d)^y} \qquad (14.8)$$

where:

$FTAX_{cti,c}$ = present value of future U.S. income tax to C corporation shareholders on export profits currently allocable to DISC under the CTI method, assuming a profit margin of 8 percent or more

$FTAX_{cti,i}$ = present value of future U.S. income tax to individual shareholders on export profits currently allocable to DISC under the CTI method, assuming a profit margin of 8 percent or more

$FTAX_{gr,c}$ = present value of future U.S. income tax to C corporation shareholders on export profits currently allocable to DISC under the GR method, assuming a profit margin of 4 percent or less

$FTAX_{cti,c}$ = present value of future U.S. income tax to individual shareholders on export profits currently allocable to DISC under the GR method, assuming a profit margin of 4 percent or less

$d$ = applicable discount rate

$y$ = years DISC-related tax liability is deferred

---

**EXAMPLE**

In addition to the prior example's facts, assume the DISC plans to retain its export earnings for five years and the applicable discount rate is 13 percent. The deferred DISC income equals \$4,720 (\$10,000 − \$5,280 Globalite's taxable export income for year the export sale occurs), and the DISC-related deferred tax liability, still assuming 35 percent as Globalite's applicable tax bracket, is \$1,652 (\$4,720 × 35%). On a present value basis, this future tax equals \$897 (\$1,652 ÷ $1.13^5$). Equation 14.2 results in the same present value amount:

$$\text{FTAX}_{cti,c} = 0.35 \frac{(0.4706 \times \$10,000) + (0.0941 \times \$150)}{(1 + .13)^5} = \$897$$

Equations 14.9 through 14.12 present the final component of the MTR calculation. The interest charge applies each year, beginning with the DISC's second year. For instance, 10-year deferrals result in interest charges in years 2 through 11. The numerator's second factor in equations 14.9 and 14.11 reflects the deductible nature of interest charges C corporate shareholders pay. The numerator's bracketed factor equals the U.S. tax on the corresponding numerators of equations 14.5 through 14.8 and reflects the deferred tax on deferred DISC income in the export year.

$$\text{INT}_{cti,c} = \sum_{n=2}^{y+1} \frac{\text{BILL}_n (1 - t_{us})[t_{us}(0.4706\ \text{CTI} + 0.0941\ \text{EPE})]}{(1 + d)^n} \qquad (14.9)$$

$$\text{INT}_{cti,i} = \sum_{n=2}^{y+1} \frac{\text{BILL}_n [t_{us}(0.5\ \text{CTI} + 0.1\ \text{EPE})]}{(1 + d)^n} \qquad (14.10)$$

$$\text{INT}_{gr,c} = \sum_{n=2}^{y+1} \frac{\text{BILL}_n (1 - t_{us})\left[t_{us}\left(\text{CTI} \times \dfrac{16}{17}\right)\right]}{(1 + d)^n} \qquad (14.11)$$

$$\text{INT}_{gr,i} = \sum_{n=2}^{y+1} \frac{\text{BILL}_n [t_{us}(\text{CTI})]}{(1 + d)^n} \qquad (14.12)$$

where:

$\text{INT}_{cti,c}$ = present value of future after-tax interest charges on shareholders' DISC-related deferred tax liability

$\text{INT}_{cti,i}$ = present value of future after-tax interest charges on shareholders' DISC-related deferred tax liability

$INT_{gr,c}$ = present value of future after-tax interest charges on shareholders' DISC-related deferred tax liability

$INT_{gr,i}$ = present value of future after-tax interest charges on shareholders' DISC-related deferred tax liability

$BILL_n$ = applicable T-bill rate in year $n$

---

## EXAMPLE

In addition to the facts in the two prior examples, assume the applicable T-bill rate is 7 percent during the export year and following two years and 9 percent in later years. Equation 14.9 yields the following results:

$$INT_{cti,c} = \frac{0.07(1 - 0.35)[0.35(0.4706 \times \$10,000) + (0.0941 \times \$150)]}{(1 + .13)^2}$$

$$+ \frac{0.07(1 - 0.35)[0.35(0.4706 \times \$10,000) + (0.0941 \times \$150)]}{(1 + .13)^3}$$

$$+ \frac{0.09(1 - 0.35)[0.35(0.4706 \times \$10,000) + (0.0941 \times \$150)]}{(1 + .13)^4}$$

$$+ \frac{0.09(1 - 0.35)[0.35(0.4706 \times \$10,000) + (0.0941 \times \$150)]}{(1 + .13)^5}$$

$$+ \frac{0.09(1 - 0.35)[0.35(0.4706 \times \$10,000) + (0.0941 \times \$150)]}{(1 + .13)^6} = \$269$$

---

Equation 14.13 yields the MTR for export sales involving a DISC. The MTR equals the sum of three components—current tax plus the present value of future tax plus present value of the interest charge—divided by the profit attributable to qualified export receipts during the year at issue. Equations 14.1 through 14.12 provide these components, which depend on the export profit margin and shareholder type. For instance, when the export profit margin is 8 percent or higher and a C corporation owns the DISC, the numerator in equation 14.13 equals the summed results from equations 14.1, 14.5, and 14.9.

$$MTR = \frac{CTAX + FTAX + INT}{CTI} \qquad (14.13)$$

**EXHIBIT 14.3**   Sample Marginal Tax Rates for DISC Exports[a]

| Type Shareholder | Deferral Years | Export Profit Margin | MTR |
|---|---|---|---|
| Individual | 5 | $\leq 4\%$ | 25.6% |
| Individual | 5 | $\geq 8\%$ | 30.7% |
| Individual | 10 | $\leq 4\%$ | 20.9% |
| Individual | 10 | $\geq 8\%$ | 28.6% |
| C Corporation | 5 | $\leq 4\%$ | 23.4% |
| C Corporation | 5 | $\geq 8\%$ | 29.2% |
| C Corporation | 10 | $\leq 4\%$ | 17.7% |
| C Corporation | 10 | $\geq 8\%$ | 26.3% |

[a]All MTRs assume a 35 percent U.S. effective tax rate for both individual and corporate shareholders, 15 percent discount rate, 8 percent T-bill rate, and no export promotion expenses.

---

**EXAMPLE**

Based on the calculations in the prior three examples, the exporter can determine its MTR from DISC-related exports. Using Equation 14.13, the MTR falls below Globalite's 35 percent U.S. tax rate:

$$\text{MTR} = \frac{\$1,848 + \$897 + \$269}{\$10,000} = 30.14\%$$

---

Different combinations of the salient factors change the MTR. Longer deferral periods decrease the MTR; and the greater the spread between an exporter's cost of capital (i.e., discount rate) and the T-bill rate, the lower the MTR. Also, the MTR is lower for export profit margins below 8 percent than for higher margins. Finally, the interest deduction often causes MTRs for DISCs with C corporate shareholders to be lower than MTRs for other DISCs. Exhibit 14.3 provides sample MTRs.

# CHAPTER 15

# U.S. Individuals Abroad

**U.S.** companies conducting business in foreign countries often send executives, managers, technicians, and other personnel abroad for extended periods. Sometimes, the transfers are part of a global expansion plan to open new markets. At other times, U.S. companies wish to develop their human resources through valuable international experiences. Regardless of the reason, U.S. individuals living abroad for extended periods (known as **expatriates**) face significant tax issues.

Some employers adopt a laissez-faire approach to expatriate tax issues—employees assume responsibility for whatever taxes they incur while working abroad. However, most U.S. multinationals maintain tax reimbursement policies providing either tax protection or equalization. **Tax protection plans** reimburse employees for most or all taxes they incur while working abroad that exceed the taxes they would have paid without the foreign assignment. Nonetheless, employees transferred to low-tax jurisdictions that, as a result, incur lower tax liabilities keep the difference. Thus, tax protection plans shield employees from increased tax burdens while working in high-tax foreign countries, but employees retain the windfall benefits from assignments in low-tax jurisdictions. Like protection policies, **tax equalization plans** reimburse employees for additional taxes they incur from working abroad. However, equalization plans require expatriates to reimburse employers if actual tax burdens decline as the result of working in low-tax countries. In effect, tax equalization plans keep employees "whole," providing neither incentives nor disincentives to work abroad.

---

### EXAMPLE

Trent and Catie work for the same international accounting firm, receive the same compensation package, and pay $40,000 federal income, state income, and Social Security taxes in 2003. At the beginning of 2004, their employer transfers Trent to Japan and Catie to Jamaica. As a result, Trent's worldwide taxes increase to $50,000, while Catie's declines to $12,000. The firm's human resource department is debating the merits of converting their current tax protection plan to a tax equalization plan. Under their current plan, the accounting firm reimburses Trent for his additional $10,000 tax liability but allows Catie to keep her $28,000 windfall. Under the proposed tax equalization plan, the employer reimburses Trent (the same as with a tax protection plan) but reduces Catie's compensation for the $28,000 tax decrease or requires Catie to reimburse the firm.

Tax protection and equalization plans have their respective pros and cons and advocates among human resource experts. From a behavioral perspective, employers' tax reimbursement policies often affect the expectations, motivations, and job satisfaction of expatriate employees and, so, must receive careful attention. U.S. multinationals cannot ignore expatriate tax issues since companies with reimbursement plans, not their employees, often bear the incremental taxes attributable to foreign assignments. Thus, employers must understand the special tax issues their U.S. employees abroad face.

This chapter explains the **foreign earned income exclusion,** a special incentive encouraging U.S. individuals to work in foreign countries. A brief discussion of the special provisions applicable to expatriates in U.S. possessions follows. The last section explains the Social Security tax implications of working abroad.

## FOREIGN EARNED INCOME EXCLUSION

American workers abroad, especially those in procurement positions, send business orders for materials, products, and services to U.S. companies, increasing U.S. exports and creating U.S. jobs. To encourage employment abroad (and, thus, to stimulate exports and jobs), the United States allows qualifying U.S. individuals to exclude part or all of their **foreign earned income (FEI).** Since many countries provide similar tax benefits to their expatriates, the FEI exclusion makes U.S. workers price-competitive and, thus, achieves a rough form of capital import neutrality. Without the exclusion, many U.S. expatriates working in low-tax countries, such as Saudi Arabia, would become more expensive to hire vis-à-vis their European counterparts. As a result, fewer American workers would choose to expatriate, U.S. companies would receive fewer orders from abroad, and the U.S. economy would lose an important stimulus to exports and jobs.[1]

---

**FLASHBACK**

As Chapter 2 discussed, the United States has jurisdiction to tax the worldwide income of its U.S. citizens and residents. Without some double tax relief, the United States and the foreign host country tax the same income of U.S. expatriates. The FEI exclusion provides a territorial form of relief.

---

Only qualified individuals can elect the FEI exclusion, and electing expatriates can exclude only FEI.[2] Once made, the election applies to the current and later taxable years unless revoked. Taxpayers can revoke an election for any year after the election year. However, U.S. expatriates revoking an election without IRS consent must wait five years before they can reelect the exclusion.[3]

**COMPLIANCE POINTER:** U.S. individuals elect the FEI exclusion using Form 2555, Foreign Earned Income, even if they exclude all income.[4] To be valid, expatriates must attach the election to a timely filed return (including extensions), an amended return, or a late return made within a year following the original due date. Taxpayers missing these deadlines still can make the election in two situations. First, U.S. expatriates who do not owe income tax after considering the FEI exclusion can make the election at any time. Second, those owing income tax can elect the FEI exclusion if the election precedes IRS discovery of their omission.[5]

---

[1] John Mutti, *The American Presence Abroad and U.S. Exports*, Office of Tax Analysis Paper 33 (U.S. Department of the Treasury, October 1978). For a complete overview of the economic arguments supporting this analysis, see David Hamod, "Section 911 Coalition's Remarks at Ways & Means Hearing on International Competitiveness," *Worldwide Tax Daily* (July 2, 1999), 1999 WTD 127–146.

[2] IRC §911(a), (d)(7).

[3] IRC §911(e).

[4] IRC §6012(c).

[5] Reg. §1.911-7(a)(2). In determining whether expatriates file timely returns, Reg. §1.6081-5(a)(5) grants those with tax homes outside the United States and Puerto Rico two additional months to file.

### Qualified Individuals

To qualify for the FEI exclusion, individuals must shift their tax homes to foreign countries.[6] **Tax homes** exist at the location of the taxpayer's regular or principal place of business.[7] Temporarily working abroad does not cause the tax home to change, whereas indefinite stays do cause a shift.

Absent contrary facts and circumstances, foreign assignments that expatriates realistically expect to last no more than a year that, in fact, do last one year or less are **temporary work assignments**. They do not result in a foreign tax home or qualify the worker for the FEI exclusion. In contrast, foreign stays expatriates realistically expected to last more than one year are **indefinite work assignments** regardless of the actual duration. As indefinite assignments, they result in foreign tax homes and qualify U.S. workers for the FEI exclusion if they meet other requirements (explained later). When U.S. expatriates initially expect their foreign assignment to last a year or less but later realistically expect the assignment to exceed one year, the IRS treats their employment abroad as temporary until the change in expectation, and indefinite after the change.[8]

Notwithstanding the preceding guidelines, anyone with a U.S. abode cannot possess a foreign tax home.[9] An **abode** is wherever an individual's domestic ties exist.[10] Thus, the IRS might consider individuals working abroad but spending substantial time living in the United States as not possessing the required foreign tax home.

---

### EXAMPLE

Christie, a U.S. citizen, lives with her family in Detroit but regularly commutes to her full-time job in Toronto. Even though she principally works in Canada, she does not have a foreign tax home since her abode exists in the United States. Thus, Christie cannot exclude FEI.

---

[6]IRC §911(d)(1).

[7]Reg §1.911-2(b).

[8]Rev. Rul. 93-86, 1993-2 CB 71.

[9]IRC §911(d)(3).

[10]*Harrington v. Comm.*, 93 TC 297 (1989); *Lemay v. Comm.*, 837 F.2d 681 (CA-5, 1988). The abode depends on economic, family, social, and personal ties (e.g., location of personal bank account and membership in social clubs). In contrast, the tax home depends on business ties.

In addition to the tax home requirement, U.S. expatriates must meet either a bona fide resident or physical presence test. They need not meet the same test each year. Thus, a U.S. individual satisfying the physical presence requirement in 2002 and 2004 and the bona fide residence test in 2003 can exclude FEI all three years if they possess a foreign tax home.

To meet the **bona fide resident test,** individuals must be U.S. citizens residing in one or more foreign countries for an uninterrupted period including within it an entire taxable year.[11] Mere transients or sojourners in a foreign country do not qualify as foreign residents.[12] The United States considers many factors in determining residency status. For instance, the location and residence of family members, the nature and duration of foreign stays, the assumption of economic burdens abroad, and the place of social and cultural ties serve as important factors.[13] Nonetheless, U.S. citizens submitting statements to foreign governments claiming nonresidency and, as a result, avoiding foreign income tax, cannot assert their bona fide foreign residency to the United States, so they also avoid U.S. income tax via the FEI exclusion.[14] In short, U.S. citizens cannot play the residency card both ways.

---

## EXAMPLE

Timothy accepts an 18-month appointment to Singapore under his company's international executive training program. He can select the program starting and ending dates from these possibilities:

|          | *Starting Date*    | *Ending Date*     |
|----------|--------------------|-------------------|
| Choice 1 | June 1, 2003       | November 30, 2004 |
| Choice 2 | September 1, 2003  | February 29, 2005 |

Assume he will be a Singaporean resident and have a foreign tax home regardless of his selection. Under the first choice, he will not meet the bona fide resident test for either 2003 or 2004 since his period of

---

[11]IRC §911(d)(1)(A). Though the statute limits the availability of the bona fide resident test to U.S. citizens, Rev. Rul. 91-58, 1991-2 CB 340, indicates that resident aliens can assert equal standing to the extent U.S. tax treaties extend nondiscriminatory treatment to them.
[12]Reg. §1.911-2(c), referring to Reg. §1.871-2(b).
[13]*Sochurek v. Comm.*, 300 F.2d 34 (CA-7, 1962).
[14]IRC §911(d)(5). *Riley, Jr. v. Comm.*, 74 TC 414 (1980), clarifies that qualifying for a treaty exemption is not equivalent to making a prohibited statement to the host country.

residency will not include either the entire 2003 or 2004 taxable years. To exclude FEI under choice 1, Timothy will have to meet the alternative physical presence test. However, Timothy can meet the bona fide resident test if he selects the second option since it includes the entire 2004 taxable year. Thus, choosing the September 1 starting date allows Timothy to qualify as a bona fide Singaporean resident during four months of 2003, all of 2004, and two months of 2005 (i.e., the entire period of his foreign residency).

To satisfy the **physical presence test**, a U.S. citizen or resident must be physically present in one or more foreign countries for at least 330 full days during a 12-month period.[15] Counting as one of the 330 days abroad requires only physical presence. Thus, days of foreign presence when expatriates do not perform services apply toward the threshold. For instance, days U.S. individuals vacation abroad, even when vacations occur in a different foreign country from the one of employment, help in qualifying for the exclusion.

## EXAMPLE

Nancy is a U.S. citizen working as a tour guide in the Bahamas. Except for 20 days when she visits her family in Atlanta, she lives in Nassau. She actually performs services 200 days during 2003. Even if Nancy does not qualify as a bona fide Bahamian resident, she meets the physical presence test. She can identify a 12-month period during which she is bodily present in the Bahamas.

**COMPLIANCE POINTER:** U.S. expatriates can document the number of days present in a foreign country using custom stamps on passports.

U.S. individuals do not qualify for the FEI exclusion if their residence or presence in a foreign country violates regulations interpreting the Trading with the Enemy Act or the International Emergency Economic Powers

---

[15]IRC §911(d)(1)(B). In prior years, approximately 60 percent of U.S. expatriates electing the FEI exclusion qualified under the bona fide resident test. For example, see U.S. Treasury, *Taxation of Americans Working Overseas: The Operation of the Foreign Earned Income Exclusion in 1987* (January 1993), table 7.

Act.[16] However, U.S. citizens and residents whose foreign residence or presence does not violate these regulations sometimes must leave their foreign host countries due to war, civil unrest, or similar adverse conditions precluding normal business activities. When such exits occur before meeting either the bona fide resident or physical presence test but the affected individuals would have met at least one test absent the adverse conditions, they qualify for the FEI exclusion during their shortened periods of foreign residence or presence.[17]

## Qualified Income

To benefit from the FEI exclusion, satisfying the bona fide resident or physical presence test is an essential but insufficient requirement. In addition to meeting one of these tests, U.S. citizens and residents must earn income they derive from foreign sources.[18] U.S. individuals cannot exclude foreign source investment income or U.S. source earned income.

**Earned income** is compensation received for rendering personal services such as wages, base salary, professional fees, and noncash remuneration (e.g., rent-free housing). Also, earned income includes allowances and reimbursements related to overseas assignments.[19] These additional amounts sometimes exceed employees' base salaries, more than doubling the size of the total compensation package. For instance, U.S. expatriates often receive overseas allowances for inconveniences and cultural shock, hardship premiums for adverse living conditions abroad, cost-of-living allowances, housing allowances, education allowances for children to receive American-style schooling, home leave allowances for periodic returns to the United States, and reimbursements for additional taxes due to the foreign assignment. Spouses with community property rights cannot split FEI between them to increase and, perhaps, double the amount of their combined tax benefits.[20]

## KEY CASE

A U.S. citizen and Swiss resident creates artistic works and afterward seeks a buyer; he does not perform contract work. His sales occur through both private purchases and art galleries, acting as agents, that display his con-

---

[16]IRC §911(d)(8).
[17]IRC §911(d)(4). For instance, Rev. Proc. 2002-20, 2002-1 CB 732, waives the normal qualification periods for individuals leaving Macedonia after July 26, 2001.
[18]IRC §911(b)(1)(A).
[19]IRC §911(d)(2)(A).
[20]IRC §911(b)(2)(C).

signed creations and receive commissions. The taxpayer argues that gain from selling art he creates in his Swiss studio is personal service income and, thus, qualifies for the FEI exclusion. The government contends that the gain is not earned income since service recipients do not exist, only buyers of property (i.e., artistic creations). The court holds that gain from selling the taxpayer's creations results in earned income. Personal effort, time, and energy produced the earned income, not capital.[21]

Earned income does not include "disguised dividends" (i.e., amounts shareholders receive for personal services to their corporations that, in fact, represent distributions from E&P).[22] When independent contractors perform services in a trade or business in which capital is a material income-producing factor, the Code treats a reasonable allowance as earned income. However, the reasonable allowance cannot exceed 30 percent of the self-employed individual's share of the business's net profit.[23] Whether capital constitutes a material income-producing factor is a question of fact.

## EXAMPLE

Thelma Lou, a U.S. citizen, moves to Uruguay to start a computer service and repair business with a Uruguayan resident. During 2004, her share of the business fees and related deductions equal $150,000 and $60,000, respectively. Based on the facts and circumstances, $35,000 is a reasonable allowance for her service contributions. If capital is a material income-producing factor in the business, Thelma Lou treats $27,000 as earned income [30% × ($150,000 − $60,000)]. If capital is not a material income-producing factor, she treats $90,000 ($150,000 − $60,000) as earned income. If Thelma Lou meets the bona fide resident or physical presence test and derives her earnings from foreign sources, she can exclude part or all of her earned income (i.e., either $27,000 or $90,000).

---

[21]*Tobey v. Comm.*, 60 TC 227 (1973), *acq.* Similarly, *Robida v. Comm.*, 460 F.2d 1172 (CA-9, 1972), held that a professional gambler using his ingenuity and expertise to manipulate slot machines can treat his winnings as earned income. Also, see *Cook v. U.S.*, 599 F.2d 400 (Ct. Cl., 1979), involving a sculptor, and Rev. Rul. 80-254, 1980-2 CB 222, dealing with book royalties.
[22]IRC §911(d)(2)(A).
[23]IRC §911(d)(2)(B).

## KEY CASE

A U.S. citizen owns an auto body repair business in Canada, which requires several pieces of equipment and spare parts inventory to operate. He estimates repair work, supervises his workers, and inspects finished repairs. The court opines that capital is a material income-producing factor when it accounts for a substantial portion of the business's income or when operations require a substantial investment in inventories, equipment, or machinery, whether owned or leased. In this case, the taxpayer's total material charges exceed his total labor charges, and the book value of equipment, machinery, and inventory is substantial vis-à-vis the business's net earnings. Thus, the court holds that capital is a material income-producing factor in this business, and the owner's foreign earned income cannot exceed 30 percent of his net earnings.[24]

To be foreign source income, U.S. individuals must earn it rendering personal services outside the United States.[25] When expatriates earn some income within the United States and some abroad, they allocate their compensation between U.S. and foreign sources on a reasonable basis.[26] For instance, the number of days worked in each location usually is acceptable as an allocation basis.

**PLANNING POINTER:** Some tax professionals argue that expatriates should not allocate foreign allowances between U.S. and foreign sources like base salary. Since companies pay these amounts only because the recipients perform services abroad, this argument treats allowances as foreign source income in their entirety, often increasing the FEI exclusion.

## EXAMPLE

Virginia, a U.S. citizen and Estonian resident, receives a $60,000 base salary plus $25,000 foreign allowances. During 2004, she works 208 days in Estonia and 24 days in the United States. She calculates FEI as follows:

$$\text{FEI} = \left( \$60,000 \times \frac{208}{208 + 24} \right) + \$25,000 = \$78,793$$

---

[24]*Rousku v. Comm.*, 56 TC 548 (1971).
[25]IRC §861(a)(3).
[26]IRC §863(b)(1).

> The alternative interpretation, which the IRS may prefer, considers the entire compensation package as allocable between U.S. and foreign source income. Under this approach, FEI declines:
>
> $$\text{FEI} = \left( \$85,000 \times \frac{208}{208 + 24} \right) = \$76,207$$

By definition, foreign earned income does not include any amount a qualified individual receives:

- As a pension or annuity (including Social Security benefits),
- From a nonexempt trust or nonqualified annuity,
- As a government employee from the United States or its agencies (e.g., foreign service offices and diplomats), or
- After the year following the year in which the expatriate earns the income.[27]

### EXAMPLE

After working most of her career in foreign locations, Carolyn, a U.S. citizen, retires to Paris, France. She receives an annual pension of $100,000, 60 percent attributable to foreign services. Though $60,000 is foreign source income, it is not FEI by definition. Thus, she cannot exclude any portion of her pension benefits.

### EXAMPLE

Mary is a U.S. expatriate who earns a $30,000 bonus in 2003 while working abroad. She receives one-third of the bonus in 2003, one-third in 2004, and the remaining third in 2005. Only the $20,000 she receives in 2003 and 2004 is FEI. Mary receives the 2005 portion more than a year following 2003 (i.e., the year she earns it). By definition, the last installment is not FEI.

---

[27]IRC §911(b)(1)(B); Reg. §1.911-3(c). IRC §912 allows certain U.S. civilian officers and employees and Peace Corps volunteers to exclude specified foreign allowances.

The tax law applicable to partnerships and partners raises interesting expatriate issues. For instance, FEI a partnership earns via one of its partners stationed abroad, passes through the entity, and is allocable among the partners according to their respective distributive shares.[28] It does not pass through to the specific partner working abroad except to the extent of his or her distributive share. In these cases, any FEI allocable to partners living in the United States provides no tax benefit since they meet neither the bona fide resident nor the physical presence test. Also, the partner stationed abroad receives a distributive share in the FEI for only a fractional part attributable to his or her personal services abroad.

## EXAMPLE

A domestic partnership with five equal U.S. partners earns $500,000 gross income. One partner, Charles, works abroad the entire year and qualifies for the FEI exclusion. As a result of his assignment, the partnership receives $150,000 of its $500,000 gross income (or 30 percent) from foreign sources. Under the partnership agreement, Charles's distributive share of partnership income equals $100,000 (20% × $500,000) of which $30,000 is FEI (30% × $100,000). Each of the other four partners receives identical distributive shares.[29]

**PLANNING POINTER:** To avoid losing tax benefits, partnerships can make guaranteed payments to their expatriate partners for their work abroad. Such amounts are FEI to recipient partners in their entirety since U.S. law views them as payments to nonpartners.[30]

### Exclusion Benefit

Qualified U.S. expatriates can elect to exclude FEI. For employees, the maximum available exclusion equals $80,000 plus an amount based on excess housing expenses.[31] Similarly, self-employed individuals exclude $80,000

---

[28]Reg. §1.702-1(a)(8)(ii).
[29]This example follows Rev. Rul. 75-86, 1975-1 CB 242, in allowing the taxpayer to claim the FEI exclusion against the partnership's gross income. For a different approach for years preceding this ruling, see *Vogt v. U.S.*, 537 F.2d 405 (Ct. Cl., 1976).
[30]*Miller, Jr. v. Comm.*, 52 TC 752 (1969), *acq.*, and *Carey v. U.S.*, 427 F.2d 763 (Ct. Cl., 1970).
[31]IRC §911(a).

and deduct excess housing expenses.[32] A qualified individual's FEI sets the upper limit on these aggregate benefits.[33] In effect, expatriates cannot exclude U.S. source income or any unearned income.

U.S. individuals qualifying for the entire year exclude up to $80,000 before considering any additional exclusion or deduction based on housing expenses. Those qualifying for less than an entire year must pro rate the $80,000 on a daily basis.[34] Beginning in 2008, the $80,000 receives cost-of-living adjustments.

---

**EXAMPLE**

Before her transfer overseas on December 30, 2003, Priscilla (a U.S. citizen) managed the export division of a U.S. multinational company. During 2004, she qualifies as a bona fide foreign resident for the entire year and receives $90,000 compensation. If she makes the election, Priscilla excludes $80,000 and reports the remaining $10,000 as gross income. If her housing expenses exceed a base amount, Priscilla omits an additional amount. However, she cannot exclude more than $90,000, her FEI.

---

**EXAMPLE**

Rebecca, a U.S. employee working abroad, qualifies as a bona fide Kuwaiti resident during the last three months of 2003, all of 2004, and the first four months of 2005. Her maximum exclusion before considering excess housing expenses equals $20,164 ($80,000 × 92/365) in 2003 and $80,000 in 2004. In 2005, her maximum exclusion before housing expenses equals $26,301 ($80,000 × 120/365). If her 2005 FEI equals $25,000, she excludes $25,000. However, if her 2005 FEI equals $30,000, she excludes $26,301 plus excess housing expenses, if any, up to $3,699 ($30,000 − $26,301).

---

[32]IRC §911(c)(3).
[33]IRC §911(d)(7).
[34]IRC §911(b)(2)(A), (D).

Assuming a foreign tax home, U.S. expatriates physically present in a foreign country or countries for 330 days in a 12-month period can elect the FEI exclusion. Which 12-month period should the taxpayer select? The optimal choice is the 12-month period overlapping the greatest portion of the taxable year.[35] If the chosen 12-month period overlaps 90 percent of the taxable year, the taxpayer's maximum exclusion before considering housing costs equals $72,000 (90% × $80,000).

> **PLANNING POINTER:** To extend their qualifying period, some U.S. expatriates can count days before their arrival in the host country and after their departure date, maximizing their exclusion.[36] Especially during the first and last years abroad, the amount excludable under the physical presence test may exceed the available exclusion under the bona fide resident test.

## EXAMPLE

Mark arrives in Liechtenstein on April 1, 2004, and departs May 1, 2005. During this foreign assignment, Mark's compensation equals $240,000. To meet the physical presence test, he identifies a 12-month period during which his Liechtenstein presence totals at least 330 days. He also uses this period to calculate his maximum exclusion. For 2004, he can point to the 12-month period from February 26, 2004 to February 25, 2005, during which he is present in Liechtenstein for exactly 330 full days.

---

[35]Though not clear from the current statutory construction, IRC §911(b)(2)(A) prior to the Tax Reform Act of 1986 reads as follows: "The foreign earned income of an individual which may be excluded under subsection (a)(1) for any taxable year shall not exceed the amount of foreign earned income computed on a daily basis at the annual rate set forth in the following table for each day of the taxable year *within the applicable period* [emphasis added] described in subparagraph (A) or (B) of subsection (d)(1)." The "applicable period" refers to the period of bona fide residence or physical presence. Thus, U.S. expatriates receive the exclusion benefit for the 12-month period rather than the days physically present in foreign countries. Regulations condone calculating the maximum exclusion based on the 12-month period during which the U.S. expatriate establishes 330 days of physical presence.

[36]Reg. §1.911-2(d)(1) states that a U.S. individual's 12-month period "may begin before or after arrival in a foreign country and may end before or after departure."

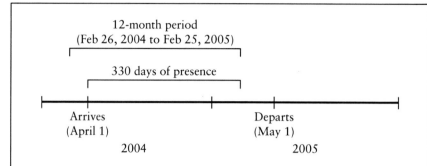

This 12-month period allows Mark to count 36 days in his 12-month period even though they occur before his arrival. Assuming no excess housing expenses, Mark's 12-month period includes 310 days during 2004, and he can exclude $67,760 ($80,000 × 310/366) FEI in 2004.

## EXAMPLE

Assume the same facts as the previous example. For 2005, Mark's optimal 12-month period runs from June 5, 2004, to June 4, 2005, during which he is present in Liechtenstein for exactly 330 full days.

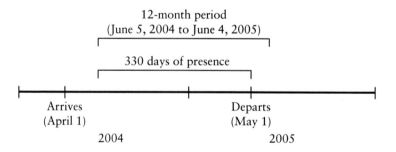

This 12-month period allows Mark to count 35 days in his 12-month period even though they occur after his departure. Assuming no excess housing expenses, Mark's 12-month period includes 155 days during 2005, and he can exclude $33,973 ($80,000 × 155/365) FEI in 2005.

In addition to the $80,000 exclusion, U.S. employees working abroad can exclude a housing cost amount, and independent contractors working abroad can deduct a housing cost amount for adjusted gross income.[37] The **housing cost amount** equals the excess of reasonable housing expenses over a base housing amount.[38] The **base housing amount** equals 16 percent of a U.S. government employee's salary at step 1 of grade GS-14.[39] Like the annual $80,000 exclusion, the taxpayer allocates the base housing amount on a daily basis when the expatriate's qualifying period overlays less than the entire taxable year.[40]

---

**EXAMPLE**

Thomas, a U.S. citizen, qualifies as a bona fide Saudi resident during the entire taxable year. His company pays him a $70,000 base salary and a $20,000 housing allowance (i.e., FEI totals $90,000). He spends $15,000 for actual housing expenses. Assuming the U.S. government salary at step 1 of grade GS-14 equals $84,732, he can exclude $1,443 ($15,000 − 16% of $84,732) as a housing cost amount and $80,000. Thus, his gross income is $8,557 ($90,000 − $1,443 − $80,000).

---

**EXAMPLE**

Peter, a U.S. citizen, maintains a foreign tax home and qualifies as a bona fide Latvian resident for 73 days in 2004 (and all of 2005). His 2004 FEI equals $27,000, which includes a $4,000 housing allowance. He spends $3,500 for foreign housing expenses in 2004. Assuming the U.S. government salary at step 1 of grade GS-14 equals $84,732, he can claim an exclusion of $16,000 ($80,000 × 1/5) plus $789 [$3,500 − (16% × $84,732 × 1/5)]. Thus, Peter excludes $16,789 and reports gross income of $10,211 ($27,000 − $16,789) in 2004.

---

[37] IRC §911(a)(2), (c)(3)(A).
[38] IRC §911(c)(1). The amount employers designate or pay as a foreign housing allowance (if anything) does not affect the housing cost amount.
[39] The U.S. Office of Personnel Management publishes government salary information at www.opm.gov/oca/payrates/index.htm. Salary levels vary by region. For instance, the 2002 salaries for step 1 of grade GS-14 are $77,043 in Atlanta and $81,473 in Los Angeles.
[40] IRC §911(c)(1)(B)(ii).

Reasonable housing expenses include rental payments for lodging, fair rental value of employer-provided housing; rental payments for furniture and appliances; real and personal property insurance premiums; utility expenses other than telephone, repair, and maintenance costs; and residential parking fees. Housing expenses do not include the purchase price of lodging, cost to make capital improvements, otherwise deductible mortgage interest and real estate taxes, expenses to obtain domestic help, depreciation expense, subscription fees for cable or satellite television service, or any lavish or extravagant expense.[41] When the qualified individual's family maintains a second foreign abode because of dangerous, unhealthful, or otherwise adverse living conditions in the host country, the taxpayer treats the expenses of the second household as reasonable housing expenses too.[42]

The $80,000 exclusion (or pro rata portion for partial-year qualifiers) plus the housing cost amount cannot exceed FEI.[43] Thus, expatriates cannot exclude U.S. source income or foreign unearned income. Self-employed individuals carry forward for one year on a last-in, first-out basis any housing cost amount this FEI limit precludes them from deducting.[44] The carryforward necessitates some ordering rules: Qualified individuals exclude the housing cost amount if an employee, then claim the $80,000 exclusion, and last deduct the housing cost amount if self-employed. Thus, qualified employees exclude the housing cost amount, then claim the $80,000 exclusion; qualified self-employed individuals claim the $80,000 exclusion, then deduct their housing cost amount.[45]

---

**EXAMPLE**

---

Jenny, a U.S. resident alien physically present in Singapore the entire year, has FEI of $83,000. Her foreign housing expenses total $19,060 and the U.S. government salary at step 1 of grade GS-14 equals $84,732. If Jenny is an employee, she excludes her housing cost amount of $5,503 [$19,060 − (16% × $84,732)] plus $77,497 ($83,000 − $5,503). That is, she excludes her entire $83,000 FEI but no more. She cannot carry over any portion of the $2,503 ($80,000 − $77,497) the

---

[41]Reg. §1.911-4(b)(1), (2).
[42]IRC §911(c)(2)(B).
[43]IRC §911(d)(7).
[44]IRC §911(c)(3)(C). No comparable carryforward applies for the $80,000 exclusion or the housing cost amount of employees.
[45]Reg. §1.911-4(f)Ex.(8) illustrates these ordering rules when a U.S. expatriate receives FEI in his or her capacity as both an employee and an independent contractor.

FEI limit disallows. However, if Jenny is self-employed, she excludes $80,000, deducts $3,000 ($83,000 − $80,000) of her housing cost amount, and carries forward the residual $2,503 [$19,060 − (16% × $84,732) − $3,000] housing cost amount for one year.

To prevent double tax benefits, the Code disallows deductions and credits allocable to excluded FEI.[46] Thus, electing the FEI exclusion results in the loss of otherwise deductible employee and self-employment expenses and foreign tax credits. In effect, **U.S. expatriates** decide to:

- Elect the FEI exclusion, deduct employee and self-employment expenses allocable to included FEI, and claim creditable taxes allocable to included FEI, or
- Report all FEI as gross income, deduct all employee and self-employment expenses, and claim all foreign income taxes as creditable.

In high-tax jurisdictions, forgoing the FEI election and claiming the deduction for employee expenses and the foreign tax credit often yields the optimal result, especially for U.S. expatriates who can absorb the resulting excess credits against their U.S. tax on other foreign source income. The lower the effective foreign income tax rate, the more likely the election to exclude FEI minimizes worldwide taxes.

## EXAMPLE

His employer transfers Alvin, an unmarried U.S. citizen, to Hong Kong on December 30, 2003. He expects to stay abroad approximately 18 months and, thus, qualifies for the FEI exclusion. His lodging expenses do not result in a housing cost amount. Alvin provides the following information for 2004:

| | |
|---|---|
| FEI | $100,000 |
| Foreign travel expenses | 12,000 |
| Other employee expenses | 5,000 |
| Hong Kong income taxes | 16,000 |

If Alvin does not elect the FEI exclusion, he reports $100,000 gross income, deducts $5,000 employee expenses, and claims $16,000 cred-

---

[46]IRC §911(d)(6).

itable taxes. He cannot deduct foreign travel expenses since his expected stay in Hong Kong results in a foreign tax home. Without a U.S. tax home, he cannot deduct meals and lodging expenses since he will not incur them away from home.[47] If Alvin elects to exclude FEI, he excludes $80,000 and reports $20,000 gross income. He determines deductible employee expenses and creditable taxes as follows:

$$\text{Deductible employee expenses: } \$5,000 - \left(\$5,000 \times \frac{\$80,000}{\$100,000}\right)$$
$$= \$1,000$$

$$\text{Creditable foreign tax: } \$16,000 - \left(\$16,000 \times \frac{\$80,000}{\$100,000}\right) = \$3,200$$

Since Hong Kong is a low-tax jurisdiction, Alvin probably minimizes his tax liability if he elects the FEI exclusion.

**PLANNING POINTER:** U.S. individuals working in high-tax countries and, thus, forgoing the FEI election to exclude FEI may wish to establish, based on facts and circumstances, that they do not have a foreign tax home. If successful, they can deduct lodging, meals, and other travel expenses while abroad. Expatriates whose foreign stays approximate one year stand the best chance of establishing a U.S. tax home.

## INCOME SOURCED IN U.S. POSSESSIONS

U.S. expatriates working in U.S. possessions cannot elect the FEI exclusion since it requires bona fide residence or physical presence in one or more foreign countries. However, these individuals often qualify for separate exclusions that implement territorial tax principles to accomplish the following objectives:

- Equalize the competition between U.S. and foreign businesses operating in U.S. possessions,

---

[47]IRC §162(a)(2). See the earlier discussion in this chapter regarding tax homes and their locations.

▨ Redirect federal tax revenues to U.S. possession treasuries, and

▨ Alleviate the burden of filing tax returns in both the United States and U.S. possessions.

The Code treats nonresident aliens residing in American Samoa (AS) and Puerto Rico (PR) for the entire taxable year similarly to U.S. residents (e.g., taxable on worldwide income).[48] Also, U.S. citizens, U.S. residents, and nonresident aliens residing in AS for the entire taxable year exclude Samoan source income and income effectively connected with a Samoan trade or business.[49] Similarly, U.S. individuals and nonresident aliens residing in PR for the entire taxable year exclude all Puerto Rican source income.[50] The combined effect of these provisions exempts all Samoan residents from U.S. taxation if they derive virtually all their income from AS, and all Puerto Rican residents from U.S. taxation if they derive nearly all their income from PR. Thus, these individuals often do not file U.S. tax returns but, instead, pay tax to AS or PR, placing U.S. and foreign individuals residing in these possessions on an equal competitive footing.[51]

---

## EXAMPLE

Nathaniel, a U.S. citizen, resides in AS for the entire taxable year. He earns $120,000 from performing services as a marine biologist and derives $15,000 income from AS investments. He has no other income. Nathaniel excludes $135,000 for U.S. income tax purposes, and AS taxes it instead. Since Nathaniel has no U.S. gross income, he does not file a U.S. income tax return.

---

[48]See IRC §876.

[49]IRC §931(a). This provision also will apply to individuals residing in Guam and the Northern Mariana Islands once these possessions enter implementing agreements with the United States to develop tax systems not mirroring the U.S. tax system. **Mirror codes** are identical to the U.S. Code except they substitute the name of the possession for "United States" wherever it appears in the U.S. law, and substitute "United States" for the name of the possession.

[50]IRC §933(1).

[51]IRC §6012(a)(1). Without these exclusions, U.S. individuals residing in American Samoa or Puerto Rico would report worldwide income on their U.S. tax returns and claim foreign tax credits for possession income taxes they pay. In fact, this procedure also applies to U.S. individuals residing in lesser-known U.S. possessions not mentioned here.

U.S. individuals residing in the U.S. Virgin Islands (USVI) on the last day of the taxable year, reporting their worldwide income to the USVI, and paying USVI tax on such income do not file a U.S. tax return.[52] U.S. citizens and residents not residing in the USVI at the close of the taxable year but deriving USVI source income or income effectively connected with a USVI trade or business file identical U.S. tax returns with both the United States and the USVI.[53] These taxpayers split their income tax liabilities between the United States and the USVI based on the source of adjusted gross income (AGI). The Code allows the portion payable to the USVI as a credit against the U.S. tax.[54] Individuals determine the amount payable to the USVI as shown in equation 15.1:

$$\text{Taxes payable to USVI} = \frac{\text{USVI AGI}}{\text{AGI}} \times \text{U.S. tax before USVI credit} \quad (15.1)$$

## SOCIAL SECURITY CONCERNS

In addition to income tax concerns, some U.S. individuals working abroad encounter Social Security tax issues. For instance, double taxation can occur if both the United States and the foreign host country impose Social Security taxes on the same income. Also, payment of foreign Social Security taxes does not assure receipt of a future Social Security benefit. Thus, objectives of U.S. expatriates and their tax advisers often include avoiding double Social Security taxation and obtaining future benefits commensurate with Social Security tax liabilities.

U.S. citizens and residents working abroad for American employers must pay Federal Insurance Contribution Act (FICA) tax on their compensation, including foreign allowances and tax reimbursements, even if they exclude part or all compensation as FEI.[55] In addition, American employers can elect FICA coverage for U.S. individuals employed by their 10-percent-owned foreign affiliates.[56] The potential for double taxation exists in these

---

[52]IRC §932(c)(4).
[53]IRC §932(a)(2).
[54]IRC §932(b).
[55]IRC §3121(b). IRC §3121(h) defines **American employers** to include the federal government and its instrumentalities, U.S. residents, partnerships if at least two-thirds of the partners are U.S. residents, trusts if all the trustees are U.S. residents, and U.S. corporations.
[56]IRC §3121(l).

**EXHIBIT 15.1** U.S. Totalization Agreements

*Panel A: Countries Entering Agreements*

| | | |
|---|---|---|
| Australia | Germany | Norway |
| Austria | Greece | Portugal |
| Belgium | Ireland | Spain |
| Canada | Italy | Sweden |
| Chile | Korea | Switzerland |
| Finland | Luxembourg | United Kingdom |
| France | Netherlands | |

*Panel B: Countries Discussing Agreements*

| | | |
|---|---|---|
| Argentina | Israel | Mexico |
| Brazil | Japan[a] | New Zealand |
| Denmark | | |

[a]Japan is actively negotiating an agreement.

situations since most countries impose Social Security tax on compensation foreign nationals earn within their borders. Also, depending on the foreign Social Security law, the U.S. expatriate's foreign assignment may be too short to qualify for a future Social Security benefit.

Special international agreements called totalization agreements satisfactorily resolve these issues for many U.S. expatriates.[57] These agreements seek to avoid double Social Security taxation and provide for a totalized (i.e., partial) benefit when an individual pays Social Security taxes to more than one country. The United States has concluded totalization agreements with 20 countries and entered discussions with several others. Exhibit 15.1 lists these countries.

Most totalization agreements allow U.S. employees whose American employers "send" or transfer them abroad to pay Social Security taxes only in the United States. However, agreements extend this privilege only to U.S. expatriates on temporary foreign assignments of five years or less.[58] In most other cases, U.S. expatriates pay the host country's Social Security tax. Thus, totalization agreements do not apply to foreign stays exceeding five years and U.S. individuals accepting employment with foreign companies (i.e., those American employers do not send).

---

[57]The Social Security Administration provides information about U.S. totalization agreements and Social Security tax systems around the world at www.ssa.gov/international/status.html.

[58]For instance, see the U.S.-U.K. totalization agreement, TIAS 11086 (1984), Article 4(2).

# Related Person Transactions

# Transfer Prices

The IRS scrutinizes controlled person transfers closely since these transactions provide opportunities for taxpayers to manipulate intercompany prices artificially, shift taxable income to controlled persons with low marginal tax rates, and deprive the U.S. Treasury of tax revenue.[1] However, when shifts occur between two domestic corporations, departures from "true taxable income" often make little difference since, within the United States, affiliated companies can file consolidated returns. In many cases, income shifted among domestic corporations does not materially change the U.S. tax liability the controlled group owes. Also, controlled corporations not qualifying to file consolidated returns because of significant minority holdings cannot shift income among themselves unconstrainedly without raising the ire of minority owners. When majority shareholders artificially shift income away from the entity in which minority owners hold stock, the latter rightfully resent losing wealth and, in egregious cases, can take legal action to protect the value of their holdings. In short, consolidated returns and watchful minority shareholders often minimize or restrict the potential tax savings from inappropriately shifting income between domestic corporations.

In contrast, foreign corporations cannot file consolidated returns with U.S. affiliates.[2] Thus, IRS concern and intervention usually occur in transactions between a domestic person and a controlled foreign person, particularly when their marginal tax rates differ significantly. Specifically, when

---

[1] Reg. §1.482-1(i)(4) defines "controlled taxpayer" as two or more taxpayers that the same interest directly or indirectly owns or controls. The regulation treats taxpayers owning or controlling the other taxpayers as controlled taxpayers also. Reg. §1.482-1(i)(3) clarifies that "control" means the reality of control and includes direct and indirect control of all kinds, even if not legally enforceable and regardless of how one exercises it. Arbitrary income shifting establishes a presumption of control. Thus, this chapter considers the concept of control to include within it the concept of relatedness. Controlled persons certainly include related persons but can include unrelated persons to the extent contractual or other control devices cause persons to act in concert to reduce U.S. taxes in much the same manner as related persons might.
[2] IRC §1504(b)(3). A narrow exception exists in IRC §1504(d).

the U.S. tax rate exceeds the foreign tax rate, the rate differential creates an incentive for taxpayers—whether U.S. or foreign persons—to shift income abroad. When the foreign tax rate exceeds the U.S. tax rate, the rate differential motivates taxpayers to shift income into the United States.[3] When U.S. and foreign tax rates are roughly equal, the incentive to shift income in either direction diminishes.

Foreign tax authorities fret about income shifting to the United States since it deprives their treasuries of tax revenues. The IRS worries primarily about outbound income shifting since it reduces U.S. tax revenues.[4] However, the IRS also examines prices in foreign-to-foreign transfers since income shifting among controlled foreign entities can affect U.S. tax revenues in several ways. First, taxpayers may manipulate intercompany prices between foreign affiliates to shift passive income away from foreign corporations precariously close to meeting the income test for passive foreign investment company (PFIC) or foreign personal holding company (FPHC) status. Second, U.S. persons can shift income away from controlled foreign corporations (CFCs) near the 5-70 thresholds. Third, U.S. shareholders may shift earnings and profits (E&P) among CFCs to reduce future dividend income or increase deemed paid credits. Fourth, pricing policies might reduce foreign entities' U.S. source income or income effectively connected with U.S. trades or businesses.

## FLASHBACK

As Chapter 13 explained, U.S. law treats foreign corporations as PFICs if at least 75 percent of their income is passive. Also, foreign corporations meeting an ownership test and whose foreign personal holding company income equals or exceeds 60 percent of gross income qualify as FPHCs. In Chapter 12, the 5-70 rule ignores Subpart F income when gross insurance income plus foreign base company income falls below the lesser of $1 million or 5 percent of gross income while treating all gross income as Subpart F income when the sum exceeds 70 percent of gross income.

---

[3]From a policy perspective, Code amendments that drop U.S. tax rates decrease the motivation for taxpayers to shift income abroad, reducing government resources necessary to monitor taxpayer compliance. Conversely, increasing U.S. tax rates might stoke incentives to shift income abroad.
[4]Though politicians sometimes assert that foreign corporations with U.S. subsidiaries engage in abusive pricing policies that cost the United States billions of tax revenue dollars, the evidence is inconclusive. One study suggests that low U.S. incomes are

Market forces assure that uncontrolled persons adopt appropriate pricing and do not artificially shift income. Thus, U.S. law treats charges between uncontrolled persons as arm's-length prices. In contrast, controlled persons may make decisions as single entities, artificially inflating or deflating intercompany or **transfer prices** to minimize taxes, increasing their combined wealth.[5] Controlled persons arrive at their **true taxable incomes** only when they determine intercompany charges using the arm's-length standard.[6]

---

### EXAMPLE

Payload, Ltd., a Taiwanese corporation, produces a fireworks display package at a cost of $25,000, which it sells to its wholly owned domestic corporation, Fanfare, Inc., for $42,000. Fanfare, a distributor, resells the fireworks display package for $43,000 to a married couple (unrelated to Payload and Fanfare) using it to celebrate their fiftieth wedding anniversary.

*(continues)*

---

not necessarily due to transfer price manipulations. See Julie H. Collins, Deen Kemsley, and Douglas A. Shackelford, "Transfer Pricing and the Persistent Zero Taxable Income of Foreign-Controlled U.S. Corporations," *Journal of the American Taxation Association*, 19 (Supplement 1997), pp. 68–83. Nonetheless, tax rate differentials seem to explain a significant portion of U.S. subsidiaries' reported incomes, suggesting that foreign companies do use transfer pricing policies and other means to shift income away from the United States. See Lillian F. Mills and Kaye J. Newberry, "Do Foreign Multinationals' Tax incentives Influence Their U.S. Income Reporting and Debt Policy," Working Paper: University of Arizona, 2003.

[5]For evidence that U.S. multinationals engage in such behavior, see John Jacobs, "Taxes and Transfer Pricing: Income Shifting and the Volume of Intrafirm Transfers," *Journal of Accounting Research*, 34 (Autumn 1996), pp. 301–312, and Julie Collins, Deen Kemsley, and Mark Lang, "Cross-Jurisdictional Income Shifting and Earnings Valuation," *Journal of Accounting Research*, 36 (Autumn 1998), pp. 209–229.

[6]In a survey of multinational enterprises, transfer pricing headed the list as the most important tax issue. Eighty-five percent of parent companies ranked transfer pricing as the most important current issue, and 61 percent ranked it as the most important future issue. Among subsidiaries, 94 and 66 percent ranked transfer pricing as the most important current and future issue, respectively. See Ernst & Young, *Transfer Pricing 2001 Global Survey: Making Informed Decisions in Uncertain Times* (November 2001), pp. 14–16.

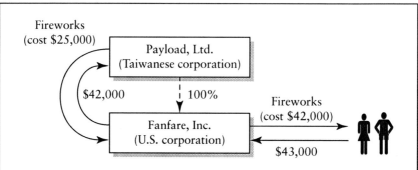

The combined profit of Payload and Fanfare from these transactions totals $18,000 ($43,000 price to couple − $25,000 production cost). Of this combined profit, Fanfare's share equals only $1,000 ($43,000 price to couple − $42,000 transfer price). The related corporations may have set the transfer price between them artificially high to shift more profit to Payload, the Taiwanese corporation. Assume an arm's-length price equals $36,000. If left uncontested, the artificially high transfer price might allow the related persons to avoid U.S. tax during the current year on $6,000 income they shift to Payload ($42,000 transfer price − $36,000 arm's-length price).

## GENERAL PRINCIPLES

U.S. law endows the IRS with broad powers to thwart artificial attempts to shift income. Specifically, the IRS can reallocate gross income, deductions, credits, allowances, basis, or other items affecting taxable income between controlled persons if necessary to prevent tax evasion or clearly reflect income.[7] Thus, U.S. law empowers the IRS to determine arm's-length prices. When taxpayers disagree with a reallocation, their rebuttal should show the IRS adjustments are arbitrary, unreasonable, or capricious and their own methodologies result in arm's-length prices.[8]

Transfer prices between controlled persons meet the arm's-length standard when consistent with those of uncontrolled persons engaging in the same transaction under the same circumstances. However, identical transactions often do not exist, so prices uncontrolled persons charge in comparable transactions under comparable circumstances often represent the

---

[7]IRC §482; Reg. §1.482-1(a)(2). See Robert Feinschreiber, *Transfer Pricing Handbook*, 3rd ed. (Hoboken, NJ: John Wiley & Sons, Inc., 2001).
[8]*Bausch & Lomb, Inc. v. Comm.*, 92 TC 525 (1989), *aff'd*, 933 F.2d 1084 (CA-2, 1991).

yardstick.[9] Under the **best method rule**, taxpayers use the methodology resulting in the most reliable measure of arm's-length pricing. The best method sometimes results in an arm's-length range rather than a single-point estimate. In these cases, the IRS cannot adjust transfer prices within the range.[10] Also, the IRS must consider the effect of foreign legal restrictions on transfer prices to the same degree such restrictions affect uncontrolled persons engaging in similar transactions.[11]

> **PLANNING POINTER:** Never include terms such as "tax haven" or "artificial prices" in correspondence or working papers involving international tax issues. One company's internal memo suggested that setting a low transfer price might escape IRS scrutiny.[12] Even if inconsistent with corporate policy, such language can prove damaging.

To determine the best method, two principles apply.[13] First, transfer prices consistent with prices set in comparable transactions with uncontrolled persons increase reliability. *Ceteris paribus*, U.S. law prefers methods relying on such comparables when they exist. Comparability depends on the functions each person performs, contractual terms, risks each person assumes, existing economic conditions, and the property or services involved.[14] Second, reliability varies with the completeness and accuracy of data and the validity of assumptions.[15] Beyond these guidelines, no strict hierarchy of methods exist.[16]

> **COMPLIANCE POINTER:** Based on differing transfer prices, some multinationals keep two sets of records, one to evaluate performance and one for tax. However, approximately three-fourths of surveyed multinationals maintain just one set despite the differing management

---

[9]Reg. §1.482-1(b)(1).
[10]Reg. §1.482-1(e). When data are sufficiently complete so that the taxpayer (or IRS) likely has identified all material differences between controlled and uncontrolled transactions and made appropriate adjustments, the arm's-length range includes the results of all uncontrolled comparables. However, when the taxpayer (or IRS) cannot identify all material differences or make appropriate adjustments, they must treat the interquartile range of controlled comparables as the arm's-length range. If the taxpayer's transfer price falls outside the arm's-length range, the IRS ordinarily will adopt the range's median as the arm's-length price.
[11]Reg. §1.482-1(h)(2).
[12]*E.I. Du Pont de Nemours & Company v. U.S.*, 608 F.2d 445 (Ct. Cl., 1979).
[13]Reg. §1.482-1(c)(2).
[14]Reg. §1.482-1(c)(2)(i), (d).
[15]Reg. §1.482-1(c)(2)(ii).
[16]Reg. §1.482-1(c)(1). See Reg. §1.482-8 for examples of choosing the best method.

and tax objectives.[17] Keeping only one set reduces complexity, and companies taking this approach use additional metrics to assist with performance evaluation.

After transfer pricing audits, the IRS allocates gross income to taxpayers not following arm's-length standards. In addition to these **primary allocations**, the IRS must permit **collateral adjustments**. Collateral adjustments include correlative allocations, conforming allocations, and setoffs.[18] To some extent, these adjustments reduce double tax problems otherwise arising from primary allocations.

> **COMPLIANCE POINTER:** In a recent survey, U.S. multinational companies reported that 30 percent of IRS examinations involving transfer pricing issues resulted in tax adjustments. Of those adjustments, double tax resulted 22 percent of the time.[19]

**Correlative allocations** affect the records of controlled persons engaging in the transfer with the taxpayer receiving the primary allocation. The nature of correlative allocations differs depending on the situation. While the primary allocation usually increases the taxpayer's gross income, correlative allocations allow deductions, increase basis, or decrease earnings and profits (E&P) of the other controlled person involved in the adjusted transaction. Thus, correlative allocations do not always reduce taxable income in the same year the primary allocation increases taxable income.[20]

---

### EXAMPLE

Daring Designs, Inc., a U.S. corporation, allows Fab Fabrics, Ltd., a CFC not engaged in a U.S. trade or business, to use foreign office space rent free. Following an audit, the IRS increases Daring's gross income for the arm's-length rental value (primary allocation) and allows Fab to decrease its E&P (correlative allocation). Even if the E&P reduction does not currently reduce U.S. tax, it may affect Daring's constructive

---

[17]Ernst & Young, *Transfer Pricing 2001 Global Survey: Making Informed Decisions in Uncertain Times* (November 2001), p. 6.
[18]Reg. §1.482-2(g)(1).
[19]Ernst & Young, *Transfer Pricing 2001 Global Survey: Making Informed Decisions in Uncertain Times* (November 2001), pp. 22–24.
[20]Reg. §1.482-2(g)(2).

dividend or deemed paid credit in the future. If the rent-free transaction had related to Fab's conduct of a U.S. trade or business, the correlative allocation might have taken the form of a deduction, reducing Fab's effectively connected income.

**PLANNING POINTER:** Seeking deductions under foreign law for primary allocations to U.S. taxpayers can relieve double tax problems. Requesting competent authority assistance through U.S. treaties increases the likelihood of consistent treatment between the United States and foreign jurisdictions.[21] In fact, failing to invoke competent authority procedures can endanger the U.S. foreign tax credit that a foreign tax deduction would have reduced.[22]

**Conforming adjustments** make a controlled person's books and records consistent with primary allocations. Conformity sometimes requires controlled persons to treat primary allocations as dividends or contributions to capital. At other times, conformity necessitates that controlled persons recognize receivables so later receipts do not trigger tax consequences.[23]

## EXAMPLE

Fresh Veggies SA, a foreign corporation, sells inventory to Dynamic Diet, Inc., its wholly owned U.S. subsidiary. On audit, the IRS determines that the transfer price exceeded the arm's-length price by $375,000, understating Dynamic's true taxable income. The primary allocation attributes $375,000 additional income to Dynamic. To conform its accounts, Dynamic requests IRS permission to establish a $375,000 account receivable from Fresh Veggies and accrue interest from the transaction date. Without this conforming adjustment, the IRS might treat Fresh Veggies' later reimbursement for the overcharge as a taxable dividend.

---

[21]See Rev. Proc. 96-13, 1996-1 CB 616. Some U.S. treaties allow transfer pricing adjustments to foreign returns even after the foreign statute of limitation expires.

[22]Rev. Rul. 92-75, 1992-2 CB 197. Foreign tax deductions reduce foreign income taxes. In excess limit situations, reducing foreign income taxes lowers the U.S. foreign tax credit.

[23]Reg. §1.482-2(g)(3).

Setoffs affect controlled persons receiving primary allocations and in-volve netting the effects of two or more nonarm's-length transactions. Thus, if one nonarm's-length transaction understates true taxable income while another overstates it, the IRS must permit the latter transfer to offset the for-mer. To qualify for setoffs, taxpayers notify the IRS within 30 days after re-ceiving either an examination report or notice of deficiency, whichever they receive earlier, about transfer pricing adjustments. The notification provides details about the requested setoff and all correlative allocations resulting from the setoff.[24]

---

### EXAMPLE

Delish Bakery, Inc., a U.S. corporation, makes an interest-free loan to Fiber Buyers, a Slovenian foreign affiliate. The IRS audits Delish's U.S. return and adjusts gross income upward $80,000 based on an arm's-length interest rate. After receiving the auditor's examination report, Delish notifies the IRS that it bought long-grain rice from Fiber during the same year, paying $110,000 when an arm's-length price equaled $125,000. Assuming Delish provides all required documentation, the IRS should allow a $15,000 setoff against the $80,000 primary alloca-tion, a net adjustment of $65,000 to Delish's taxable income.

---

## LOAN OF FUNDS

Interest is a charge for the use of money in transactions involving loans, ad-vances, or indebtedness arising in the ordinary course of business (e.g., in-terest on an installment sale). When loans occur between controlled persons, taxpayers must determine the arm's-length interest rate based on independ-ent transactions between uncontrolled persons in similar situations. To iden-tify similar situations, relevant factors include the principal amount, indebtedness period, security involved, debtor's creditworthiness, and pre-vailing interest rates.[25]

For creditors not in the business of making loans, safe harbor rules es-tablish ranges of acceptable interest charges for dollar-denominated indebt-edness between controlled entities.[26] Exhibit 16.1 provides the ranges of

---

[24]Reg. §1.482-2(g)(4).
[25]Reg. §1.482-2(a)(2)(i).
[26]Reg. §1.482-2(a)(2)(iii)(D), (E).

**EXHIBIT 16.1** Safe Harbor Interest Rate Limits[a]

| Indebtedness | Lower Limit | Upper Limit |
|---|---|---|
| Term loan ≤ 3 years | 100% of federal short-term rate | 130% of federal short-term rate |
| Term loan > 3 but ≤ 9 years | 100% of federal midterm rate | 130% of federal midterm rate |
| Term loan > 9 years | 100% of federal long-term rate | 130% of federal long-term rate |
| Demand loan | 100% of average market yield on federal short-term securities over period demand loan has been outstanding | 130% of average market yield on federal short-term securities over period demand loan has been outstanding |
| Sale- or exchange-related debt | Lowest applicable federal rate (short-, mid-, or long-term) for three calendar months before binding written contract | 130% of applicable federal rate (short-, mid-, or long-term) |

[a]These limits do not apply if the debt instrument denominates either the principal or interest in a foreign currency or the controlled creditor regularly engages in the business of lending or advancing money to uncontrolled persons.

arm's-length interest rates for various indebtedness forms and periods. When controlled entities charge interest above the upper (below the lower) limit, the arm's-length rate equals the upper (lower) limit. If the interest rate actually charged falls above the upper limit but below the established arm's-length rate or below the lower limit but above the established arm's-length rate, the IRS accepts the controlled entities' interest rate.[27]

A special rule applies for certain back-to-back loans. When a controlled creditor loans or advances funds to a controlled borrower and the creditor obtains the funds at the borrower's situs, the arm's-length rate equals the creditor's borrowing rate increased to cover expenses the creditor incurs in obtaining and reloaning the funds.[28] Though this rule mitigates abusive income shifting, it omits profit from the arm's-length rate, treating the controlled creditor as a mere middleman.

---

[27]Reg. §1.482-2(a)(2)(iii)(B), (C).
[28]Reg. §1.482-2(a)(2)(ii).

---

**EXAMPLE**

---

Cachalot Whale Company, Inc., a domestic corporation, sells deep-water fishing gear and supplies. To obtain capital for Reelemin Quik SA, its Chilean affiliate, Cachalot borrows capital from a Chilean bank at 9.2 percent and immediately reloans the funds to Reelemin. The arm's-length interest rate equals 9.4 percent, where the extra two-tenths of a percentage point reflect the expenses Cachalot incurred obtaining and reloaning the funds.

---

## PERFORMANCE OF SERVICES

The IRS can reallocate items when controlled group members perform services for other members but do not charge arm's-length prices. The arm's-length price equals the amount an uncontrolled performer would have charged in an independent transaction under similar circumstances.[29] However, when parent companies provide general supervisory services to their subsidiaries, the expense often benefits only the parent company and, in those cases, does not require intercompany charges.[30] Similarly, U.S. law does not require service charges when the recipient's expected benefit is so indirect or remote that an uncontrolled person would not have charged for similar services. Also, services between controlled persons duplicating services the recipient already has performed do not require charges.[31]

---

**EXAMPLE**

---

Ace Accountants, a U.S. company, owns all interests in Finesse Financial, a Hong Kong enterprise. After year-end, Finesse's qualified tax staff prepares the company's tax return and submits it to Ace for review before filing with Hong Kong's Inland Revenue Department. Since Ace's review duplicates Finesse's tax preparation services, the IRS cannot require a service charge.

---

[29]Reg. §1.482-2(b)(3).
[30]*Young & Rubicam v. U.S.*, 410 F.2d 1233 (Ct. Cl., 1969). However, specific managerial services that benefit the recipient do require an arm's-length charge.
[31]Reg. §1.482-2(b)(2).

When services are not an integral part of either controlled entity's business activities, the safe harbor price equals the direct and indirect costs of performance and, thus, excludes profit. Nonetheless, the IRS accepts other transfer prices when the taxpayer establishes them as more appropriate.[32] U.S. law requires an arm's-length charge (including a profit element) for managerial, administrative, marketing, technical, or other services constituting an integral part of the business activity of either the performer or the recipient.[33]

## KEY CASE

U.S. Steel is a vertically integrated steel producer owning iron ore mines in the United States and abroad. To exploit its mines in Venezuela, the company establishes a wholly owned U.S. subsidiary, Orinoco. To transport the Venezuelan ore to the United States, U.S. Steel organizes Navios, a wholly owned Liberian subsidiary chartering vessels from unrelated shippers. The foreign flag of the chartered fleet results in cost savings, presumably from lower registration and labor expenses. Navios sets transportation charges so its sum with the cost of Orinoco ore equals the price of U.S. mined iron ore. This pricing policy protects U.S. Steel's domestic mining operations; that is, it does not undercut U.S. ore prices with foreign ore prices. In addition to the taxpayer, unrelated persons buy ore from Orinoco and use Navios' transport services. Both subsidiaries charge unrelated persons the same prices they charge U.S. Steel. The taxpayer argues that the price it charges unrelated persons for transportation services controls, while the government adopts a profit split approach regarding Navios' pricing policies. In reversing the Tax Court, the Second Circuit agrees with the taxpayer. Independent parties purchase Orinoco ore and hire Navios for transportation services frequently and in sufficient volume to establish an arm's-length price. The court finds no evidence the taxpayer or its policies require independent purchasers of Orinoco ore to hire Navios. In fact, some purchasers use another transportation company to transport Orinoco ore. The independent purchasers have sufficient financial sophistication to secure a substantially lower rate than the one Navios offers if one is available.[34]

---

[32]Reg. §1.482-2(b)(3).
[33]Reg. §1.482-2(b)(7).
[34]*United States Steel Corporation v. Comm.*, 617 F.2d 942 (CA-2, 1980). This decision dealt with years preceding the CFC rules. If the same situation arose today, U.S. Steel would pay tax on Navios' foreign base company shipping income under Subpart F, regardless of transfer pricing indiscretions (if any).

## RENTAL OF TANGIBLE PROPERTY

Rent is a charge for possessing, using, or occupying tangible personal or real property. In leases between controlled persons, an arm's-length price equals the rent that would have applied to the same or similar property in an independent lease involving uncontrolled persons under similar circumstances. Factors affecting the arm's-length price include the duration of the rental agreement, anticipated maintenance expenses, location of the property or its use, and the property's condition.[35] When the lessor or lessee engages in a leasing business, comparable rentals may exist that establish the arm's-length charge.

A special rule applies when a controlled person (lessee) rents tangible property from an uncontrolled person and then transfers it to a controlled user through a sublease or other arrangement. In these cases, U.S. law treats the sum of all deductions the lessee claims attributable to the property as the arm's-length charge. Thus, the arm's-length charge includes the lessee's rent payment to the uncontrolled person and any other direct or indirect expenses the lessee deducts in relationship to the transferred property (e.g., maintenance, repair, utility, and management expenses).[36]

In effect, this special sublease rule treats the lessee as a middleman receiving no profit allocation on the sublease or other arrangement. Nonetheless, this special sublease rule does not apply if the taxpayer establishes a more appropriate rental charge. Also, if the lessee or controlled user regularly engages in the business of leasing similar property to uncontrolled persons, this rule does not apply.[37]

---

### EXAMPLE

Perimeter Properties, Inc., a U.S. corporation, rents warehouse space in Panama's Colón Free Zone for one year starting January 1, 2004. The unrelated lessor charges $180,000, and Perimeter also pays $15,000 in indirect expenses related to the warehouse facilities. Perimeter later deducts these amounts on its U.S. return. Beginning January 1, 2004, Perimeter allows its wholly owned Panamanian subsidiary to use the warehouse rent-free for storage and packaging. This arrangement lasts the entire year and, if left unchallenged, effectively shifts taxable income

---

[35]Reg. §1.482-2(c)(2)(i).
[36]Reg. §1.482-2(c)(2)(iii)(A).
[37]Reg. §1.482-2(c)(2)(iii)(B).

from the United States to Panama. However, the IRS audits the return and treats $195,000 as the arm's-length charge between Perimeter and its subsidiary.

## SALE OR LICENSE OF INTANGIBLE PROPERTY

**Intangible properties** consist of rights and other assets with value but no physical substance. Manufacturing intangibles include patents and secret formulae; marketing intangibles include trademarks and franchises; and artistic intangibles include copyrights. Absent some restrictions, U.S. persons can deduct their research and development expenditures against U.S. source income, transfer resulting intangible assets to offshore affiliates in tax-free transactions, and indefinitely defer the U.S. residual tax on profits derived from the intangible properties.[38]

Thus, the IRS pays particularly close attention to transfers of intangible properties between controlled persons. When controlled persons transfer intangible properties (or partial interests in such properties) between themselves for nonarm's-length prices, the IRS can reallocate income or other items. Owners transfer intangible properties (or partial interests) through sale, assignment, loan, or license.[39]

Controlled persons determine arm's-length prices for intangible property transfers using one of the following methods:

- Comparable uncontrolled transaction,
- Comparable profits,
- Profit split, and
- Unspecified (i.e., any other method).

U.S. taxpayers adopt the method coming closest to an arm's-length price (i.e., the most reliable or best method).[40] Thus, if an unspecified method (one regulations do not specifically describe) provides a result approximating an arm's-length price better than any of the other three, taxpayers use that method.

---

[38]The restrictions cited in Chapter 17 may affect the tax-free nature of outbound transfers. Also, Chapter 12 explained how the Subpart F rules sometimes prevent deferral.
[39]Reg. §1.482-2A(d)(1)(i).
[40]Reg. §1.482-4(a).

The reference point for the **comparable uncontrolled transaction (CUT)** method is the arm's-length price in a comparable transaction between uncontrolled persons. This method's reliability is highest when relying on uncontrolled transactions with the same intangible property transferring under substantially the same circumstances. Reliability declines when based on comparable intangibles transferring under comparable circumstances, but the method still might be the best one. To be comparable intangibles, properties in both controlled and uncontrolled transactions must affect similar products or processes in the same industry or market and possess similar profit potential. To be comparable circumstances, intangibles in both controlled and uncontrolled transactions must involve similar contract terms and occur under similar economic conditions. For instance, contractual differences in exploitation rights, exclusivity guarantees, rights to property updates and revisions, contract duration, and product liability risks reduce comparability.[41]

---

### EXAMPLE

AirNet, Inc., a U.S. corporation, develops an Internet-access device the size of a credit card and secures patent protection in Korea, Japan, and the United States. The company licenses manufacturing and marketing rights within Korea to a wholly owned subsidiary, SeoulNet. Also, Air-Net licenses production and marketing rights within Japan to an unrelated Japanese company. The estimated production costs, market demand, and profit potential in Korea and Japan are about the same. If the licensing terms with the unrelated Japanese company are similar to those with SeoulNet, the CUT method requires that the royalty rates in the two licensing agreements be approximately the same.

---

### EXAMPLE

Assume the same facts as the prior example except that AirNet licenses exclusive rights to its Internet-access device to SeoulNet; no license agreement occurs with unrelated persons. Thus, uncontrolled transactions do not exist involving the same intangible property. On audit, the IRS identifies potentially comparable licensing agreements for the same

---

[41]Reg. §1.482-4(c).

years and similar products on Securities and Exchange Commission (SEC) filings. After eliminating those agreements with dissimilar contract terms and those concluded under dissimilar economic conditions, 13 licensing agreements remain with royalty rates ranging from 12.5 to 7 percent. Since some of these agreements may contain undisclosed material differences, the IRS identifies the interquartile range of these 13 agreements (12 to 8.5 percent) as the arm's-length range. If the contractual royalty rate falls outside this range, the IRS selects the median (11 percent) as the arm's-length royalty rate.

The **comparable profits method (CPM)** determines a controlled person's transfer price based on profitability comparisons with uncontrolled persons engaging in similar business activities under similar circumstances.[42] CPM presumes that similar persons will earn similar profits over time. Applicable to either tangible or intangible property transfers, the IRS considers this a method of last resort.[43]

CPM involves several steps. First, it identifies the controlled person with the more verifiable profit data (i.e., requiring fewer and more reliable adjustments). This "tested party" usually is the controlled person with the less-complex business activities and, preferably, without valuable intangibles or other unique assets requiring adjustments.[44] Of course, determining the tested party's profit from controlled transactions also determines the other controlled person's profit from the same transactions. Second, CPM selects the most appropriate **profit-level indicator** such as rate of return on capital (i.e., operating income to operating assets), operating profit to sales, or gross profit to operating expenses.[45] Third, it determines the profit-level indicator for comparable uncontrolled companies over a reasonable time (e.g., three years) and applies this external indicator to the tested party's financial data to obtain comparable profit measures.[46] Since CPM relies on external market benchmarks, this method increases in reliability the more similar the controlled and uncontrolled persons.[47]

---

[42]Reg. §1.482-5(a). The biggest difference between CUT and CPM is the latter's focus on comparable uncontrolled persons rather than comparable uncontrolled transactions.

[43]TD 8552, 1994-2 CB 93, 109.

[44]Reg. §1.482-5(b)(2). For instance, the activities of wholesale distributors usually are less complex than those of related manufacturers.

[45]Reg. §1.482-5(b)(4).

[46]Reg. §1.482-5(b)(1).

[47]Reg. §1.482-5(c)(2).

## EXAMPLE

Custom Tools, a U.S. corporation, develops, manufactures, and distributes machinist tools. Custom develops a new tool, the Pry Master, and transfers the manufacturing know-how to HK Tools, its wholly owned Hong Kong subsidiary, in return for a royalty equal to 4 percent of the Pry Master's sales. HK Tools manufactures the new tool and sells it to unrelated distributors. After determining that CPM is the best method, the IRS examines whether the 2003 royalty represents arm's-length compensation for the know-how. The IRS chooses HK Tools as the tested party and selects return on capital as the most appropriate profit level indicator. HK Tools' financial disclosures for 2003 and the two preceding years provide the following information:

|                  | 2001 | 2002 | 2003 | Average |
|------------------|---------|---------|---------|---------|
| Operating assets | $100,000 | $150,000 | $170,000 | $140,000 |
| Operating profit | 22,000 | 35,000 | 45,000 | 35,000 |
| Royalties at 4%  | 8,000 | 10,000 | 12,000 | 10,000 |

Financial data exist for five unrelated Hong Kong tool manufacturers in similar circumstances, and the data are sufficiently complete to identify and adjust for all material differences between HK Tools and the uncontrolled comparable companies. The uncontrolled comparables' return on capital for the combined 2001 through 2003 years and the ratio's application to HK Tools' average operating assets for the same period yield the following results:

| Uncontrolled Comparables | Return on Capital | Operating Assets of HK Tools | Comparable Operating Profits |
|--------------------------|-------------------|------------------------------|------------------------------|
| A | 12.0% | $140,000 | $16,800 |
| B | 13.2% | 140,000 | 18,480 |
| C | 13.5% | 140,000 | 18,900 |
| D | 14.1% | 140,000 | 19,740 |
| E | 17.0% | 140,000 | 23,800 |

Thus, comparable operating profits range from $16,800 to $23,800. Since HK Tools' $35,000 average operating profit lies above the arm's-length range, an audit adjustment might be appropriate.[48] Based on its

---

[48]When the IRS (or taxpayer) cannot identify and make appropriate adjustments for all material differences, the arm's-length range of comparable operating profits consists of the interquartile range. For instance, the IRS (or taxpayer) must use the

analysis, the IRS decides to increase the 2003 royalty by $26,100 (the difference between HK Tools' $45,000 operating profit in 2003 and the $18,900 median comparable operating profit). Thus, the adjusted 2003 royalty equals $38,100 ($12,000 preadjustment royalty + $26,100 audit adjustment).

Under the **profit split method,** taxpayers allocate controlled persons' combined operating profit or loss from controlled transactions per the relative contribution of each controlled person to the profit or loss.[49] The relative value of each person's contribution depends on functions performed (e.g., manufacturing or distribution), risks taken, and resources used in the relevant business activity. Applicable to either tangible or intangible property transfers, this method does not support arbitrary percentage allocations including equal sharing of combined profit or loss. For instance, the IRS (or taxpayer) cannot simply split income 50-50 between controlled persons without sound economic basis. The profit or loss allocation reflects the results from uncontrolled persons performing similar functions, taking like risks, and using similar resources.[50]

Profit split allocations follow either of two methods: comparable profit split or residual profit split.[51] Under the **comparable profit split,** the IRS (or taxpayer) identifies uncontrolled persons with similar transactions and activities to controlled persons. Since contracts specify who performs which functions and assumes which risks, a principal consideration is the extent of similarity between the uncontrolled persons' legal agreements and the contractual terms between controlled persons. Also, comparability requires that uncontrolled persons' combined operating profits as a percentage of combined operating assets do not differ significantly from the same ratio for controlled taxpayers. Next, the IRS (or taxpayer) determines each uncontrolled person's percentage share of combined operating profit or loss from similar activities and uses the percentages to divide the controlled person's combined operating profit or loss. The reliability of the resulting allocation depends on data quality and assumptions. For instance, one must adjust for differences in accounting practices materially affecting the profit or loss

---

interquartile range when differences in geographic markets exist. So, if the financial data had related to controlled comparable companies in Singapore rather than Hong Kong, the IRS (or taxpayer) may have narrowed the range of comparable operating profits to its interquartile numbers.

[49] Reg. §1.482-6(a).
[50] Reg. §1.482-6(b).
[51] Reg. §1.482-6(c)(1).

allocation. Like some other methods, the comparable profit split relies entirely on external market benchmarks (i.e., profit measures from uncontrolled persons) for the allocation.[52]

---

### EXAMPLE

Home Zone, a U.S. corporation, manufactures and markets home products in the United States. It also licenses the right to manufacture and sell its products in Latin America to its subsidiary, Abode Décor SA. The controlled group does not own unique assets or intangibles causing their profits to differ significantly from those of similar activities between uncontrolled persons. On audit, the IRS decides on the comparable profit split as the best method and obtains a sample of uncontrolled persons in the same industry. The comparable companies perform manufacturing-distribution activities under similar circumstances (e.g., the licensed rights are similar), and the ratio of combined operating profit to combined operating assets for each pair does not differ significantly from that of Home Zone and Abode Décor. Based on the sample data, the IRS concludes that the U.S. licensor normally earns 40 percent of combined operating profits in the relevant business activity and reallocates income between Home Zone and Abode Décor accordingly.

---

The second profit split method is the **residual profit split**. This approach involves two steps. Step 1 allocates combined operating income between controlled persons for the routine contributions each makes. **Routine contributions** include those attributable to tangible properties, intangibles uncontrolled persons engaged in similar activities often own, and services. When the controlled transferor incurs no direct expense related to the sales or licensing agreement or any other expense related to the transferee's marketing efforts, the transferor's routine contributions might be zero. Like the comparable profit split approach, the first step allocation results in a market return based on profit measures of comparable companies (i.e., external market benchmarks).[53]

After step 1, unallocated operating profit often remains, and this method attributes such residual profit to valuable, unique intangibles. Step 2 divides the residual profit between controlled persons based on the relative contributions unique intangibles make toward the relevant business activ-

---

[52]Reg. §1.482-6(c)(2).
[53]Reg. §1.482-6(c)(3)(A).

ity's operating profit. If only one of the controlled persons owns unique intangibles, the method allocates the entire residual profit to that person. When both controlled persons own unique intangibles, the regulations suggest three approaches for determining their relative contributions: using external market benchmarks establishing the unique intangibles' fair market values (preferred when available), capitalizing intangible property development costs for each person and subtracting appropriate amortization, and relying on intangible property development expenditures of each person from recent years.[54]

---

## EXAMPLE

Assume the prior example's facts except the sample of comparable companies yield an average market return of 15 percent (i.e., operating profit over operating assets) for routine contributions in Latin America, Abode Décor's operating assets total $500,000, and combined operating profits of the controlled persons equal $200,000. Also, assume Home Zone and Abode Décor each own a valuable, unique intangible. No external market data establish the fair market value of either intangible. So, to estimate respective fair market values, the IRS capitalizes the costs incurred for each intangible and, based on age, subtracts a reasonable amount for amortization. The unique intangibles' resulting values equal $78,000 and $22,000 for Home Zone and Abode Décor, respectively. Step 1 allocates $75,000 of the combined operating profits to Abode Décor ($500,000 operating assets × 15% market return), and step 2 allocates $27,500 of residual profits to Abode Décor [($200,000 – $75,000) × 22%]. If the annual royalty differs from $102,500 ($75,000 routine contribution + $27,500 unique intangible contribution), the IRS can reallocate income between Home Zone and Abode Décor.

---

Regardless of the transfer pricing method, the Code requires that profit allocations from intangible property sales or licenses to controlled persons be **commensurate with income** transferees eventually derive from the property.[55] This antiabuse rule arose from concerns that controlled persons sometimes transfer intangibles with low current values but very high-profit potentials to offshore affiliates in low-tax jurisdictions. For those intangibles

---

[54]Reg. §1.482-6(c)(3)(B).
[55]Last sentence of IRC §482.

later proving very valuable and resulting in higher-than-expected profits, taxpayers pleaded their inability to predict the intangible asset's later success and value when signing the licensing agreement. Thus, according to this argument, the original agreement should stand since it satisfied arm's-length principles when signed.

To combat this perceived abuse, U.S. law now stipulates that any initial gain or future royalties might require adjustment based on the intangible property's later profitability. In effect, the IRS can retroactively change gain or royalties applicable to sales or licensing agreements between controlled persons. U.S. firms licensing intangibles to foreign affiliates later proving very successful must increase their royalty income commensurately, resulting in **super royalties**.[56]

---

**EXAMPLE**

---

Elixir, Inc. is a U.S. pharmaceutical company owning a Hong Kong subsidiary, Panacea, Ltd. In 2002, Elixir licenses the secret formula for a new antibiotic, RevilDoc, to Panacea for 10 years at an annual fee of $200,000, which represented a fair price at the time. Early in 2004, an Elixir scientist discovers that RevilDoc cures some cancers, increasing the license's annual value to $5 million. U.S. law requires that Elixir recognize $5 million income from the licensing arrangement in 2004. In other words, Elixir must recognize income from its secret formula each year commensurate with its profitability.

---

**PLANNING POINTER:** When U.S. taxpayers receive super royalties under the commensurate with income standard, jurisdictions where the controlled licensees reside may be less than enthusiastic about allowing correlative deductions for the increased royalties. In these cases, some double tax may result. When treaties exist, U.S. taxpayers should appeal to competent authorities early in the process to secure the foreign deduction or, failing that, to treat the entire foreign income tax as a creditable tax for U.S. purposes.

Taxpayers entering qualified cost-sharing arrangements avoid many of the pricing issues involving intangible assets. **Cost-sharing arrangements** require participants to share the costs of developing intangible assets in proportion to the reasonably anticipated benefits each participant expects to

---

[56]Reg. §1.482-4(f)(2)(ii) describes five situations in which taxpayers need not make periodic adjustments.

derive from their use.[57] For instance, a foreign affiliate expecting to derive 20 percent of the total benefits from a patentable drug should bear 20 percent of the research and development expenses related to the drug's development. To be qualified, participants must document their arrangements contemporaneously, and agreements must specify the method for calculating each participant's share of development costs and modifying such calculations due to changes in economic conditions, business activities, and ongoing development. The agreement also must describe the research undertaken and specify the agreement's duration.[58]

## SALE OF TANGIBLE PROPERTY

When individuals or entities sell tangible assets to controlled persons, the IRS can reallocate income or other items if the controlled seller does not charge an arm's-length price. To protect U.S. revenue, the IRS pays particularly close attention to transfer prices set too low on outbound transfers and prices set too high on inbound transfers. In fact, the transfer price on inbound items cannot exceed the value U.S. Customs assigns.[59] For tangible property sales, taxpayers choose the best method from the following list:

- Comparable uncontrolled price,
- Resale price,
- Cost-plus,
- Comparable profits,
- Profit split, and
- Unspecified (i.e., any other method, such as return on investment).

The prior section explained the comparable profits and profit split methods. Thus, this section deals only with the first three methods.

The **comparable uncontrolled price (CUP)** method uses prices in comparable uncontrolled transactions as the basis for arm's-length pricing. Comparability between controlled and uncontrolled transactions depends on the similarity of products, contractual terms, transportation costs, business activities (e.g., wholesaling), geographic markets, sale dates, intangibles transferred, foreign currency risks, and other economic conditions. The CUP method is very reliable when these factors are substantially the same or taxpayers can reasonably adjust for minor differences. When taxpayers cannot make reasonable adjustments, they still can use the CUP method, but its reliability declines.[60]

---

[57]Reg. §1.482-7(a)(1).
[58]Reg. §1.482-7(b).
[59]IRC §1059A(a).
[60]Reg. §1.482-3(b)(2).

### EXAMPLE

Honshu Swish Swash, a Japanese corporation that manufactures electrical appliances, sells laundry washers to its wholly owned U.S. distributor, USA Swish Swash, which resells the appliances to retail outlets in the southeastern United States. Honshu also sells laundry washers to Appliance Suppliers, Inc., an unrelated distributor in California, for $750 each.

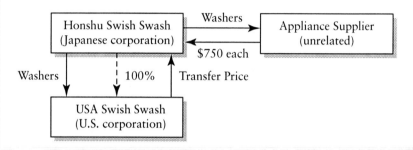

If the washers Honshu sells to USA and Appliance Suppliers are identical, and the transactions and economic conditions do not differ, the CUP method yields a very reliable arm's-length price of $750 for Honshu sales to USA. However, differences may require adjustments. For instance, if the price to USA is FOB (free on board) destination while the price to Appliance Suppliers is FOB factory, USA can adjust for the difference in transportation and insurance charges and its effect on price, resulting in an arm's-length price higher than $750. Similarly, USA probably can reasonably adjust for price differences, if any, attributable to the differing geographical markets (i.e., California versus the Southeast). However, if Honshu places its valuable trademark on washers it sells to USA but not on washers it sells to Appliance Suppliers, the trademark's effect on price, if material, may be difficult to establish. In that case, the controlled group probably cannot make appropriate adjustments, making the CUP method unreliable.

Public exchange prices and industry quotations provide CUPs when the data meet three conditions. First, businesses must widely and routinely use the data to negotiate prices in uncontrolled sales. Second, the taxpayer must use the data in the same way to set prices for the controlled sales at issue. Third, the taxpayer must appropriately adjust for differences between controlled and uncontrolled sales. Fungible commodities, such as natural resources and farm products, often satisfy these conditions. Nonetheless, public exchange prices and industry quotations may not reflect CUPs under extraordinary conditions that disrupt the market's equilibrium (e.g., during wartime conditions).[61]

The **resale price method** usually applies to tangible property sales between controlled persons in which purchaser-resellers function as mere middlemen or distributors. Ordinarily, taxpayers cannot use this method if the purchaser-reseller physically alters the product. Distributors can package, repackage, or label the product or engage in minor assembly since these activities do not involve physical alteration. However, if the purchaser-reseller uses intangibles to increase the tangible product's value substantially, the resale price method usually is inappropriate.[62]

When the controlled purchaser resells the property to an uncontrolled person, an appropriate gross profit reduces the applicable resale price, backing into the arm's-length price between the controlled persons. The appropriate gross profit equals the applicable resale price times a gross profit margin the taxpayer (or IRS) derives from comparable uncontrolled transactions, preferably involving the controlled reseller.[63] Exhibit 16.2 illustrates the general approach.

Comparability under the resale price method depends particularly on similarities in business functions, risks assumed, and contractual terms. Product similarity is less important under the resale price method than under the CUP method; nonetheless, the IRS expects comparable uncontrolled transactions to involve products in the same general category (e.g., consumer electronics). Taxpayers should not overlook other factors. For instance, differences in cost structures (e.g., as evidenced in the age of plant and equipment), business experience (e.g., new versus mature companies), and management efficiency (e.g., as evidenced in executive compensation

**EXHIBIT 16.2**   Resale Price Method

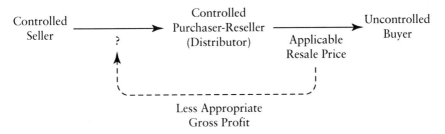

---

[61]Reg. §1.482-3(b)(5).
[62]Reg. §1.482-3(c)(1).
[63]Reg. §1.482-3(c)(2).

packages or sales) may suggest that controlled and noncontrolled transactions materially differ. Also, inventory methods and cost accounting practices often vary. Taxpayers must reasonably adjust for material differences so uncontrolled transactions remain comparable and yield the requisite gross profit margins.[64]

---

### EXAMPLE

Kimchon Raingear, a South Korean corporation manufacturing protective clothing, sells 2,000 pairs of galoshes to Stormy Weather, Inc., its wholly owned U.S. subsidiary. Stormy Weather, without altering the galoshes or enhancing their value, resells them to High Fashion, Inc., an unrelated U.S. clothing boutique, for $40,000.

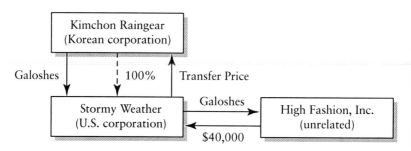

On audit, the IRS questions Kimchon's transfer price of $38,000. Relying on the resale price method to provide the best measure of true taxable income, the IRS determines that comparable uncontrolled transactions yield a 20 percent gross profit margin and that no material differences exist between the controlled and uncontrolled sales requiring adjustments. Thus, an appropriate gross profit for the controlled transaction is $8,000 ($40,000 applicable resale price × 20%), and the arm's-length price equals $32,000 ($40,000 − $8,000).

---

Survey data indicate that taxpayers use the cost-plus method most often.[65] The **cost-plus method** ordinarily applies to manufacturing, assembly, or other production operations selling their output to controlled entities that may further process or substantially transform the goods before reselling them to uncontrolled persons. Under this method, the arm's-length

---

[64]Reg. §1.482-3(c)(3).
[65]Ernst & Young, *Transfer Pricing 2001 Global Survey: Making Informed Decisions in Uncertain Times* (November 2001), p. 19.

price equals the production cost plus an appropriate gross profit. The gross profit equals the controlled seller's production cost times a gross profit markup percentage derived from comparable uncontrolled transactions, preferably of the controlled person.[66] Exhibit 16.3 summarizes the general approach under the cost-plus method.

Like the resale price method, similarities of business functions, risks assumed, and contractual terms are particularly important in establishing comparability. Close physical likeness of the product is unnecessary, but substantial differences may suggest dissimilarities between controlled and uncontrolled persons' business functions. Thus, goods involved in the controlled and uncontrolled transactions ordinarily fall in the same product categories. Other factors the taxpayer (or IRS) considers when evaluating comparability include intangibles, cost structures, business experience, management efficiency, and accounting practices. Material differences affecting the gross profit markup require adjustments.[67]

---

**EXAMPLE**

Storage and Structure Solutions (SSS) is a U.S. manufacturer of partitions, shelving, and similar store fixtures. On a sale of metal display cases to its Canadian subsidiary, SSS uses the cost-plus method to establish the transfer price. The production cost of the display cases total $72,000. Based on comparable uncontrolled transactions between SSS and unrelated Canadian customers, 30 percent represents a reasonable gross profit markup. No material differences exist between the uncontrolled transactions and SSS's sale to its subsidiary. Thus, the appropriate gross profit equals $21,600 ($72,000 production cost × 30%), and the transfer price equals $93,600 ($72,000 + $21,600).

---

**EXHIBIT 16.3**  Cost-Plus Method

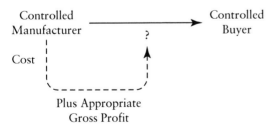

Controlled Manufacturer → Controlled Buyer

Cost

Plus Appropriate Gross Profit

---

[66]Reg. §1.482-3(d)(1), (2).
[67]Reg. §1.482-3(d)(3).

## VALUATION MISSTATEMENTS

When taxpayers substantially misstate transfer prices, the IRS imposes a stiff accuracy-related penalty equal to 20 percent of the tax underpayment.[68] **Substantial valuation misstatements** occur if the:

- Transfer price for a transaction lies outside the range of 50 to 200 percent of the IRS-determined arm's-length price or
- Aggregate net increase in taxable income from transfer price adjustments for the year exceeds the smaller of $5 million or 10 percent of total gross receipts.[69]

Gross valuation misstatements result in an even more severe penalty equal to 40 percent of the tax underpayment.[70] **Gross valuation misstatements** arise when the:

- Transfer price for a transaction falls outside the range of 25 to 400 percent of the IRS-determined arm's-length price or
- Aggregate net increase in taxable income from transfer price adjustments for the year exceeds the smaller of $20 million or 20 percent of total gross receipts.[71]

A de minimis safe harbor shields taxpayers from the accuracy-related penalty when the taxable year's aggregate tax underpayments attributable to substantial valuation misstatements do not exceed $5,000 (or $10,000 for C corporations other than personal holding companies).[72] Also, taxpayers demonstrating reasonable cause and good faith can avoid these penalties.[73] For instance, reliance on a transfer pricing study a qualified professional conducts may constitute reasonable cause and good faith.[74]

For inbound transfers, the IRS watches for inflated prices reducing U.S. tax revenues. As noted, transfer prices 200 percent or more above the correct price result in accuracy-related penalties. For outbound transfers, the IRS's focus switches to understatements, and transfer prices at least 50 percent below the correct price lead to penalties. Thus, the penalty provisions are more forgiving for inbound transfers.

---

[68]IRC §6662(a).
[69]IRC §6662(e)(1)(B).
[70]IRC §6662(h)(1).
[71]IRC §6662(h)(2)(A).
[72]IRC §6662(e)(2).
[73]IRC §6664(c)(1).
[74]Reg. §1.6664-4(c).

## EXAMPLE

Digital Net, Inc., a U.S. corporation in the 35 percent tax bracket, owns all stock of Comp Concepts, a Latvian corporation, and Design Pros, Ltd., a Singaporean corporation. During 2004, the IRS determines that the corporate group did not charge arm's-length prices for two transactions. First, on computer sales to Comp Concepts, Digital Net charged $160,000 though the arm's-length price was $400,000. Second, Digital Net paid $750,000 for services it received from Design Pros when the arm's-length price was $400,000.

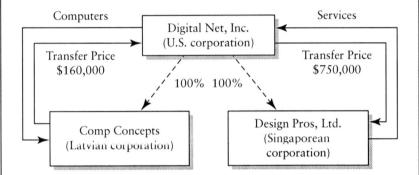

The IRS adjusts the $160,000 transfer price upward $240,000, resulting in $84,000 ($240,000 × 35%) additional tax and a $16,800 ($84,000 × 20%) accuracy-related penalty since the group's transfer price is $200,000 ($400,000 correct price x 50%) or below. It also adjusts the $750,000 transfer price down $350,000, producing additional tax of $122,500 ($350,000 × 35%); but no accuracy-related penalty is charged since the group's transfer price falls below $800,000 ($400,000 correct price × 200%). Even though the correct price is $400,000 in both transactions, the $240,000 understated transfer price results in an accuracy-related penalty, while the $350,000 overstated price does not.

**PLANNING POINTER:** To avoid penalties, minimize instances of double tax, and seize tax-saving opportunities, multinationals should include tax and finance directors early in strategic planning and decision making involving intercompany, cross-border payments.

## ADVANCE PRICING AGREEMENTS

Identifying the best method and arriving at true taxable income is an art fraught with substantial uncertainty. Taxpayers and the IRS often disagree about appropriate methodologies and their applications. In addition to the substantial tax dollars at stake, transfer pricing issues involve the possibility of double taxation, misstatement penalties, costly IRS audits, and prolonged settlement procedures.

Advance pricing agreements (APAs) represent one means of reducing risk and cost when establishing transfer pricing policies. As negotiated, binding agreements between taxpayers and the IRS, they establish acceptable transfer prices prospectively, reducing audit uncertainties and instances of settlement disputes.[75] APAs vary in their scope. They can cover all types of transfer payments or limit coverage, for instance, to payments for intangible property transfers. Similarly, they can cover all product lines or only selected ones, and they can extend to all affiliates or just chosen entities.[76] Unilateral APAs involve only the taxpayer and the IRS as contractual parties. When tax authorities from one or more foreign jurisdictions also participate, the resulting bilateral or multilateral APA reduces uncertainty and cost even further.[77]

> **PLANNING POINTER:**  Through a **rollback procedure,** taxpayers can request application of APAs to prior open tax years, even when APAs do not specifically cover such years.[78] If granted, this procedure can settle disputes otherwise lasting for several years.

To obtain an APA, taxpayers first request one or more prefiling conferences with the IRS. If desired, taxpayers remain anonymous during these preliminary discussions, sending their attorneys, accountants, or other representatives. However, taxpayers revealing their identities can assure that the IRS personnel attending include district office and competent authority analysts. Prefiling conferences provide opportunities to explore documentation and analysis issues, acceptable transfer pricing methodologies, the advisability of pursuing bilateral or multilateral APAs, the use of competent authority to address double tax issues, the necessity of hiring independent experts, and procedural issues in submitting and evaluating APA proposals.[79]

---

[75]Rev. Proc. 96-53, §1, 1996-2 CB 375.
[76]Id. at §10.03.
[77]Id. at §§3.02, 7.
[78]Id. at §§3.06, 8.01.
[79]Id. at §4.

After the prefiling phase, taxpayers submit formal APA applications to the IRS and user fees ranging from $5,000 to $25,000. For bilateral or multilateral proposals, the IRS forwards application packages to the appropriate foreign tax authorities. Applications describe the business activities and functions of the taxpayer and covered affiliates, provide an economic or industry analysis of the relevant markets and geographical areas, identify major competitors, propose transfer pricing methodologies, apply the methodologies to three years of financial and tax data, identify comparable transactions, list critical assumptions, and provide relevant documentation. Also, applications identify the years the APA will cover (usually three to five) and, if desired, request competent authority assistance.[80] After receiving an application and evaluating the proposal, the IRS asks follow-up questions, requests further documentation, and, perhaps, offers a counter or modified proposal. The entire process from application submission to a completed APA typically takes one year or less.[81]

> **COMPLIANCE POINTER:** Small business taxpayers and those submitting applications for bilateral or multilateral agreements may qualify for simplified procedures.[82]

Completed APAs represent binding agreements between the parties involved.[83] As part of these agreements, taxpayers agree to file annual reports to demonstrate compliance.[84] The IRS agrees to accept transfer prices that APAs cover. Also, APAs and related documentation are confidential return information the IRS cannot disclose.[85]

> **PLANNING POINTER:** Negotiating APAs entails some risks since taxpayers submit information the IRS otherwise might not possess. The disclosed information can raise prior-year issues about which the IRS is unaware, or provide helpful guidance in conducting future audits. Thus, taxpayers should consider the cost-benefit trade-offs before pursuing APAs.

---

[80]Id. at §5.
[81]Id. at §6.
[82]Id. at §3.09.
[83]Id. at §10.01.
[84]Id. at §11.01.
[85]Id. at §12.

# CHAPTER 17

# Asset Transfers

International tax professionals often view the Code as collections of separate realms, each with distinct rules for taxing income. Absent some constraint, rules applicable to domestic, foreign, and controlled foreign corporations (CFCs) create incentives for taxpayers to transfer appreciated assets among these three realms, secure more favorable gain treatment on eventual sale, and avoid U.S. tax. The asset transfer provisions in this chapter curb the tax incentives to transfer assets between realms.

In the domestic realm, U.S. corporations pay U.S. income tax on worldwide incomes.[1] However, asset transfers among related persons often avoid immediate U.S. taxation. For instance, Subchapter C allows taxpayers to transfer appreciated assets without recognizing gain when contributing capital to controlled corporations, restructuring affiliated groups, and liquidating subsidiaries.[2] Gains from these nontaxable transactions do not permanently avoid U.S. tax since basis adjustments preserve the income for later recognition.[3]

As Chapters 7 and 8 explained, foreign corporations do not pay U.S. income tax except on U.S. source income and income effectively connected with U.S. trades or businesses.[4] Most foreign source income escapes U.S. taxation. Thus, without some legislative restraints, potential gain that taxpayers shift from the domestic to the foreign realm may avoid U.S. tax permanently.

U.S. law taxes CFCs the same as noncontrolled foreign corporations— only on U.S. source and effectively connected income. So, one reasonably can view the CFC realm as a subset of the foreign realm. However, as Chapter 13 discussed, U.S. shareholders recognize constructive dividends when CFCs earn Subpart F income or invest earnings in U.S. property.[5] Earnings not constituting Subpart F income and not invested in U.S. property allow

---

[1]Reg. §1.11-1(a).
[2]See IRC §§332, 351, 354, 355, 356, and 361.
[3]IRC §358.
[4]IRC §§881 and 882.
[5]IRC §951(a)(1).

U.S. shareholders to avoid U.S. taxation until they receive dividends or sell shares. When U.S. shareholders liquidate their holdings, the Code may convert capital gain into constructive dividends to the extent of earnings and profits (E&P) not previously recognized as actual or constructive dividends.[6] Exhibit 17.1 facilitates comparisons among the three realms' tax rules.

Since the three realms—domestic, foreign, and CFC—involve different rules for taxing income, absent some restrictions, they create incentives for taxpayers to transfer appreciated assets to more favorable realms. The incentives take three forms. First, potential gain that taxpayers shift from the domestic to the foreign realm (**outbound asset transfers**) might permanently escape U.S. taxation if later sales of appreciated assets yield foreign source gain. Second, assets transferred from CFCs to the domestic realm (**inbound asset transfers**) may carry with them E&P that skips the U.S. corporate-level tax. Third, when CFCs transfer assets to noncontrolled foreign corporations (**external asset transfers**), the potential conversion of capital gain to dividend income on disposition of CFC shares can disappear.

Chapters 13 and 14 dealt with restrictions on income-shifting behavior applicable to CFCs, foreign personal holding companies, and passive foreign investment companies. This chapter explains asset transfer restrictions that curb incentives for taxpayers to shift potential gains to more favorable realms or avoid U.S. tax in other ways. The restrictions, known collectively as **toll charges**, often require taxpayers to recognize gain or dividend income immediately. Exhibit 17.2 depicts transfers frequently requiring a toll charge.

**EXHIBIT 17.1**  Differences among U.S. Tax Realms

| U.S. Tax Realms | Corporation Treatment | Shareholder Treatment |
|---|---|---|
| Domestic | Taxable on worldwide income | 1. Taxable on actual dividends<br>2. Capital gain from selling shares |
| Foreign | Taxable on U.S. source and effectively connected income | 1. Taxable on actual dividends<br>2. Capital gain from selling shares |
| Controlled foreign corporation | Taxable on U.S. source and effectively connected income | 1. Taxable on actual and constructive dividends<br>2. Capital gain from selling shares may be converted into dividends |

---

[6]IRC §1248.

**EXHIBIT 17.2**   Asset Transfers among U.S. Tax Realms Subject to Toll Charges

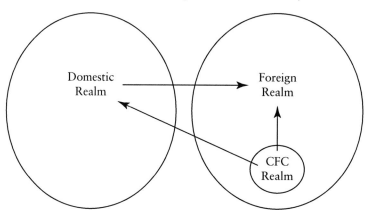

The three arrows represent outbound, inbound, and external asset transfers. These transfers occur as part of larger transactions involving capital contributions, affiliated group restructurings, or liquidations.

For each type of transfer, U.S. law only forces recognition of gain. Realized losses continue unrecognized if a transfer within the domestic realm would have gone unrecognized.[7] Thus, taxpayers cannot deduct potential losses on assets transferred abroad in otherwise nontaxable transactions. To segregate gains from losses, the Code views outbound transfers of partnership interests as pro rata transfers of the partnership's underlying assets.[8]

Statutory and regulatory rules dealing with asset transfers among realms involve some of the more brain-numbing convolutions under U.S. law. Part of the complexity arises from superimposing rules addressing income-shifting and other tax avoidance concerns over already-intricate Subchapter C and N provisions. Also, the different U.S. policy objectives underlying outbound, inbound, and external transfers[9] confuse the uninitiated and cause the regulations to appear even more indecipherable. (The regulations even intimidate many tax veterans.) Thus, in keeping with the text's broader purpose, this chapter resists the temptation to delve into all the reader-tormenting aspects of international asset transfers and adopts a more conceptual approach. It provides a general framework for thinking about outbound, inbound, and external asset transfers and the issues they raise.

---

[7]Temp. Reg. §1.367(a)-1T(b)(3)(ii) and Reg. §1.367(b)-1(b)(1)(ii)(B).
[8]IRC §367(a)(4).
[9]IRC §367(a) deals with outbound transfers, while IRC §367(b) deals with inbound and external transfers.

## OUTBOUND ASSET TRANSFERS

When U.S. persons transfer appreciated assets abroad, realized gain escapes U.S. taxation permanently if Subchapter C's nontaxable exchange rules apply. Asset transfers occur in relation to capital contributions to foreign corporations, mergers with foreign corporations, and liquidations into foreign parent companies. To prevent tax avoidance and safeguard tax revenue in these transactions, the Code requires that transferors recognize gain for the excess of the appreciated property's fair market value over its adjusted basis. The requirement to recognize gain supersedes Subchapter C's nontaxable exchange provisions normally applying in the domestic realm.[10]

### Capital Contributions

In the domestic realm, a person recognizes neither gain nor loss when transferring property to a U.S. corporation in exchange for stock if the person controls the corporation afterward.[11] The gain or loss does not permanently escape U.S. tax. Rather, shareholders adjust their stock basis to defer gain or loss.[12] Similarly, when existing shareholders contribute appreciated property to a U.S. corporation without receiving shares in return, the shareholders do not recognize gain or loss.[13]

---

### EXAMPLE

Universal Finance, Inc., a U.S. corporation, transfers securities (basis $100,000 and value $180,000) and other business assets to a newly established subsidiary in return for all the subsidiary's shares. The subsidiary does not use the securities in its trade or business but holds them for long-term appreciation. However, the subsidiary is not an investment company. If Universal organizes its subsidiary in the United States, it does not recognize the $80,000 gain. However, if Universal organizes the subsidiary as a foreign corporation, it reports the $80,000 gain.

---

[10]To reach this result, IRC §367(a)(1) treats foreign corporate transferees as though they are not corporations. This treatment makes the nontaxable exchange rules in Subchapter C inapplicable. Thus, the transferor must recognize gain under the broad provisions of IRC §1001(c).

[11]IRC §351(a). IRC §368(c) defines control as owning at least 80 percent of the corporation's voting power and nonvoting shares.

[12]IRC §358(a)(1).

[13]Such contributions often involve asset transfers to wholly owned corporations, where the transferor is indifferent about receiving additional shares.

This nonrecognition provision does not apply when U.S. persons transfer appreciated assets to foreign corporations. In these transfers, potential gain leaves the domestic and enters the foreign realm. Since the United States does not tax all income foreign persons earn, the potential gain might escape U.S. taxation on a later disposition. So, except as noted later, U.S. law requires transferors to recognize gain on such transfers.[14]

### Reorganizations

Mergers, consolidations, and other reorganizations involving only domestic corporations often occur tax-free.[15] For instance, when a U.S. target corporation transfers all assets to another U.S. corporation in return for the latter's stock, which the target distributes to its former stockholders, the target corporation does not recognize gain or loss.[16] Also, the target's stockholders do not recognize gain or loss for exchanging the target's shares (an asset transfer) for shares in the surviving corporation.[17] Thus, wholly domestic restructurings involving asset transfers often avoid gain or loss recognition.

In contrast, mergers of domestic corporations into foreign corporations and other restructurings in which appreciated assets leave the domestic realm involve taxable exchanges. In short, the U.S. persons transferring appreciated assets to the foreign realm recognize gain even though they defer gain on identical transactions in the domestic realm.[18]

Two exceptions to gain recognition may apply when the outbound assets are securities or stock.[19] First, U.S. transferors may defer gain recognition when they transfer appreciated securities or stock to foreign corporations involved in stock-for-stock restructurings.[20] Specifically, U.S. transferors do not recognize gain if:

- They own less than 5 percent of voting power and stock value in the transferee foreign corporation afterward or
- They enter **gain recognition agreements** with the IRS, obligating U.S. transferors to recognize gain if the foreign transferee disposes of transferred securities or stock (or underlying assets) within the next five years and pay an interest charge on the deferred gain.[21]

---

[14]IRC §367(a)(1), (c)(2), (f).
[15]IRC §368(a).
[16]IRC §361(a).
[17]IRC §354(a)(1).
[18]IRC §367(a)(1).
[19]For this purpose, Temp. Reg. §1.367(a)-1T(c)(3)(ii)(C) treats regularly traded interests in domestic limited partnerships as corporate securities and stock.
[20]IRC §367(a)(2).
[21]Reg. §1.367(a)-3(b)(1). For ownership interests below the 5 percent threshold, the

**COMPLIANCE POINTER:** U.S. transferors must attach gain recognition agreements to their timely filed U.S. tax returns for the taxable year in which transfers occur.[22]

---

### EXAMPLE

Garland Designs, Inc., a U.S. corporation, owns all shares of Wreath Enterprises SA, a CFC with no current or accumulated earnings and profits. Garland's basis in Wreath's shares equals $78,000, and the current value is $100,000. In a Type B stock-for-stock reorganization, Garland exchanges all its Wreath shares for 22 percent of Festoon Decor, Ltd., a foreign corporation previously unrelated to Garland and Wreath. Unrelated foreign persons own the other 78 percent of Festoon's shares; thus, Festoon is not a CFC.

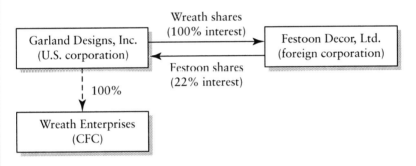

Since Garland owns at least 5 percent of Festoon after the restructuring, Garland either recognizes $22,000 gain ($100,000 − $78,000) currently or enters a gain recognition agreement obligating it to recognize gain if Festoon disposes of Wreath shares within five years.

---

Second, U.S. transferors may escape gain recognition when they transfer appreciated securities and stock in domestic target corporations to foreign corporations. For a given U.S. transferor, the conditions for avoiding gain recognition include:

---

United States stands to lose relatively little tax revenue from deferring gain and, thus, chooses not to burden minority shareholders with the monitoring and reporting requirements that gain recognition agreements require.
[22]Reg. §1.367(a)-8.

- The U.S. transferor either owns less than 5 percent of the foreign corporation's voting power and stock value after the restructuring or enters a gain recognition agreement;
- U.S. transferors aggregately receive 50 percent or less of the foreign corporation's voting power and stock value in the restructuring;
- U.S. target company's officers, directors, and 5 percent stockholders aggregately own 50 percent or less of the foreign corporation's voting power and stock value after the restructuring;
- The foreign transferee engages in a foreign active business during the 36 months preceding the restructuring and plans to continue the business after the restructuring; and
- The fair market value of the foreign transferee equals or exceeds the fair market value of the domestic target company.[23]

---

## EXAMPLE

Delphi, Inc. owns all shares of Oracle, Inc. Both entities are U.S. corporations. Delphi's basis in Oracle shares is $1.8 million, and the shares' fair market value equals $3 million. Delphi exchanges all its Oracle shares for 3 percent of Apollo, Ltd., a foreign corporation worth $10 million. Before the exchange, neither Oracle (the target) nor Delphi owned equity in Apollo. After the exchange, foreign persons own 97 percent of Apollo. Apollo conducted a foreign business for the three years before restructuring, which it plans to continue.

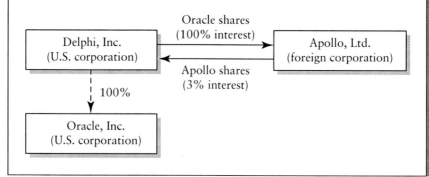

---

[23]Reg. §1.367(a)-3(c). The 50 percent thresholds assure dilution of U.S. ownership. Absent these thresholds, U.S. persons might transfer ownership in a domestic corporation to a foreign corporation they control and force the foreign corporation to immediately sell the domestic corporation's stock, resulting in foreign source gain that avoids U.S. tax.

> Since Delphi, Oracle, and Apollo meet the five requirements, Delphi does not recognize the $1.2 million gain ($3 million − $1.8 million). Neither must Delphi enter a gain recognition agreement.

**COMPLIANCE POINTER:** Domestic target companies in stock-for-stock acquisitions must attach sufficient information to their U.S. returns to verify that they can forgo gain recognition. In limited situations, the IRS may provide advance rulings.[24]

## Liquidations

When 80-percent-owned U.S. subsidiaries liquidate into their domestic parents, the subsidiaries recognize no gain or loss.[25] They treat the liquidating distribution of their assets as nontaxable exchanges. To preserve the potential gain or loss, domestic parent companies take carryover bases in assets they receive in liquidation.[26]

In contrast, U.S. subsidiaries liquidating into foreign corporations recognize gain since assets transfer from the domestic to the foreign realm.[27] Nonetheless, 80-percent-owned U.S. subsidiaries avoid gain recognition if:

- They use the assets in U.S. trade or business activities before liquidation and
- Foreign parent companies use the assets in U.S. trade or business activities for 10 years after liquidation.[28]

### FLASHBACK

Assets a foreign corporation uses in a U.S. trade or business may trigger the branch profits tax described in Chapter 10 when the foreign corporation removes the assets from U.S. operations. Also, if the foreign corporation sells the assets, the asset use test explained in Chapter 8 assures U.S. taxation of any gain as effectively connected income.

---

[24]Reg. §1.367(a)-3(c)(6), (7), (9).
[25]IRC §337(a).
[26]IRC §334(b)(1).
[27]IRC §367(e)(2).
[28]Reg. §1.367(e)-2(b)(2). This nonrecognition rule does not apply to intangible assets that the domestic subsidiary distributes in liquidation.

---

## EXAMPLE

Holliday, Ltd., a U.K. corporation, owns all the stock of Cassidy, Inc., its U.S. subsidiary. In complete liquidation, Cassidy distributes the following assets to Holliday:

|            | Fair Market Value | Adjusted Basis |
|------------|-------------------|----------------|
| Cash       | $ 12,000          | $ 12,000       |
| Buildings  | 700,000           | 820,000        |
| Land       | 280,000           | 200,000        |

Before the liquidation, Cassidy used these assets in its U.S. business. If Holliday plans to sell the assets or use them in its foreign business, Cassidy recognizes $80,000 gain on transferring the land to Holliday. Cassidy cannot deduct the $120,000 loss on transferring the building. If Holliday uses the assets in a U.S. trade or business after the liquidation for 10 years, Cassidy avoids recognizing the $80,000 gain and Holliday takes a $200,000 basis in the land.

---

### Foreign Business Exception

As indicated, appreciated assets that taxpayers transfer from the domestic realm to foreign corporations often trigger gain recognition. However, transferors do not recognize gain on some appreciated assets foreign corporations use in active foreign trades or businesses.[29] Thus, when a legitimate business reason exists for transferring assets to the foreign realm, the transferor presumably lacks a tax avoidance motive and does not recognize gain.

Nonetheless, in two areas, the Code requires transferors to recognize gain even when foreign transferees use assets in active foreign businesses. First, transferors must recognize gain on the following assets:

- Inventory and similar assets held for sale to customers,
- Installment obligations,
- Accounts receivables,
- Foreign currencies,
- Certain leased properties, and
- Intangible assets.[30]

---

[29]IRC §367(a)(3)(A).
[30]IRC §367(a)(3)(B) and Temp. Reg. §1.367(a)-5T. For this purpose, intangible assets include creative, manufacturing, and marketing intangibles. This chapter explains the special treatment of intangibles later.

Also, taxpayers recognize depreciation recapture on appreciated assets they transfer to the foreign realm.[31] Gain beyond depreciation recapture remains unrecognized for assets transferees use in active foreign businesses.

---

**EXAMPLE**

Copperhead Construction, Inc., a domestic corporation, transfers steel and new earth-moving equipment to its wholly owned Nigerian subsidiary, Cobra Construction, Ltd., in return for all of Cobra's stock, worth $3,500,000. Copperhead originally purchased the steel for $1,200,000 (current value $1,500,000) and the equipment for $1,900,000 (current value $2,000,000). If this transaction had occurred between two domestic corporations, Copperhead would recognize no gain and take a $3,100,000 basis in new Cobra shares ($1,200,000 + $1,900,000) since it transferred property to a controlled corporation solely for stock. However, U.S. law requires Copperhead to recognize $300,000 gain since the steel crossed into the foreign realm and constitutes raw materials inventory. Copperhead does not recognize the equipment's $100,000 gain if Cobra uses the equipment in its Nigerian business.

---

Second, U.S. corporations transferring foreign branch assets to foreign corporations recognize gain to the extent of their branches' net losses deducted against U.S. income.[32] This recapture rule assures that U.S. companies do not benefit from foreign losses and then avoid reporting foreign income when branch operations turn profitable.

---

**EXAMPLE**

Systems Control, Inc., a U.S. corporation, conducts its European operations through a Finnish division. Since beginning business, the company has experienced the following operating results:

|      | *U.S. Profit (Loss)* | *Finnish Profit (Loss)* |
|------|---------------------|-------------------------|
| 2002 | $130,000            | $(120,000)              |
| 2003 | 190,000             | ( 40,000)               |

*(continues)*

---

[31]Temp. Reg. §1.367(a)-4T(b)(1).
[32]IRC §367(a)(3)(C).

Systems Control deducts each year's Finnish loss against U.S. profit. The company expects its Finnish division to turn profitable in 2004 and, so, incorporates it. The division purchased land two years ago for $480,000, which now appraises for $690,000. On the transfer of land to its new Finnish subsidiary, Systems Control realizes $210,000 gain ($690,000 − $480,000). The company recaptures and recognizes $160,000 of this gain ($120,000 + $40,000). Systems Control defers the remaining $50,000 gain ($210,000 − $160,000).

### Intangible Assets

Special tax benefit measures prevent taxpayers from developing intangible assets in the United States, deducting the development expenses against U.S. taxable income, and transferring the assets to foreign persons at little or no gain just before they become really valuable. The rules apply to capital contributions and reorganizations involving outbound transfers of marketing, manufacturing, and other intangible assets. Rather than demanding gain recognition for the excess of an intangible's fair market value over its adjusted basis, the Code requires U.S. persons to treat such transfers as contingent sales. Thus, U.S. transferors receive constructive royalties contingent on the future productivity, use, or disposition of the intangible assets.

The annual royalties U.S. transferors report must be commensurate with the profitability of the intangibles to the transferees.[33] So, if an intangible asset becomes more valuable after its transfer abroad, the constructive royalty the U.S. transferor must report increases. Royalties continue for the intangible asset's useful life, but not more than 20 years.[34]

> **PLANNING POINTER:** Taxpayers may decide to pay actual royalties under the arm's-length principles described in Chapter 16. In contrast to constructive payments, foreign countries usually allow deductions for actual royalties but also may impose withholding

---

[33]IRC §367(d). Under regulatory authority that IRC §367(d)(3) grants, the IRS may implement similar rules for U.S. persons transferring intangible assets to partnerships when a foreign partner may receive the gain allocation.
[34]Temp. Reg. §1.367(d)-1T(c)(3).

taxes. Especially in high-tax countries with low royalty withholding taxes, executing a formal licensing agreement may reduce the overall foreign tax liability.

## INBOUND ASSET TRANSFERS

For outbound transfers, the United States denies access to the Subchapter C nonrecognition provisions. Thus, the outbound rules require immediate gain recognition when U.S. persons transfer appreciated assets to foreign persons. This approach prevents U.S. persons from transferring potential gain to the foreign realm where the United States cannot reach the income and collect tax on later dispositions.

U.S. concern about inbound transfers differs considerably since, by definition, assets enter the domestic realm where U.S. jurisdiction permits taxation of later dispositions. For inbound transfers, the United States seeks to assure that profits earned in the foreign realm do not skip a level of U.S. taxation as they enter the domestic realm. Specifically, the tax law prevents foreign transferors' E&P, which the United States has not yet taxed, from mixing with domestic transferees' E&P, which the United States has taxed, before extracting a toll charge.

As Exhibit 17.2 illustrates, toll charges do not apply to inbound transfers from most foreign corporations. They apply only when foreign transferors are current or former CFCs.[35] Toll charges usually take the form of constructive dividends and apply to U.S. shareholders' otherwise nontaxable exchanges.[36] Thus, the following inbound transfers may cause U.S. shareholders of CFCs to report constructive dividends:

- Reorganization in which CFC's assets transfer to a domestic corporation and
- Liquidations of CFCs into domestic parent companies.

---

[35]Since IRC §332(b)(1) protects parent companies (transferees) against gain recognition only when 80-percent-owned subsidiaries liquidate, a domestic parent and foreign subsidiary satisfying this ownership requirement means that the subsidiary also qualifies as a CFC (which requires only a 50 percent threshold). Thus, the inbound provisions focus on transfers from the CFC to the domestic realm, as Exhibit 17.2 highlights, rather than on transfers from the entire foreign realm to the domestic realm.
[36]Reg. §1.367(b)-3(b)(3)(ii). For share holdings worth $50,000 or more, Reg. §1.367(b)-3(c) clarifies that U.S. persons (other than U.S. shareholders who, by definition, own 10 percent of the CFC's voting power) recognize gain unless they elect to report constructive dividends.

## EXAMPLE

Encore, Inc., a U.S. corporation, owns all stock of Ovation SA, a Peruvian CFC engaged in manufacturing with $20 million E&P. Encore does not recognize constructive dividends from Ovation since the latter, as a manufacturer, never earns Subpart F income and never invests its profits in U.S. property. Thus, the United States has not taxed Ovation's E&P.

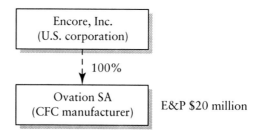

If Ovation distributes its E&P, Encore must recognize $20 million as gross income. Assuming Encore's U.S. tax rate is 35 percent, Encore pays $7 million U.S. income tax on the dividend ($20 million × 35%), and the after-tax dividend of $13 million increases Encore's E&P ($20 million − $7 million). However, absent a toll charge, Encore possesses a tax incentive to liquidate Ovation rather than receiving its E&P as taxable dividends. Specifically, the liquidation occurs tax-free, the $20 million increases Encore's E&P, and Encore avoids the U.S. corporate-level tax. To prevent this end run, the asset transfer rules require Encore to recognize a $20 million constructive dividend when Ovation transfers its assets to Encore in liquidation.

## FLASHBACK

Chapter 12 explained that constructive dividends often bring with them deemed paid credits.[37] So reporting constructive dividends from low-tax countries and claiming a deemed paid credit usually results in a U.S. residual tax. However, if the U.S. shareholder possesses excess credits within the same basket (e.g., from activities in high-tax countries), the excess credits reduce or eliminate the U.S. residual tax otherwise due from the constructive dividends.

---

[37]IRC §960(a)(1).

## EXTERNAL ASSET TRANSFERS

In contrast to outbound and inbound transfers, the Code and regulations dealing with external (i.e., foreign-to-foreign) asset transfers prevent the disappearance of Section 1248 earnings through extracting a toll charge. When applicable, the toll charge takes the form of a constructive dividend and applies only when earnings move from the CFC realm to the non-CFC portion of the foreign realm.[38] Usually, U.S. law does not require a toll charge when earnings remain in the CFC realm and Section 1248 earnings do not disappear or become diluted.

### FLASHBACK

As Chapter 12 explained, U.S. shareholders selling foreign stock recognize constructive dividends for Section 1248 earnings (i.e., gain attributable to earnings and profits accumulated while the corporation was a CFC, accumulated while the U.S. seller qualified as a U.S. shareholder, and not previously taxed as constructive dividends).[39]

External asset transfers commonly triggering a constructive dividend include:

- Capital contributions from CFCs to foreign corporations that are not CFCs and
- Reorganizations in which current or former U.S. shareholders exchange shares with Section 1248 earnings for shares without such earnings.[40]

### EXAMPLE

Metal Art, Inc., a U.S. corporation, owns 100 percent of Hephaestus AE, a Greek CFC. In a Type C asset-for-stock reorganization, Hephaestus transfers all its assets to Vulcan SpA, an Italian corporation, and liquidates. Metal Art exchanges its Hephaestus shares for Vulcan voting shares. After the reorganization, Metal Art owns 40 percent of Vulcan, and unrelated foreign persons own the remaining 60 percent.

*(continues)*

---

[38]Reg. §1.367(b)-4(b).
[39]IRC §1248(a).
[40]Reg. §1.367(b)-4(b)(1)(i).

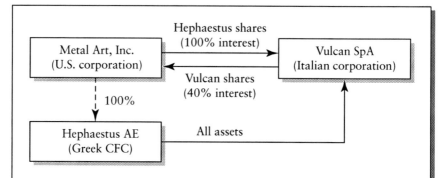

Thus, Vulcan is not a CFC, and the Section 1248 earnings disappear. Absent a toll charge, Metal Art can sell its Vulcan shares and avoid Section 1248 treatment. However, to prevent tax avoidance, the asset transfer rules require Metal Art to recognize a constructive dividend for the Section 1248 earnings attributable to its prereorganization holding in Hephaestus.

# Glossary

**Abode**  Location of an individual's domestic ties.

**Active foreign business test**  Test that, when satisfied, converts interest received from resident aliens or domestic corporations to foreign source income.

**Administrative assistance article**  Treaty clause that, when invoked, enlists the assistance of a treaty country in efforts to collect tax liabilities.

**Advance pricing agreement (APA)**  Negotiated, binding agreement between the United States and the IRS establishing acceptable transfer prices prospectively.

**Aggregate amount of interest**  For passive foreign investment company purposes, summed interest charges on the aggregate increases in taxes using a rate three percentage points higher than the federal short-term rate.

**Aggregate increases in taxes**  For passive foreign investment company purposes, portion of excess distribution allocable to each prior year times the highest statutory rate applicable to each such year and then summed together.

**Alien**  Individual without U.S. citizenship.

**Allocation**  Process of assigning expenses to classes of gross income based on their degree of relatedness to each class.

**American employers**  For FICA tax purposes, the federal government and its instrumentalities, U.S. residents, partnerships if at least two-thirds of their partners are U.S. residents, trusts if all their trustees are U.S. residents, and U.S. corporations.

**Applicable determination dates**  Dates on which corporations must test for U.S. real property holding corporation status.

**Applicable earnings**  Current and accumulated E&P of CFC that limits constructive dividends from increased investments in U.S. property.

**Apportionment**  Process (after allocation) of assigning expenses to a statutory or residual grouping based on each expense's relationship to each grouping.

**Arm's-length price**   In a transaction between related or controlled persons, the amount that would have been charged if the transaction had occurred between unrelated and uncontrolled persons. *Same as* Section 482 pricing.

**Asset tax**   In Latin American countries, a tax paid on the value of assets owned.

**Asset use test**   Test that treats U.S. source income as effectively connected when a foreign person derives income from assets used or held for use in a U.S. trade or business.

**Back-to-back loans**   Two loans among three persons of similar terms in which the same person (e.g., a bank) acts as the borrower under one loan and the creditor under the second loan. Sometimes used to obtain treaty or other tax benefits not available through a single direct loan between related persons.

**Bareboat charter**   Agreement in which lessee provides the crew when renting a ship rather than using the lessor's crew.

**Base housing amount**   Sixteen percent of a U.S. government employee's salary at step 1 of grade GS-14.

**Basket**   Intended to restrict cross-crediting strategies, category of foreign income for which taxpayers separately measure creditable taxes and determine the foreign tax credit limitation.

**Best method rule**   In transactions between related or controlled persons, taxpayers must use the methodology resulting in the most reliable measure of arm's-length prices.

**Blocked income**   Controlled foreign corporation's earnings that cannot be distributed as dividends because of foreign legal restrictions such as currency controls.

**Bona fide resident test**   Test allowing U.S. citizens with foreign tax homes to exclude foreign earned income when they reside in one or more foreign countries for an uninterrupted period that includes an entire taxable year.

**Branch interest tax (BIT)**   U.S. tax on interest that the U.S. business of a foreign corporation (i.e., U.S. branch) pays as well as excess interest.

**Branch operations**   Extension of corporate business activities consisting of an office, division, or other unincorporated place of business in a different location from the corporation's main office or headquarters.

**Branch profits tax (BPT)**   Foreign corporation's dividend equivalent amount times 30 percent (or lower treaty rate).

**Branch rule**  Rule preventing CFCs from shifting income to branches in low-tax jurisdictions while avoiding its characterization as foreign base company sales income.

**Business activities test**  Test that treats U.S. source income as effectively connected when the activities of a foreign person's U.S. trade or business are a material factor in realizing the income.

**Capital export neutrality**  Policy standard for which domestic and foreign income is taxed at the same overall effective rate. Thus, tax rules meeting this standard create neither an incentive nor a disincentive for conducting business or investing abroad.

**Capital import neutrality**  Policy standard for which companies based in different countries experience the same overall tax burden in a given market. Thus, tax rules meeting this standard foster global competitiveness.

**Captive insurance company**  Insurance company that primarily insures the risks of its own shareholders or persons related to its shareholders.

**Cascading royalties**  Back-to-back licensing contracts in which the same person acts as licensor under one agreement and licensee under the second agreement, both having similar terms.

**Check-the-box**  Procedure for foreign business entity to elect treatment as corporation or partnership.

**Citizenship**  Constitutional rights individuals possess who are born or naturalized in a country. *Same as* nationality.

**Closer connection exception**  Exception to the substantial presence test that treats an alien individual as a nonresident based on U.S. presence less than 183 days, foreign tax home, closer connection to a foreign country, and no attempt to become a U.S. resident.

**Coastwise transportation**  Travel or shipping in which both the departure and termination points lie within the same country.

**Collateral adjustment**  Correlative allocation, conforming adjustment, or setoff that reduces double tax problems following an IRS primary allocation.

**Combined taxable income (CTI)**  Aggregate net profit for a domestic international sales corporation and its related supplier attributable to qualified export receipts.

**Combined taxable income (CTI) method**  Transfer pricing method under the domestic international sales corporation (DISC) regime that allocates 50 percent of combined taxable income attributable to qualified export receipts plus 10 percent of export promotion expenses to the DISC.

**Commensurate with income**   Standard requiring controlled persons to periodically adjust royalty payments to reflect changes in an intangible asset's value.

**Commercial traveler article**   Treaty provision exempting individuals from host country taxation when traveling abroad for short periods.

**Committee on Foreign Relations**   *See* Senate Foreign Relations Committee.

**Comparable profit split**   One of two acceptable means of allocating controlled persons' combined profit or loss under the profit split method, it relies entirely on external market benchmarks for the allocation percentages.

**Comparable profits method (CPM)**   Method that determines a controlled person's transfer price based on profitability comparisons with uncontrolled persons engaging in similar business activities under similar circumstances.

**Comparable uncontrolled price (CUP) method**   Pricing method for tangible property transfers between controlled persons that relies on prices in comparable uncontrolled transactions as the basis for arm's-length pricing.

**Comparable uncontrolled transaction (CUT) method**   Transfer pricing method relying on transactions between uncontrolled persons involving the same or comparable intangible properties transferring under substantially the same or comparable circumstances.

**Competent authority**   Treaty procedure that taxpayers invoke to resolve issues not otherwise addressed.

**Conforming adjustment**   Collateral adjustment to the controlled person receiving a primary allocation that causes the person's books and records to be consistent with the primary allocation.

**Consent dividend**   For foreign personal holding companies, earnings that common shareholders agree to treat as dividends though no actual distribution occurs.

**Constructive ownership**   Under the Subpart F provisions, stock ownership through five complex attribution rules.

**Continuum rule**   Regulatory provision that begins U.S. residency in the current year on January 1 when an alien individual also qualified as a U.S. resident in the previous year. Similarly, the rule extends U.S. residency to December 31 for any year in which an alien individual qualifies as a U.S. resident in the following year.

**Controlled foreign corporation (CFC)**   Foreign corporation that U.S. shareholders control through more than 50 percent of either voting power or stock value.

**Correlative allocation**  Collateral adjustment to a controlled person's records that usually allows deductions, increases basis, or reduces earnings and profits following a primary allocation of income to the other controlled participant in the adjusted transaction.

**Cost-plus method**  Transfer pricing method applicable to manufacturers selling to controlled persons that may further process the goods before resell, the arm's-length price equals production cost plus an appropriate gross profit based on comparable uncontrolled transactions.

**Cost-sharing arrangement**  Agreement requiring participants to share the costs of developing an intangible asset in proportion to the reasonably anticipated benefits each participant expects to derive from its use.

**Creditable**  Type of foreign government levy that is an income tax or that substitutes for an income tax; thus, it qualifies for the foreign tax credit.

**Cross-credit**  Process of intermingling low-taxed and high-taxed foreign income in the same basket to obtain a higher foreign tax credit.

**Cruises to nowhere**  Cruises that depart from and terminate in the host country with no foreign port calls.

**DISC**  *See* domestic international sales corporation.

**Deemed paid credit (DPC)**  Foreign tax credit that a U.S. corporation claims attributable to foreign income tax that its foreign subsidiary pays. *Same as* indirect foreign tax credit.

**Deemed paid tax (DPT)**  Creditable taxes that a U.S. corporation claims for foreign income tax that its foreign subsidiary pays. Deemed paid taxes result in a deemed paid credit unless Section 904 limits the foreign tax credit.

**Deemed sale election**  Election that U.S. investors in unpedigreed QEF make to recognize built-in gain (but not loss) as though they sold their shares.

**Deferred DISC income**  Accumulated income of domestic international sales corporation from previous taxable years that has not been taxed.

**Deferred tax amount**  Consisting of deferred tax and interest charges, amount the U.S. owner of passive foreign investment company shares pays on excess distributions and gain from disposing of shares.

**De minimis rule**  Provision that waives normal rules when the activity or amount triggering the normal rules is trivial or immaterial.

**Dependent agents**  Persons (e.g., employees) who regularly exercise authority to conclude contracts on behalf of their principals and, thus, represent permanent establishments. *Compare* independent agents.

**Developed countries**   Nations that are economically advanced (e.g., the OECD countries) and generally export large amounts of capital. Once called *industrialized countries. Contrast with* developing countries.

**Developing countries**   Nations that are economically poorer than developed countries and generally are net capital importers. Once called *third-world countries* and *undeveloped countries.*

**Direct investment abroad**   Foreign investment holdings greater than 10 percent. *Contrast with* portfolio investments.

**DISC-related deferred tax liability**   Difference between the U.S. income tax liability of a domestic international sales corporation (DISC) shareholder and the hypothetical tax resulting when deferred DISC income is added to the shareholder's other taxable income.

**Distributee**   Shareholder recipient of a corporate distribution of earnings and profits.

**Distributor**   Corporation distributing earnings and profits to its shareholders.

**Dividend-equivalent amount (DEA)**   Foreign corporation's effectively connected E&P plus decreases (minus increases) in its U.S. net equity. Basis for calculating branch profits tax.

**Dividend paid deduction**   For foreign personal holding companies, the sum of dividends actually paid during the year, dividends actually paid in the two and a half months following the year that the corporation chooses to apply to the preceding year, and consent dividends.

**Dividend received deduction**   Corporate deduction for dividends received that mitigates effect of double U.S. taxation.

**Domestic corporation**   Corporation organized within the United States. *See also* legal domicile.

**Domestic international sales corporation (DISC)**   Export entity that defers the U.S. income tax on a substantial portion of export profit.

**Domestic partnership**   Partnership created or organized in the United States.

**Double taxation**   Situation in which the United States and a foreign country (or U.S. possession) taxes the same income stream.

**Dual capacity taxpayer**   For foreign tax credit purposes, a person paying a foreign government levy that is partially a tax and partially in return for a specific economic benefit received.

**Dual resident**   Taxpayer who, under the laws in two countries, qualifies as a resident in both countries simultaneously.

**Dual status alien**   Alien individual who has started or terminated U.S. residency during the year and, as a result, is treated as a nonresident alien part of the year and a resident alien for the rest of the year.

**Earned income**   Compensation received for rendering personal services such as wages, base salary, professional fees, and noncash remuneration.

**Earnings and profits (E&P)**   Economic measure of a corporation's capacity to pay dividends to shareholders without impairing capital.

**Earnings stripping**   Use of debt or other contractual arrangements to siphon a related company's earnings in deductible forms such as interest and royalties. *Compare* interest stripping.

**Effective tax rate (ETR)**   Tax liability divided by income.

**Effectively connected income**   Income of a nonresident alien or foreign corporation related to U.S. business activities.

**80-20 company**   Domestic corporation meeting the active foreign business test for sourcing interest income.

**Eurobond market**   Source of debt financing in Europe.

**European Union (EU)**   Organization of approximately 15 Western European nations seeking economic integration and, to a lesser degree, political unification.

**Excess credit**   Amount by which creditable foreign taxes exceed the Section 904 limitation.

**Excess distribution**   For passive foreign investment company purposes, portion of total excess distribution allocable to a given distribution during the taxable year.

**Excess interest**   Under the branch interest tax, the excess of the foreign corporation's deduction for interest against effectively connected income over the interest the foreign corporation's U.S. branch pays.

**Excess interest expense**   Under the interest stripping rule, the amount by which net interest expense exceeds half of adjusted taxable income and the excess limitation carryforward.

**Excess limit**   Amount by which the Section 904 limitation exceeds creditable foreign taxes.

**Exchange of information agreement**   Agreement between nations for sharing taxpayer information to discourage tax evasion.

**Exchange of information article**   Article in an income tax treaty providing similar benefits to a separately negotiated exchange of information agreement.

**Exempt persons**   Foreign government officials, students, teachers, trainees, or professional athletes competing in charitable sports events whose days of U.S. presence are ignored when conducting the substantial presence test.

**Exemption method**   Unilateral or bilateral method for eliminating double taxation in which a country forgoes the tax on a specified income stream.

**Expatriates**   Individuals living outside their home country.

**Export financing interest**   Bank's interest income from financing the sale of goods produced in the United States for use or consumption abroad.

**Export promotion expense**   Expense that domestic international sales corporation incurs to distribute or sell export property for use, consumption, or distribution abroad, including half of transportation expenses on aircraft that U.S. persons own and operate and U.S. registered ships.

**Export property**   Asset producing qualified export receipts eligible for domestic international sales corporation (DISC) benefits if a person other than a DISC manufactures, produces, grows, or extracts it domestically; the DISC or its related supplier holds it primarily for sale, lease, or rent in the ordinary course of business for direct use, consumption, or disposition abroad; and its fair market value consists of 50 percent or more domestic content.

**Export sale**   Outbound sale to a location or customer in another country.

**Export terminal rule**   Rule applicable to profit from most natural resources that bases source on the natural resource's value at the export terminal point.

**Expropriation**   Similar to eminent domain, a foreign government's seizure of a company's assets.

**External asset transfer**   Transfer of assets from controlled foreign corporation realm to foreign realm, subject to toll charge, to prevent loss of Section 1248 earnings.

**Extraterritorial income exclusion (EIE)**   Tax exemption ranging between 15 and 30 percent that the World Trade Organization declared an illegal export subsidy in 2002.

**Fair market value method**   Method for valuing assets when allocating and apportioning interest deductions.

**FDAP income**   *See* fixed or determinable, annual or periodical income.

**50-50 method**   Method for sourcing inventory profit in which half of the gain is sourced based on where production occurs and half based on the place of sale.

**FIRPTA**   *See* Foreign Investment in Real Property Tax Act of 1980.

**FITA**   *See* Foreign Investors Tax Act of 1966.

**Financial services entity**   Person deriving at least 80 percent of its gross income from financing activities.

**Financial services income**   Income of financial services entities falling into a separate foreign tax credit basket and consisting of income from banking, insurance, financing, and similar activities.

**First-year election**   Election alien individuals make that accelerates residency starting date into the election year and causes electing persons to file as dual status aliens for that year rather than nonresident aliens for the entire year.

**Fiscal domicile**   The country from where an entity's central management occurs. *Contrast with* legal domicile.

**Fiscally transparent entity**   Entity that a jurisdiction ignores for tax purposes (e.g., a partnership), allowing profit, loss, and other items to flow through to owners. *Same as* a flow-through entity.

**5-70 rule**   Controlled foreign corporation provision ignoring Subpart F income when gross insurance income plus foreign base company income falls below the smaller of $1 million or 5 percent of total gross income and treating all gross income as Subpart F income when the same sum is more than 70 percent of gross income. The latter provision is the full-inclusion rule.

**Fixed or determinable, annual or periodical income (FDAP)**   Income that the Code taxes at 30 percent when derived from U.S. sources but not from a U.S. trade or business.

**Flow-through entity**   Entity that a jurisdiction ignores for tax purposes (e.g., a partnership), allowing profit, loss, and other items to flow through to owners. Same as a fiscally-transparent entity.

**Force of attraction rule**   Stopgap measure that causes U.S. source income that the Code does not explicitly tax or exempt to be drawn toward the taxpayer's U.S. trade or business and taxed as effectively connected income.

**Foreign base company (FBC) income**   One component of Subpart F income consisting of five separate categories of gross income, each reduced by allocable deductions.

**Foreign base company (FBC) oil-related income**   Foreign source income from processing, transporting, distributing, or selling minerals extracted from oil or gas wells.

**Foreign base company (FBC) sales income**   Income resulting from related person sales of personal property that a controlled foreign corporation neither manufactures within its country of organization nor sells to customers for use within the same country and, thus, part of foreign base company income.

**Foreign base company (FBC) services income**   Compensation, commissions, and fees from rendering services outside a controlled foreign corporation's country for or on behalf of a related person and, thus, part of foreign base company income.

**Foreign base company (FBC) shipping income**   Except for coastwise travel, income from using, hiring for use, or leasing for use aircraft or vessels to transport people or cargo and, thus, part of foreign base company income.

**Foreign corporation**   Corporation organized in a foreign country or U.S. possession. *See also* legal domicile.

**Foreign direct investment**   Ownership of ten percent or more of a foreign entity that resides in another country. Contrast with portfolio investment.

**Foreign earned income (FEI)**   Compensation received for rendering personal services outside the United States.

**Foreign earned income exclusion**   Provision allowing qualified U.S. expatriates to exclude up to $80,000 personal service income derived from foreign sources, plus an additional amount based on excess foreign housing expenses.

**Foreign Investment in Real Property Tax Act of 1980 (FIRPTA)**   Legislation that added Section 897 to the Code, which provides rules for taxing real estate gains of foreign persons.

**Foreign Investors Tax Act of 1966 (FITA)**   Legislation that introduced the concept of effectively connected income and, to a large extent, eliminated the force of attraction principle.

**Foreign partnership**   Partnership created or organized outside the United States.

**Foreign personal holding company (FPHC)**   Foreign corporation that five or fewer U.S. individuals control through more than 50 percent of either voting power or stock value and that derives at least 60 percent of its gross income from passive sources and certain personal service contracts.

**Foreign personal holding company income (FPHCI)**   Under the controlled foreign corporation regime, interest, dividends, annuities, rents, royalties, and net gain from investment-oriented transactions in stocks, bonds, commodities, and foreign currencies. Under the foreign personal holding company regime, interest, dividends, annuities, rents, royalties, net gain from investment-oriented security and commodity transactions, income from estates and trusts, and certain personal service income.

**Foreign persons**   Nonresident aliens, foreign partnerships, and foreign corporations.

**Foreign Relations Committee**   *See* Senate Foreign Relations Committee.

**Foreign sales corporation (FSC)**   Export entity that excludes some export profit from U.S. income tax. Congress repealed the FSC in 2000 after the World Trade Organization held that it was an illegal export subsidy.

**Foreign source income**   Income derived from sources outside the United States.

**Foreign tax credit (FTC)**   Dollar-for-dollar reduction of resident's tax liability for foreign income tax resident pays or accrues.

**Foreign tax credit basket**   Intended to restrict cross-crediting strategies, category of foreign income for which taxpayers separately measure creditable taxes and determine the foreign tax credit limitation.

**Foreign tax credit limit**   Section 904 limitation on the foreign tax credit that prevents taxpayers from using creditable taxes to reduce the U.S. tax on U.S. source income.

**Foreign trading gross receipts (FTGRs)**   Amounts received from export sales qualifying for the extraterritorial income exclusion.

**Full-inclusion rule**   Controlled foreign corporation provision treating all gross income as Subpart F income when insurance income plus foreign base company income is more than 70 percent of total gross income. *See also* 5-70 rule.

**Gain recognition agreement**   In international reorganizations, an agreement in which a U.S. transferor agrees to recognize gain later if the foreign transferee disposes of the asset it receives within a stated period.

**General Agreement on Tariffs and Trade (GATT)** Assimilated in 1994 as part of the pact creating the World Trade Organization, an international agreement to discourage income tax laws from erecting trade barriers or creating export incentives.

**General basket** Foreign tax credit basket containing most business profit and any other income not falling into the other baskets. *Same as* overall basket and residual basket.

**Global system** Type of jurisdiction that seeks to tax the worldwide income of a country's taxpayers.

**Goods and services tax (GST)** Tax that Australia and other countries impose on the value of transferred goods and services. *Similar to* value-added tax.

**Green card test** Same as the lawful permanent residence test for U.S. residency.

**Gross income** Income (before deductions) that the Code does not exclude.

**Gross income method** Method for apportioning R&D deductions that apportions 25 percent of R&D wherever it occurs and the remainder based on gross income.

**Gross receipts (GR) method** Transfer pricing method under the domestic international sales corporation (DISC) regime that allocates 4 percent of qualified export receipts plus 10 percent of export promotion expenses to the DISC.

**Gross receipts test** With some flexibility, requirement that a foreign tax must begin with gross receipts as a tax base to be creditable.

**Gross up** When receiving dividends from foreign subsidiaries, the amount Section 78 requires U.S. corporations to include in gross income, which is equal to deemed paid taxes.

**Gross valuation misstatement** Transfer pricing misstatement that results in penalty equal to 40 percent of the tax underpayment.

**High withholding tax interest basket** Foreign tax credit basket containing interest income subject to a foreign withholding rate of 5 percent or more.

**Home country** Country where the taxpayer resides.

**Home office** Term sometimes used in referring to place of corporate residence to distinguish it from the location of foreign subsidiary or branch activities. The place to which foreign businesses eventually remit profits.

**Hopscotch rule**   When second- or lower-tier foreign subsidiaries generate Subpart F income or invest earnings in U.S. property, their U.S. parent corporations recognize constructive dividends that seemingly "hop over" intervening foreign subsidiaries.

**Host country**   Country (outside the home country) where the taxpayer conducts business or makes investments. Some international works use the term *source country* instead.

**Housing cost amount**   Excess of reasonable foreign housing expenses over a base housing amount.

**Hybrid entity**   Foreign business entity that the home country treats as a corporation but the United States treats as a partnership or branch. *Compare* reverse hybrid entity.

**Inbound asset transfer**   Transfer of assets from controlled foreign corporation realm to domestic realm, subject to toll charge, to prevent earnings and profits from skipping the U.S. corporate-level tax.

**Inbound transaction**   Transaction in which a nonresident alien or foreign entity invests or does business in the United States.

**Inbound transfer**   Transfer of foreign-located property to a place within the United States.

**Income tax treaty**   Negotiated agreement between two countries to mitigate the effect of double income taxation and prevent tax evasion.

**Indefinite work assignment**   Foreign assignment that the worker expects will last more than one year, resulting in a foreign tax home.

**Independent agents**   Persons (e.g., independent contractors) who work for multiple principals in the course of their own business and are not permanent establishments. *Compare* dependent agents.

**Independent factory price (IFP) method**   Based on regular sales from manufacturers to unrelated distributors, elective source of income method applicable to inventory profit.

**Indirect foreign tax credit**   Foreign tax credit that a U.S. corporation claims attributable to foreign income tax that its foreign subsidiary pays. *Same as* deemed paid credit.

**Indirect ownership**   Under the Subpart F rules, stock ownership through one or more foreign entities.

**Insurance income** Controlled foreign corporation's income from issuing or reissuing insurance or annuity contracts if attributable to risks outside the corporation's country of organization.

**Intangible property** Right or other asset with value but no physical substance.

**Inter vivos gifts** Gifts donors make while still living.

**Interest stripping** Use of debt obligations to shelter a related company's taxable income from tax by siphoning earnings as deductible interest. *Compare* earnings stripping.

**International boycott** Refusal to deal with companies conducting business in designated countries (e.g., Israel) or companies with directors, managers, owners, or employees from designated nationalities, races, or religions. Participating in or cooperating with a boycott results in Subpart F income and the loss of foreign tax credits.

**International shipping and aviation agreement** Agreement that precludes the host country from taxing certain international transportation income.

**Jurisdiction to tax** Power of government to impose its taxes on a person or transaction.

**Kick-out rule** Statutory provision placing high-taxed passive income in the residual basket rather than the passive income basket.

**Later-in-time rule** Principle that resolves conflicts between Code and treaty provisions. Generally, the most recently enacted provision prevails.

**Lawful permanent resident** Individual to whom the federal government grants the right to permanently reside in the United States. *Same as* permanent immigrant.

**Legal domicile** The country in which an entity organizes or incorporates. *Contrast with* fiscal domicile.

**Limitation amounts** Dollar limits that, if exceeded, trigger determination dates on which corporations must test their U.S. real property holding corporation status.

**Listed countries** List of countries that a national tax system specifically identifies from which certain foreign source income receives special treatment (e.g., exemption for foreign dividends). The tax laws of most countries do not contain such a list.

**Loan-out schemes** Use of shell corporation in favorable treaty country to contract for services of sole shareholder who is often a highly compensated athlete or entertainer. If successful, the treaty precludes host country taxation.

**Look-through rule**  Code provision that determines the character of income received by examining (or looking through to) the payor's or distributor's underlying assets, income, or activities.

**Manufacturing**  Activity involving substantial transformation of raw materials, substantial conversion costs, or major assembly.

**Marginal tax rate (MTR)**  Present value of taxes applicable to incremental income divided by incremental income.

**Mark-to-market election**  Election U.S. investor makes simultaneously with the qualified electing fund election that requires immediate recognition of built-in gain or loss on investor's passive foreign investment company shares.

**Medical emergency**  Provision that ignores U.S. days during which alien individuals are ill when conducting the substantial presence test.

**Mirror code**  Tax law in some U.S. possessions identical to the U.S. Code except that it substitutes the name of the possession for United States wherever it appears in the U.S. law and substitutes United States for the name of the possession.

**Model treaty**  Prototype tax treaty that countries use as a basis for tax treaty negotiations.

**Multinational company**  Headquarters company for a chain of related entities performing production, distribution, and other business functions in several countries.

**Mutual agreement article**  Treaty clause that establishes the procedures for clarifying issues and resolving conflicts between taxpayers and taxing authorities.

**National neutrality (NN)**  Policy standard allowing taxpayers to deduct foreign tax levies, a disincentive for conducting business or investing abroad vis-à-vis domestic activities with comparable before-tax rates of return.

**Nationality**  Same as citizenship when used in reference to an individual.

**Net income test**  With some flexibility, requirement that a foreign tax must allow recovery of significant costs and expenses to be creditable.

**Net profit margin**  Under the domestic international sales corporation regime, an export sale's net profit divided by sales receipts.

**Neutrality**  *See* capital export, capital import, or national neutrality.

**New resident election**   Election dual status aliens make that accelerates residency starting date to January 1 and allows them to file jointly.

**No loss rule**   Limit on commissions that related suppliers can pay to domestic international sales corporation equal to export profit (i.e., combined taxable income).

**Noncontrolled section 902 corporation**   For foreign tax credit purposes, foreign corporation in which a U.S. company holds a significant but noncontrolling interest of 10 to 50 percent. *Same as* 10-50 company.

**Nondiscrimination clause**   Treaty provision that prevents a treaty country from imposing more tax burden on the other country's residents than it imposes on its own taxpayers.

**Nonresident**   Taxpayer who does not reside in the country at issue.

**Nonresident alien**   Individual who is neither a U.S. citizen nor resident.

**Nonresident election**   Election nonresident aliens make that treats them as U.S. residents and allows them to file jointly.

**Notional loan**   Hypothetical loan that helps to explain the tax treatment of an interest payment.

**OECD**   *See* Organisation for Economic Co-operation and Development.

**Offshore**   Characterization of activity taking place, property located, or entity established outside the United States.

**One-taxpayer rule**   Provision requiring affiliated companies to allocate and apportion interest expense as though the affiliated companies' assets belong to a single corporation.

**Operative section**   Code section requiring allocation or apportionment of deductions.

**Organisation for Economic Co-operation and Development (OECD)**   Members include major developed nations.

**Outbound asset transfer**   Transfer of appreciated assets from domestic realm to foreign realm, subject to toll charge, to prevent avoidance of gain.

**Outbound transaction**   Transaction that involves a U.S. individual or entity investing or doing business outside the United States.

**Outbound transfer**   Transfer of U.S. property to a location outside the United States.

**Overall basket**   Foreign tax credit basket containing most business profit and any other income not falling into the other baskets. Same as *general basket* and *residual basket.*

**Overall foreign loss**   Excess of deductions apportioned to foreign source gross income over such income for all foreign tax credit baskets combined.

**Paper entity**   Legal entity with little or no physical substance, such as most domestic international sales corporations.

**Parent company**   Corporation that controls another company through stock ownership.

**Passive assets**   In testing for passive foreign investment company status, property that produces passive income or that the foreign entity holds to produce passive income.

**Passive foreign investment company (PFIC)**   Foreign corporation with either passive gross income that is at least 75 percent of its total gross income or passive assets that are at least 50 percent of its total assets.

**Passive gross income**   In testing for passive foreign investment company status, dividends, interest, annuities, and nonbusiness rents and royalties, and net gain from disposing of stocks, bonds, commodities, currencies, and other investment assets.

**Pedigreed QEF**   For a particular U.S. investor, passive foreign investment company (PFIC) that has been a qualified election fund during all PFIC years in the investor's holding period and, thus, is free from deferred tax and interest charges.

**Per se corporation**   Foreign business entity that the United States always treats as a corporation.

**Permanent establishment (PE)**   Fixed place of business such as a factory or office, certain projects lasting more than 12 months, or a dependent agent who regularly concludes contracts.

**Permanent immigrant**   Individual to whom the federal government grants the right to permanently reside in the United States. *Same as* lawful permanent resident.

**Physical presence test**   Test allowing U.S. citizens with foreign tax homes to exclude foreign earned income when they are bodily present in one or more foreign countries for at least 330 days during a 12-month period.

**Portfolio interest**   Exempt U.S. source interest that foreign persons receive from a corporation or partnership in which they own less than a 10 percent interest.

**Portfolio investment**   Less than 10 percent ownership of an entity residing in another country. *Contrast with* foreign direct investment.

**Possession corporation**   Domestic corporation conducting business in Puerto Rico or the U.S. Virgin Islands and receiving tax credits under Section 936.

**Preservation clause**   Treaty provision preventing an inadvertent denial of benefits, otherwise available under local law, due to a strict reading of the treaty. *Same* as statutory allowance clause.

**Primary allocation**   IRS allocation of gross income to taxpayers not following arm's-length standards in transactions between related or controlled persons.

**Profit-level indicator**   Under the comparable profits method, profitability measures in the form of financial ratios.

**Profit split method**   Transfer pricing method that allocates controlled persons' combined operating profit or loss from controlled transactions per the relative contribution of each controlled person to the profit or loss.

**Protocol**   Amendment to existing treaty that must be separately negotiated and ratified to become effective.

**Qualified electing fund (QEF)**   Stock in current or former passive foreign investment company for which U.S. persons elect to flow through their pro rata share of ordinary income and net capital gain each year.

**Qualified export asset**   Property related to export activities that qualifies a corporation as a DISC if totaling at least 95 percent of all assets.

**Qualified export receipt**   Sale producing profit allocable between DISC and its related supplier and, thus, eligible for deferral benefits; also, qualifies a corporation as a DISC if totaling at least 95 percent of all receipts.

**Qualified nonrecourse indebtedness**   Debt financing the acquisition, construction, or improvement of depreciable personal property, real estate, or amortizable intangible, and acting as the property's sole security.

**Qualified resident**   Foreign corporation that, since it resides in a treaty country and meets certain other requirements, can use a U.S. income treaty to reduce or eliminate its U.S. branch profits tax.

**Qualifying foreign trade property (QFTP)**   Exported goods that yield foreign trading gross receipts and, thus, qualify for the extraterritorial income exclusion.

**Ratification**   Process of treaty approval. In the United States, ratification requires a two-thirds favorable vote in the Senate.

**Realization test**   Requirement that a realization event or qualified prerealization event must trigger a foreign tax for it to be creditable.

**Related person insurance income (RPII)**   Foreign corporation's insurance income from U.S. persons owning its stock and persons related to such owners. Component of Subpart F income if U.S. persons own more than 25 percent of foreign corporation's stock value or voting power.

**Resale price method**   Transfer pricing method often appropriate when the controlled purchaser resells tangible property as a mere middleman, it involves subtracting an appropriate gross profit, based on comparable uncontrolled transactions, from the resale price.

**Resident**   Under U.S. law, non-citizen who qualifies as a lawful permanent resident or meets a substantial presence test. Same as resident alien.

**Resident alien**   Individual without U.S. citizenship who resides in the United States.

**Residual basket**   Foreign tax credit basket containing most business profit and any other income not falling into the other baskets. *Same as* general basket and overall basket.

**Residual grouping**   Grouping to which all expenses not apportioned to the statutory grouping are assigned.

**Residual profit split**   One of two acceptable means of allocating controlled persons' combined profit or loss under the profit split method, it allocates routine contributions based on external market benchmarks and any remaining profit attributable to unique intangibles based on either external or internal data, whichever is more appropriate.

**Residual U.S. tax**   The incremental U.S. tax due when a taxpayer remits relatively low-taxed foreign income to the United States.

**Reverse hybrid entity**   Foreign business entity that the home country treats as a flow-through structure but the United States treats as a corporation. *Compare* hybrid entity.

**Rollback procedure**   Procedure allowing the application of advance pricing agreements to prior taxable years.

**Routine contributions**   Under the residual profit split method of allocating profit between controlled persons, the contributions to operating profit of each person attributable to tangible properties, intangibles that uncontrolled persons engaged in similar activities often own, and services.

**Sales method**   Method for apportioning R&E deductions that apportions half of R&E wherever it occurs and the remainder based on sales.

**Savings clause**   Treaty provision that allows the United States to tax its own persons as though the treaty does not exist.

**Seat of effective management**   Geographic place from which a company is managed, which may depend on criteria such as the location of the company's head office or where the board of directors meets.

**Section 78 gross-up**   When receiving dividends from foreign subsidiaries, the amount Section 78 requires U.S. corporations to include in gross income, which is equal to deemed paid taxes.

**Section 482 pricing**   In a transaction between related or controlled persons, the amount that would have been charged if the transaction had occurred between unrelated and uncontrolled persons. *Same as* arm's-length pricing.

**Section 904 limitation**   Limitation on the foreign tax credit that prevents taxpayers from using creditable taxes to reduce the U.S. tax on U.S. source income.

**Section 1248 earnings**   Portion of U.S. shareholder's gain from disposing of stock in current or former CFC that Code taxes as dividend income rather than long-term capital gain.

**Senate Foreign Relations Committee**   Senate committee that evaluates proposed U.S. treaties.

**Setoff**   Collateral adjustment to the controlled person receiving a primary allocation that partially or entirely offsets the primary allocation.

**Shell corporation**   Corporation that generally owns few business assets (if any), has few employees (if any), and performs few business functions (if any). Normally established to obtain tax benefits through exalting form over substance, as in treaty shopping.

**Shipping and aviation agreement**   Agreement that precludes the host country from taxing certain international transportation income.

**Shipping income**   Income falling into a separate foreign tax credit basket and consisting of income from using, hiring for use, or leasing aircraft or vessels in foreign commerce, as well as income from space and ocean activities.

**Soak-up tax**   Intended to siphon tax revenues from the home country to the host country, foreign tax designed to apply only to the extent the taxpayer can receive an offsetting credit against its home country income tax.

**Source country**   Country (outside the home country) where the taxpayer conducts business or makes investments. *Same as* host country.

**Source of income rules**   Rules U.S. taxpayers use to determine their foreign tax credits and foreign taxpayers use to calculate their U.S. tax liabilities.

**Specific economic benefit**   For foreign tax credit purposes, a benefit received in return for a foreign government levy that is not available on substantially the same terms to substantially all other taxpayers or the general public.

**Standard Industrial Classification (SIC)**   Numerical codes that classify businesses into industry groups. Taxpayers allocate R&E deductions to product lines based on SIC codes.

**Statutory allowance clause**   Treaty provision preventing an inadvertent denial of benefits, otherwise available under local law, due to a strict reading of the treaty. *Same as* preservation clause.

**Statutory grouping**   Grouping based on gross income from a particular activity or source to which an operative section requires that expenses be apportioned.

**Subchapter N**   Portion of the Code applicable to international transactions and events.

**Subpart F income**   Income of a controlled foreign corporation resulting in a constructive dividend to U.S. shareholders.

**Subsidiary company**   Corporation that a parent company controls through equity ownership.

**Substantial presence test**   Test for U.S. residency based on the number of days an alien individual spends in the United States during the current and two preceding calendar years.

**Substantial transformation**   Process by which finished units become sufficiently distinguishable from raw materials or component parts, indicating that manufacturing has occurred.

**Substantial valuation misstatement**   Transfer pricing misstatement that results in penalty equal to 20 percent of the tax underpayment.

**Super captive insurance company**   Insurance company that primarily insures the risks of its own shareholders (or persons related to its shareholders) but spreads its voting power and shares so that U.S. shareholders own no more than 25 percent. Thus, the company avoids status as a controlled foreign corporation.

**Super royalty**   Per the commensurate with income standard, royalty exceeding the amount that controlled persons set in their original licensing agreement.

**Supremacy clause**   Article VI, clause 2 of the U.S. Constitution, declaring that the Constitution, federal laws, and treaties comprise the supreme law of the United States.

**Tainted income**   *See* Subpart F income.

**Tax**   For foreign tax credit purposes, compulsory payment made pursuant to a government's authority to levy taxes.

**Tax book value method**   Method for valuing assets at their adjusted bases when allocating and apportioning interest deductions.

**Tax equalization plan**   Plan under which employers reimburse expatriate employees for additional taxes they incur from working abroad, and expatriate employees reimburse employers when they incur fewer taxes from working abroad.

**Tax haven**   Country in which a taxpayer or type of transaction is subject to little or no taxes.

**Tax holiday**   Period over which a jurisdiction waives part or all of a foreign investor's normal tax obligations.

**Tax home**   Located where the taxpayer's regular or principal place of business exists.

**Tax nothing**   Vernacular for a foreign branch, which is not considered a separate taxable entity in the United States.

**Tax protection plan**   Plan under which employers reimburse expatriate employees for additional taxes they incur from working abroad.

**Tax-sparing credit**   Credit for foreign income tax that taxpayers do not pay, for example, because of a tax holiday.

**Tax treaty**   Bilateral negotiated agreements specifying reciprocal rules for two countries to follow in taxing residents from the other country.

**Temporary work assignment**   Foreign assignment that the worker expects will last no more than a year and actually does last one year or less, resulting in a U.S. tax home.

**10-50 company**   For foreign tax credit purposes, foreign corporation in which a U.S. company holds a significant but noncontrolling interest of 10 to 50 percent. *Same as* noncontrolled section 902 corporation.

**Territorial system**  Type of jurisdiction that seeks to tax income from all transactions occurring within a country's borders and exempting income from all transactions occurring abroad.

**Testing period**  Period over which some test is performed (e.g., the active foreign business test uses income for a three-year period).

**Thin capitalization rules**  Maximum debt-to-equity ratios that nations set to limit the debt in corporate capital structures.

**Tie-breaker rules**  Treaty rules that countries use to classify dual residents as residents of only one country.

**Title passage rule**  Sales occur and, thus, inventory profit is sourced where title to goods changes hands.

**Toll charge**  Restrictions, such as immediate gain recognition, applicable to asset transfers between different tax regimes, such as from domestic to foreign corporations.

**Total excess distribution**  Portion of aggregate distributions a U.S. person receives from a PFIC during the taxable year that exceeds 125 percent of average distributions includable in gross income over the preceding three taxable years.

**Totalization agreement**  Negotiated agreement between two countries, mitigating the effect of double Social Security taxation and, under some circumstances, securing benefits from each country when the worker has paid taxes to both.

**Trade or business**  For-profit activity that is regular, continuous, and considerable.

**Transfer price**  Price charged between related persons on the transfer of property.

**Transient exception**  Exception to the substantial presence test that ignores U.S. days during which alien individuals commute to work, experience brief U.S. layovers, or work as crew members on foreign vessels engaged in international transportation.

**Transparent entity**  Entity that a jurisdiction ignores for tax purposes (e.g., a partnership), allowing profit, loss, and other items to flow through to owners. *Also known as* look-through entity.

**Treaty shopping**  Establishment of a company in a favorable treaty country (other than the country where the owners reside) through which investment or business activities are conducted.

**True taxable income**   Taxable income of controlled persons when they transact intercompany business using arm's-length pricing.

**Undistributed foreign personal holding company (FPHC) income**   Measure of foreign personal holding company's dividend-paying ability.

**United States**   Includes the 50 states, the District of Columbia, the airspace over these land masses (other than outer space), and 12 nautical miles from shores. Generally does not include U.S. possessions.

**Unpedigreed qualified electing fund (QEF)**   For a particular U.S. investor, passive foreign investment company (PFIC) that has not been a qualified election fund during all PFIC years in the investor's holding period and, thus, is still subject to deferred tax and interest charges on some earnings.

**U.S. continental shelf**   Seabed and subsoil of ocean areas adjacent to U.S. territorial waters over which the United States claims exclusive rights in exploring for and exploiting natural resources.

**U.S. expatriate**   U.S. citizen or resident individual living outside the United States.

**U.S.-owned foreign corporation**   Foreign corporation in which U.S. persons directly or indirectly own 50 percent or more of the voting power or stock value.

**U.S. individuals**   U.S. citizens and U.S. residents.

**U.S. persons**   U.S. citizens, U.S. residents, domestic partnerships, domestic corporations, or nonforeign estates and trusts.

**U.S. possession**   Territory that the United States owns, including American Samoa, Guam, the Northern Mariana Islands, Puerto Rico, and the U.S. Virgin Islands.

**U.S. property**   Type of asset that may trigger a constructive dividend if a CFC invests in it.

**U.S. real property holding corporation (USRPHC)**   Corporation in which U.S. real property interests are at least half of the aggregate sum of U.S. real property interests, foreign real estate, and business assets.

**U.S. real property interest**   Either a direct interest in U.S. real estate or an interest in a domestic corporation that is a U.S. real property holding corporation.

**U.S. residents**   Permanent U.S. immigrants and individuals living in the United States for extended periods.

**U.S. shareholder**   Regarding controlled foreign corporations (CFCs), a U.S. person owning 10 percent or more of CFC voting power.

**U.S. source income**   Income derived from sources within the United States.

**U.S. trade or business**   U.S. for-profit activity engaged in continuously and regularly.

**Valuation misstatements**   Differences between transfer prices between controlled persons and arm's-length prices that lead to accuracy-related penalties.

**Value-added tax (VAT)**   Tax that European and other countries impose on the value manufacturers add to a product. *Similar to a goods and services tax.*

**Voting power**   Authority to elect, replace, or appoint directors to a corporation's board or similar governing body.

**Withholding tax**   Tax that purchasers of U.S. real property interests and payors of interest, dividend, and royalty income collect and remit.

**World Trade Organization (WTO)**   Umbrella organization that monitors international trade and disciplines member nations that violate accepted tenets.

# Table of Statutes

# Table of Regulations

# Table of Cases

# Table of Rulings

# Index

Printed in the United States
145782LV00001B/55/A